Ordinary
Enchantments

Ordinary Enchantments

*Magical Realism
and the Remystification
of Narrative*

Wendy B. Faris

Vanderbilt University Press

NASHVILLE

© 2004 Vanderbilt University Press
Second printing 2013

This book is printed on acid-free paper.
Manufactured in the United States of America

Library of Congress Cataloging-in-Publication Data

Faris, Wendy B.
Ordinary enchantments : magical realism and the
    remystification of narrative / Wendy B. Faris.
    —1st ed.
p. cm.
Includes bibliographical references and index.
ISBN 0–8265–1441–3 (alk. paper)
ISBN 0–8265–1442–1 (pbk. : alk. paper)
1. Magic realism (Literature) 2. Fiction—
20th century History and criticism. I. Title.
PN56.M24F37 2004
809.'915—dc21

                                    2003002250

For the birds . . .

Contents

Acknowledgments   ix

Preface
Permissible Savag'ry   xi

Introduction   I

1 **Definitions and Locations**   7
*Magical Realism between Modern
and Postmodern Fiction*
 Definitions
 Locations

2 **"From a Far Source Within"**   43
Magical Realism as Defocalized Narrative
 Defocalization
 Postmodern Primitivists
 The Presence of Spirit
 Shamanistic Narrative Healing

3 **Encoding the Ineffable**   88
A Textual Poetics for Magical Realism
 Magical Details, Naïve Narrators,
  Indeterminate Spaces and Times, the Oneiric Optic
 Bridges
 Two-Way Streets
 Narrative Distances and Chinese Boxes
 Mirroring

4 **"Along the Knife-Edge of Change"**   133
   Magical Realism and the
   Postcolonial Dynamics of Alterity
       Decolonization
       Historical Realities
       Ventriloquism
       Transculturation
       Recent Literary History and Cultural Politics

5 **"Women and Women and Women"**   170
   A Feminine Element in Magical Realism
       Housekeeping
       "Virgin Paper"; or, Inhabiting Female Bodies
       The Female Body of Writing
       Cooking
       Territorial Magic
       "La Mystérique"

   Notes   221

   Works Consulted   279

   Index   301

Acknowledgments

Many thanks to Stacy Alaimo, Jon Thiem, and Lois Zamora for their thoughtful readings of parts of the book and their helpful suggestions, and to Dave Faris for presenting me with several of the books that eventually became central to this study. Special thanks to Emma Kafalenos, for her reading of the entire book in the midst of a busy teaching schedule, as well as for sharing her knowledge of narratology, and to Steve Walker, for his numerous valuable ideas and clarifications. I am also grateful to Michael Ames, director of Vanderbilt University Press, and my editor, Betsy Phillips, for their constructive comments, their encouragement, and their patience, and to the University of Texas at Arlington, which provided me with a grant to aid in publication costs, and two faculty leaves to work on this project (which has taken more time than I could ever have imagined).

I wish to thank Duke University Press for permission to include here modified versions of my essay "Scheherazade's Children: Magical Realism and Postmodern Fiction," in *Magical Realism: Theory, History, Community,* ed. Lois Parkinson Zamora and Wendy B. Faris (1995), and the editors of *Janus Head* for permission to include sections of my article "The Question of the Other: Cultural Critiques of Magical Realism" (5, 2 [2002]).

Preface

Permissible Savag'ry

This book probably has its distant origins in the Fijian cannibal fork with which my mother livened up her performance during the "show and tell" period at her girls' school in Australia. The fork, given to my grandfather by the native Fijians, so the story goes, had been used to eat an earlier missionary. That the story may be apocryphal makes it all the more intriguing, of course, especially in the context of magical realism and narrative invention. Even if the Fijians had invented that other, that eaten missionary in order to cement more closely their friendship with, or alternately, to terrorize and thus to colonize the current one (my grandfather), the story was passed down and believed by my mother, her sisters, their schoolroom audiences, and me. That attraction, of the postcolonial English schoolgirls for the permissible savag'ry of the Fijian cannibal and, more generally, our overcivilized century's attraction to the "primitive" arts is the starting point for substantial parts of this critical narrative, and also for much—though not all—of the magical realist fiction I consider here. To be deployed fruitfully, this attraction must be understood to contain not only projections of selves but also genuine appreciation of others.

Introduction

   In this book I investigate magical realism in contemporary literature.
The term *magical realism,* coined in the early twentieth century to describe a
new, neo-realistic, style in German painting, then applied to Latin American
fiction, now designates perhaps the most important contemporary trend in
international fiction. Magical realism has become so important as a mode
of expression worldwide, especially in postcolonial cultures, because it has
provided the literary ground for significant cultural work; within its texts,
marginal voices, submerged traditions, and emergent literatures have developed and created masterpieces.
   Why has it been able to do this? Magical realism radically modifies and
replenishes the dominant mode of realism in the West, challenging its basis of representation from within. That destabilization of a dominant form
means that it has served as a particularly effective decolonizing agent. Very
briefly defined, magical realism combines realism and the fantastic so that
the marvelous seems to grow organically within the ordinary, blurring the
distinction between them. Furthermore, that combination of realistic and
fantastical narrative, together with the inclusion of different cultural traditions, means that magical realism reflects, in both its narrative mode and its
cultural environment, the hybrid nature of much postcolonial society. Thus
the mode is multicultural in its very nature, but because it achieved that
distinction before that now-ubiquitous term was current, it has played a
significant role in the development of a multicultural literary sensibility.[1] In
other words, magical realism occupies a pivotal position, both reflecting the
cultural moment of postcolonialism and achieving substantial work within
it. In addition, because of its discursive heterogeneity, magical realism has
also contributed to the growth of a postmodern literary sensibility.[2] Indeed,

it constitutes a point of convergence between postmodernism and postcolonialism.[3] We should note at the outset, however, that magical realism is not just a postcolonial style. It also represents innovation and the re-emergence of submerged narrative traditions in metropolitan centers. In turn, that phenomenon can be understood in part in the context of literary globalization as a writing back from the peripheral colonies, but only in part.

Magical realism's widespread distribution means that in attempting to define the term and explain the particular power of the mode we need a theoretical perspective that includes the study of formal characteristics spanning different traditions but one that also takes account of interactions between different cultures. My approach, then, combining close analysis of narrative technique with ideas from postcolonial theory, permits an increased understanding of the formal characteristics and cultural work of magical realism, and most important, of the relationship between them, of the ways in which literary forms develop in response to cultural conditions.[4] It illustrates how modifications of realistic narrative technique in magical realism are both an index and a result of its cultural situation.[5]

In developing my ideas about magical realism, the novels on which I have focused include (in chronological order) Juan Rulfo, *Pedro Páramo* (1955), Günter Grass, *The Tin Drum* (1959), Wilson Harris, *Palace of the Peacock* (1960), Gabriel García Márquez, *One Hundred Years of Solitude* (1967), Robert Pinget, *That Voice* (1975), Maxine Hong Kingston, *The Woman Warrior* (1976), Milan Kundera, *The Book of Laughter and Forgetting* (1979), Salman Rushdie, *Midnight's Children* (1980), Carlos Fuentes, *Aura* (1962) and *Distant Relations* (1980), D. M. Thomas, *The White Hotel* (1981), Isabel Allende, *The House of the Spirits* (1982), William Kennedy, *Ironweed* (1983), Patrick Süskind, *Perfume* (1985), Toni Morrison, *Beloved* (1987), Ben Okri, *The Famished Road* (1991), Ana Castillo, *So Far from God* (1993), and Marie Darrieussecq, *Pig Tales* (1996).[6] Other eminent precursors and contemporaries I recall more peripherally are Nikolai Gogol, Henry James, Franz Kafka, Alejo Carpentier, Jorge Luis Borges, Octavio Paz, Julio Cortázar, André Schwarz-Bart, John Updike, Lawrence Thornton, José Saramago, Francine Prose, Louise Erdrich, Abby Frucht, Laura Esquivel, and Cristina García. There are many more; the list is constantly growing.[7] Although magical realism has been most widespread in Latin America, my aim here is to continue the critical trend that extends the mode beyond that region, beyond "el boom," which popularized the term. For that reason I have included relatively few Latin American examples.[8] *That*

Voice appears partly for shock value, because it is not ordinarily considered magical realist writing and is not very similar to its canonical texts. Yet for those very reasons, given its significant points of contact with magical realism through its creation of material metaphors, and its use of voices from beyond the grave, it underscores ways in which magical realism is interwoven with many strands of contemporary fiction. As the preceding list suggests, while I claim to discuss magical realism as a worldwide phenomenon, except for *Midnight's Children* and *The Famished Road*, I have followed my own limitations and confined myself to texts from Europe, the United States, and Latin America. A truly comprehensive study of magical realism in world literature would need to range much more widely and, I suspect, could be extended into other literatures, especially in the Near and Far East.[9]

I begin my investigation of magical realism by formulating a brief working definition of the mode. In Chapter 1 I propose five characteristics of magical realism and locate it at the intersection of modernism and postmodernism, engaging both sets of agendas and aesthetics. Working from that basis, in Chapter 2, I then discuss the way in which magical realism destabilizes realistic representation by means of what I call its "defocalized" narrative. As I explain in more detail there, because it reports events that it does not empirically verify through sensory data, within a realistic, empirically based, fiction, the narrative voice seems to be of uncertain origin, and the narrative is "defocalized." In addition, because it witnesses and reports events that humans ordinarily do not, and therefore suggests the existence of forces that are not encompassed by reference to ordinary human perceptions of a strictly material reality, magical realism is also imbued with a certain visionary power. Thus the mode constitutes what we might term a remystification of narrative in the West.[10]

In Chapter 3 I propose a textual poetics for magical realism by investigating a series of narrative techniques that it employs. Because magical realism is important as an international style, even though I consider the subject matter of magical realist fictions, my primary concern here is to study how this mode operates as discourse, irrespective of specific thematic content. This approach to magical realism thus corresponds in a comparative context to the kind of cultural analysis James Clifford proposes in studies of cultural identity: an investigation of "what processes rather than essences are involved."[11]

After discussing narrative strategies in magical realism, I next investigate the cultural politics of the mode. Because magical realism is frequently a cultural hybrid, it exemplifies many of the problematic relations that exist between selves and others in postcolonial literature. And because its narrative mode destabilizes the dominant mode of realism, it implicitly attempts to abolish the ethnographic literary authority of Western representation. However, a study of its cultural assumptions and narrative practices reveals that it is also a living record of the difficulties and failures of that attempt, because it cannot help being caught in the very appropriation it seeks to destroy. Such is the case with much of modern and postmodern literature and art. This is the issue I investigate in Chapter 4, on the postcolonial dynamics of alterity. The chapter deals with the continuing process of literary decolonization, and the complex project of speaking of/with/for cultural others that it entails.

The processes that contribute to the decolonizing force of magical realism can also be seen to operate in relation to gender. In that context, magical realism continues the process of patriarchal culture's disenchantment with itself and its dominant forms of realistic representation begun by surrealism. It has therefore adopted what can be regarded in this context as various traditionally female ways of being and knowing. For example, feminist theoreticians, including Julia Kristeva, Luce Irigaray, and Elaine Showalter, among others, have proposed that to speak with a voice that "is not one" within patriarchal culture is a female strategy, so that the multivocal and defocalized narrative of magical realism, which bridges the diverse worlds of realism and fantasy, is double-voiced in the way that female voices have been, integrating both a dominant and a muted mode in a given text. However, like surrealism, magical realism also perpetuates some of patriarchal culture's stereotypes, using female bodies as a bridge to the beyond, for instance. Because of the importance of these gender issues, in Chapter 5 I investigate whether it is possible to discern the presence of a female voice in magical realism. In addition to considering novels by women, I also investigate the use of women as narrative enablers in the texts of male magical realists.

In short, my basic aims in this study are to explore the importance of magical realism in contemporary literature and its power as a postcolonial narrative style by describing the characteristics that define, the techniques that enable, and the cultural issues that traverse it. Throughout this discussion, I suggest connections between magical realist practices and various strands of contemporary thought, most notably with selected accounts of postmodernism, with postcolonial theory, and (in Chapter 5) with several issues in feminist theory and criticism, but, clearly, a thorough investigation of such connections would be a whole other book. Since I began the study of magical realism as a global trend with a paper given at the International Comparative Literature Association in 1985, nearly twenty years ago, the number of its narrative fictions and the amount of critical analysis devoted to those fictions, as well as theoretical considerations of the genre and its cultural meanings, have increased substantially, providing additional proof of the significance of magical realism in contemporary literature.

1 ক্ষ

Definitions and Locations

*Magical Realism between Modern
and Postmodern Fiction*

Definitions

The Irreducible Element

As a basis for investigating the nature and cultural work of magical realism, I suggest five primary characteristics of the mode. First, the text contains an "irreducible element" of magic; second, the descriptions in magical realism detail a strong presence of the phenomenal world; third, the reader may experience some unsettling doubts in the effort to reconcile two contradictory understandings of events; fourth, the narrative merges different realms; and, finally, magical realism disturbs received ideas about time, space, and identity.

The "irreducible element" is something we cannot explain according to the laws of the universe as they have been formulated in Western empirically based discourse, that is, according to "logic, familiar knowledge, or received belief," as David Young and Keith Hollaman describe it.[1] Therefore, the reader has difficulty marshaling evidence to settle questions about the status of events and characters in such fictions. We must take Gabriel García Márquez's very old man with enormous wings, for example, "as a given, accepted but not explained."[2] The narrative voice reports extraordinary—magical—events, which would not normally be verifiable by sensory perception, in the same way in which other, ordinary events are recounted. The account often involves concretely detailed descriptions of phenomena that are not articulated in such detail or so completely integrated into everyday reality in other narrative traditions—mythical, religious, folkloric. This irreducible element goes beyond the uncanny, which, as Tzvetan Todorov explains, exists as an incidental element in various kinds of narrative.[3] According to

Amaryll Chanady, "while the implied author is educated according to our conventional norms of reason and logic, and can therefore recognize the supernatural as contrary to the laws of nature, he tries to accept the world view of a culture in order to describe it.[4] He abolishes the antinomy between the natural and the supernatural on the level of textual representation, and the reader, who recognizes the two conflicting logical codes on the semantic level, suspends his judgment of what is rational and what is irrational in the fictitious world."[5] Brenda Cooper, writing of magical realism in West African fiction, similarly sees "the relationship between the magical and the scientific" as central to magical realism; "it is the narrative space where the educated writer's simultaneous ironic distance from and acceptance of, pre-scientific worldviews negotiate the magical realist stance."[6] The narrator's presentation of the irreducible element on the same narrative plane as other, commonplace, happenings means that in the terms of the text, magical things "really" do happen: young Victor and André in Carlos Fuentes's *Distant Relations* "really" become a twinned fetus floating in a pool; Remedios the Beauty in García Márquez's *One Hundred Years of Solitude* "really" ascends heavenward; Saleem Sinai in Salman Rushdie's *Midnight's Children* "really" is made invisible by his future wife, Parvati; Grenouille in Patrick Süskind's *Perfume* "really" distills a powerful and intoxicating human scent from the bodies of virgins. And so on.

These irreducible elements are well assimilated into the realistic textual environment, rarely causing any comment by narrators or characters, who model such an acceptance for their readers. Paradoxically, though, because they also nevertheless frequently surprise those readers and their realistic expecta-tions, they also say, in almost existential fashion, "I EKsist," "I stick out." Here we might detect the remnants of existential anguish at an un-co-optable world, but tempered by the more playful side of surrealism (or the intersection of diverse cultural traditions). In *So Far from God*, for example, Ana Castillo specifically confirms the irreducible nature of a dead person's reappearance by verifying her sighting by several people, as if to convince any skeptics in her audience: "Esperanza [who has died] was also occasionally seen. Yes, seen, not only by La Loca, but also by Domingo who saw her from the front window. . . . And once, although she had thought at first it was a dream, Es-peranza came and lay down next to her mother."[7] In short, the magic in these texts refuses to be entirely assimilated into their realism; it does not brutally shock but neither does it melt away, so that it is like a grain of sand in the oyster of that realism. And because it disrupts reading habits, that irreducible grain increases the participation of readers, contributing to the postmodern proliferation of writerly texts, texts co-created by their readers.

Magical images or events, glowing alluringly from within the realistic matrix, often highlight central issues in a text. The song Sethe's daughter miraculously begins to sing in Toni Morrison's *Beloved* underlines a female line of descent and the ways it is transmitted: "Leaning forward a little, Beloved was humming softly. . . . / 'I made that song up,' said Sethe. 'I made it up and sang it to my children. Nobody knows that song but me and my children.' / Beloved turned to look at Sethe. 'I know it,' she said."[8] Similarly, the trail of blood that miraculously travels across town from son to mother in *One Hundred Years of Solitude* underlines the unusually close, even incestuously involuted nature of the Buendía family, whose ties are especially strong. Examples of those ties abound: Colonel Aureliano predicts from a distance his father's death, announcing on his arrival home that he has come for "the obsequies of the king"; José Arcadio Segundo and Aureliano Segundo share Petra Cotes for almost two months until they both contract "a low life disease," but having "submitted to burning baths of permanganate and diuretic waters, . . . both were cured separately after three months of secret suffering" and years later die at the same instant.[9]

In *Perfume,* Grenouille's magical talent that permits him to construct scents for himself that abolish his problematic status as a nonperson, to which his odorless body had consigned him, highlight the novel's questioning of our notions about unique and naturally formed individuals and their socially determined relationships because they totally change his status. One "perfume in his arsenal was a scent for arousing sympathy that proved effective with middle-aged and elderly women. It smelled of watery milk and fresh, soft wood. The effect Grenouille created with it—even when he went out unshaved, scowling, and wrapped in a heavy coat—was of a poor, pale lad in a frayed jacket who simply had to be helped. Once they caught a whiff of him, the market women filled his pockets with nuts and dried pears because he seemed to them so hungry and helpless."[10]

In *The Stone Raft* by José Saramago, the issue of marginality is underlined by directly motivating the magic in the text. The novel narrates events during the magical severance of the Iberian Peninsula from the rest of Europe, which creates a larger and larger chasm between them. That rift dramatizes the sense of cultural isolation experienced by Spaniards and Portuguese in relation to the rest of Western Europe. But it is also extended in a more general and cosmic sense to encompass divisions between people, and existential questions of connection. Near the end of the novel, the peninsula has stopped drifting, but the narrator tells us as he leaves us that the travelers whom we have followed "will travel on their way, who knows what future awaits them, how much time, what destiny." Just before this ending, one of these travelers dies, and somehow the obvious extraordinariness of the stone island is abandoned for—and mysteriously seems to enhance—the quotidian strangeness of death, for both Pedro Orce and his companions. Before dying Pedro "stretched out" on the ground, "his white hair mingling with fresh shoots, flowering at a time when it should have been winter." After he is dead and they are taking him to be buried, we hear that "such a thing has never happened to them before," and the women both weep, thinking "dear God, how all things in this world are linked together, and here we are thinking that we have the power to separate or join them at will, how sadly mistaken we are, having been proved wrong time and time again, a line traced on the ground, a flock of starlings, a stone thrown into the sea, a blue woolen sock, but we are showing them to the blind, preaching to the deaf with hearts of stone."[11] The uncertain connection between this death and the "stone raft" whose progress we have been following throughout the novel is made explicit with the mention of a line traced on the ground, which recalls the boundary between the peninsula and Europe that did not behave according to expectations, and the stone thrown into the sea. Once again, a magical event highlights the extraordinary nature of reality.

In the course of highlighting such issues, irreducible magic frequently disrupts the ordinary logic of cause and effect. Lisa's pains in D. M. Thomas's *The White Hotel* appear before she experiences the atrocities at Babi Yar that cause them and kill her. Melquíades's manuscript turns out to be a prediction as well as a recording of events in *One Hundred Years of Solitude*, implicitly asking whether he, and we, are the masters or the victims of our fates. We wonder whether Grenouille's perfuming skills are a cause or a result of his own perfumeless persona. In Ben Okri's *The Famished Road*, the text presents Azaro's visions in such a way that we question whether Azaro's own visionary skills conjure the images he presents or whether they result from the effects on him of people or of phenomena he encounters. In one of many sequences in which he journeys into the forest, a mask "with eyes both daunting and mischievous" falls on him, so that when he puts it on, "the forest became as night," and he "sees a different world. There were beings everywhere in the darkness and the spirits were each of them a sun." But even before he encounters the mask, he twice recounts entering "another reality, a strange world," in which he sees strange things, such as "nude women [who] appeared and vanished before my gaze," and "my eyes became charged too and I saw people with serene bronze masks emerging from trees." Shortly, however, "my wonder turned to bewilderment. When I took off the mask the darkness was the same. Patches of light came over the wind. I had begun to lose my sense of reality, confused by the mask." Furthermore, at one point near the end of this sequence of events, when Azaro attempts to remove the mask, it "stuck to my face," which "felt somewhat raw" when it was removed, suggesting the possibility that mask and face are one, questioning the source—and cause—of his visions. He sees different things, or things transformed into others when he wears the mask, but the speed of the transitions, the statement that it remained dark when he removes it, and the visionary nature of the images he sees without it confuses our sense of cause and effect, and we are led to ask whether the mask has caused the visions or forms part of them, caused by his own visionary powers as an *abiku* or spirit child.[12]

In the light of disruptions of cause and effect and irreducible elements of magic recounted with little or no comment, in conjunction with accounts of extraordinary but actual phenomena and events, the real as we know it may seem amazing or even ridiculous.[13] As Erik Camayd-Freixas expresses it, summarizing the thesis of Irlemar Chiampi, magical realism contains the "coexistence of the natural and the supernatural in a narrative that presents them in a nondisjunctive way, in which the natural appears strange, and the supernatural pedestrian."[14] Throughout *One Hundred Years of Solitude,* for example, as Robert Anderson points out, the rationally expected is often contradicted by the surprises of the actual. Sentences like "Rebeca, contrary to what might have been expected, was the more beautiful," occur over and over again (59).[15] In *Midnight's Children,* Rushdie implies the interchange of the ordinary and the extraordinary when he describes a hummingbird as "a creature which would be impossible if it did not exist."[16] And just before we are told of his magical journey in which he is invisible inside a basket as fact, Saleem describes the city of Dacca under Indian occupation, where he "saw many things which were not true, which were not possible, because our boys would not could not have behaved so badly; we saw men in spectacles with heads like eggs being shot in side-streets, we saw the intelligentsia of the city being massacred by the hundred, but it was not true because it could not have been true, . . . we moved through the impossible hallucination of the night" (449). (The magical is factual and the historical is impossible.) The bureaucratic red tape that Nikolai Gogol's man in "The Nose" encounters in his attempts to report the loss of his nose seems more outrageous than the magical disappearance of the nose itself. The lies of the Pakistani government about the number of Indian aircraft shot down in the Indo-Pakistani War (in *Midnight's Children*), and the discovery of ice, the properties of magnets and movies, or the government's denial of the deaths in the banana company's massacre of workers in Macondo (in *One Hundred Years of Solitude*), achieve an equality of strangeness with Saleem's magical voices or Macondo's flying carpets.[17] Embodying the spirit of this marvelous everyday magic is the description in "Light Is Like Water," by García Márquez, of "household objects, [which,] in the fullness of their poetry, flew with their own wings through the kitchen sky."[18]

In a metafictional gloss on this kind of rhetoric that tends to blur distinctions between the marvelous and the ordinary, Saleem claims he has adopted "matter of fact descriptions of the outré and bizarre, and their reverse, namely heightened, stylized versions of the everyday" (261). And in *The Moor's Last Sigh* Rushdie's protagonist explains the strategy to us.

> I had never been up in a plane before, and the experience of passing through clouds . . . was so spookily like the images of the After Life in movies, paintings and story-books that I got the shivers. Was I traveling to the country of the dead? I half expected to see a pair of pearly gates standing on the fluffy fields of cumulus outside my window. . . .
>
> "I feel as if I have slipped in time," I told the friendly stewardess some while later. "But whether into the future or the past, I cannot say."
>
> "Many passengers feel that way," she reassured me. "I tell them, it is neither. The past and future are where we spend most of our lives. In fact, what you are going through in this small microcosmos of ours is the disorienting feeling of having slipped for a few hours into the present." Her name was Eduviges.[19]

The Moor will, in some sense, enter the realm of the dead before his time, for the principal irreducible magic in the book is that his life is rushing toward his death at twice the normal human rate of aging. And immediately after this scene, the rest of the airplane's crew deny the existence of Eduviges. So, perhaps she really was a dream, or, as the Moor speculates, "a sort of phantom of the air, called forth by my own desires. No doubt such houris did float up here, above the clouds. They could pass through the aircraft's walls whenever they chose" (283). As often before, then, the magic surrounding this now ordinary but amazing phenomenon of airplane travel renders it newly strange. Rushdie also shows us where he got the idea, conjuring a bit of intertextual magic by plumbing Hispanic literary history: this interchange takes place as the Moor is flying to Benengeli and speaking to Eduviges: the first is the name of the fictional author of Don Quixote, and the second of a character in Juan Rulfo's *Pedro Páramo*. Perhaps, with the Moor, magical realism and its irreducible element enter the mainstream of metafictional satire: "the centrality of the magical image" and "the logic of dream" are terms bandied about by a stream of "dope-fiends and professors and journalists and celebrities and critics" who appear in a send-up of postcolonial theory in Rushdie's novel (201).

In magical realism, reality's outrageousness is often underscored because ordinary people react to magical events in recognizable and sometimes also in disturbing ways, a circumstance that normalizes the magical event but also defamiliarizes, underlines, or critiques extraordinary aspects of the real. Grenouille's perfuming abilities and the uncannily entrancing scent he manufactures for himself are magical, but the mass hysteria that they engender, tearing him literally limb from limb and devouring him at the end of the novel, if exaggerated, is real, and all too familiar as an analogue for the power of charismatic leaders and the malleability of crowds, as well as for the persecution and scapegoating that has resulted from such adulation in recent history.

> Meanwhile the masses on the other side of the barricade were giving themselves over ever more shamelessly to the uncanny rush of emotion that Grenouille's appearance had unleashed. Those who at the start had merely felt sympathy and compassion were now filled with naked, insatiable desire. . . . They all regarded the man in the blue frock coat as the most handsome, attractive, and perfect creature they could imagine . . . as their ideal image of themselves. . . . The result was that the scheduled execution of one of the most abominable criminals of the age degenerated into the largest orgy the world had seen since the second century before Christ. (238–39)

Magic thus also serves the cause of satire and political commentary. Similarly, in García Márquez's story "A Very Old Man with Enormous Wings," Pelayo and Elisenda exploit the miraculous old man as factory owners do their workers. A passage from André Schwarz-Bart's novel *A Woman Named Solitude* also exemplifies this highlighting of political atrocity by magic. At the start of the section where the narrator will describe the massacre of blacks by French forces in Guadeloupe, a magical event occurs: "Early one afternoon, on a day like other days, a peal of thunder shook the great trees, sending a rain of leaves down on the astonished fugitives. The animals whimpered and slunk away into the copse. Surprised in her sleep, a dead woman suddenly flew up to the sky, her breasts flapping like wings. . . . / This cannonade on the Côte-sous-le-Vent was the beginning of the end of an episode in history which, though unknown to the fugitives, was to be their death."[20] The magic grows almost imperceptibly out of the real, and the narrator registers no surprise, with the result that the element of surprise is redirected onto the history we are about to witness, which constitutes the nasty shock.

The Phenomenal World

A second characteristic of magical realism is that its descriptions detail a strong presence of the phenomenal world. This is the realism in magical realism, distinguishing it from much fantasy and allegory. It appears in several ways. Realistic descriptions create a fictional world that resembles the one we live in, often by extensive use of detail. On one hand, this attention to sensory detail continues and renews the realistic tradition. On the other hand, in addition to including magical events (such as Beloved's appearances and Frances Phelan's conversations with the dead) or phenomena (such as Melquíades's manuscript, Saleem's transmitting and receiving radio head, and Grenouille's nose), magical realist fiction includes intriguing magical details. Because these magical details represent a clear departure from realism, detail is freed from a traditionally mimetic role to a greater extent than it has been before. This is still true even from the Barthesian perspective that questions the site-specific mimesis of realism. Roland Barthes claims that realism endows details with an "effet de réel" (reality effect), which conveys not any particular information but rather the idea that this story is real.[21] In addition to projecting that message with detailed descriptions, the irreducible details of magical realism can lead in the opposite direction, signaling that this may be imaginary. The sense of the magical growing within the real was articulated early on by Franz Roh in his initial discussion of magical realism in painting: "with the word 'magical,' as opposed to 'mystical,' I wish to indicate that the mystery does not descend to the represented world, but rather hides and palpitates behind it."[22]

A graphic illustration of this commingling phenomenon is the way in which magical events are usually grounded textually in a traditionally realistic, even an explicitly factual, manner. Furthermore, as Brenda Cooper has stated it, "the mysterious, sensuous, unknown, and unknowable are not in the subtext, as in realist writing, but rather share the fictional space with history."[23] Within the fiction, Felipe Montero in Carlos Fuentes's *Aura* reads in a newspaper of the magically potent job he will eventually take; similarly, Remedios the Beauty's levitation in *One Hundred Years of Solitude* starts quite concretely, when Fernanda, as she is hanging out the laundry, feels a "delicate wind of light pull the sheets out of her hand and open them up wide" (222). With respect to history, *The White Hotel* begins with fictional letters from the historical figures of Ferenczi and Freud; in *Midnight's Children,* Rushdie carefully situates his narrative in the events surrounding India's independence and the turmoil that followed it. Remnants of this quality, of magic's solid grounding in reality, persist even when the fantastical element shows its colors quickly and clearly. In *Perfume,* for example, Grenouille, with his magically powerful and discriminating sense of smell, is born in carefully located space and time: in geographical space "in Paris under the sway of a particularly fiendish stench," and in textual time immediately after the opening catalogue of stenches "barely conceivable to us modern men and women," a formulation that locates both him and us historically (3). Like the perfumers whose ranks he joins, Grenouille is a product of this smelly environment—perhaps even compensating for his mother's "utterly dulled" sense of smell (5).

If we focus on reference rather than on description, we may witness idiosyncratic recreations of historical events, but events grounded firmly in historical realities, often alternate versions of officially sanctioned accounts.[24] This grounding in history grows out of realism's frequent "embedding of random persons and events in the general course of contemporary history," as Erich Auerbach expressed it.[25] García Márquez's rewriting of the history of Latin America in that of Macondo, for example, including a massacre that has been elided from the public record, and the opening of Milan Kundera's *The Book of Laughter and Forgetting,* which replaces a man airbrushed out of history by party doctrine, are elements that differ from the mythical components of those tales, though they are related to them. The combination implies that historical events and myths are both essential aspects of our collective memory. As we hear in *Midnight's Children,* "sometimes legends make reality, and become more useful than the facts" (48). Thus these histories may include magic and folk wisdom, like events told from Ursula's or Melquíades's point of view in *One Hundred Years of Solitude,* for example. But history is the weight that tethers the balloon of magic, and as if to warn against too great a lightness of mythic or magical being, both Fuentes and Kundera include dangerous sets of floating angels in their novels, angels that represent the lightness of ahistorical irresponsibility. The twin fetus at the end of Fuentes's *Distant Relations,* the remainder of old Heredia's desire to create an angel, floats "with a placidity that repudiates all past, all history, all repentance," a dangerously unanchored position.[26] At the end of the first section on "the angels" in *The Book of Laughter and Forgetting* the narrator tells us that "from the day they excluded me from the circle, I have not stopped falling, I am still falling . . . away from my country and into the void of a world resounding with the terrifying laughter of the angels that covers my every word with its din," a laughter that is virtually diabolic in its erasure of historical consciousness.[27] Because it shows the clock being forcefully returned to the decay of actual time passing, the description of Oskar's first scream in Günter Grass's *The Tin Drum* seems to recognize both the danger of encapsulation in a timeless realm, and the delicate task of balancing between magic and history: at the sound of the scream, "the polished round crystal which protected the honey-colored dial of our clock from dust and moribund flies burst and fell to the floor."[28]

Historical anchoring is well demonstrated in what John Foster calls "felt history," whereby a character experiences historical forces bodily: Anna Karenina, for instance, is crushed by a train, which in this context represents European modernizing forces in Russia.[29] This phenomenon is exaggerated and particularized in magical realist fictions. Clear examples are Lisa's pains that anticipate her death at Babi Yar in *The White Hotel,* Grenouille's magical nose born from the smells of Renaissance Europe in *Perfume,* and Saleem's literal dismemberment as a result of his sympathetic identification with the forces dividing his country at the end of *Midnight's Children.*

Unsettling Doubts

A third quality of magical realism is that before categorizing the irreducible element as irreducible, the reader may hesitate between two contradictory understandings of events, and hence experience some unsettling doubts. The question of belief is central here, this hesitation frequently stemming from the implicit clash of cultural systems within the narrative, which moves toward belief in extrasensory phenomena but narrates from the post-Enlightenment perspective and in the realistic mode that traditionally exclude them. And because belief systems differ, clearly, some readers in some cultures will hesitate less than others, depending on their beliefs and narrative traditions. Even so, much of magical realism is encompassed by Tzvetan Todorov's formulation of the fantastic as existing during a story when a reader hesitates between the uncanny, where an event is explainable according to the laws of the natural universe as we know it, and the marvelous, which requires some alteration in those laws.[30] In other words, magical realism expands fictional reality to include events we used to call magic in realism.[31]

This is a difficult matter, however, because many variations exist. Hesitation may obscure the irreducible element, which consequently is not always so easily perceived as such. The contemporary Western reader's primary doubt is most often between understanding an event as a character's dream or hallucination and, alternatively, understanding it as a miracle. The mysterious character of Beloved in Morrison's novel of that name slithers provokingly between these two options, playing with our rationalist tendencies to recuperate, to reconcile antinomies or co-opt the marvelous. Women outside of Sethe's house ask themselves, "Was it the dead daughter come back? Or a pretend? Was it whipping Sethe?" (258). A little later "Paul D knows Beloved is truly gone. Disappeared, some say, exploded right before their eyes. Ella is not so sure. 'Maybe,' she says, 'maybe not. Could be hiding in the trees waiting for another chance'" (268). And at the end of the book, we hear, "They forgot her like a bad dream." We readers ask ourselves, "Was she no more than that?" "It took longer for those who had spoken to her, lived with her, fallen in love with her, to forget, until they realized they couldn't remember or repeat a single thing she said, and began to believe that, other than what they themselves were thinking, she hadn't said anything at all" (274).

Magical realist scenes may seem dreamlike, but they are not dreams, and the text may both tempt us to co-opt them by categorizing them as dreams and forbid that co-option. Magical realist narratives almost seem to bring up the possibility of interpreting what they chronicle as a dream in order to forestall that interpretation, after having first aired it as a possibility. That strategy, while allaying the reader's doubts, also calls them into being, causing the reader to hesitate. At the start of Kafka's *The Metamorphosis* we are told that this was no dream, and the same words appear near the end of *Perfume* as Grenouille is undergoing his dismemberment. As Saleem says, at one point, of "the invasion of dreams—or a mother's knowledge, or a woman's intuition," "there was no proof," this is "not something that will stand up in court" (60), and at another, regarding the ability of midnight's children "to look into the hearts and minds of men," "don't make the mistake of dismissing what I've unveiled as mere delirium" (240). When Saleem is telling how Parvati made him invisible so that he could return to India from Pakistan undetected, Padma interrupts and questions him, and they ponder the magic of his transformation:

> Then Parvati whispered some other words, and, inside the basket of invisibility, I, Saleem Sinai, complete with my loose anonymous garment, vanished instantly into thin air.
>
>   "Vanished? How vanished, what vanished?" Padma's head jerks up; Padma's eyes stare at me in bewilderment. I shrugging, merely reiterate: Vanished, just like that. Disappeared. Dematerialized. Like a djinn: poof, like so. . . .
>
>   . . . I was in the basket, but also not in the basket. . . . I was tossed with the basket, but also not tossed. Afterwards, Picture Singh said, "No, captain, I couldn't feel your weight." (455)

So we are often literally instructed by the text to hesitate. But even if we are not, we may hesitate, both in doubt because we are unsure about the nature of the events and in wonder, in awe, at their remarkable properties.[32] We do so as we wonder whether Oskar could actually have ceased to grow as a result of the fall he orchestrates for himself, and started again after being hit on the head with a rock, and as we behold the yellow butterflies that appear with Mauricio Babilonia every time he comes to visit Meme Buendía, and "who did not give him a moment's peace" until his death: "The yellow butterflies would invade the house at dusk. Every night on her way back from her bath Meme would find a desperate Fernanda killing butterflies with an insecticide bomb" (271). The phenomenon of the butterflies seems to be a marvelous one but the fact that they die from an insect bomb subjects them to the rules of the physical universe, so we are puzzled about their status. Similarly, we wonder whether it is possible for a woman to live to be more than 145, as Pilar Ternera is reported to have done. The way she is described shortly before we hear of her death locates her both in actual time and in a magical mythical time: "Years before, when she had reached one hundred forty-five years of age, she had given up the pernicious custom of keeping track of her age and she went on living in the static and marginal time of memories, in a future perfectly revealed and established, beyond the futures disturbed by the insidious snares and suppositions of her cards" (363). García Márquez continues to play this game with his readers by beginning *Of Love and Other Demons* with a newspaper story he claims to have covered in 1949, which inspired the novel, and which he in turn links to his grandmother's now legendary tales. He witnesses the unearthing of the tomb of a young girl whose twenty-two meters and eleven centimeters of brilliant coppery hair flow out of her coffin.

> The chief of excavations calmly explained to me that human hair grows one centimeter a month even after death, and twenty-two meters seemed to him a reasonable amount for two hundred years. To me, on the other hand, it didn't seem so trivial, for as a child my grandmother had told me the legend of a little twelve year old marquise whose hair dragged her along like a bride's train, who had died of rabies from a dog bite, and who was worshipped in Caribbean villages for the miracles she performed.[33]

We hesitate on three accounts, most important, because we wonder whether the events the novel narrates are possible and therefore could be true. That initial hesitation increases the intensity of the two other, more pragmatic, speculations about whether García Márquez actually witnessed the phenomenon, and whether the introduction is fact or fiction. With *Aura*, we hesitate at first and then begin to comprehend slowly, because the details of Felipe Montero's transformation into General Llorente are given camouflaged and piecemeal, so that the awareness of the transformation dawns on the reader in the same way it does on Felipe, bit by bit.

In many instances, however, the magic in magical realism is clear and we barely hesitate, the narrator's acceptance of the magic modeling our own, a strategy that I examine in more detail in Chapter 3 in a discussion of narrative techniques.[34] For now, a few briefly noted instances: in *One Hundred Years of Solitude* the flying carpets, Remedios's ascension to heaven, and José Arcadio's blood traveling across Macondo to find Ursula are clearly magic, as is the transformation of the Automobile Club pool into a jungly swamp in *Distant Relations,* the arrival of the title character of García Márquez's "A Very Old Man with Enormous Wings" in Pelayo and Elisenda's courtyard, the "two tiny handprints [that] appeared in the cake" at the start of *Beloved,* or the revival of dead people at the end of *The White Hotel,* and they are presented matter-of-factly by the narrators. This manner of presentation is an essential defining characteristic for Chanady in her distinction between magical realism and the fantastic. In magical realism "authorial reticence . . . naturalizes the supernatural" so that it "does not disconcert the reader." Because the fantastic encodes hesitation, Chanady argues, it presents antinomy, "the simultaneous presence of two conflicting codes in the text," as unresolved. In contrast, because the magical realist narrator accepts the antinomy and promotes the same acceptance in the reader, the antinomy is resolved.[35] Although many magical realist narrators accept the disjunction between realism and magic, thereby tempting their readers to do likewise, many others do not and thus promote hesitation. Another reason this distinction, while generally valid, seems not entirely unproblematic is that even when the text does not entice us to hesitate, we readers' investment in the codes of realism is still so strong, and if they are present in the text we are reading, even the narrator's acceptance of antinomy does not overcome our hesitation completely; thus the hesitation tends often to remain rather than being totally resolved. Brenda Cooper's idea that "it is precisely the mix of authorial reticence with authorial irony that is a defining feature of the magical realist text" takes account of this strange combination of acceptance and skepticism that characterizes the reader's experience in magical realism.[36]

Another possible strategy for the reader is to interpret a particular instance of magic in an otherwise realistic fiction as nothing more than allegory. This kind of interpretation is tempting in Kundera's *The Book of Laughter and Forgetting,* when we see people rise above the ground in a charmed circle of ideological bliss—for Kundera an example of the "unbearable lightness" that totalitarian ideologies will tend to engender. Even so, since the magic here is presented clearly as magic within an otherwise realistic narrative, it belongs on the fringes of magical realism. For Camayd-Freixas, among the essential criteria of magical realism is the reader's simultaneous adoption of a literal and an allegorical perspective.[37] In other words, the weight of the nonallegorical thrust of realistic narrative conventions works against a reduction of the magic in magical realism to a primarily allegorical mode.

Merging Realms

Fourth (in this list of characteristics), we experience the closeness or near-merging of two realms, two worlds, another aspect of magical realism that I examine more closely in Chapter 3.[38] The intermittent and uncertain nature of the narrator's metamorphosis into a sow in *Pig Tales* means that (as Catherine Rodgers formulates it) "the tale opens a space of the in-between ["l'entre-deux"], a space of uncertainty. The narrator herself is captive between two worlds, the human and the animal, not belonging really to one or the other." Marie Darrieussecq regards this situation as symptomatic of certain aspects of contemporary life, such as living in a suburb, which "is a rather undifferentiated in-between . . . a space of all possibilities, sometimes frightening, since one can forget where one comes from there and become lost."[39] For Brian McHale, describing what he terms the postmodern fantastic, "another world penetrates or encroaches upon our world (as in 'House Taken Over' [by Julio Cortázar]), or some representative of our world penetrates an outpost of the other world, the world next door (as in *Aura*). Either way, this precipitates a confrontation between real-world norms (the laws of nature) and other-worldly, supernatural norms."[40] In terms of cultural history, magical realism often merges ancient or traditional—sometimes indigenous—and modern worlds. Ontologically, within the texts, it integrates the magical and the material.[41] Generically, it combines realism and the fantastic. We might say of it, in the words of H. P. Duerr in his *Dreamtime,* that in many of these texts "seeing takes place only if you smuggle yourself in between worlds, the world of ordinary people and that of the witches."[42] Perhaps the magical realist narrative line is analogous to the axis of the world that in many systems of thought is imagined to join the realms of the underworld, the earth, and the heavens.

The magical realist vision thus exists at the intersection of two worlds, at an imaginary point inside a double-sided mirror that reflects in both directions. Ghosts and texts, or people and words that seem ghostly, inhabit these two-sided mirrors, many times situated between the two worlds of life and death; they enlarge that space of intersection where a number of magically real fictions exist. André Breton imagines techniques that will fix the attention "not any longer on what is real, or on the imaginary, but . . . on the other side of reality."[43] Fluid boundaries between the worlds of the living and the dead are traced only to be crossed in *Pedro Páramo, Palace of the Peacock, One Hundred Years of Solitude, The House of the Spirits, Midnight's Children, That Voice, Distant Relations, The White Hotel, Ironweed,* and *So Far from God.* From a metafictional perspective, if fiction is exhausted in this world, then perhaps these texts create another contiguous one into which it spills over, so that it continues life beyond the grave, so to speak.

From the first sentence, William Kennedy's *Ironweed* weaves a web of connections between the land of the living and the land of the dead: the novel begins by telling us that "riding up the winding road of Saint Agnes Cemetery in the back of the rattling old truck, Francis Phelan became aware that the dead, even more than the living, settled down in neighborhoods." As he approaches "the neighborhood of the Phelans," "Francis's mother twitched nervously in her grave as the truck carried him nearer to her." Later on, Francis sees in his mind's eye "his mother and father alight from their honeymoon carriage in front of the house and . . . climb . . . the front stairs to the bedroom they would share for all the years of their marriage, the room that now was also their shared grave, a spatial duality as reasonable to Francis as the concurrence of this moment both in the immediate present of his fifty-eighth year of life and in the year before he was born."[44] This sense of an interchange of worlds is expressed in Isabel Allende's *The House of the Spirits* by Clara, who, during her lifetime, communicated with the spirits. As she is dying "she added that if she could easily communicate with those from the Hereafter, she was absolutely convinced that afterward she would be able to do the same with those of the Here-and-Now." When her husband is old, she appears to him first "just as a mysterious glow, but as my grandfather slowly lost the rage that had tormented him throughout his life, she appeared as she had been at her best, laughing with all her teeth and stirring up the other spirits as she sailed through the house."[45]

The unmediated way in which these different realities are presented means that magical realism also blurs the boundary between fact and fiction, another characteristic that locates magical realism within postmodernism.[46] Following his discussion of the postmodern fantastic, McHale explores the generalized effect of a fantastic " 'charge' [that] seems to be diffused throughout postmodernist writing," though he claims that the hesitation in traditional fantastic writing between this world and the next has been displaced by "the confrontation between different ontological levels in the structure of texts."[47] His formulation thus ultimately stresses the magic *of* fiction rather than the magic *in* it. Similarly, Marie Darrieussecq sees the way in which she writes, between realism and the fantastic, as a reflection of current discourse: "today there exists, even in ordinary life, a way of speaking of reality that always makes a detour through the fantastic, with a lot of realism, as if the fantastic were already an almost trite element of reality."[48]

As we are seeing, with respect to the realm of the referent, reports of irreducible elements of magic question post-Enlightenment science's empirical definition of the world. With respect to the realm of the discourse, those reports of magic question the code of realism, and the texts foreground the constructed nature of fiction. In both cases, magical realism blurs borders between categories. It also begins to erode the categories themselves because the link between empirically constructed perceptions of reality and realistically constructed fictional discourse means that to question one is to question the other.[49]

Disruptions of Time, Space, and Identity

Finally, in addition to merging different worlds, these fictions disturb received ideas about time, space, and identity.[50] With "four years, eleven months, and two days" of rain, an insomnia plague that erases the past and the meaning of words, and a room where it is "always March and always Monday," our usual sense of time is shaken throughout *One Hundred Years of Solitude*. Our sense of space is disrupted when tropical plants grow over the automobile club's pool in Paris at the end of *Distant Relations*, when Cortázar's axolotl and his observer seem to change places on either side of the glass in the aquarium, and when Grenouille smells virgins across town. As Fredric Jameson sets out the project of realism, one thing it achieves is "the emergence of a new space and a new temporality" because realism's spatial homogeneity abolishes the older forms of sacred space. Likewise the newly measuring clock and measurable routine replace "older forms of ritual, sacred, or cyclical time."⁵¹ Even as we read Jameson's description, we sense the erosion of this program by magical realist texts—and by other modern and postmodern ones as well.

Like their nineteenth-century Gothic predecessors, many magical realist fictions delineate near-sacred or ritual enclosures, but these sacred spaces are not watertight; they leak their magical narrative waters over the rest of the texts and the worlds they describe, just as that exterior reality permeates them. As Felipe enters Consuelo's house (in Fuentes's *Aura*), for example, it is presented as a realm apart from the noisy outside street: "Before going in you give a last look over your shoulder, frowning at the long line of stalled cars that growl, honk, and belch out the unhealthy fumes of their impatience. You try to retain some single image of that indifferent outside world." That world contrasts with "the mold, the dampness of the plants, the rotting roots, the thick drowsy aroma," an interior Gothic-like world that increasingly encloses Felipe. And yet Felipe's clothes from his room in the city mysteriously appear at the house.⁵² Bluestone Road is the scene of Beloved's mysterious haunting presence and the magical events that it engenders, and Sethe thinks that "Whatever is going on outside my door ain't for me. The world is in this room." But Sethe, Denver, and Paul D come and go at will, indicating that the house is not entirely a realm unto itself—although we also hear at one point that when Denver "left the house she neither saw the prints nor heard the voices that ringed 124 like a noose" (183). At another point, Stamp Paid talks about Beloved at 124 to Ella, indicating Stamp's familiarity with the territory, and its lack of total isolation, a phenomenon that helps Sethe in the end.

> "Somebody new in there. A woman. Thought you might know who is she."
>
> "Ain't no new Negroes in this town I don't know about," she said. "What she look like? You sure that wasn't Denver?"
>
> "I know Denver. This girl's narrow.'
>
> "You sure?"
>
> "I know what I see."
>
> "Might see anything at all at 124."
>
> "True." (185)

The same sense of magical and yet permeable interiors characterizes Saleem's pickle factory, Branly's house (in *Distant Relations*), and the actual houses in

The White Hotel and *The House of the Spirits,* as I explain in more detail in a discussion of magically real houses in Chapter 5.

Magical realism reorients not only our habits of time and space but our sense of identity as well.[53] The multivocal nature of the narrative and the cultural hybridity that characterize magical realism extends to its characters, which tend toward a radical multiplicity. With over five hundred children of midnight talking through his head, for example, is Saleem himself anymore? And we hear him question his identity in other ways as well. At one point, he reports, " 'I am glad,' my Padma says, 'I am happy you ran away.' But I insist: not I. He. He, the buddha. Who, until the snake, would remain not-Saleem" (431). And he expands on this idea of multiple and mobile identity: "Who what am I? My answer: I am the sum total of everything that went before me, of all I have been seen done, of everything done-to-me. I am everyone everything whose being-in-the-world affected was affected by mine. I am anything that happens after I've gone which would not have happened if I had not come. Nor am I particularly exceptional in this matter; each 'I,' every one of the now-six-hundred-million-plus of us, contains a similar multitude. [54] I repeat for the last time: to understand me, you'll have to swallow a world" (457–58).[55] He actualizes the potential in that statement about personal multiplicity with the midnight's children inside his head, but in addition to them, he says that his mother's "inside-voice is bouncing against the inside of my head," his "favorite uncle's sadness is pouring into me," and he has "Mary Pereira's dreams inside my head" (202, 203).[56] Similarly, in *The Famished Road,* people may be taken over by other beings or phenomena. A mysterious sense of fluid identities and interconnectedness appears in this passage:

> The night filled the room and swept over us, filling our space with light spirits, the old forms of animals; extinct birds stood near Dad's boots, a beautiful beast with proud eyes and whose hide quivered with gold-dust stood over the sleeping forms of Mum and Dad. A tree defined itself over the bed where I lay. It was an ancient tree, its trunk was blue, the spirit sap flowed in many brilliant colours up its branches, densities of light shone from its leaves. I lay horizontal in its trunk. The darkness moved; future forms, extinct tribes, walked through our landscape. They traveled new roads. They traveled for three hundred years and arrived in our night-space. I did not have to dream. It was the first time I realized that an invisible space had entered my mind and dissolved part of

the interior structure of my being. The wind of several lives blew into my eyes. The lives stretched far back and when I saw the great king of the spirit-world staring at me through the open doors of my eyes I knew that many things were calling me. It is probably because we have so many things in us that community is so important.[57]

The extinct birds and beautiful beasts hover over the sleeping and therefore more available forms of Mum and Dad, the wind of several lives blows over Azaro's eyes, and the great king of the spirit-world stares at Azaro through his own eyes. And all the while he lies inside the trunk of the blue tree. Thus not only are the living spaces and minds of Azaro and his parents peopled by humanlike spirits and cosmic forms but they also inhabit them. The permeability is mutual and incessant.

In a less multiple but similarly interchangeable manner, the merging and changing of identities is central to the magic in Cortázar's story "Axolotl." When, after having witnessed what seems to be the transformation of the narrator into an axolotl, we hear the narrator's final ambiguous speculation about whether "he" on the other side of the glass who has presumably been an axolotl moments before "is going to write a story about us, that, believing he's making up a story [but actually recounting what has happened to him and that he no longer consciously recalls], he's going to write all this about axolotls," we wonder about the identities of both narrator and axolotl. And this narrator (now an axolotl) further deconstructs the notion of separate selves by speculatively musing, "or I was also in him, or all of us were thinking humanlike." And we are even further confused when we hear this sentence: "I am an axolotl for good now, and if I think like a man it's only because every axolotl thinks like a man inside his rosy stone resemblance."[58] When he begins the sentence, he seems to refer to his transformation from human to axolotl, confirming the difference between then, but as the sentence progresses, he seems to deconstruct that transformation and to merge humans and axolotls.

Similarly deconstructive of individuality, with their reversal of skin colors, Tristão and Isabel in John Updike's novel *Brazil* achieve a partial, at least a social, exchange and merging of identities. Just before those changes of skin, Isabel says of herself and the shaman who seems responsible for the changes that "something in the smoke had eaten away at the boundary between their minds."[59] That example reminds us that often those multiple identities are constructed. Grenouille's creation of a scent for himself out of the distilled essences of the most diverse substances exemplifies that idea. And as we see in more detail shortly, we ask ourselves who is the voice in *That Voice,* and who or what are the relations in *Distant Relations.* According to Linda Hutcheon, "in *The White Hotel,* the realist novel's concept of the subject, both in history and in fiction, is openly contested."[60] That challenge is particularly effective because it operates from within; the magic questions individual identity from a realistically rendered historical fiction and a realistically detailed character.[61]

Locations

Geographical stylistics are problematic, but one might speculate about the existence of a tropical lush and a northerly spare variety of the magical realist plant.[62] In the northerly variety, there is less magic and its range is more circumscribed: the ingenious and rather programmatic magic of smell in *Perfume,* and the very small intrusions of magical event in *The Book of Laughter and Forgetting,* for example, contrast with the more pervasive magic in García Márquez and Rushdie; the occasional magic of *Beloved* is somewhere in between the two. Jean Weisgerber makes a similar distinction between two types of magical realism: the "scholarly" type, which "loses itself in art and conjecture to illuminate or construct a speculative universe," and which is mainly the province of European writers, and the mythic or folkloric type, found mainly in Latin America.[63]

These two strains of scholarly and mythic roughly coincide with the two types of magical realism that Roberto González Echevarría proposes: the epistemological, in which marvels stem from an observer's vision, and the ontological, in which America is considered to be itself marvelous (Alejo Carpentier's "lo real maravilloso"[the marvelous real]).[64] The trouble is, it is often difficult to distinguish between these two strains. Two of Cortázar's stories, otherwise quite similar, illustrate the difficulty. "Axolotl," on one hand, is set in Paris, in the aquarium section of the Jardin des Plantes zoo, but the axolotl itself is an American organism, with an Aztec name, so that categories begin to crumble—just as I was about to put this story nearer the European, epistemological branch of the genre. Following my initial impulse, however, we can note that it is the narrator's identity with the amphibian rather than its continent of origin that begins the magic. In "The Night

Face Up," on the other hand, perhaps the extraordinarily strong presence of the Aztec past in modern Mexico motivates the magical transportation of the narrator back into that past, or conversely, the brutal irruption of that Aztec past into the modernizing program of the European Renaissance is responsible for the movement forward into the modern present. Like the atmosphere of belief in Haiti in Carpentier's *The Kingdom of This World,* this strong Aztec element is a particularly American phenomenon. Thus these categories of European versus American have a certain validity. Whether one chooses Carpentier's ontological "marvelous real" or the epistemological view that the magic inheres in the words and the vision rather than in the world, magical realism flowers in culturally hybrid ground. As Chanady has noted, a major force contributing to the development of magical realism in Latin America was the perception of that continent as exotic and the consequent desire to describe this unfamiliar reality to Europe.[65] Similarly, whatever cultural agendas more recent magical realist texts such as *Midnight's Children* and *The Famished Road* serve in the former colonies where their authors were born, the texts also present those postcolonial cultures to an international reading public. But as I show in a later discussion, such a postcolonial agenda does not appear in all magical realist fictions, because they also exist outside postcolonial environments.

These questions of location suggest that much of magical realism may resemble Caliban, now something of an icon of new world, or postcolonial, writing, who learns the master's language, then uses it to curse. Magical realism has mastered the European discourse of realism and now uses it not to curse, exactly, but to undermine some of its master's assumptions. Just as Caliban's swear words are not the combinations of sounds Prospero intended for him to use, so magical realism's use of realistic detail to describe an impossible event, which moves us beyond everyday reality, rather than anchoring us in it, was not realism's original program. Allied to the modernist "ruin of representation," which occurred largely in the realm of formal structure and syntax, this current challenge operates more radically in the register of phenomena, of semantics, and might almost be called a partial ruin of the represented.[66] It challenges the assumptions of realistic representation but is enraptured with its practices. Realism, for example, does not believe in miracles, but it has given the magical realist the means to describe them. Thus even when a magical realist text overturns the assumptions of Western empiricism and questions the binary opposition of magic and realism from the perspective of another cultural or narrative tradition that lacks those assumptions and that opposition, they persist, because they are embedded within the conventions of realism the text employs.[67]

In addressing the question of location, then, we continue to see how, in addition to combining the genres of realism and the fantastic, magical realism is also often culturally hybrid. Because magical and realistic narrative modes frequently come from different cultural traditions, their amalgamation makes magical realism a liminal mode, in the sense of Victor Turner's "liminal entities," which "are neither here nor there; they are betwixt and between the positions assigned and arrayed by law, custom, convention, and ceremonial."[68] In other words, much of magical realism is multicultural in its structure and its history *avant la lettre* and has therefore contributed substantially to the development of contemporary multicultural fiction and criticism. Thus magical realism partially reverses the process of cultural colonization.

Magical realism's multicultural perspective often originates in the peripheral and colonized regions of the West: Latin America and the Caribbean, India, Eastern Europe, Africa. But the mode is becoming less and less marginal, even though it retains the charm of the marginal position. In 1980, John Barth rejected membership in any imaginary writer's club that did not include García Márquez, praising *One Hundred Years of Solitude* as a prime example of replenished postmodern fiction. Barth's statement represents an important shift in literary relations and signals an increased worldwide recognition of magical realism—according to John Updike, writing in 1988, "a now widely available elixir."[69] Both a cause and an effect of magical realism's international success, its decentering of contemporary literary discourse, is the fact that its mastertexts are widely dispersed. The novel that put the term *magical realism* on the international literary map, *One Hundred Years of Solitude*, comes from the small Latin American country of Colombia. What seems to be increasingly regarded as a second definitive example, *Midnight's Children*, is from India. Both of these are aggressively postcolonial texts. A third, Grass's *The Tin Drum*, is from Germany and locates the final (albeit chronologically first) apex of this far-flung triangle in Europe, so that it is not only a postcolonial style.[70] Furthermore, the presence of magical realist films such as *The Witches of Eastwick, Field of Dreams, Ironweed, Wolf, Thinner, Like Water for Chocolate* and its spin-offs *Woman on Top* and *Chocolat*, among others, in the cinematic mainstream, further attest to its increasing dispersion throughout all contemporary culture.

In terms of literary history, magical realism in the West develops from a combination of realism and surrealism, often with an infusion of pre-Enlightenment or indigenous culture. Rushdie claims, for example, that his writing comes from a combination of Gogol and Dickens—"on the edge between the surreal and the real"—and the *Arabian Nights*—"flying horses and invisible cloaks."[71] Located within postmodernism, it nevertheless has strong roots in modernism, situating it at the intersection of those two modes.[72] In articulating the position of magical realism as growing out of modernism into postmodernism, it is useful to consider Brian McHale's idea that modernism is epistemological, concerned with questions of knowledge, while postmodernism is ontological, concerned with questions of being.[73] (In the one we ask how we know something and in the other we ask what it is.) McHale locates a point in William Faulkner's *Absalom, Absalom!* where this line is crossed. It is the moment when Quentin and Shreve leave off their attempts to remember and reconstruct and begin self-consciously to invent. That moment of invention, the realization of an imaginary realm, can help to distinguish magical realism from realism. In the former, it happens not provisionally in the voices of narrators but concretely in the reality depicted.[74]

Especially with regard to the questioning of time, space, and identity, it is possible to see how magical realism has its roots in modernism and its branches and leaves in postmodernism, as it were. If we contrast magical realist presentations of space and time with modernist paradigms, we can see that in modernism, readers are brought into surreptitious contact, through, as Virginia Woolf expressed it, a kind of mental tunneling process within the discourse, with mythical, historical, or, most frequently, personal pasts—a depth of perception characteristic of modernism, whereas in magical realism, those temporal realms are brought to life in the referential realm of the text. The Greece of *The Odyssey*, for example, is endlessly evoked in *Ulysses*, and Clarissa's past at Bourton resonates in present-day London in her mind in *Mrs. Dalloway*, but they are not magically conjured into concrete existence as are time and space in "The Night Face Up" in which the protagonist shuttles between the temporal spaces of a realistically described Aztec ritual and a similarly actualized modern hospital, or in *The White Hotel*, in which Lisa's future death from a bayonet is magically present in the premonitory pains in her womb and breast.[75] Similarly, in *Pedro Páramo*, the voices of the past live again in the present, and Juan Preciado seems to pass between those times as they are spatially embodied in the town of Comala. First, we hear from him what seems to be his passing between the spaces of life and death or present and past-in-the-present through the medium of air.

> There wasn't any air. I had to swallow the same air I breathed out, holding it back with my hands so it wouldn't escape. I could feel it coming and going, and each time it was less and less, until it got so thin it slipped through my fingers forever.
>
> Forever.
>
> I remember seeing something like a cloud of foam, and washing myself in the foam, and losing myself in the cloud. That was the last thing I saw.

Then, a bit later, those temporal spaces are again concretely inhabited as Dorotea tells Juan that "They buried me in your grave, and I fit very well into the hollow of your arms. Only it occurs to me that I ought to be embracing you, not he other way around. Listen. It's raining up there. Can't you feel the raindrops falling?" / [And Juan answers] "It feels as if somebody were walking over us."[76]

Following McHale's distinction between the modernist epistemological and the postmodernist ontological, then, readers experience the engagement of the spectators in the sky-writing in *Mrs. Dalloway* as an epistemological question of viewing, whereas in addition to the epistemological orientation that is achieved by the presence of different voices in *Pedro Páramo,* through the way those voices are embodied in beings with concretely described attributes, readers also confront ontological questions of being. In the first example our attention is focused on *how*—through whose eyes—we perceive the writing, whereas in the second we wonder what kind of beings we are seeing. It is not so much a question of how but of what. As Saleem said, "who what am I?" The same is true, however briefly, in the case of the two circles of dancers that rise into the air in *The Book of Laughter and Forgetting,* which the reader experiences both in an epistemological way, as a figment of the narrator's imaginative distance from the communist ideology to which the dancers subscribe, and in an ontological sense as a different spatial mode of being in the world.

With regard to questions of identity as well, these fictions greatly resemble modernist ones, their closest precursors. It is not so much the existence of these multiple times, places, or identities in magical realism as it is the way in which they are portrayed that distinguishes magical realism from modernism. To continue with our two salient examples, Leopold Bloom in *Ulysses* as a bricolage of (among other things) *l'homme moyen sensual,* the Wandering Jew, the flaneur, an Irish Christ, and a unique and realistically described Dubliner is very similar to the Buendías as biblical dynasty, Latin American colony, twentieth-century oligarchy, or Melquíades as magician, scribe, Saint John writing the apocalypse, and friend to José Arcadio Buendía; but García Márquez's inclusion of the birth of the prophesied child with the pig's tale as the realization of a family curse, the repetition not only of names but of character traits and activities, such as the repetition of incestuous urges between aunts and nephews, especially in the male members of the family, the blood trail that joins mother and son, among other events, questions the boundaries of the individual self in more radical form than Joyce does. In *Mrs. Dalloway,* Woolf questions the separateness of our identities through Clarissa's sympathetic identification with Septimus, especially in the moment when she imagines to the point of vicariously performing his death. And Woolf's own excursion into the fantasy of changing identity in Orlando has been seen as a precursor to magical realism.[77] But in Laura Esquivel's *Like Water for Chocolate,* the way in which the identity of Tita as Pedro's beloved and true, cosmically correct wife is conflated with that of his official wife, Rosaura, through the phenomenon of Tita's milk being magically generated to feed Rosaura and Pedro's baby as if it were hers and Pedro's, or the way that Consuelo and Aura, like Felipe and the General, alternately separate and combine in Fuentes' *Aura* extends that questioning of boundaries even further and in more concrete detail. The modernist tendency toward revealing psychic depth of personality implies the existence of multiple selves within one individual and mysterious connections between different people, but these principles are not actualized to the same extent that they are in much of magical realism, which, like postmodernism generally, often radically extends modernism's tendency toward multiplicity and collectivity in its portrayal of fictional character. If in modernism character generates story out of psychic depth, and in postmodernism story generates character out of events and histories and intertextual bricolage, then once again, magical realism mediates between those modes.[78]

In short, the epistemological concerns, along with the mythic elements, the primitivism, the psychological interiors and depths, align magical realism with much of modernism; the ontological questions raised by the presence of magical events, and the confrontations between different worlds and discourses, together with the collective spirit and political pointedness of the writing, align it with postmodernism.[79] In magical realism, the mythic patterns glimpsed behind modernism's realistic texts emerge as magical elements on its surface. Aschenbach in Thomas Mann's *Death in Venice* mentally activates the antique Dionysian while Rushdie's Saleem with his large nose comes near to actually re-embodying in human form the elephant-nosed authorial persona of Ganesh, and, like Sinbad from the *Thousand and One Nights,* is literally transported in a basket. The magical, irreducible elements in magical realism inherit modernism's search beyond the rational into the unconscious, but they bring more than an individual's hidden scenarios to the postmodern surface of the text. In other terms, the autonomy of discourse that magical realism implicitly proposes through the irreducible element means that it mediates the modernist organization of the world's chaos through art and the postmodern occlusion of the world by the text. In the end, though, in the way that its texts slither dizzyingly between modern and postmodern sensibilities, magical realism exemplifies the way in which those very categories destabilize themselves the longer we look at them.[80]

As we have been observing, contemporary magical realism has developed as a narrative mode that produces fictions in diverse cultural traditions, its continuing popularity ensuring those productions a growing international audience. As part of that literary history, Latin American magical realist writing grew out of the first wave of postcolonial romantic primitivism, which affirmed the sense of a usable, natural, and indigenous past but had not yet articulated a distinctive style in which to portray that sensibility. It thus developed as a response to the conjunction of indigenist and avant garde modes, and through a combination of Latin American and European inspiration. It responded to the questioning of the novel of the land by writers influenced by European and U.S. modernism and surrealism, and their consequent production of a more psychological realism in the 1930s and 1940s, together with a revalidation of the land and culture of Latin America.[81] Even though Franz Roh had coined the term *magical realism* and his essay had been translated into Spanish and published by the influential *Revista de Occidente* in 1927, according to Erik Camayd-Freixas, the essential link in the dissemination of the idea of magical realism was Arturo Uslar-Pietri, who was a close friend of Massimo Bontempelli's and also knew Carpentier and Miguel Angel Asturias in Paris.

The origin of the term *magical realism* and the history of the dissemination of the concept aside, the surrealism that was current in Europe during the 1920s and that challenged the tradition of realism, encouraging excursions into the surreal, beyond conscious reason into realms of dream, myth, the unconscious, and "primitive" culture, led Carpentier and Asturias to exploit and affirm what America had to offer in those areas.[82] Hence Asturias's inclusion of magical images drawn from Mayan mythology in his fiction and Carpentier's idea of "the marvelous real" as a distinctly American phenomenon where church sculptures depicted the intercultural phenomenon of angels playing the maracas, where outrageous otherworldly plants grew in profusion and that therefore was in no need of the kind of artificial juxtaposition, such as sewing machines and umbrellas on dissecting tables, to which European surrealists had recourse in their desperate search for the extraordinary. In contrast to the surprising images constructed by surrealism out of ordinary objects, which aim to appear virtually unmotivated and which programmatically resist interpretation, magical realist images, while projecting a similar initial aura of surprising craziness, tend to reveal psychological, social, emotional, and political motivations after some scrutiny. (Recall the trail of Aureliano José's blood, which suggests the incestuous passions of the Buendías and the close ties between mothers and sons, and the levitation of Madame Raphael and a few of her pupils, which suggests the heartless power of a party line.) But that initial craziness points to the carnivalesque side of magical realism, the way in which its realistic fictional language is partially freed from its habitual mimetic constraints. But only partially. According to Carpentier the problem with European surrealists is that "many of them disguise themselves cheaply as magicians, forgetting that the marvelous begins to be unmistakably marvelous when it arises from an unexpected alteration of reality (the miracle), from a privileged revelation of reality, an unaccustomed insight that is singularly favored by the unexpected richness of reality or an amplification of the scale and categories of reality, perceived with particular intensity by virtue of an exaltation of the spirit that leads it to a kind of extreme state [*estado límite*]."[83] Essential here for the development of magical realism in general is the idea of the marvelous growing within the richness of reality. In addition, the repudiation of the metropolitan paradigm, while at the same time speaking with that paradigm in mind, is of specific importance for its efficacy as a postcolonial style. The affirmation of the local, together with its attachment to the cosmopolitan, with which magical realism began, continues to characterize it.

Following this initial impetus, Latin American magical realism as it developed in the 1950s and 1960s in the fiction of Rulfo, García Márquez, Fuentes, and Cortázar, among others, then combined the cosmopolitanism of Jorge Luis Borges's universally oriented speculative philosophical fictions with the more specifically American perspective of Asturias and Carpentier, who discovered in myth the possibilities of reconciling the universal and the autochthonous and experienced a renewed validation of Latin American nature and culture. As I suggest above, that revalidation—ironically enough—received a seminal impetus from European modernist surrealism and primitivism, from the ideas of Pierre Mabille, for example, who located an important source for the marvelous in folklore, as well as those of the primitivist anthropologists Lucien Lévi-Bruhl and G. W. Frazer, and in Latin America, especially, the Marxist theoretician and activist José Mariátegui, who advocated an Indian utopia, and culminating with the ideology of the mestizo as a legitimate rather than merely a degenerate source of Latin American identity in the work of Arturo Uslar-Pietri and others. Those early theories also reflected the widespread attempt (by such writers as José Enrique Rodó and José Vasconcelos) to reconstruct a positive idea of America, overturning Eurocentric stereotypes of native "barbarism." Out of that context, the "'abnormality' and 'distortion,' formerly condemned as deviations from a given model, were now considered excellent aesthetic effects."[84]

Thus magical realism was culturally hybrid from the start and has been instrumental in temporarily alleviating the universalist/nativist controversy central to the development of a modern Latin American literary identity, a controversy that has resurfaced recently with respect to magical realism itself. It combines the telluric force of novels of the land that undergirded movements of national independence in the nineteenth century with modernist innovations such as stream-of-consciousness narration, nonlinear temporal sequencing, surrealist imagery, and a primitivist ethnographic consciousness. García Márquez, for example, has said that reading a sentence of Woolf's *Mrs. Dalloway* completely changed his sense of time and may have given him the idea for Macondo's process of decomposition and also that he thinks the Caribbean taught him "to see reality differently, to accept supernatural elements as part of our everyday life."[85] Camayd-Freixas locates the central Latin American texts by Carpentier, Asturias, Rulfo, and García Márquez that he studies within the discourse of primitivism and maintains that the reader familiarizes extraordinary events by categorizing them as the manifestations of a primitive mentality alien to his or her own. But as magical realism moves out of that primitivist phase, as it is currently doing, such a distancing mechanism lessens in importance, and the otherness moves closer to the self-same. In any case, its frequent alliance to literary identity politics, an alliance strengthened by its narrative encoding of alterity, has made magical realism a powerful decolonizing mode. That it continues to serve such a function and that this function is tied to the magical realist portrayal of worlds of the spirit is suggested by a recent article describing fiction by a new generation of post-apartheid black South African writers, many of whom claim that their writing is more nuanced in a society whose primary concern is no longer the relatively clear-cut injustice of the racist regime but the complex intraracial tensions that have succeeded them. Thus, according to the reporter Rachel Swarns, many young black writers are "abandoning a rigidly realist style to incorporate a sense of the spiritualism that pervades rural villages. Lightning is hurled to kill an enemy. Birds carry messages of good and evil. And the dead fuss over the living as they watch from the other side."[86]

If we take these developments into account, it is clear that magical realism in Latin America and elsewhere belongs largely in the second wave, in Kwame Anthony Appiah's terms, of "postrealist writing, postnativist politics, a transnational rather than a national solidarity—and pessimism: a kind of post optimism . . . a post that challenges earlier legitimating narratives," a wave that is continued but changed in nature by the general shift toward the documentary realism that has followed magical realism in Latin America in the texts of Carpentier (*Rite of Spring*), García Márquez (*The General in His Labyrinth*), Cortázar (*Manual for Manuel*), and Fuentes (in *Terra Nostra* and *The Campaign*).[87] In *Midnight's Children* this sense of postcolonial pessimism, of the betrayals of supposed liberation, coexists with the celebration of ancient patterns (Saleem's nose as a reincarnation of Ganesh's, Dr. Narliker's huge emblems of birth control transformed into fetishes connected with ancient fertility worship). It resembles Yambo Ouologuem's *Bound to Violence* as interpreted by Appiah to represent "a challenge to the novels of the first stage"; Ouologuem's novel identifies "the realist novel as part of the tactic of nationalist legitimation and so it [like magical realism] is . . . postrealist."[88] Thus, like magical realism in Latin America, and in partial response to it, African magical realism developed out of a first wave of postcolonial indigenist novels inspired by traditional myth and oral narrative, such as *The Palm Wine Drinkard* and *My Life in the Bush of Ghosts* by Amos Tutuola or *The Forest of a Thousand Daemons* by D. O. Fagunwa, and the nationalistically oriented fictions of Chinua Achebe and Wole Soyinka, but also indirectly fed on earlier surrealist impulses imbibed by negritude poets such as Léopold Sédar Senghor.[89] Similarly, Margaret Cezair-Thompson, though she does not deal with magical realism as such, studies the development of Okri's fiction out of earlier nonmagical postcolonial fiction. She proposes that through Azaro, who wants "to find and create new roads from this one which is so hungry, this road of *our refusal to be*," Okri "proceeds beyond the road of incessant hunger, beyond the postcolonial's actual and discursive 'refusal to be,' and beyond the crises of history" that overwhelmed earlier postcolonial fiction, but without ignoring them.[90]

In the fifties, sixties, and seventies, then, when magical realism as a liminal mode was growing in Latin America, and beginning to spread abroad, it may have been a source of strength in the definition of a continental literary identity, contributing to a sense of community with its consequent mutual support of Latin American writers during the boom. This sense of community now spans the globe, whether or not it is affirmed by its practitioners, and is exemplified in P. Gabrielle Foreman's claim that Allende uses magical realism consciously as a literary technique to draw her readers into the text of *The House of the Spirits* before presenting her political message near the end of the novel, a strategy that builds on but contrasts with what Foreman claims is García Márquez's earlier and less explicitly political use of magic and with Toni Morrison's simultaneous use of magic and history.[91] But the moment of defining a continental identity passes, and the sense of solidarity, together with the revolutionary impact of the style is less prominent when the mode is more solidly established.[92] A similar process, and a confirmation of the idea that magical realism has frequently played a significant role in emergent or replenished literatures, can be discerned in the way in which *The Tin Drum* is often considered to be a blueprint for the formation of German literary identity after the Second World War, and *Midnight's Children* an enabling model for the second generation of postindependence Indian novelists.[93]

Following this developmental pattern, we might imagine a magically real decolonizing pen as having been passed from Grass, García Márquez, and Fuentes, among others, to Rushdie and other magical realists, including Okri.[94] For Fuentes, the magical realism he seemed to implicitly champion over twenty years ago in his essay on the new Latin American novel with his references to the death of bourgeois realism and to novels that invent "a second reality,"[95] and to which I would argue that *Aura,* "Chac Mool," *Distant Relations,* and *Christopher Unborn* belong, now seems to feel to him like a critically imposed straitjacket.

> Gabriel García Márquez's *The General in his Labyrinth* managed to close, with a historical scar, the wounds emanating from the so-called "magical realism," which, invented by Alejo Carpentier, had been applied indiscriminately as a label to too many Hispanic American novelists, although truly it became the personal stamp of only one: Gabriel García Márquez. The first surprising thing, in starting to read *The General in His Labyrinth* is, precisely, the lack of elements associated with "magical realism." García Márquez's narrative, this time, is directly and historically localized.[96]

The mistake is perhaps, as Fuentes suggests, to label novelists rather than texts, because magical realism may appear, disappear, and reappear within an author's oeuvre. Fuentes himself, like Rushdie, Morrison, Allende, and others, has developed an increasingly historicized magical realism. Indeed, the messianic tone of Fuentes' recent fiction, especially *Christopher Unborn,* a masterful post-Joycean historical fantasy that grows out of magical realism, suggests that magic still enlivens politically engaged narrative.

The force of magical realism as a decolonizing agent, its passage from Latin America eastward, is documented by Rushdie in a 1982 review of García Márquez's *Chronicle of a Death Foretold:* "El realismo magical [*sic*], magical realism, at least as practiced by Márquez, is a development out of Surrealism that expresses a genuinely 'Third World' consciousness.[97] It deals with what Naipaul has called 'half-made' societies, in which the impossibly old struggles against the appallingly new."[98] Note how Rushdie's formulation of "impossibly old" combined with "appallingly new" aptly encapsulates both the themes and styles of magical realism: literally dead people or metaphorically buried beliefs—that are "impossibly old"—may be revived to question "appallingly new" realities of contemporary life in narratives that combine post-Enlightenment realistic descriptions with pre-Enlightenment elements of magic. Perhaps Rushdie is guilty of the very critical error Fuentes objects to, of continuing to invoke the label of magical realism when it may no longer apply to the fiction in question. However, that very mislabeling, the fact that Rushdie manages to squeeze a reference to magical realism into this review of a book that does not exemplify that mode particularly well, suggests both the enabling force of magical realism and the bonding of its new practitioners with its more experienced ones. Rushdie invokes its communal support as he writes his own postcolonial magical realist masterpiece. And his (mis)use of Spanish underscores the strength of his desire to absorb its general decolonizing power, irrespective of his familiarity with its particular language or history. That the decolonizing force of magical realism began its cultural work in Latin America and has spread from there to other postcolonial sites helps to explain why, as Fredric Jameson has formulated it, "Latin American literature since the boom has today become perhaps the principal player on the scene of world culture, and has had an unavoidable and inescapable influence, not merely on other Third World cultures as such, but on First World literature and culture as well."[99]

Throughout its history, an erosion of clear distinctions plagues the term *magical realism* itself, which is flawed for many reasons. It began in art history, having been coined, to repeat, by Franz Roh in 1925 to describe European painting's movement back toward realism after expressionism, but also virtually simultaneously used by Bontempelli to describe both painting and literature in 1926. It therefore carries burdens from visual history that its verbal embodiments cannot well bear. Following that, it has migrated from continent to continent and has suffered from inexact definitions.[100] Nevertheless, it seems that the term *magical realism,* while confusing, hybrid, imprecise, will not go away.[101] It continues to hold, as Jameson has said, "a strange seductiveness" for both readers and critics.[102] Why?

First, and most important, the term persists because it is useful as a description of a worldwide trend.[103] As such, its hybrid nature, originating between painting and literature, describing European and third world literatures, suits the mixture of genres, perspectives, and cultures in postcolonial writing.[104] Moreover, the very oxymoronic nature of the term suggests its capacity for including multiple worlds and discourses.

A second, and contrasting, reason for the seductive persistence of the term *magical realism* is that it suggests ways in which this genre can be related to and traced back to earlier modes of fiction, which also contain combinations of realism and fantasy. While it is too anachronistic to label *The Odyssey,* for example, or *The Inferno* magical realism, because they are informed by pre-Enlightenment systems of belief in which the terms *magic* and *realism* were not so sharply distinguished as they subsequently became in post-Enlightenment thought, they can be seen as precursors of magical realism, in the sense that Borges describes writers such as Kafka as creating their own precursors by achieving similar effects even though they might not have had the imaginary precursors specifically in mind.

Finally, like the fiction it labels, the combination of materialism and mystery in the term *magical realism* may appeal to us because it suggests a possible approach to the realm of the spirit in western critical discourse. Virginia Woolf prefigures this idea when she characterizes Joyce and the modernists as "spiritual" in contrast to the late nineteenth-century "materialists"— H. G. Wells, Arnold Bennet, and John Galsworthy, so that here again, we can discern seeds of this aspect of magical realism in modernism. Outrageously enough, the term *magical realism* may persist not because it helps to formulate clear distinctions or coherent analyses but because it provides the hint of an escape from them into another discursive space not dominated by them or by material reality and reason. As Jean-Pierre Durix has proposed, "perhaps the merit of the phrase 'magic realism' is to suggest a field of possibilities in which the term will no longer be an oxymoron."[105] Within the realm of critical discourse, then, an investigation of the general significance of the mode of magical realism can begin to address the lack of attention given to the spirit in contemporary theory. In his description of the fantastic, Tzvetan Todorov, for example, associates the phenomena he discusses as "the fragility of the limit between matter and mind" with the worlds of the child and the psychotic or the drugged, but not in any explicit way with the domain of spirit or mystery.[106]

To continue using the term *magical realism* raises several additional problems. The difficulty one faces in studying magical realism globally is that it serves different cultural needs and agendas in different times and places. Especially important to note but also especially difficult to encompass in a single discussion is its presence in societies at all stages of development—in both "First" and "Third" Worlds. The term thus underlines the danger that to treat magical realism in this way, from a broad, comparative perspective, is to colonize the diverse cultural traditions of these texts by considering them under a general rubric. That is, the attempt to define the general characteristics and significance of magical realism as a worldwide trend will necessarily involve the neglect of many local particularities. There is really no satisfying solution to this problem, except, perhaps, to keep it constantly in mind. According to Stephen Slemon, "the critical use of the concept of magical realism can . . . signify resistance to monumental theories of literary practice—a way of suggesting there is something going on in certain forms of literary writing, and in the modalities of cultural experience that underlie those forms, that confounds the capacities of the major genre systems to come to terms with them. At the same time, of course, the concept of magic realism itself threatens to become a monumentalizing category for literary practice and to offer to centralizing genre systems a single locus upon which the massive problem of *difference* in literary expression can be managed into recognizable meaning in one swift pass."[107]

Nevertheless, despite such cultural differences and particularities, one can recognize significant similarities that indicate a worldwide trend. It is useful to register that fact and to speculate about its meaning. Cultural imperialisms are to be avoided, but fear of them should not cloud a sense of genuine cultural community, which may eventually help to increase our understanding of a common genre and to dissolve imperialisms.[108] To begin with, because its strongest literary associations are Latin American, the term *magical realism* reverses the direction in which critical formulations have tended to migrate, so that it can be seen as constituting a partial critical "writing back." That all these terms—primitivism, First and Third Worlds, centers and margins—elicit quotation marks around themselves confirms the sense of how spheres of influence have shifted in contemporary culture. The increasing visibility of magical realism in the international literary marketplace has contributed substantially to that cultural reorientation. According to Edna Aizenberg, the spread of magical realism "is a development of revolutionary magnitude . . . and we should not take it for granted"; it "suggests that Latin American magical realism may well be the first contemporary literary mode to break the hegemony of the center by forcing the center to 'imitate' the periphery, and by allowing a vibrant, innovative intertextuality of the margins—between Latin America and Africa, for instance."[109] Similarly, Franco Moretti maintains that with magical realism, "for the first time in modern history, the center of gravity of formal creation leaves Europe."[110]

However, that success and popularity are not without their costs and (as I point out in Chapter 4) have also occasioned protests and accusations of commodification and commercialization. In addition, there is also the risk of subscribing to the modernist critical program as Meyer Schapiro formulates it, in which, " 'the highest praise' of a modern work of art 'is to describe it in the language of magic and fetishism.' "[111] I use the term, however, not as a category of praise, and I discuss the colonizing tendencies within the mode. Even with these reservations, I think it is not too much to propose that because of the high quality and widespread diffusion of the texts that it has been producing, magical realism may constitute the single most important trend in contemporary international fiction.

"From a Far Source Within"

Magical Realism as Defocalized Narrative

Defocalization

In magical realism, the focalization—the perspective from which events are presented—is indeterminate; the kinds of perceptions it presents are indefinable and the origins of those perceptions are unlocatable.[1] That indeterminacy results from the fact that magical realism includes two conflicting kinds of perception that perceive two different kinds of event: magical events and images not normally reported to the reader of realistic fiction because they are not empirically verifiable, and verifiable (if not always ordinary) ones that are realism's characteristic domain.[2] Thus magical realism modifies the conventions of realism based in empirical evidence, incorporating other kinds of perception. In other words, the narrative is "defocalized" because it seems to come from two radically different perspectives at once.[3] Therefore, I have coined the term *defocalization* to take account of the special narrative situation that seems to me to characterize magical realism as a genre.[4] In addition to suggesting the special nature of magical realist narrative, *defocalization* has the advantage of differentiating its qualities from the narrative perspective within realism that Gerald Prince characterizes as "non-focalized" or as having "zero focalization," which designates omniscient narration.[5] More important, I use *defocalization* generically, broadening the sense of focalization from its usual designation of individual perspectives within a narrative to characterize the way in which magical realism constitutes a particular way of focalizing as a genre, irrespective of the particular perspectives and narrators in individual texts. In short, my discussion of defocalization here attempts to describe in modified narratological terms the strangely indeterminate nature of magical realism's generic narrative stance.

Because realism attempts to create an accurate picture of the world as it is experienced by ordinary human consciousness, readers of realistic fiction are most familiar with focalizations that seem to be grounded in empirical evidence, the quantity of sensory data enhancing the reader's confidence that this representation is accurate and causing the reader to invest the narrative's picture of the world with authority. And the prevailing realism in magical realism, with its many sensory details, reinforces those habits. The combination of that grounding in empirical evidence with reports of phenomena that are not real and verifiable, such as Melquíades's knowledge of the end of Macondo, Grenouille's knowledge of the world of scents, or Saleem's hearing the voices of midnight's children in his head, disrupts our normal sense of where such reports are coming from, and so the narrative that includes them is what I am calling defocalized. This defocalization may include the perceptions of more than one perceiver and shift—sometimes without warning—from one perceiver to another. But that is not so different from what happens in other modernist and postmodern narratives, such as Virginia Woolf's *Mrs. Dalloway*, William Faulkner's *As I Lay Dying*, or Alain Robbe-Grillet's *In the Labyrinth*, for example. Most important, some of those perceptions do not reflect empirically based knowledge of events—they are irreducible elements—and the reader is not sure from what perspective such events are viewed or where such a perspective might originate. Oskar's drum, which can be seen as an analogue for his narrative art, is in a sense a figural representation of defocalized narrative. Oskar is the narrator but his drum, in Alexander Gelley's words, "is the symbol of evocative memory," a "channel," "a trivial and patently inadequate symbol of a pervasive demonic force for which Oskar is more an instrument than a conscious agent."[6]

Focalization is usually imagined to originate in an individual's consciousness, but as we have seen, magical realism often questions our habitual notions of individual characters, so it is appropriate that this new kind of focalization should accommodate that dimension of the genre. What kind of perceiver, for example, in *One Hundred Years of Solitude*, sees both magic carpets and massacres, ghosts and golden fishes? Or can hear, as Oskar in *The Tin Drum* reports he did, what his parents discuss immediately after his birth, as well as chronicle the details of the war that preceded it? "I may as well come right out with it: I was one of those clairaudient infants whose mental development is completed at birth and after that merely needs a certain amount of filling in. The moment I was born I took a very critical attitude toward the first utterances to slip from my parents beneath the light bulbs."[7] In a similar way, but incorporating very different cultural traditions, *The Famished Road* achieves its particular variety of defocalization primarily through the special nature of Azaro the *abiku* or spirit-child, who exists between and mediates the everyday and the spirit worlds.[8] Again, in a culturally very different text, but one that is similarly evocative of special perceptive qualities and perceived realities, as Francis Phelan in *Ironweed* steps up to his son's grave, with no transition, the narrator recounts that "in his grave, in a cruciformed circle, Gerald [the buried baby] watched the advent of his father and considered what action might be appropriate to their meeting," an account that has switched from focalizing through Francis's mind to focalizing through that of his dead baby son. And the narrative continues, in this same vein, presenting Gerald's magical qualities in the same matter-of-fact and detailed way that it tells us of ordinary events: "Denied speech in life, having died with only monosyllabic goos and gaahs in his vocabulary, Gerald possessed the gift of tongues in death. His ability to communicate and to understand was at the genius level among the dead. He could speak with any resident adult in any language, but more notable was his ability to understand the chattery squirrels and chipmunks, the silent signals of the ants and beetles, and the slithy semaphores of the slugs and worms that moved above and through his earth."[9] Thus, while magical realism builds on the multivocal techniques of modernist fiction, the nature and origin of narrative voice in magical realism, compared with that of its modernist precursors, is more radically destabilized because of the presence of irreducible elements within an otherwise realistic narrative environment.[10] Because it questions the norms of realistic representation that is based on sensory data, the defocalized narrative that results from such a destabilized origin undercuts the assumed reliability of realism from within it. Furthermore, that the narrative voice reports events that cannot be empirically verified disrupts the identification of reliable representation in narrative with ordinary human consciousness.

Thus, apparently grounded in sensory data, yet moving beyond them, but not consistently into any recognizable supernatural realm, such as a secret garden, heaven, the underworld, or a mythical past (although it may use elements from such realms), magical realist narrative conjures a narrative space that we might call the "ineffable in-between." It is not the magical events themselves that are ineffable, because they are often described in detail, but the fact that they are present within an otherwise realistic narrative makes that narrative the space of the ineffable in-between, a space in which the realistic and the magical coexist. We might say that defocalization creates a narrative space of the ineffable in-between because its perspective cannot be explained, only experienced.[11] Within it, one does not know quite where one is, what one is seeing, or what kind of voice one is hearing. It is therefore a space that figures a sense of the mysterious within the ordinary. I am thus positing something similar for magical realism to what Bruce Kawin posits for the self-reflexive text, which tends "to project an extratextual order of presence," which he also terms the ineffable, and which he describes as ever absent. The texts on which Kawin bases his analyses are the pre-texts of the ones I analyze here, and most of them are realistic—although at the magical end of realism.[12] That is perhaps why the ineffable exists outside of them. In magical realism, however, just as the magic is enmeshed within the real, so the sense of the ineffable is created within the text, not outside it, as Kawin proposes for the self-reflexive texts that he discusses. In any case, however, magical realist texts seem to challenge Wittgenstein's notion regarding the ineffable that "what can be shown, cannot be said."[13] Small irreducible intrusions suggest that perhaps it can begin to be said. These texts, in Kawin's words describing the teaching of Castañeda's Don Juan, "present the reason with something paradoxical and incontestable, something it simply cannot explain but also will not allow itself to deny."[14]

Combining as it does the concrete and the magical to create a sense of the ineffable, such a narrative infuses reliable portraiture with visionary power. In other words, the magical nature of these irreducible elements intensifies them and endows them with a large imaginative charge—paradoxically, because at the same time they are integrated into the surrounding depictions of material reality. For example, the music that emanates from Wilson Harris's palace of the peacock (that gives the novel its title), comes "from a far source within—deeper than every singer knew."[15] Similarly, André Breton's description of "the voice which it is everyone's prerogative to hear, if only he will, a voice which converses with us most specifically about something other than what we believe we are thinking, and upon occasion assumes a serious tone when we feel most light-hearted or deals in idle prattle when we are unhappiest" suggests the defocalized nature of magical realist narrative, especially since "we still know as little as we ever did about the *origin* of it" (my emphasis).[16]

Oskar, with his (tin) drum, and, especially, his literal refusal to grow up, and his magical vocal chords, constitutes a good early example of magical realism as defocalized narrative. The reader is kept wondering exactly what kind of a person Oskar is and where his extraordinary bodily and vocal powers come from. He tells us that "forever after the story was: on his third birthday our little Oskar fell down the cellar stairs, no bones were broken, but he just wouldn't grow any more. / And I began to drum" (63). Note the three shifts in focalization here. Those shifts do not create the defocalized quality of the narrative, because that is a result of the dissonance between the realistic detail and the impossible events, but they do contribute to it.[17] Beginning through his own perspective, characteristically ironic with respect to "the story" that is being fabricated by his family, he moves momentarily—after the colon—to focalizing through the resident adults in his household, who condescendingly characterize him as "our little Oskar," and returns in the last sentence to his own perspective, recounting simply, "I began to drum." That he refuses to grow up can of course be interpreted as a political statement against fascism, a refusal to join the adults who are moving toward it, and the magical way in which his body obeys him can be seen as confirmation of his point of view. Alternatively, we can view this story as the later fabrication of the dwarf, claiming agency where there was none in order to assuage the pain he feels because of his size. Following this line of thought, perhaps Oskar doth protest too much, when he tells us explicitly, "I declared, resolved, and determined that I would never under any circumstances be a politician, much less a grocer, that I would stop right there, remain as I was" (60). However seriously we choose to take Oskar's statements, the metafictional implications of Oskar's body language, because they are synecdochally linked to his drum, point toward his narrative art. He will not grow up but he will talk drum—or drum talk. Furthermore, as he subsequently recounts:

> The ability to drum the necessary distance between grownups and myself developed shortly after my fall, almost simultaneously with the emergence of a voice that enabled me to sing in so high-pitched and sustained a vibrato, to sing-scream so piercingly that no one dared to take away the drum that was destroying his eardrums; for when the drum was taken away from me, I screamed, and when I screamed, valuable articles burst into bits: I had the gift of shattering glass with my singing: my screams demolished vases, my singing made windowpanes crumple and drafts prevail. (64)

Oskar describes the results of his talents in concrete detail, as would the first-person narrator of a realistic novel who perceives and describes ordinary events, but he also perceives and describes in detail the magical element of his screams' shattering glass. The reader accepts the events since the narrator leaves no room for doubt. However, including as it does different kinds of perceptions, realistic and fantastical, historical events and irreducible elements, such as the drum's near-miraculous number of replacements and Oskar's glass-shattering voice, the nature and origin of this narrative voice is indeterminate, and so the narrative is defocalized. The fact that Oskar presents the arrival of his drumming as "developing" and, even more significant, his ability to shatter glass with his screams as "emerging" increases the sense of mystery surrounding his talents, and consequently of the kind of perspective from which we hear about them, thus contributing to the defocalization of the narrative. That this defocalized narrative nevertheless "speaks" forcefully and grounds itself in numerous historical names, dates, and places infuses it with an authority that seems to be born of substantial worldly experience and that therefore validates its implicit criticism of the events that Oskar witnesses.

In his seminal discussion of magical realism as postcolonial discourse, Stephen Slemon helps to explain what I call magical realism's generic defocalization by stressing its permanent embodiment of alterity. Even though the empirical paradigm with its realist narrative traditions prevails—this is magical *realism,* after all—the radical move of presenting the unverifiable as real profoundly questions that prevalence. Thus, as Slemon has stated it, in magical realism the two separate modes of realism and fantasy "never manage to arrange themselves into any kind of hierarchy," and so the "sustained opposition" between them "forestalls the possibility of interpretive closure through any act of naturalizing the text to an established system of representation."[18] The anchoring in concrete reality created by such an established system of representation based on a common acceptance of scientific fact is dislodged, and yet nothing like a complete rhetoric of fantasy takes its place. Rather, an aura of unknowability and mystery transfuses the narrative.[19] Furthermore, this is not only a question of rhetoric; these two modes of realism and fantasy often reflect the presence of different belief systems, which question post-Enlightenment categories of fact and fantasy. Yet even when a magical realist text includes the perspective of a non-Western system of belief, and questions such categories, their forms and the assumptions behind them are still present in the realism that the text employs, so it does not belong entirely to that non-Western system either.

These pragmatic considerations are fragile, however, as we noted in our initial discussion of hesitation as a defining characteristic of magical realism (the most problematic characteristic, as we are finding out), because the effects of this narrative voice depend on habits and conventions that are constantly changing in response to cultural transformation. As Western readers become increasingly accustomed to irreducible elements of magic, their surprise and hesitation may begin to disappear. Similarly, as authors and readers from non-Western cultures develop new and distinctive narrative traditions that both reflect belief in non-material phenomena and use realistic narrative resources, the hesitation often induced by adherence to realistic narrative codes may also fade away. This complex process of cultural interchange is the context in which magical realism is growing and changing.

Wilson Harris is particularly good at creating and metafictionally alluding to the frequently camouflaged voice in defocalized narrative that projects a sense of the ineffable. What might be described as virtual descriptions of this defocalized narrative, emanating from an indeterminate source, appear several times in *Palace of the Peacock*. For example, the palace of the title is described near the end of the novel as a rock wall with windows in it. That imaginary landscape symbolizes both the trajectory of man's journey through the world and a magical spirit house of fiction: "This was the palace of the universe and the windows of the soul looked out and in" (146). The peacock palace comes into being before our eyes through the narrator's vision of it. Music issues from it, and it is described as growing from a distant tree. The narrator sees that tree (magically) "wave its arms and walk when I looked at it through the spiritual eye of the soul" (146). The fact that this arboreal palace moves as the narrator looks at it suggests that its music symbolizes the lyrical music of Harris's novel. Its indeterminate and defocalized nature is affirmed by the way the narrator "knew it came from a far source within—deeper than every singer knew" and by the way it represents "the inseparable moment within ourselves of all fulfillment and understanding" (151).[20] Combining individual and communal knowledge and imagination, it is both powerful and ineffable. Earlier on, one of the characters is described as resting "against the wall and cliff of heaven as against an indestructible mirror and soul in which he saw the blind dream of creation crumble as it was re-enacted" (124). That wall and cliff are a premonition, still blind, of the wall in which we later see the windows of narrative creation; both of them picture the mysterious origin of the text. This space abuts a still inaccessible and therefore indeterminate realm, which is both background of enticement outward and mirror of self-revelation. Harris evokes the prophetic nature of this vision, which embodies the mysterious origin and imminent mystery of the voice, when he characterizes the peacock as an image of potentiality: "the colours of the peacock may be equated with all the variable possibilities or colours of fulfillment we can never totally realize."[21]

If we turn to another Caribbean text, and if we examine the accounts of the flights attributed to Mackandal and Archbishop Cornejo Breille in Alejo Carpentier's *The Kingdom of This World,* those flights can be seen as symbolic analogues for defocalized magical realist narrative and thus can contribute to our understanding of it. As we have been observing, this perspective suggests the existence of a different dimension within the ordinary coordinates of the sensory world and its realistic representation. The defocalized narrative of magical realism, with its nonverifiable phenomena—magical loves, political ideologies, psychological states, ghosts—however different and differently valued they may be, empowers readers accustomed to realistic narrative with an appealing sense of elation. Still tied to those realistic traditions, they journey imaginatively beyond them, but not too far. In other words, they achieve a special kind of defamiliarization, not only with respect to familiar events and images but with respect to habitual realistic narrative referentiality, knowledge, and authority.

Some details about how Mackandal is presented are relevant here. When we hear of Mackandal's metamorphoses, the way we enter the focalization, gradually, progressing from the narrator to the slaves, draws us into their community of belief.

> They all knew that the green lizard, the night moth, the strange dog, the incredible gannet, were nothing but disguises. As he had the power to take the shape of hoofed animal, bird, fish, or insect, Mackandal continually visited the plantations of the Plaine to watch over his faithful and find out if they still had faith in his return. In one metamorphosis or another, the one-armed was everywhere, having recovered his corporeal integrity in animal guise. With wings one day, spurs another, galloping or crawling, he had made himself master of

the courses of the underground streams, the caverns of the seacoast, and the treetops, and now ruled the whole island. His powers were boundless. [22]

Because of its aura of communal assertiveness, the expression "todos sabían" (they all knew; everyone knew) seems to step up the authority of the slaves' perspective. In addition, it is not entirely clear whether this expression represents the narrator's or the slaves' point of view, because it could be a description from the outside of what the narrator is reporting about the slaves (the "they all knew" option), or it could represent a focalization based within that group (the "everyone knew" option), so that it provides a bridge between them. Thus when we hear about Mackandal's visiting his followers in the form of a bird, fish, or insect, the origin of that information is less easily located than the earlier characterization of "some thought he had taken refuge in the interior" and "others stated that the houngan had got away on a schooner, and was operating in the region of Jacmel."[23] That he is described as making himself master ("se había adueñado") of the rivers, caverns, and treetops in animal form so that he "now ruled the whole island" suggests recuperation of power by the land itself and its original inhabitants, a mysterious rather than a clearly magical event, but one that can be seen as allied to his supposed flight as experienced by people whose sympathies are connected to that recuperation (42, 56). And soon we hear that "through his offices a black woman gave birth to a child with a wild boar's face" (42). By that time we have been gradually connected to the community that believes in such a birth.

The scene of Mackandal's execution also provides intriguing details with respect to its narrative mode. After Mackandal has been captured and condemned to death for inciting slaves to rebellion, he is lashed to a post for burning.

> The fire began to rise toward the Mandingue, licking his legs. At that moment Mackandal moved the stump of his arm, which they had been unable to tie up, in a threatening gesture which was none the less terrible for being partial, howling unknown spells and violently thrusting his torso forward. The bonds fell off and the body of the Negro rose in the air flying overhead, until it plunged into the black waves of the sea of slaves. A single cry filled the square:
> "Mackandal saved!"
> Pandemonium followed. The guards fell with rifle butts on the howling

blacks, who now seemed to overflow the streets, climbing toward the windows. And the noise and screaming and uproar were such that very few saw that Mackandal, held by ten soldiers, had been thrust head first into the fire, and that a flame fed by his burning hair had drowned his last cry. (51–52)

The narrative shifts of perspective in this episode, as Amaryll Chanady has pointed out, ultimately allow the reader to recuperate the magical event of Mackandal's airborne escape as someone else's belief, so the irreducible element of Mackandal's flight can be re-entered into a realistic point of view.[24] Nevertheless, that perspective is undermined in various ways. Once again, the perspectives change without clear demarcations, leaving us disoriented as we move between them. In the paragraph preceding the account of Mackandal's "flight," the competing perspectives of masters and slaves are relatively clear, although the perspective of the slaves is given precedence, and the prediction that "Mackandal, transformed into a buzzing mosquito, would light on the very tricorne of the commander of the troops to laugh at the dismay of the whites" is presented as "what their masters did not know" (51). But then there is a paragraph break, with the result that the collective focalization of the magical event through the minds of the slaves is experienced as a fact presented by a seemingly omniscient narrator who includes it in his otherwise realistic account of the scene. We hear of Mackandal's flight first and therefore are led to believe it initially, even if we are subsequently told of his capture and burning. Since the shifts in focalization are camouflaged to some extent, the reader may continue to experience the flight as having actually happened since he or she initially read of it that way.[25] The perspective of the community of slaves is further valorized by the greater moral authority with which they, in contrast to their masters, are endowed, so that the reader's experience of the event is not only a narratological but also a cultural matter. The reader is induced to identify culturally with the crowd of believers for whom Mackandal is saved rather than with the very few empiricists who see his last cry suffocated by flames. And the chapter title, "The Great Flight," carrying an air of authority with it, contributes to that inducement. But this is not a simple matter. That only a small number sees this event can be interpreted two ways. On one hand, that they are few can be seen as weakening their perspective; on the other hand, that perspective can be seen also as a privileged one, the same one that holds the power. Despite this complexity, I would argue that the narrative, while ultimately validating the realistic paradigm, destabilizes it to some extent by the way in which it presents this event through its shifting and varied focalizations.

It seems in keeping with this varied focalization that Carpentier himself has written twice about this episode, and with slightly varying implications. First, in the original preface to the novel, published in 1949, he says that during his stay in Haiti, "I found myself in daily contact with something that could be defined as the marvelous real. I was in a land where thousands of men, anxious for freedom, believed in Mackandal's lycanthropic powers to the extent that their collective faith produced a miracle on the day of his execution."[26] He does not qualify that statement with a disavowal and lets the miracle stand, as it were, on its own terms, even though it is clear that they are not his own. The collective faith produced a miracle, not a "seeming" or an "apparent" miracle. Later on, however, in an essay on the baroque and the marvelous real, originally published in 1975, he cites several phenomena he considers examples of the marvelous real in America, among them "Mackandal's revolt, which makes thousands and thousands of slaves in Haiti believe that he has lycanthropic powers, that he can change into a bird or a horse, a butterfly or an insect, whatever his heart desires. So he foments one of the first authentic revolutions of the New World."[27] Which is the correct gloss, the first one, in which the faith produces a miracle, or the second, in which the revolt produces a belief in a miracle?

Later on in the novel from the account of Mackandal's death, Ti Nöel's transformations, which the reader perceives from his perspective and therefore initially accepts on their own terms, are preceded by the surveyors measuring everything and noting it down, prefatory to the imposition of forced labor on the native population. The implied association between noting down the facts and imposing labor on people implicitly vitiates that notational enterprise and perhaps by implication the narrative mode of realism, since both notation and realism can be seen to rely perhaps too heavily on the mimetic function of language. Therefore, even though the reader is given the option of distancing himself or herself from the slaves' beliefs in the miracles of transformations, thereby revalidating a modern empirically oriented perspective, that perspective has already been devalued. Thus, despite the problematic status of these irreducible elements, I would include *The Kingdom of This World* among these defocalized magical realist texts, especially given its ending, which we examine shortly.[28]

If we continue to entertain the idea that images of flight can be seen as emblematic of a new narrative perspective, the figures of Mackandal and Archbishop Breille also weigh in according to plan. The archbishop, after scaring Henri Christophe half to death, is reported flying up onto the rafters in the roof of the church and looking down at the king from there. That height, like Mackandal's, suggests his power in a realm that extends beyond that of sensory reality. It contrasts with the material power of Henri Christophe, who operates very much in the lower registers. He aspires to heights, building his castle as high as he can on the mountain, but we hear at length about its construction, which is anything but a lofty endeavor: people are forced to neglect their crops as they laboriously carry its bricks up the mountainside. The description of the fortress makes it metaphorically into a new Macchu Picchu as it was recreated poetically by Neruda in his poem "The Heights of Macchu Picchu," built on the oppression of its workers—both of them places where lives are lost in constructing a castle of power.

Appropriately enough, the descriptions of Henri Christophe in his decline emphasize his weight, the sign of a monarch who is about to fall, but also, I would argue, an indication of his spiritual bankruptcy, and a contrast to the spiritual authority of his opponents. His carriage is heavy, he has to be lifted, he falls into bed "like a sack of chains" (139); he turns over "clumsily" ("dando pesadas [heavy] vueltas") in bed (141, 153). Later on, we hear that "the king drew in deep breaths of the afternoon air, and the oppressions that had weighed down his breast began to lift" (141–42). (The Spanish word "pesada," describing his turning over, emphasizes his weight.) The king's pages sit with their bottoms on the first step of the cold marble staircase—at least they have gotten that far. They are implicitly in tune with where they sit, unlike the inflated king, whose sign, ironically, is a crowned phoenix, with the emblem *"I rise from my ashes."* He will never be able to rise because he is too weighted down with a "heavy coffer," from which he takes "several solid gold crowns of different weight." One of those crowns rolls down the stairs on which he later falls as he shoots himself. Henri subsequently recalls "his fortress up there above the clouds. But at that moment the night grew dense with drums" (147). That "but" denies him the right to occupy the heights he has mistakenly marked out for himself and gives them to the voices of his enemies, the supporters of the leaders of the revolution. As he is carried into his citadel, his cadaver is "heavier with each step" (153), as if to reconfirm his fate as a heavy earthling.

Ti Nöel's house, in contrast, specifically designated as having no roof, is open to the sky, to the traditional realm of the vague and yet powerful forces of the spirit. Furthermore, Ti Nöel hopes to establish a peaceful government by issuing "orders to the wind" (172) and then, inspired by the thought of Mackandal, decides to take on animal form, given the trials of forced labor that are once again becoming inescapable for humans. As proof of his magical powers of transformation, again reported as fact, "he climbed a tree, willed himself to become a bird, and instantly was a bird" (178). Later on he becomes more specific, changing into a goose, because he likes the social system of geese. They, alas, will not have him, just as they would not accept a goose from another clan, because he was "an upstart, an intruder" ("un meteco") (184, 143). Ti Nöel's subsequent fatigue, in realizing that he has erred in his escapist transformation, is figured as "a cosmic weariness, as of a planet weighted with stones," which "fell on his shoulders shrunk by so many blows, sweats, revolts" (184). It affirms the human task of improving the kingdom of life in this world rather than the dream of flying to the kingdom of heaven. Even so, a prophetic wind comes from the sea, implicitly affirming a complementary and mysteriously undefined task; and we are told that Ti Nöel's armchair—Is he in it? The text does not say—together with various of his possessions, "rose in the air" ("echaron a volar de golpe") (186, 144), and he is heard of no more, except, in the words that end the novel, by "that wet vulture who turns every death to his own benefit and who sat with outspread wings, drying himself in the sun, a cross of feathers which finally folded itself up and flew off into the thick shade of Bois Caiman" (186). The narrator reports the armchair's flight (with or without Ti Nöel in it) as actual but leaves the reader in doubt about whether he—or the legend from which he draws his story—may have mistaken the flight of the armchair for that of the vulture. Because this flight ends the novel, it is more ambiguous than the other two, leaving the reader in doubt also about its status as actual—irreducible—event or senile hallucination. That doubt, I would argue, contributes to the defocalized nature of this narrative, because the origin of the perception of this event is indeterminate. Nonetheless, aspiration toward a mysterious realm of the spirits is both concretized with realistic details and ironized: the geese refuse to adopt Ti Nöel, and a cross of feathers turns out to be a wet vulture. Magical realism often combines such concreteness and irony with a hint of mystery.

I have traced the dynamics of lightness and weight in some detail in *The Kingdom of This World* to illustrate one covert way that this early magical realist fiction expresses a sense of the ineffable. The values assigned the physical properties reverse those in Milan Kundera's novels, with their post-romantic, post-Nietzschean spatial semiology of unbearable lightness and salutary weight, but the presence of the dynamic suggests that—largely hidden—sense in these texts, different as they are, that coexists with but is not identical to their more obvious political agendas. By contrast, Toni Morrison pays great attention to shoes in *Beloved,* most understandably, perhaps, in rational terms, because slaves did not usually own any. Baby Suggs mends shoes for white people—ironically, since her family has none to wear; Amy manufactures makeshift shoes (from shawl and leaves) for Sethe (a slight amelioration of Sethe's racially dictated disadvantages); Beloved arrives with beautiful new shoes (suggesting, in addition to the idea that she has not walked to her destination, hope for at least a partial redressing of historical wrongs?). More covertly, however, in addition to these historical concerns, taken as a group, the attention to shoes is a counterweight to the complementary pole, to the world of spirit that Morrison also celebrates in her text in the figure of Baby Suggs, holy, preaching.[29] In this text, then, as in others, we can see how magical realism articulates an interchange between rising and tethering, between the ineffable and the concrete, the eternal and the historical, spirit and body, in short, between wings and shoes.

There are many winged creatures and flights in magical realist fictions. Salman Rushdie's *Satanic Verses* begins with the account of "the angel Gibreel" Farishta and his friend Saladin Chamcha falling out of the sky rather than rising up into it, but as they fall they encounter a deceased woman on a flying carpet; the gypsies bring a magic carpet to Macondo, where later Remedios the Beauty ascends with the sheets; Paul Eluard and a dancing circle of communists rise above the ground in *The Book of Laughter and Forgetting.* (One needs to distinguish between these two levitations, however; the first is presented as a popular miracle, arising out of Macondo's community of belief, whereas the second appears within Kundera's political critique and serves a more clearly political purpose.) These postmodern "angels" can be seen as thematizing magical realism's defocalized narrative mode that encodes the ineffable, although the symbolic meaning of the fliers rarely points them explicitly in this direction.[30] Finally, even more than Mackandal, perhaps, because of his indeterminate nature and origin, the "very old man with enormous wings" in Gabriel García Márquez's story of that name, with his mysterious and inexplicable wings, his lice, and his unpleasant odor, can serve as an emblem of the defocalized nature of magical realist narrative. Even though the story is not told from his perspective, it is centered on him, and we sympathize with his plight, even though we have no idea of where he came from or where he is off to at the end. More generally, he also embodies the miraculous nature of everyday life, and the unexpectedly mundane appearance of its miracles.

A final example of the thematic attraction to flight in magical realism, a magically real angel, appears early in Isabelle Allende's *The House of the Spirits*. But as with García Márquez's old man with enormous wings, the category no sooner appears than it is problematized. First we hear that "this child of hers seemed to have been made of a different material from the rest of the human race. Even before she was born, Nívea had known she was not of this world, . . . and rumors quickly spread that Nívea had borne an angel." Then we are told that

> the tone of her skin, with its soft bluish lights, and of her hair, as well as her slow movements and silent character, all made one think of some inhabitant of the sea. There was something of the fish to her (if she had had a scaly tail, she would have been a mermaid), but her two legs placed her squarely on the tenuous line between a human being and a creature of myth. Despite everything, the young woman had led a nearly normal life.[31]

Precise description there is, but the kind of solid empirical evidence that leads readers to posit a familiar kind of narrative voice that shares their sense of what is possible in this world evaporates in the description of this relentlessly hybrid being. Nor does the description enable us to classify the creature within known mythic or religious traditions. And soon another flyer appears, and his hybrid nature is underlined: Uncle Marcos disappears on his homemade "bird of prehistoric dimensions, with the face of a furious eagle, wings that moved, and a propeller on its back."[32]

The experience of what we might characterize as a magic that "rises" beyond the real in these fictions contrasts with the impulse that Roberto González Echevarría discusses as the archival. According to González Echevarría, the archival comes largely from Europe and is concerned with writing down, or grounding: "writing is bound to the founding of cities." The narrative mode we are examining here frequently combines the realism and surrealism of European origin with indigenous beliefs and practices—or at least the memory or the fantasy of them—and can be seen to be concerned with metaphorically rising up, with powers of the imagination not grounded in sensory data, perhaps even with the escape from written archives. If, as González Echevarría argues, Carpentier's *The Lost Steps* is "the founding archival fiction" of Latin American literature, then *The Kingdom of This World* might be one of its initial non-archival fictions.[33] Following Jurij Lotman's idea that "worldview invariably acquires features of spatial characteristics," both grounding and rising are instrumental in the development of post-colonial narratives with their newly developing world views.[34] Interestingly enough, in this context, there is a flight near the end of *The Lost Steps,* but it is a very concrete one and not at all magical. For one thing, it is in an airplane, and for another, that airplane returns the narrator and the reader to the modern city. As he journeys from the jungle to the town, the narrator lies down on the floor of the plane and sleeps, with the result that neither he nor the reader participates imaginatively in the plane's ascent, which is symbolically a descent, into time and history. As it takes the narrator toward existentially conceived burdens of temporality and history, and away from primitivistic fantasies and the wellsprings of creative inspiration, that descent contrasts with the image of rising as a spatial model for the ineffable element figured by the defocalized narrative voice of magical realism, which modifies even while remaining connected to the materially grounded aesthetic of realism.

Such an ascending mode is problematic, however, as Heidegger, Nietzsche, and their existentialist successors have pointed out. That is why Kundera condemns it; it may evade issues of mortality and history, a problem that we confront in Chapter 4.[35] In *The Book of Laughter and Forgetting,* Raphael, ironically recalling the angel from the Apocrypha who accompanies Tobias on his journey to the past, takes Tamina to the dystopic island of children, where she would have to forget her past. This is a light option she refuses in favor of the heavier alternative of death by drowning, which at least preserves "her body and a great desire for life," which she wants to get away from the island: "that hollow feeling in her stomach comes from the unbearable absence of weight. And just as one extreme may at any moment turn into its opposite, so this perfect buoyancy has become a terrifying *burden of buoyancy,* and Tamina knows she cannot bear it another instant. She turns and runs" and eventually jumps into the water, where she drowns, "afraid that they [the island's children] would try to save her and she would have to play with them again."[36] In *Perfume,* Süskind also presents an angel of doom. Grenouille with his virgin-scented perfume so brutally distilled is a frightening "angel of a man" who provokes violence. All of his skill is worthless because he cannot smell and love himself, so when he puts on his miraculous perfume the torrent of adoration it unleashes is really his suicide: the people "lunged at the angel; pounced on him, threw him to the ground. Each of them wanted to have a piece of him, a feather, a bit of plumage, a spark from that wonderful fire." They attack "like hyenas," and "in very short order, the angel was divided into thirty pieces."[37] The vultures have become hyenas, and the angelic figure of feathers and fire is reduced to an earthly image of betrayal. These troubling images of undesirable angels dramatize the idea that one of magical realism's paradoxical projects is how to be grounded in history but not crushed by it and, alternatively, how to rise above it enough to re-imagine it without shortchanging its intractability. Thus magical realism's generic complexity underlines in its particular way the eternal question of how to live fruitfully on the earth and in the air, in the body and the imagination, in the sensory and the ineffable, and how to express that experience. Different as they are, magical realist texts can be seen to embody those issues through their defocalized narrative mode.

Postmodern Primitivists

In its frequent though not constant fascination with pre-Enlightenment culture, nonscientific belief systems, and the narrative strategies associated with them, magical realism continues the tradition of modernist primitivism, our attraction to it resulting from the lure of foreign stories.[38] In that context, it raises some of the same questions that anthropologists, such as James Clifford, Sally Price, and others, have been asking about twentieth-century primitive art collections.[39] Although themes in magical realism contain many elements taken from indigenous cultures, magical realism also embodies a specifically narrative primitivism, irrespective of theme.[40] Because the moments of magic exist within the narrative environment of realism, often disrupting both its spatial and its temporal conventions, they resemble artifacts from a different narrative culture, existing in something like the artificially created "ethnographic present" of anthropological museums. Here again, the question of cultural perspective arises because the belief systems of readers will differ. This description of the isolation of magical moments in magical realism applies more to Western readers than to non-Western ones. However, the strength of the realistic tradition that surrounds those moments means that even readers whose systems of belief cause them to accommodate such moments more easily than Western readers do enter the realistic tradition and implicitly subscribe to its conventions as they read these fictions. Thus, a sense of cultural hybridity still obtains. Working from a definition of animism as "the belief in a spiritual vitality lying behind all natural objects," Ato Quayson signals the semi-anthropological aura and the hybrid nature of Okri's work, which projects an "impression that all things from trees to photographs have a potential spiritual vitality," and in which "the literary expression of such animism is clearly meant to stand as a surrogate for indigenous beliefs in spirits." However, according to Quayson, the novels "should be read more as a literary defamiliarization of indigenous beliefs than a true replica of such beliefs in reality."[41]

To continue the analogy between the ethnographic aura of magical realism and museum collections of primitive art, a "proper" collection, James Clifford maintains, is supposed to evolve in "a pedagogical, edifying manner," "private fixation on single objects" being "negatively marked as fetishism."[42] In their resistance to classification and their surprising, often repetitive appearances, and in the way they lurk within their realistic surroundings, magical realist images, such as the pig's tail or the trail of blood in *One Hundred Years of Solitude,* the tick in *Perfume,* the scar on Beloved's neck, or the shiny spherical object in *Distant Relations,* may belong not to the "classification and display" that obtain in "proper" collections but rather to the more deviant "accumulation and secrecy" that characterize fetishism.[43] In the domain of narrative, then, perhaps they serve a fetishistic function. Like fetish statues, objects endowed with magical powers, part of their charm is, despite their realistic qualities and their imbrication into everyday reality, a certain aura of secrecy and inscrutability, which protects those powers. Just why does García Márquez's "very old man" have "enormous wings"? Or the narrator of Julio Cortázar's story "Letter to a Young Lady in Paris" vomit baby rabbits? Why does Remedios the Beauty levitate? Why is Grenouille able to smell the scent of a virgin across all of Paris? Why does Saleem's grandfather's snot turn to rubies? In their initial mysterious opacity (I say initial because they do reveal reasons on scrutiny; this is their main difference from much of surrealism), these images allow the reader to fetishize, to fixate on them as objects of narrative power emanating from a hidden source. Thus the images possess the power that Clifford allows for collections, the power "to fixate rather than simply the capacity to edify or inform."[44] This power of attraction is enhanced because an irreducible element, like a good fetish, keeps incompatible ideas alive.[45]

Such narrative fetishization, which sustains incompatible realities, may explain Rushdie's distinction between the programmatic, systematized magic of professional magicians, whose verbal sign is abracadabra, and the unsystematic magic Saleem implicitly wills to his son, "who will have to be a magician to cope with the world I'm leaving him" (547), the kind of magic he uses in his text. He makes a similar distinction between systematic trickery and mysterious artistry for Parvati-the-witch, born in the ghetto of the magicians, raised

> amid ventriloquists who could make stones tell jokes and contortionists who could swallow their own legs and fire-eaters who exhaled flames from their arseholes and tragic clowns who could extract glass tears from the corners of their eyes; she had stood mildly amid gasping crowds while her father drove spikes through her neck; and all the time she had guarded her own secret, which was greater than any of the illusionist flummeries surrounding her; because to Parvati-the-witch . . . had been given the powers of the true adept, the illuminatus, the genuine gifts of conjuration and sorcery, the art which required no artifice. (239)

In invoking an art that requires no artifice but that nonetheless conjures and enchants, Rushdie suggests magical realist magic palpitating behind the real and associates it with ancient and eternal arts, which contrast with the systematic procedures of either science or publicly recognized magic.

Because they incorporate eccentric ways of writing, these texts can be seen as a kind of willful narrative insanity, a mode that recalls the romantic variety of primitivism that includes glorifications of mental deviance and that Edward Dudley and Maximilian Novak claim brought the wild man within the mind in the nineteenth century.[46] In this way, magical realism continues that primitivist retreat within the self that engendered the literary wild man of the mind but projects that wild self onto the surface of the text. As people living in the wilderness become fewer and less "wild," their appeal increases, but now, in addition to serving only as theme, something comparable to verbal wildness is textualized as a defocalized voice and permeates the very self of narrative.

Magical realism, however, is moving beyond its earliest ties with a primitivist ideology and aesthetic. The recent novel *Pig Tales* by Marie Darrieussecq, in which a young cosmetics saleswoman slowly and with many reversals becomes increasingly like a pig, is a good example of contemporary magical realism's moving substantially beyond the archaic while still remaining in touch with it. The impulse for the narrator's transformation, the source of the magic in the novel, is not her proximity to ancient culture or nature but her role—salesperson, consumer, and, ultimately, consumed commodity—in the cosmetics industry that sells products that alter, display, and market female bodies. (The fact that we never hear her name clearly reflects her commodified status.)

And her transforming into an animal and becoming increasingly comfortable in nature could be seen to echo the atavistic origins of magical realism as well as of an eco-politics, which desires a reconnection with nature. But it also echoes Franz Kafka and belongs to a whole line of modern distopic fiction. And though the novel includes various ecological concerns, the point of the comfort she experiences in the natural world is not only a nostalgic proximity to animal and other nature as such but her need to learn to live in the physical self that she has become as a result of social conditioning. Because it ultimately can be categorized as a female-centered modernization of *The Metamorphosis* and the whole classical tradition that precedes Kafka's text, this novel, like *The Book of Laughter and Forgetting*, exists on the fringe of magical realism that is contiguous to the mode of sociopolitical allegory. But because of the way Darrieussecq juxtaposes actual and imagined worlds, integrating irreducible elements of the narrator's porcine persona into contemporary Parisian life, the novel can be included in the genre of magical realism.

The same lack of primitivist magic characterizes *Ironweed,* William Kinsella's *Field of Dreams,* and Francine Prose's *Bigfoot Dreams,* in which magic is not archaic but psychological, Rushdie's intensive use of cinematic imagery and technique as a source of narrative magic in *Midnight's Children,* and *The White Hotel* and *Beloved,* in which magic is engendered by the pain of history. Similarly, in the short story "The Enormous Radio," by John Cheever, a radio in one apartment (in New York) receives and broadcasts events in various others—clearly a magical phenomenon but not so far from telephone and computer scrambling as to be undeniably fantastic. Edna Aizenberg notes a similar presence of technology in magical realism but in entirely different socioeconomic contexts with different agendas: with respect to the electricity, record player, and car in *The Famished Road,* "as in *One Hundred Years of Solitude,* technology, brought in from the outside anachronistically, forms part of magical realism's enactment of the deliriums of a colonized world."[47] We should note here that the sound of the ancestor ghost Maxine Hong-Kingston describes in *The Woman Warrior* is compared to the sound of electric wires in the city, and that the main irreducible elements in both *Midnight's Children* and *The Moor's Last Sigh* are magic inspired by technology. The voices in Saleem's head are compared over and over again to a radio: "By sunrise, I had discovered that the voices could be controlled—I was a radio receiver, and could turn the volume down or up; I could select individual voices; I could even, by an effort of will, switch off my newly-discovered inner ear. . . . by morning, I was thinking, 'Man, this is better than All-India Radio, man; better than Radio Ceylon!' " (193). That the Moor ages at twice the normal rate is described as if "somebody somewhere has been holding down the button marked 'FF,' or to be more exact, 'x2'."[48] That association with virtual reality is meaningful and perhaps prophetic. It exemplifies the way in which contemporary international magical realism is not necessarily tied to a nostalgic primitivism.[49]

The Presence of Spirit

Perhaps the factual uncertainty in magical realism, the defocalization (as well as the difficulty of defining the term) not only point toward the general modern and postmodern condition of indeterminacy but also suggest, in a very general way, the existence of a mysterious realm of the spirit, even a hidden presence of the sacred within the profane, which inhabits the narrative space of the ineffable in-between.[50] Such a presence emerges because the narrative voice in the defocalized mode of magical realism often speaks what it cannot have perceived directly, so that it loosens the narrative's connection to the ordinary world of sense perceptions, and because of that extraordinary kind of perception, it makes room for readers to entertain the general idea of a different kind of especially gifted perceiver and a present realm of extraordinary event from where the narrative voice emanates.

The idea of the ineffable does not necessarily imply the sacred, although more often than not it has done so. In the introduction to a collection of essays that investigates the ineffable in literary texts, Peter Hawkins and Anne Schotter distinguish between the positive ineffable, the "nothing that is," which is usually religious, and the negative ineffable, the "nothing that is not," the former exemplified by Dante's *Paradiso* and the latter by Beckett's fictions, among other texts.[51] The *genre* of magical realism, as opposed to most of the particular texts studied in that collection, in which the *subject* of the ineffable is addressed, cannot be definitively categorized as either one or the other. However, since the notion of the ineffable has so often been associated with a sacred realm in Western literature, it is reasonable that such an association may persist here. Nonetheless, the sense of the ineffable (however defined) that results from the combination of the magical and the real in magical realism supplements our habitual experience of concrete reality.

Even though a magical realist narrative may contain no explicit references to spirits of any kind, and may even be critical of particular religious traditions, the irreducible elements and the defocalized mode cause the reader to feel a sense of contact with an indeterminate and undefinable domain, a feeling that endows the text with a slight and occasional mysterious aura. In short, it may even present readers with glimpses of the transcendent within the everyday. For example, Grass makes no specific reference to supernatural powers in *The Tin Drum* (and Oskar's "spiritual development in the course of the novel is [even]a regressive one"), but the fact that the narrative is focalized through Oskar who reports on the superhuman qualities of his voice, infuses the narrative with a mysterious charge.[52] Similarly, even though García Márquez shows the priest in "A Very Old Man with Enormous Wings" engaging in ridiculous machinations as he attempts to obtain official classification of what he wishes to consider an angel, the defocalized narrative that reports not only on those machinations but also on the puzzlingly incongruous attributes of the angel's wings and his lice, details that validate the old man's delicately undefinable nature, lend the story its particular tone that combines the mysterious with the ironic.[53]

Magical realism, in the words of Arturo Uslar-Pietri, takes account of "man as a mystery in the midst of realistic facts."[54] By incorporating a mysterious dimension into the discourse of literary realism, magical realism both questions and replenishes it. Magical realism would then represent a moment of cultural retrospection that is a reverse image of the "moment of desacralization" that Fredric Jameson investigates in drawing his "realist floor-plan" as part of the "bourgeois cultural revolution."[55] Thus it might even begin to reverse the progressive secularization that M. H. Abrams sees as the cause of early nineteenth-century supernaturalism. From this perspective, magical realism would constitute a latent tendency to include a spirit-based element within contemporary literature—a possible remystification of narrative in the West.

The habitually secular Rushdie seems to suggest just such a process, implying the presence of a spirit world within magical realism, when he asks whether art can be "the third principle that mediates between the material and spiritual worlds, . . . [offering] us something that might even be called a secular definition of transcendence." By "transcendence" he means "that flight of the human spirit which all of us, secular or religious, experience on at least a few occasions." Although Rushdie is speaking of all art, his statements are related to his own practice, and that of his contemporaries, and he finally proposes a "form of fiction in which the miraculous might coexist with the mundane."[56] Similarly, Harris's characterization of the "palace of the universe" in which "the windows of the soul looked out and in" (146) and the way he looks at a tree waving its arms "through the spiritual eye of the soul" (151) suggest a generalized sense of ineffable mystery in the world and the self.[57]

Descriptions of techniques for achieving the combination of miraculous and mundane worlds that Rushdie proposes permeate the 1925 essay in which Franz Roh coins the term *magical realism* to describe the new post-expressionist style in painting, which emphasized sharply focused representation, in contrast to the near-abstractions of expressionism.[58] An overly earthbound orientation is intriguingly represented—and perhaps even implicitly critiqued?—in a collage by Roh himself. In the collage, an anatomically correctly drawn human body contains an eye placed just above the rectum (which is identified as such). The drawing is entitled "She saw the World only from the Perspective of the Lower Organs" ("Sie sah die Welt nur von den unteren Organen her").[59] The magical realist painters Roh describes in his 1925 essay, however, seem closer to the implicit program of contemporary magical realism; even though they reveal a new reverence for everyday life by creating the exterior world "most precisely," they retain the orientation of expressionism toward a realm of the spirit: in Roh's words, "the point is not to discover the spirit beginning with objects but, on the contrary, to discover objects beginning with the spirit."[60] Roh describes the interchange between ordinary and mysterious domains with respect to the painter Georg

Schrimpf: even though Schrimpf paints inside his studio, he wants the painting to be "real." While he wants it "to impress us as something ordinary and
familiar, . . . nevertheless, he tries for it to be a magic world, that is to say,
that by virtue of that isolation in the room, even the last little blade of grass
can refer to the spirit."[61]

The culturally inclusive nature of the mysterious charge in recent magical
realist fiction surfaces explicitly in Lawrence Thornton's *Imagining Argentina*
as the narrator asks himself, "had St. Jude empowered Carlos Rueda to restore
the child, or was the man who had foreseen this a shaman who belonged
in a smoky hut deep in the jungle?"[62] Even the otherwise secularly oriented
Oskar in *The Tin Drum* has some textual roots that suggest the existence of
a sacred realm within the ordinary world. According to Grass, Oskar appeared first in a long poem "as a stylite saint," who "in the middle of a small
town . . . built himself a pillar and chained himself to the top of it." Even
though in the end Grass decided that "the stylite's elevated standpoint was
too static," his stance is distantly felt in the novel's magical realism. Oskar
does not live at the top of a pillar but his screams shatter glass. The force and
indeterminate origin of Oskar's voice is commensurate with Grass's idea that
"the only interesting feature of [the poem] was my quest for a perspective."[63]
One of the perspectives he ultimately creates is embodied in the novel's defocalized narrative, which, although very different in tone, can be compared
in its slightly other-worldly—though also heavily ironic—coloring, to "the
exultation of the spirit" that Alejo Carpentier claimed a few years earlier for
the marvelous real as a description of the new world.[64] Another small and
ironized but still suggestive mysterious dimension to Oskar's text appears in
the surrealists' portraits of him paired with the ethereal Ulla, a series that
culminates in the image of Oskar as Christ the drummer.

The increased nuance of spirit that I am suggesting exists in the narrative
mode of contemporary magical realism as it contrasts with modernist fiction can perhaps be measured by the distance between the endings of André
Gide's *The Immoralist* and Tahar Ben Jelloun's *The Sacred Night*. In Gide's
novel, having willfully peeled off his layers of bourgeois culture and Protestant ethics, Michel is left with the epidermal sensory—and secular—project
of warming and cooling stones in his hands. The narrator of Ben Jelloun's
novel, by contrast, after her travels, imprisonment, and involuntary clitoral
circumcision, somehow enters a community of pilgrims, magically including at least one woman who has died. At the end of the novel, she awaits the

arrival of her blind lover, "the saint," in a luminous temple in a "thin layer of mist of darkness" "between life and death," "between reality and appearance."[65] Thus Ben Jelloun reveals with resources of lyrical realism similar to Gide's but with a small intrusion of magical possibility the latent presence of spirit in the indigenous culture of the colony, which the great modernist primitivist seems largely to have bypassed in his sensual awakening to North Africa.[66] Thus here again we see how magical realism develops out of modernism: through its narrative mode that encodes the ineffable, magical realism can be seen to mine the hidden and often demonized veins of the spirit in modernist primitivism tapped there by figures such as Narouz in Lawrence Durrell's *Mountolive,* Kurtz in *Heart of Darkness,* or even the series of messengers from Hades in *Death in Venice.*

In the epilogue to his study of the progression from the sublime to the uncanny in modernist narrative, one that implies "an opening outward, . . . a suggestion of what the contemporary inheritance of Modernist uncanniness might be," David Ellison delineates a similar movement out of modernism to the one I have been tracing. In so doing, he furnishes another way to understand how contemporary magical realism moves beyond its modernist precursors as it constitutes an encoding of the ineffable. He discerns a movement in Kafka's late stories and Maurice Blanchot's essays on narrative toward the textualizing of what he calls, following Blanchot, "the power and meaning of the secret, of mystery." He proposes that in the end the "tranquil indifference" of the mouse-narrator in Kafka's late short story "Josefine, the Singer, or the Mouse Folk," expresses a mystery that moves beyond the "discursive logic" and "existential despair" of Kafka's own voice, and he defines that movement as a change of mode, from novel to story—from *roman* to *récit,* or, more precisely, as a change in narrative voice, from a *voix narratrice,* localizably human (in Derrida's explication of Blanchot, which Ellison quotes, a voice that "derives from a subject . . . knowing who he is, where he is, and of what he speaks"), to a *voix narrative,* which moves beyond the human into what Blanchot calls the *neutre,* the neutral, or the void: "to write (or to read), according to the *voix narrative* as it opens up the strange space of the *récit,* is to find oneself beyond that horizon in an *unheimlich* (uncanny, unhomely) no-man's land," which, somewhat like the space of the ineffable in-between in magical realism's defocalized narrative, is "unlocatable." This change in narrative mode toward the strange and the mysterious in Kafka's story, and in Blanchot's theoretical meditation on narrative, can occur because "at the center of narrative (understood rigorously as *récit*) lies a void, a nothingness, which is untranslatable in the terms of rational discourse, . . . and that the *récit* as expression of the *neutre* is 'voiceless,' not attributable to a consciousness as human individuality." We encounter within Kafka's work as described by Blanchot, "an irreducible strangeness"; and, according to Ellison, "it is within the 'irreducible strangeness' of this interior narrative distance that the *neutre* constitutes itself and acts to overturn the centrality of subjective consciousness."[67]

I would venture that in positing the kind of narrative that encompasses this neutral zone beyond human consciousness, Ellison is postulating a narrative mode akin to what I define as defocalization in magical realism, which also overturns habitual notions of human subjectivity. And it is one that, like magical realism's defocalized narrative mode, suggests the existence not of existential nothingness and despair but of some kind of mystery. The strange doubleness of the mouse-narrator's voice in "Josefine," between animal and human and therefore between the actual and the impossible, resembles the defocalized narrative in magical realist texts, of which Kafka's stories are seminal precursors. The encoding of the ineffable in magical realism can thus be seen as taking off from what Ellison sees in Josefine as "the impossible effort of the animal narrator to rationalize through logical discourse that which is already situated in the realm of the *neutre*," which "is neither this nor that, but somewhere (where?) in between"; it is, "in Blanchot's terms, *un autre chant*," a song that encodes a sense of mystery through the indeterminate nature of its narrative voice.[68]

Thus, magical realism can be seen to open up a space of the ineffable in-between that accommodates the camouflaged presence of the spirit amid material reality. From a philosophical perspective, the irreducible element forms a counterweight to empiricism; from a narratological perspective, it represents a new kind of focalization; and from a religious perspective, it constitutes an incipient re-emergence of spirit or the sacred. And it is this last that has been the most neglected because it is the most alien to the modern Western critical tradition, including, especially, literary and cultural criticism.[69] As we hear in *Imagining Argentina*, "if, in Buenos Aires, the supernatural were woven into the daily lives of people, as it is in the Amazon where natives believe numinous spirits invade the birds and beasts, [Carlos's] accomplishments would be easier to discuss. But we have long been hostile to the things of the spirit."[70]

That hostility dictates that if the presence of a realm of the spirit exists in magical realist fictions, it may often go largely unseen by the conscious writing and reading mind. Magical realism might constitute the formerly hidden and now emergent unconscious of modernism during which such a realm has been taboo for much realistic fiction, and which has subsequently fostered a largely Freudian as opposed to a Jungian critical perspective that would be less hostile to discerning the presence of spirit. The notion of taboo means that any contact with certain things or persons or places that belong to another order of being is imagined to provoke a disastrous upheaval at the ontological level. Normally a taboo is acknowledged and anticipated. In many cultures, for example, ritual purification is required before entering a taboo space. In magical realist texts this ritual is not observed, because we usually come upon magical moments with little or no warning. The boundary between their mysterious world and realism's ordinary one are not clearly marked. Thus magical realism can be seen as embodying something like the liminal moment in Whitman's poetry as described by George B. Hutchinson, which "violates the distinction between the sacred and the profane, as quotidian affairs are inundated with spiritual realities."[71] However, as if to acknowledge our unfamiliarity with this taboo domain of the spirits, where a powerful fetish lives, magical realism presents that space sparingly. Realism now seeks the mysterious but can absorb only a small quantity of it within the everyday.[72] That minimal absorption suggests a change in the scale of the ineffable: the last century's grand natural sublime has become domestic human spirit; the deistic vista cedes to the magical detail.

Thus for the most part the moments of magic in realistic texts—handprints on a cake and Beloved's arrival in *Beloved*, descriptions of Saleem's conversations with the members of the Midnight Children's Conference in his head, blood trails or magic carpets in *One Hundred Years of Solitude*, the appearance of two halves of a magically fusing shiny object or a double fetus floating in a pool in *Distant Relations*—are small but powerful. Even when a magical phenomenon such as Grenouille's perfuming abilities and his lack of a normal human odor or Beloved's return from the past are central to the texts that contain them, we are not overwhelmed with descriptions of magical occurrences, but, instead, those phenomena are integrated in relatively small doses into realistic scenarios and events. As well as contributing to a narrative mode that suggests the existence of a mysterious realm of the spirit, they also function (although on a much smaller scale) within the narratitive like mystery festivals in ancient Greece, which, according to Walter Burkert, "should be unforgettable events, casting their shadows over the whole of one's future life, creating experiences that transform existence."[73] This notion of mystical seepage explains how the small irreducible elements in magical realist texts transform them, altering their narrative terrain. And it also corresponds to an intrapsychic process. If we adopt a Lacanian perspective for a moment, and recall Roland Barthes's suggestion that instead of carrying specific referential information, realistic details contain a charge indexing the real as such, we might see that the irruptions of magic into realism function like Jacques Lacan's imaginary does in an individual psyche. They resemble the "black hole in reality," which Slavoj Zizek sees as figuring the space of Lacanian fantasy, the nothing that makes everything different, Lacan's *objet petit a,* necessarily distorted by desire. Within the realistic narrative situation, the magical elements correspond to the *objet petit a,* a surplus element, an "elusive make-believe" that nevertheless makes all the difference in these texts.[74]

That magical supplement is small and it comes from some distance. In magical realist texts irruptions of magic sometimes constitute the surfacing of buried religious traditions, which speak independently of particular themes and styles.[75] In *Perfume,* for example, the magical quality of Grenouille's perfuming abilities transmits a trace of pre-Enlightenment belief in magical powers of enchantment, which operates within the satirical narrative that condemns the beginnings of the scientific age and its culmination in Nazi experimental atrocities, and yet it is not entirely defined by it.[76] The same is true for many magical realist texts, including *The White Hotel, Imagining Argentina, Beloved, One Hundred Years of Solitude, The Famished Road,* and (to a lesser extent) *The Book of Laughter and Forgetting,* which both use magical powers of enchantment and condemn political atrocities (an issue that we investigate in more detail in Chapter 4).

Thus a common and often noted factor in much magical realist fiction is the tapping of belief systems that predate the Enlightenment. But not always. As some examples from *Midnight's Children* and *Pig Tales* show, the exceptions are meaningful and suggest that the genre is not only a contemporary instance of nostalgic romance. Whether the magic involved stems from the system of tribal legend, political rhetoric, social stereotyping, or psychoanalytic discourse, that magic is engendered by a community of shared belief, though it may be a community the narrator or the reader does not share.

As Alejo Carpentier said in his early definition of the marvelous real, "those who don't believe in saints can't be cured by saints' miracles, and neither can those who aren't Quixotes enter body, soul, and possessions, into the world of Amadis of Gaul or Tirant lo Blanc."[77] But, we might add, they can write about it. Jorges Luis Borges, for example, at the beginnings of Latin American magical realism, inscribes elements of the Kabbalah in his fiction and says that, unlike Catholics, especially Argentine Catholics, who believe, but are not interested in its doctrines, he is interested, but does not believe.[78] And Oskar's claim that "he who doubts believes, and it is the unbeliever who believes longest" (360) aligns him with these storytellers who transmit a sense of spirit while not consciously believing in it. Magical realist magic rarely conforms to official doctrine, though it may allude to it.

That Borgesian stance, whereby the magic of belief is transmitted by an unbeliever, or by someone whose mode of narration implies some distance from the community of believers it contacts, characterizes much magical realism. Diverse as the belief systems involved are, the hint of a mysterious realm of spirit presences is transmitted by the defocalized narrative. But the distance of the narrator and the implied and actual authors from that realm differs considerably from text to text. Fuentes and Cortázar transmit the archaic spirit of southern Indo-America in texts that rarely refer to it explicitly. In *Aura,* for example, in contrast to Fuentes's early story "Chac Mool," in which an ancient rain god comes alive and takes revenge on his modern commodifiers, there are no explicit references to ancient Aztec beliefs; but Aztec resonances surface implicitly in the story's commerce between the living and the dead that formed a part of Aztec tradition and that is still present (in synchretized form) in the Mexican Days of the Dead, and even more specifically, though not explicitly, in the idea that perhaps Felipe ascends Consuelo's stairs as Aztec sacrificial victims ascended the steps of temples to be sacrificed, or that Aura with her green dress may re-embody the "lady of jade skirts," second wife of the rain god Tlaloc.[79] The name of the axolotl recalls the Aztec god Xolotl, so that, in a sense the narrator's fascination and eventual transmutation can be seen as a surreptitious encounter with divinity.[80] Native American and Catholic religious traditions in *So Far from God* and *Tracks,* and Urhobo and Yoruba beliefs in *The Famished Road,* in contrast, are explicitly evoked. Kennedy (in *Ironweed*) is close to the Catholic and Morrison (in *Beloved*) to the African and Afro-American religious traditions they transmit, so that those traditions are experienced rather than explained within their texts. The somewhat larger amount of magic in *Midnight's Children* reflects the presence of a living popular religious culture that includes supernatural narrative elements in India, but Rushdie himself operates largely from outside of that culture, even as he uses its narrative traditions and transmits something like their aura of belief through his magical realist mode. Similarly, Oskar as narrator in *The Tin Drum* reflects the beliefs and religious traditions of the "pious, thrifty, superstitious" Kashubians from whom he descends (mentioning specifically that he and his relatives, being Catholic, cross themselves differently from the Protestant nuns who nurse his dying mother), but that very formulation separates him from them.[81] In another scene, in which officially sanctified miracles are distinguished from the more ordinary and yet more appealing kind of magic tied to psychology and history, Oskar twice attempts to teach a baby Jesus on a church altar to drum. Speaking to himself about this attempt, he asks—and answers, "Will he drum now, or can't he drum, or isn't he allowed to drum? Either he drums or he is not a real Jesus; if he doesn't drum now, Oskar is a realer Jesus than he is" (143). Predictably enough, Jesus does not drum, and, especially after Oskar has been chided and cuffed for his pedagogical efforts, the reader sides with him and his marginalized magic. As a belief system, communism causes Paul Eluard, Madame Raphael, and other of the faithful in *The Book of Laughter and Forgetting* to levitate, but this irreducible magic happens only twice, and Kundera narrating in his own persona distances himself from that community of belief by clearly articulating the harm it has caused.[82] And Darrieussecq, while subscribing to a somewhat nostalgic view of the environment, clearly does not share the cultural beliefs of the cosmetics industry that commodifies women's bodies, but her protagonist consciously does, at least at first—though her libido also protests in the hostile demeanor occasionally resulting from the form of her transformation.

André Breton notices this modern tendency for the marvelous to hide itself, and in writing of seers, whom we might regard as one kind of symbolic antecedent for magical realist narrators, he describes a voice that must overcome its own reluctance to transmit a mysterious force. According to Breton in his "Letter to Seers," the seers' one error is "to have accepted the scandalous condition that is forced upon you, a relative poverty that obliges you to be 'visited' at such and such an hour, like doctors. . . . May it be that age-old persecutions will forever deter you from spreading through the world the great annunciation, despite those who do not wish to hear it?"[83] Magical realism, as perhaps the most potent and widespread descendant of Breton's desire for surreality, partially overcomes those persecutions and through its defocalized narrative voice makes way for the emergence of an ineffable presence of spirit to enter the discourse of realism, "spreading throughout the world" a vague and general "annunciation [of that presence], despite those who do not wish to hear it."

Magical realism occasionally thematizes the spirit presence that I have claimed its narrative mode surreptitiously projects. This thematizing occurs frequently in *The Famished Road,* which deals with the world of the spirits overtly and often. The confluence between concrete and spirit worlds is facilitated by the nature of the narrator, Azaro, who embodies the idea of an *abiku,* or spirit child, who repeatedly dies, returning to the world of the spirits, and is reborn again in human form.[84] Azaro seems to remain in the world of the living, but he can often see other *abiku* children. These may include the girl who appears to him outside Madame Koto's bar and stirs the pepper soup with a bone that melts into the liquid, and, especially, with his friend Ade, who continually tempts him to return to the world of the spirits. (In explaining this phenomenon in these terms, however, I am doing Okri's text something of an injustice, since the situation is experienced by the reader as a confusing mesh of realities rather than a clearly articulated theory.) This overt presence of a world of the spirits also characterizes *Palace of the Peacock,* in which near the end the narrator experiences himself drawn "away from nature's end and wish, and towards the eternal desire and spirit that charged the selfsame wish of death with shades of mediation," and who seems to experience his consciousness as linked up with some kind of spirit realm—"my consciousness which was in itself but another glimmering shadow hedging the vision and the glory and the light"(48).

In *So Far from God,* Castillo explicitly actualizes the belief in spirits and power gained from congress with their realm. Caridad, for example, undergoes a vision quest, or hermetic retreat, and is "found one day living in a cave in the Sangre de Cristo [note the name] Mountains," having survived alone there for "four seasons." This feat "seemed incredible" to everyone, and "it was said that she lifted the very horse in the air that the hermano had tried to force her to mount—with him on it—but out of benevolence brought it back down safely without so much as spooking the horse with her defiant magic."[85] She subsequently becomes a curandera: "sometimes Caridad did not even have to dream as a channeler, or as doña Felicia called her, a medium. She often fell into semiconscious trances and communicated with spirit guides as a way of communicating messages to clients" (119). And her sister La Loca, after her brush with death and her magical rise onto the roof of the church, can communicate with the wandering spirit of the mythical "La Llorona, chicana international astral-traveler" (163) who she claims (without previously having known anything about her) appeared to tell her that her sister Esperanza had died, a fact that is confirmed two weeks later by mail. In more allegorical fashion, *The White Hotel* concludes with a vision of paradise in which people are reunited and cured of their worldly ills—a possible compensation for the horrible suffering they have undergone. This scene, however, has occasioned much critical controversy and accusations of facile fantasy, in part because of Thomas's expressed "intention that the Palestine of 'The Camp' serve as a metaphor for the soul's life in eternity."[86] These thematic treatments of connections to spirit worlds in several magical realist texts seem to me to confirm the fact that magical realism encodes the ineffable, but more important, I would argue, is that it is the narrative mode of magical realism itself that does so in the way it includes irreducible elements within realism.

This presence of spirit is not, however, the only consequence of magical realism's defocalization. The partial detachment from present sensory reality that such a narrative represents also allows the incursion of several varieties of otherness, of personal, historical, cultural, or literary pasts, and of different kinds of virtual realities, including textual ones. For example, the way voices traverse Saleem's head is compared to the operations of a radio transmitter, so that the resulting text is linked not only to a world of spirits through its defocalized narrative but also to historical and interpersonal events and public discourses. Grenouille's perfuming abilities resemble those of an experimental chemist of genius, so that in addition to the magical powers of its narrative mode, the novel also takes on a quasi scientific aura, intimately connected to the concrete worlds of natural and constructed chemical compounds. The ubiquitous voice in *One Hundred Years of Solitude,* which gives evidence of having absorbed much of Western culture, means that the story of Macondo is pervaded by many other actual histories and places and texts.

Shamanistic Narrative Healing

In using the resources of realism to construct a defocalized discourse that while based in ordinary sense perceptions also seems to carry the reader beyond them, magical realist narrative resembles the performance of a shaman who constructs a persona and a discourse that imaginatively negotiate different realms, joining the everyday world of concrete reality and the world of the spirits.[87] Magical realism can be seen not only as a primitivist aesthetic but also as a manifestation of a perennial cultural need, for a sense of contact with cosmic forces that extend beyond material reality and the individual and for discourses that accommodate that contact. A comparison with shamanism thus illuminates the cultural function of magical realism generally, irrespective of the particular and extremely varied subjects of its texts.[88] Shamanic performances differ from magical realist narratives in many respects, above all because they typically take place in a climate of largely homogeneous belief in supernatural powers and the existence of magical phenomena, whereas magical realism is a more hybrid construct in which the discourse of realism with its empirical assumptions maintains an implicit distance from such belief, even though it may also be present. Now, however, because that cultural homogeneity has changed, shamanic performances often take place in culturally hybrid situations, sometimes incorporating nontraditional practices and images. And there are other similarities. A shamanic performance and magical realist fiction are both "a space where unusual and magical manifestations of physicality take place."[89] In other words, magical realist narrative resembles a shaman's account of his activities, which seems as if it "walks the 'razor's edge' between the natural and supernatural universes and is therefore capable of entering and leaving them both at will."[90] This shared act of balancing between actual and extraordinary realities means that, different as shamanic performance and magical realism are in many ways, a comparison of the two helps to explain the power and popularity of magical realism.

Beyond the connection to primitive cultures or mythologies, magical realism is a narrative in which, as in a shamanic performance, the viewing or reading community experiences a discourse that suggests the existence of a different kind of reality contiguous to or within their ordinary one. This form of discourse with its magical images of uncertain origin can also be seen to continue the tradition of a shamanistic visionary or vatic stance exemplified in the previous period by such poets as Blake, Rimbaud, and Whitman.

Because it indicates the desire for a form of discourse that reaches beyond everyday reality, but which also admits the difficulty that a modern person encounters in attempting to create such a discourse, the Rimbauldian statement "Je travaille à me rendre voyant" ("I work at becoming a seer"), prefigures the modification of realism by the fantastic and the complex combination of irony and belief with respect to the irreducible element that exists in magical realism.[91] In addition, as the discussion in Chapter 4 of magical realism as postcolonial discourse reveals, this similarity of magical realism to shamanic discourse makes it especially suitable as a counterdiscourse that questions the dominance of realism, which is based largely in concrete reality, and thereby encourages the emergence of new literary voices.

Despite the variations of irony and belief regarding the magical events in magical realist narrative, the way in which the magic appears within ordinary reality resembles the way in which magical elements, which indicate contact with non-ordinary reality, are introduced in the course of shamanic performances, for a shamanic curing ceremony is a performance. The shaman may emit the cries of birds and dance and leap as he evokes connections with different beings and realms. Take, for example, the early twentieth-century ethnographer Wenceslas Sieroszewski's description of a Siberian shaman, a classic seance, according to Mircea Eliade, who cites and comments on it. At the start of this Yakut seance, as Sieroszewski describes it, "sometimes the master of the house prepares two nooses from strong thongs; the shaman secures them to his shoulders and the others present grasp their ends to hold him back in case the spirits should try to carry him off." After the shaman stares into the hearth and is shaken from time to time by nervous tremors, and the onlookers hold their breaths, "suddenly, a succession of shrill cries, piercing as the screech of steel, sounds from no one knows where; then all is silent again." While he is "dreaming," the shaman alternately drums and emits the cries of various birds—"the croaking of eagles, mixed with the lamenting of lapwings, the piercing cries of woodcocks and the refrain of cuckoos." Next, he chants a hymn invoking the horse of the steppe to the rhythm of his drumming: "Appear, then, marvelous bull of the Universe, and answer! . . . Prepare my way for me!" When his tutelary spirit arrives, the shaman drums, dances, leaps into the air ("sometimes as high as four feet"), intones a "solemn hymn," does a "light dance during which his song becomes ironic or else diabolical, depending on the beings whose voices he is imitating." He then approaches the patient and carries away the illness. Finally, the shaman goes on an ecstatic journey to escort the soul of the sacrificed animal to the sky. In performing this part of the ceremony, he moves between three trees, which are connected by a rope. "The dance," Sieroszewski explains, "always depicts a journey through the air in company with spirits; when the expiatory beast is escorted, dancing is also obligatory. According to legend, not long ago there were shamans who really flew into the sky, and the audience saw an animal sailing through the clouds, followed by the shamanic procession. 'The drum is our horse,' the shamans say."[92]

During the curing ceremony, the shaman's alleged connection to a contiguous world of animal spirits is evoked through the bird cries he emits, but, like a magical realist text, this narrative is defocalized because, according to this account, the audience does not seem to know whether it is listening to the cries of birds transmitted by the shaman, to imitations of bird cries emitted by him, or perhaps even to the sounds made by actual birds, because they are described as coming "from no one knows where." Similarly, the inclusion of magical events within realistic fiction constitutes not a proof of their existence but rather a verbal performance. To include convincing cries of eagles and jumps into the air that resemble flights is a performance that imaginatively evokes an extraordinary reality from within the ordinary, just as García Márquez's descriptions of a blood trail, Cortázar's account that merges onlooker and axolotl, or Rushdie's story of how Saleem's sneeze sets off the Midnight Children's Conference in his head imaginatively conflate imaginary and actual spaces. That these textual performances take place within realistic narrative, in many cases specifically tied to particular history or geography, resembles the way in which shamanic ceremonies are enacted in the real world but achieve results that imply a connection to superhuman or nonhuman powers.[93]

Throughout this performance, connections between sensory and spirit worlds are acknowledged in various ways: by the thongs that tether the shaman to the earth so that he will not be carried off, by the shaman's drinking cold water even as his eyes are closing and he is entering his trance, by the audience that clashes iron over the shaman when he falls over backward at the sudden arrival of the spirits. As in magical realism, those connections are often surprising: not only do the spirits arrive so suddenly that the shaman falls backward but the shaman's shrill cries begin suddenly. This suddenness also resembles the way in which the irreducible elements in magical realism appear unannounced. These analogies mean that the reader of a magical real-

ist text participates in a textual performance analogous to a shamanic trance
in which voices that are imagined as coming from another realm are produced. Like readers of magical realist fictions, who accept the magical terms
of the text created by the particular verbal artistry of its defocalized narrative,
onlookers participate in the shaman's ritual performance of an event through
his verbal and bodily artistry as it forms part of a curing ceremony, regardless
of whether they believe that he has actually flown through the air or spoken
with a power animal.

Within this account, the shaman's chant is essential, accompanying his
movements, orchestrating his actions. The evocative power of the shaman's
words and his drum is acknowledged in the hymn when he chants, "I am
the man who has all gifts!" but his subservience to an order beyond the human is acknowledged with the next line: "I am the man created by the Lord
of Infinity." The bird voices emanating from the shaman's mouth concretize
the connection between human and animal spirit worlds; at the same time,
they constitute a multivocal discourse of indeterminate origin that resembles
what we have been seeing as the "defocalized" narrative mode of magical realism.

A second example of a shamanic text, collected by the French anthropologist Michel Perrin, confirms the common characteristics of shamanic
and magical realist discourses. It consists of a Guajiro shaman describing a
shamanic performance.

> We, the shamans, eat tobacco and sing.
> Our eyes remain closed, and we see . . .
> It is as if someone were standing in front of us.
> This is the spirit helper, the *wanuluu.*
> Its words speak through our mouths,
> But they are different from people's words.
> You can't understand them, no one knows that language.
> It's like a telephone that is attached to our head.
> When we shamans sing,
> We go far away, where the Dream (*Lapu)* is.
> Our spirit runs a lot, it goes a long way.
> It travels without stopping and comes back right away.
> It's as fast as our look.[94]

Here again, as in the preceding example, the chant facilitates contact with the world of the spirits, which is distinguished from the ordinary world in this case by the initial paradox of seeing with closed eyes. A similar duality, concretizing the connection between different realms, is that the spirits are said to speak a different language from that of ordinary people, but the image for this type of communication is an everyday modern one, the telephone. Thus, like magical realist narratives, this account uses the language of ordinary reality to create a discourse that gives a sense of moving beyond it. As in magical realism, where the extraordinary is included in the everyday, even though the shamans' spirits are said to travel constantly and far, they are imagined as being able to return immediately. The spirit realm is described as contiguous with the ordinary.

Because magical realism includes images that depart from the realistic mode, suggesting the existence of hidden or unseen worlds, its narrative situation resembles the interaction between shaman and patient, in which the shaman transmits voices of indeterminate origin. Pachita, a female shaman in Mexico City, for example, has explained that she was host during her trances to the spirit of Cuautémoc, the Aztec king who ruled immediately prior to the Spanish conquest of Tenochtitlán, and whose spirit helped her to see into the patient's body and make her diagnosis.[95] In addition to empowering the shaman, the sense of hearing voices from a powerful and mysterious realm in a shamanic performance also has an effect on the patient. Michael Harner cites Albert Schweitzer's statement: "The witch doctor succeeds for the same reason all the rest of us [doctors] succeed. Each patient carries his own doctor inside him. They come to us not knowing this truth. We are at our best when we give the doctor who resides within each patient a chance to work." Harner then comments that "perhaps the shaman is uniquely qualified among the practitioners of the healing arts to give 'the doctor inside a chance to go to work.' "[96] Extending that idea, we might imagine that that sense of psychic working from the inside out is analogous to the way irreducible elements work on the conventions of realism, modifying them from inside the genre. Schweitzer's image also figures the way in which magical realist texts suggest that the miraculous nature of life exists within reality. In these narratives, as in shamanic trance states, as described by Michael Lambek, "it is always the case that the ordinary world is illuminated by its contrast with the extraordinary."[97] In García Márquez's story "Light Is Like Water," for example, the magical way in which the light the two young boys turn on behaves like water highlights for us the amazing, and near-miraculous quality of the light that we cause to regularly inundate our houses by simply flipping an electric switch: "The boys . . . closed the doors and windows and broke the glowing bulb in one of the living room lamps. A jet of golden light as cool as water began to pour out of the broken bulb, and they let it run to a depth of almost three feet. Then they turned off the electricity, took out the rowboat, and navigated at will among the islands in the house."[98]

To continue with the curative function of shamanic practice for a moment, a shaman appears to enter "a controlled altered state of consciousness on behalf of his community," to cure individuals of diseases or to heal community wounds.[99] In terms of literary history, magical realism may begin to rid realistic fiction's communal voice of its close attachment to the exact representation of concrete reality, to achieve, as I have suggested, a remystification of narrative in the West. The attempt to work this cure is an attempt to seek power in a realm that lacks that attachment. Discursively, it constitutes a defocalized narrative; thematically, it often describes pre-Enlightenment traditions, including myths, ghosts, and journeys to the lands of the dead. Combining those two registers, we might say that defocalized narrative visits dead civilizations in order to bring back a communal voice of indeterminate origin but possessing creative authority, with which it revivifies the narrative discourse of realism. Recall in this context Pachita's "channeling" of Cuautémoc's spirit during her curing ceremony. The popularity of magical realism coincides with the current interest in shamanism, attested to by countless books, journals, and workshops on the subject (some of them with actual native shamans), which both documents and contributes to a "reinvention" of shamanism in the West "precisely because it is needed."[100] Magical realism responds to this same need for contact with alternative healers belonging to pre-Enlightenment traditions. To seek such a curative voice is to attempt a union of death and birth, in the interest of rebirth, to "remember the future"—in other words, to use the past to reorient that future. Near the start of Wilson Harris's *Tumatumari,* the narrator calls for this shamanistic, atavistic voice: he is to "crawl back into the interior (there was no other way open to him) crawl back into the womb and BEG the guardians of life who held his tongue in their keeping to blow their trumpet of recall)."[101]

In addition to this general narrative healing of the split between sensory and spirit-oriented worlds and discourses, and between present and past cultural and narrative traditions, these texts often address particular historical wounds. In *Beloved,* for example, Sethe partially exorcizes the mortal harm slavery caused her to inflict on her daughter, and in *The White Hotel* the last idyllic scenes in Israel partially—and even ironically—assuage the pain of the Holocaust. According to Hena Maes-Jellinek, *Palace of the Peacock* portrays a similar healing process: when the characters climb up the escarpment of a waterfall, "which seems to represent the great divide that tore the West Indian soul (particularly its Amerindian element) in the wake of conquest," Donne re-experiences "images of his Amerindian spiritual ancestry."[102] This is a semi-real, semi-imaginary journey that opens out from a somewhat more realistically conceived one up a river. Throughout, it has as its partial scenario vegetation that seems to refer to an actual and particular landscape but that seems even more evocative of a timeless mythical realm of visionary fulfillment into which the narrative merges its travelers. Near the beginning, "the whispering trees spun their leaves to a sudden fall wherein the ground seemed to grow lighter in my mind and to move to meet them in the air. . . . A brittle moss and carpet appeared underfoot, a dry pond and stream whose course and reflection and image had been stamped for ever like the breathless outline of a dreaming skeleton in the earth. The trees rose around me into upward flying limbs" (27). Near the end, Donne sees a tree whose "bark and wood turned to lightning flesh and the sun which had been suspended from its head rippled and broke into stars that stood where the shattered leaves had been. . . . The stars became peacocks' eyes, and the great tree of flesh and blood swirled into another stream that sparkled with divine feathers where the neck and the hands and the feet had been nailed" (146). There, the contentiousness of men's desires as they manifest themselves in historical events are annulled in a different kind of eternal soul's desire: speaking of one of his companions, Donne says, "The music of the peacock turned him into a subtle step and waltz like the grace and outspread fan of desire that had once been turned by the captain of the crew into a compulsive design and a blind engine of war. His feet marched again as a spider's toward eternity, and the music he followed welled and circumnavigated the globe" (150). The narrator feels transformed, saying, "I had started to walk at last—after a long infancy and dreaming death—in the midst of mutilation and chaos that had no real power to overcome me. . . . I had never before looked on the blinding world in this trusting manner—through an eye I shared only with the soul" (145–46). The travelers are thus now outside of time, it seems, having gone beyond it: "He stood at his window and I stood at mine, transported

beyond the memory of words" (148). They stand in the rooms of the palace
at which they have arrived and "the sound that filled us was unlike the link of
memory itself. It was the inseparable moment within ourselves of all fulfillment and understanding. . . . It was the dance of all fulfillment I now held
and knew deeply, canceling my forgotten fear of strangeness and catastrophe
in a destitute world" (151–52).

That this journey represents a re-encounter with the past directed at
healing its wounds is suggested by the description of Donne's feelings: "a
longing swept him like the wind of the muse to understand and transform
his beginnings: to see the indestructible nucleus and redemption of creation"
(130). That it is a culturally hybrid journey is suggested by Christian and
indigenous-seeming images. In addition to the previous image of what appears to be a sacrificial bird nailed at neck and hands and feet, Donne sees
an image of "a young carpenter in a room," in the cliff face, a room "as old
as a cave and as new as a study," "a long dead room in which the carpenter
was sealed and immured for good. All sound had been barred and removed
for ever, all communication, all persuasion, all intercourse" (131–33). As he
hammers against the wall to catch the carpenter's attention, the carpenter as
an image of Death stares through him. Soon what seems like an indigenous
crowd erupts on the scene: "leaves sprang up from nowhere, a stampede of
ghostly men and women all shaped by the leaves, raining and running against
the sky. / They besieged the walls of the carpenter's room, clamouring and
hammering with the waterfall. . . . The carpenter looked blind to the stum-
bling human darkness that still trailed and followed across the world. He
closed his window softly upon Donne and Jennings and daSilva," in what
suggests a re-enactment of the inadequacy of the Christian colonization of the
new world (136–37). In addition to being a culturally hybrid journey, that this
is a culturally healing journey, as Maes-Jellinek maintains, is suggested by the
narrator's description of Donne's thoughts that end the chapter in which the
group encounters the waterfall: "He had stopped a little to wonder whether
he was wrong in his knowledge and belief and the force that had divided
them from each other—and mangled them beyond all earthly hope and recognition—was the wind of rumor and superstition, and truth was they had
all come home at last to the compassion of the nameless unflinching folk"
(143). This scenario of encountering the folk supercedes the one described
near the start of the journey up the river when the narrator muses, "We're all
outside of the folk" and attempts to describe the nature of their alienation as

"fear of life, . . . fear of the substance of life, fear of the substance of the fold, a cannibal blind fear in oneself" (59). It affirms a personal and communal healing through the encounter with that folk, but not an easy reconciliation with them in the realm of social reality.

Harris's novel thus evokes a mystical feeling of healing achieved through a return to the land and an imaginative encounter with the spirit of its original inhabitants. Even more generally, perhaps magical realism appeals to the atomic age as a narrative model for healing the social, political, environmental, and religious wounds caused by warring discourses that result from increased communication between diverse communities in the global village.[103] Regardless of their specific political agendas, magical realist texts are often written in the context of cultural crises, almost as if their magic is invoked when recourse to other, rational, methods have failed.[104] From this perspective, the shamanistic voice in magical realism represents the appeal to a power from a different place: ancient "guardians of life" are invoked in order to deal with present social atrocities. As I have suggested earlier, Grass writes *The Tin Drum* in response to the Nazi period in Germany and to World War II, after it is clear that there will be no easy healing of Germany's emotional wounds; similarly, *Midnight's Children* laments that independence has not healed India's cultural wounds, even for a generation that was born into it; and *One Hundred Years of Solitude* descries the damage that the overwhelming presence of North American commercial interests has caused in Latin America. No specific solutions are proposed, but acknowledging the wounds and suggesting the inadequacy of scientifically based perspectives and forms of discourse may begin the healing process.[105]

Like Schweitzer, Gloria Anzaldúa recognizes the shaman's capacity to empower the patient. The shamanic healing she claims for all literature when she says of herself and other writers, "if we're lucky we create, like the shaman, images that induce altered states of consciousness conducive to self-healing" is especially strong in magical realist texts.[106] If we move from a consideration of narrative mode to subject matter for a moment, Süskind has created a contemporary shamanistic curing ceremony in *Perfume* by refiguring Nazi cruelty in Grenouille. Just as the Nazis wished to create a pure and perfect race, but in order to do it they had to exterminate whole categories of people, Grenouille wishes to create the perfect human perfume, but in order to do it he has to exterminate a whole category of—red-haired, gorgeous young— women. Analogous to the way that a shaman often takes the sickness of a patient into himself, while also giving the patient strength to heal himself, Süskind concentrates in Grenouille a venom that can be associated to Nazi cruelty and then has him die at the hands of the multitude he has caused to love him literally to death through his shamanistic perfuming powers. For the reader who experiences these scenes, his death symbolically exorcizes psychological wounds of guilt and self-doubt in post-post-war Germany.

Palace of the Peacock, The White Hotel, Pedro Páramo, Ironweed, and *Beloved* are also analogous to shamanistic curing ceremonies, for they involve—in their different ways—the partial magical healing of socially damaged relationships through communication with beings from beyond the grave. A settling of scores from the past, a kind of social healing process, is proposed with the initial words of *Pedro Páramo,* motivating Juan Preciado's journey to Comala, which turns out to be a land of the dead: "I came to Comala because I was told that my father, a certain Pedro Páramo, was living here. My mother told me so. . . . Before that she told me, 'Don't ask for anything that isn't ours. Just for what he should have given me and didn't. Make him pay for the way he forgot us.'" At the very end of the novel, a reckoning seems to be taking place, if not the one Juan's mother envisioned, for, after having admitted, "I know Abundio [another of his sons] will be back here in a little while with his bloody hands, to keep begging for the help I wouldn't give him. And I can't lift up my hands to cover my eyes and not see him. I'll have to listen to him until his voice fades away with the daylight. Until his voice dies out." Finally, Pedro Páramo "struck a feeble blow against the ground and then crumbled to pieces as if he were a heap of stones."[107] Still yearning after his beloved, the tyrannical cacique has merged with and thereby somewhat assuaged the pain of the land he had so long oppressed.

After the horrendous circumstances surrounding Lisa's death at Babi Yar in *The White Hotel,* when she arrives in an imaginary Palestine and encounters her mother, the pains of circumstance and psychology that separated them from each other and from her father as well are healed, mother and daughter literally suckle each other, and Lisa's mother says that "wonderful healing goes on over here." This final chapter, however, does not fit well within the mode of magical realism, because it pictures a land of the afterlife, separated from the real world, where people seem to arrive after death. Earlier on, though, the healing value of continuity with the past appears in a scene in which present and past seem to magically merge. Lisa returns to "her old home. The rambling white house had been converted into a health resort," and we surmise it is the same white hotel of the earlier parts of the narrative. Thus the earlier scenes in which magical events such as burning hair, flying breasts, and impossibly telescopic views of lake and mountains, images that picture the horrible death she eventually undergoes in terms that could also be associated with the psychic dramas and passions of her youth, as well as with events in the lives of others of the hotel's guests or their relatives, are now merged into the realistic account of Lisa's return with her husband to the white house of her childhood, in a peaceful mode. At that time, Lisa experiences a sense of personal healing that joins her present and past selves. In a particularly Proustian moment, first "she had the feeling that she was no more than a spectre," but then, all of a sudden,

> As she stood close against a pine tree and breathed in its sharp bitter scent, a clear space opened to her childhood, as though a wind had sprung up from the sea, clearing a mist. It was not a memory from the past but the past itself, as alive, as real; and she knew that she and the child of forty years ago were the same person.
>
> That knowledge flooded her with happiness. . . . there was no blank wall, only an endless extent, like an avenue, in which she was still herself, Lisa. . . . It all came from the scent of a pine tree.[108]

Similar processes of magical healing are central to *Beloved* and *Ironweed.* The horrors of slavery that caused Sethe to kill her daughter Beloved can never be entirely healed, and one of Morrison's points is that we must continue to remember these wounds. However, by re-encountering Beloved, who thereby subliminally learns of the reasons for her own death and also wreaks some revenge on her mother, in addition to witnessing her suffering, Sethe is able to partially heal the wound she inflicted on her child, and on herself as well. That healing process of reconciliation in which Sethe and Beloved and Denver are reunited in the flesh, takes place in a largely wordless realm, where "I am Beloved and she is mine"; that is why Sethe says, "She come back to me of her own free will and I don't have to explain a thing." However, the text also makes room for explanations, and at numerous points, Sethe imagines explaining her actions to her child: "I'll explain to her even though I don't have to. Why I did it. How if I hadn't killed her she would have died and that is something I could not bear to happen to her. When I explain it she'll understand, because she understands everything already. I'll tend her as no mother ever tended a child."[109] Through being confronted rather than repressed, these wounds are partially healed. Frances Phelan in *Ironweed* undergoes a similar experience: having accidentally dropped and killed his baby son, he achieves, through a visit to the cemetery, a kind of atonement and reconciliation. Although, as we have seen, *Ironweed* exists on the realistic fringes of magical realism, the way in which Francis's son is described in concrete detail underground as real and the way in which the reconciliation is focalized through the baby's mind, which seems to give Francis directions to follow (which he proceeds to do), makes it comparable to these magical realist journeys to lands of the dead. In addition, because the story allies itself with Catholic tradition, the elements of confession and directions for expiation are clearly recognizable, though transformed. Francis cries onto the grave, and then asks his son, if "you suppose now that I can remember this stuff out in the open, I can finally start to forget it?" And his son answers: "Gerald, through an act of silent will, imposed on his father the pressing obligation to perform his final acts of expiation for abandoning the family. You will not know, the child silently said, what these acts are until you have performed them all. And after you have performed them you will not understand that they were expiatory any more than you have understood all the other expiation that has kept you in such prolonged humiliation."[110]

Generalizing about the cultural work of magical realism, perhaps it can be seen, among other things, as healing fiction for a computer age: written for those who wish to hear a mystical voice from an uncertain place, it over-writes the computer's artificial, predictable, intelligence, and yet it operates from within the ordinary world that includes computers and is based in the same empirically defined reality that they are. The movie *Ghost*, in which Whoopie Goldberg plays a woman who resembles a savvy female shaman, specifically exploits this interface between the mysterious and the predictable, because the ghost in question is a computer ghost, using a keyboard to type the message that finally undoes his murderer.[111] Unlike the defocalized narra-tive mode of a magical realist fiction, in which the reader is unsure of exactly what kind of perceiver is at the origin of the information she is receiving, the original basis for the information produced by a computer program is known, even though it may seem alien to the uninitiated. In the face of a frustrating Foucaultian sense that we are always inside our own epistemes, spoken by the dominant discourses of our age, this mode allows us to experience imagina-tive flights that seem to escape that discursive domination. Such flights are partially detached from the dominant realistic form of narrative authority, yet they are still grounded in social and historical reality. Thus magical realism seems to hold out the possibility of healing the split between concrete and imaginary, or science-based and spirit-oriented worlds. It is a very appealing possibility, but it is only a possibility, and, as we see in Chapter 4, it raises a number of troubling questions.

3 ⁊

Encoding the Ineffable

A Textual Poetics for Magical Realism

"You must use language in a manner which permits God to exist —the divine to be as real as the divan I am sitting on," Rushdie writes, describing the special style he needs in order to portray contemporary India. "Realism," he continues, "can no longer express or account for the absurd reality of the world we live in—a world which has the capability of destroying itself at any moment."[1] This combination of divinity and absurdity characterizes magical realism as it attempts to bridge the gap between ancient divinity and modern absurdity, which often includes scientifically created atrocity. This bridging function motivates many of the magical realist techniques we examine in this chapter. These narrative techniques enhance the defocalization of magical realism discussed in Chapter 2 and hence particularize how magical realism constitutes a narrative space of the ineffable in-between. We might imagine these techniques as combining Rimbaud's systematic "disordering of *all the senses*" ("déreglement de *tous les sens*"), which corresponds to magical realism's dismantling of realism, and T. S. Eliot's "Shantih Shantih Shantih" at the very end of *The Wasteland*, which fills that poem's ruined space with a ritual voice.[2] This is one way in which modernism sows the seeds of participatory magic that flower in magical realism; the spirit evoked in the chanting at the end of *The Wasteland* is actualized in the irreducible elements and other textual practices of magical realism. They flesh out the textual space left vacant by the phatic skeleton of the Unnameable's words. Almost unspoken, perhaps magical realism's generic narrative voice starts where Beckett's narrator leaves off and begins to speak the unspeakable.

A scene from Rushdie's *Midnight's Children* that images the defocalized quality of magical realist narrative can serve as an introduction to several different techniques that contribute to that quality. Saleem describes his narrative powers as coming from nowhere in particular: he sits "like an empty pickle jar in a pool of Anglepoised light, visited by this vision of my grandfather, . . . which demands to be recorded, filling my nostrils with the acrid stench of his mother's embarrassment. . . . I seem to have found from somewhere the trick of filling in the gaps in my knowledge."[3] His powers come "from somewhere" undefined; in a literally receptive frame of mind, he experiences a visionary moment in which he is visited by a demanding and enabling ancestor figure, whose demands push his pen and provide him with sensory details for his story.

Borges's despair as he tries to describe his elusive Aleph in the story by that name is another appropriate introduction to our investigation of magical realist techniques that figure the ineffable.

> I arrive now at the ineffable core of my story. And here begins my despair as a writer. All language is a set of symbols whose use among its speakers assumes a shared past. How, then, can I translate into words the limitless Aleph, which my floundering mind can scarcely encompass? Mystics, faced with the same problem, fall back on symbols: to signify the godhead, one Persian speaks of a bird that somehow is all birds; Alanus de Insulis, of a sphere whose center is everywhere and circumference is nowhere; Ezekiel, of a four-faced angel who at one and the same time moves east and west, north and south.[4]

(And Borges's despair is symbolically alleviated by Rushdie's investigation of a language that encompasses both the divine and the divan.) By invoking the age-old trope "words can hardly express," which in itself is not magical, and even though it thereby emphasizes the problem of narrative stance, as many magical realist fictions do not, this passage nevertheless suggests how magical realism represents a new discursive space that satisfies the desire to encompass new realms within realism. In the passage, the word *ineffable* appears just after the narrator has seen the Aleph but before he describes it to us, foregrounding both the importance of the vision and the difficulty of writing about it. Note also how he refers to the "ineffable core of my story," indicating that, as we noticed earlier, the ineffable in magical realism is a textual matter, created within the prose, not existing outside of it. Borges approaches the subject of the sacred and its texts by posing an implicitly multicultural dilemma—the problem of shared pasts—and he begins to solve the problem by evoking two common magical realist images of birds and angels that encompass different cosmic realms. Then, as if he had conjured away any malevolent spirits that might be hovering around his endeavor by invoking the inadequacy of language, Borges creates his well-known and evocative portrait of the Aleph: Within a "small iridescent sphere of almost unbearable brilliance," he sees "the unimaginable universe," in which

> each thing . . . was infinite things. . . . I saw the teeming sea; . . . I saw bunches of grapes, snow, tobacco, lodes of metal, straw; I saw convex equatorial deserts and each one of their grains of sand; I saw a woman in Inverness whom I shall never forget; I saw her tangled hair, her tall figure; . . . I saw the circulation of my own dark blood; I saw the coupling of love and the modification of death; I saw the Aleph from every point and angle, and in the Aleph I saw the earth and in the earth the Aleph and in the Aleph the earth.[5]

In combining so many details of so many different registers in such a limited narrative time and physical space, Borges uses realistic details to reach beyond the real. With the uncertain origin and ontology of the Aleph itself, this text also embodies magical realism's typical defocalization, its erasure of narrative origins and authority. As if these doubts were not enough, at the end of the story, in his proof that Carlos Daneri's Aleph (which he has described for us) is a false Aleph, Borges posits another Aleph that the faithful can hear in a pillar in a Cairo mosque, but then, finally, he asks, "Does this Aleph exist in the heart of a stone? Did I see it there in the cellar when I saw all things, and have I now forgotten it?" (The original Spanish makes his perception of all things even vaguer, not referring explicitly to the cellar, and hence requiring us to decide for ourselves whether that is indeed the experience to which he refers.) We experience layer upon layer of doubt, and yet we receive the spirit of the Aleph, which has been momentarily embodied in words.[6]

Magical Details, Naïve Narrators, Indeterminate Spaces and Times, the Oneiric Optic

One of the most immediately striking ways in which magical realism imbricates the extraordinary within the ordinary is the accumulation of realistic details to describe an impossible event. Borges's description of the Aleph, with its myriad realistic details that concretize an unreal phenomenon, has already provided us with an example. This technique is a particular strength of García Márquez's fiction, but it appears elsewhere as well. The trail of José Arcadio's blood, by now an icon of magical realist description, is an outstanding instance.

> A trickle of blood came out under the door, crossed the living room, went out into the street, continued on in a straight line across the uneven terraces, went down steps and climbed over curbs, passed along the Street of the Turks, turned a corner to the right and another to the left, made a right angle at the Buendía house, went in under the closed door, crossed through the parlor, hugging the walls so as not to stain the rugs, went on to the other living room, made a wide curve to avoid the dining-room table, went along the porch with the begonias, and passed without being seen under Amaranta's chair as she gave an arithmetic lesson to Aureliano José, and went through the pantry and came out in the kitchen, where Ursula was getting ready to crack thirty-six eggs to make bread.[7]

Because a trail of blood cannot normally climb curbs and turn corners at right angles and does not possess a humanlike capacity to direct its own progress, the more realistic details (such as the name of the street, the kind of flowers, and the exact number of eggs) the trail of blood accumulates, the more magical its progress appears. Those details weave a textual fabric that joins different worlds, one in which such a stream of blood exists in the ordinary world of precise identities and measurements and one in which it possesses magical properties. But here those worlds are imbricated one within the other. Such a combination of the real and the magical is a central paradox of magical realism. Furthermore, because the trail of blood originates at the scene of José Arcadio's death but also participates fully in the concerns of everyday life, such as taking care not to stain the rugs and avoiding the dining table, as it traverses Macondo, it seems to join the different cosmic regions of the living and the dead. The death and its bloody and yet almost whimsical sequel is the first death we actually witness in Macondo, so the trail, described in such detail, confirms the connection between these regions; it is a trail that we have seen Prudencio Aguilar follow, that Melquíades, who "really had been through death, but he had returned because he could not bear the solitude"(55), will later tread, and that also appears when Amaranta Buendía was "receiving letters for the dead" just before she dies (262). And, because it encompasses both the household's everyday reality and the magical qualities of autonomous motion and sensibility, it also links the different discursive regions of realism and fantasy. A similar effect is achieved with all the details surrounding the insomnia and loss-of-memory plague, which causes the Macondoans to put signs on objects so they can remember what they are and how to use them, and go "on living in a reality that was slipping away, momentarily captured by words" (53). And with the details of Remedios the Beauty's fascination for men: her "suffocating odor" "was so deep in his body that the cracks in his skull did not give off blood but an amber-colored oil that was impregnated with that secret perfume" (220). The more realistic the details, the more magically amazing the phenomenon.

That same effect appears in *Ironweed* in the description of Francis's son, Gerald, who died as a baby and who is seen by Francis in his grave as having "grown a protective web which defeated all moisture, all moles, rabbits, and other burrowing creatures. His web was woven of strands of vivid silver, an enveloping hammock of intricate, near-transparent weave. . . . Gerald rested in his infantile sublimity, exuding a high gloss induced by early death, his skin a radiant white-gold, his nails a silvery gray, his cluster of curls and large eyes perfectly matched in gleaming ebony."[8] Here again, in this description, as in the blood trail, the accumulation of realistic details around the impossible event of Francis's seeing his son underground, and the son's condition resembling a saint in his niche, together with the preponderantly realistic narrative in which it appears, paradoxically concretizes the event while simultaneously endowing it with a sense of wonder and amazement. A similar accumulation of details surrounds Oskar's miraculous screams.

With my very first trim, economical scream, I cut the cabinet in which Hollatz kept his loathsome curiosities wide open, and sent an almost square pane of glass toppling to the linoleum floor where, still preserving its square shape, it cracked into a thousand pieces. Then, . . . I shattered one test tube after another.

The tubes popped like firecrackers. The greenish, partly coagulated alcohol squirted and splashed, carrying its prepared, pale, gloomy-eyed contents to the red linoleum floor, and filling the room with so palpable a stench that Mama grew sick to her stomach and Sister Inge had to open the windows.[9]

The precision of the details here, including the "almost square" pane of glass that preserves its shape on falling to the floor, the exact color and texture of the alcohol in the jars, and his mother's characteristic nausea, like the details of Gerald's appearance, ground the event in ordinary reality and enhance its magic.

The way in which these magical details described realistically project a sense of the wondrous and surprising nature of the world is sometimes reinforced in magical realist fiction by a theme of unpredictability and lack of control over events in which magic underlines the nonprogrammatic nature of reality.[10] At the end of *One Hundred Years of Solitude,* Aureliano thinks he controls the speed at which he is reading the manuscript that chronicles events in Macondo, and readers follow his lead. But perhaps he is somehow programmed by the manuscript (which foretells the town's fate) to read at a certain speed so that he and the whole of Macondo will be swallowed up at the moment he finishes it, so that his individual volition is questioned. Grenouille creates a perfume to make himself acceptable, even lovable, and he becomes so loveable that his fans devour him. Before this happens, he expresses the horror of successful intent and total control: "this was the world, and this, here and now, was his dream come true. And he had wanted it thus."[11] Lisa in *The White Hotel* thinks she is simply living a private life in which she wills her fate, but that life and its fate end up being horribly foretold in her body as part of communal history. Communists such as Paul Eluard in *The Book of Laughter and Forgetting* construct an ideology of which they imagine themselves masters, but then it levitates them. Tita and Pedro in Laura Esquivel's *Like Water for Chocolate* finally affirm and consummate their love, but in the end it also consumes them. That reversal of controller and controlled is concretized in the way that even though Pedro carries Tita over the threshold of the house where this consummation takes place, once over that physical threshold, their love carries them over another threshold that they had not planned on crossing, the one between life and death or mortality and immortality. All of these examples suggest that what we think we control may in the end control us. Individual and social wills are subject to unpredictable forces that transcend them. Like Balzac's realistic tales, with their uncanny coincidences that proclaim truth to be stranger than fiction, and God to know infinitely more than man, magical realism highlights life's surprises; but it does so with more than uncanny means.

A common technique, which is related to the first one because it concerns the way that irreducible elements are introduced into the narrative, is the narrator's use of a matter-of-fact and detached style to narrate fantastic events, presenting them without comment.[12] We have just seen a prime example of that technique in the way the narrator in *One Hundred Years of Solitude* recounts the journey of the trail of blood, passing seamlessly from ordinary events to that extraordinary one with no signal of surprise. That seamless textual fabric actualizes André Breton's idea that surrealist activities aim to find and fix the "point of the mind at which life and death, the real and the imagined, past and future, the communicable and the incommunicable, high and low, cease to be perceived as contradictions."[13]

This stance is often characterized as childlike or naïve because magical events are accepted by the narrator as children seem to accept such events in stories, without questioning their reality. And it detaches us to some extent from realism's conventional reliance on sensory verification. The opening of *The Metamorphosis* might be seen as the first modern example: "When Gregor Samsa woke up one morning from unsettling dreams, he found himself changed in his bed into a monstrous vermin."[14] It continues into the present, when Azaro in *The Famished Road* usually tells of people and spirits in one breath: "the photographer took five pictures in all and the ghosts kept falling at his feet, dazed by the flash. When he went to his studio to drop off his camera, the ghosts followed him."[15] And when crows puff on discarded cigarette butts in *So Far from God:* "anyone looking up at a row of crows puffing away at cigarette butts would only be inclined to look down to see who was supplying them."[16] Those crows appear almost without commentary, as does Oskar's statement in *The Tin Drum* that he heard and meditated on his parents' conversation immediately on emerging from his mother's womb. Similarly, later on, when Oskar has just shattered glass with his voice for the first time, he seems more concerned with the exact qualities and details of the clock and its breakage, both physical and personal, and, shortly, with cataloguing all the different kinds of glass that he subsequently shattered ("windowpanes, crystal bowls full of artificial fruit, full beer glasses, empty beer bottles, or those little flacons of vernal fragrance that laymen call perfume bottles"), than with surprise or explanation of his new-found powers: "the polished round crystal which protected the honey-colored dial of our clock from dust and moribund flies burst and fell to the floor (for the carpet did not reach all the way to the base of the clock), where the destruction was completed" (68, 66). Grass endows a child narrator with this stance, but most subsequent magical realist fictions do not. The adult Ursula is reportedly alarmed by the phenomenon of three-year-old Aureliano's predicting the spilling of a pot, but not the narrator, who reports magical events in Macondo with little comment, from Aureliano's weeping in his mother's womb at the beginning of the novel to the birth of the child with the tail of a pig at the end.

Similarly, in *The House of the Spirits,* the magical force of Alba's grandfather's voice is reported in detail but with no hesitation: "the flowers never lasted until nightfall because Esteban Trueba's thundering voice and slashing cane were even powerful enough to frighten nature. . . . Whenever Trueba was heard arriving, whoever was closest ran to hide the rubber tree out on the terrace, because as soon as the old man entered the room, the plant lowered its leaves and began to exude a whitish fluid, like tears of milk, from its stem."[17] Allende implicitly engages this issue of narrative naïveté when the narrator describes Uncle Marcos's flight on his mechanical bird: "Against all logic, on the second try the bird lifted off without mishap and with a certain elegance, accompanied by the creaking of its skeleton and the roar of its motor. It rose flapping its wings and disappeared into the clouds, to a send-off of applause, whistlings, handkerchiefs, drumrolls, and the sprinkling of holy water. All that remained on earth were the comments of the amazed crowd below and a multitude of experts, who attempted to provide a reasonable explanation of the miracle" (13–14). Subsequently, Uncle Marcos supposedly dies and is buried, but "thanks to the surreptitious prayers of the women and children, as he himself admitted, he was alive and well and in full possession of his faculties" (14). The characteristic details are reported without comment; and logic and the reasonable explanations of experts are bested by amazement and aided by faith, but they hover just offstage, slightly compromising the narrator's naïveté. In the same way, Castillo compromises the narrator's total "naïve" acceptance of the crows smoking by writing that anyone looking up at the crows smoking "would only be inclined" to look down to see who was supplying them.

In writing about J.R.R. Tolkien's *Lord of the Rings,* a cycle in which realistic techniques create a separate fantastic world, Christine Brooke-Rose suggests how the magical realist meshing of realms differs from what happens in fantasy. Brooke-Rose maintains that "the techniques of realism . . . invading the marvellous" "not only weigh down and flatten out the narrative like an iron, but actually change its genre, pushing it into allegory."[18] The impetus of magical realism seems to carry it in the opposite direction. It is a question not only of quantities but also of parameters. In fantasy, a separate realm is created, and the realistic descriptions flesh out that realm. In magical realism the narrative is anchored in this world but ventures out of it and back in; the magical elements gnaw at its flesh, as it were, partially detaching it from concrete reality, but always inserting it back in.

A variation on the childlike stance occurs when the narrator reports the doubts of other characters but registers none of his or her own, a technique that causes the reader to hesitate about what attitude to take. Oskar, for example, expresses no surprise when he shatters the glass on the clock, but he registers his parents' and uncle's shock: "they blanched, exchanged shifty, helpless glances, and reached for the nearest solid object" (67). After we hear of Remedios the Beauty's "waving good-bye in the midst of the flapping sheets that rose up with her, abandoning with her the environment of beetles and dahlias and passing through the air with her" (223) the narrator reports several reactions to her ascension but gives no explanation of his own. Similarly, as we have just seen, the narrator of *The House of the Spirits* reports the amazement of the crowd at Uncle Marcos's flight on his bird but seems unfazed by it herself. The same technique is used several times in *So Far from God:* miracles are presented as such but then are often discussed, questioned, interpreted. An example is the miracle of La Loca's ascension to the church roof. At her funeral, La Loca sits up in her coffin. She then "lifted herself up into the air and landed on the church's roof," at which point father Jerome asks, "Is this an act of God or of Satan?" and her mother screams that no, "*this* is a miracle, an answer to the prayers of a broken-hearted mother" (23). Later we hear another interpretation that attempts to bring the miracle into the realm of physical normality: "It was diagnosed that she was in all probability an epileptic." But the next paragraph provides yet another point of view, stating that "epilepsy notwithstanding, there was much left unexplained" (23). And shortly we get yet another, because La Loca's sister does not remember "el Milagro," and her doubts are registered by the quotation marks in her mind (25–29). This technique of reporting doubts but affirming magic acknowledges hesitation but also combats it by co-opting it.

Magical realist narrators are not always, however, such reticent believers in their tales, as the hesitation that readers often experience on encountering irreducible elements and the compromising of narrative naïveté attest. Oskar, for example, lingers over the incredible fact that "in the three days during which I told my keeper the story of my growth, I grew a whole inch," and with the word "whole" doubt and surprise are registered (428–29). In a similarly ambiguous maneuver, even if the narrator does not explain the magical nature of an event, he may interpret its meaning, thereby implying its oddity. In *Midnight's Children,* Saleem simply tells us that he and his companions in the forest "looked at each other and realized they were becoming transparent," but then he continues on and surmises that "this was the last and worst of the jungle's tricks; . . . as their dream-life seeped out of them they became as hollow and translucent as glass" (439). In Rushdie's novel authorial reticence is frequently tempered, and readers are coaxed into belief. When a man named "the Hummingbird" is set upon by his opponents, and hums at so high a pitch that some six thousand dogs come to his aid, we are coaxed into accepting the story by the narrator's telling us, "It is well known that this is true. Everyone in town saw it, except those who were asleep" (49). That kind of witnessing, brought to bear on an impossible event, which compromises the naïve reticence of the narrative voice, appears in a passage from *The House of the Spirits,* when the narrator is discussing the appearance of Aunt Férula "without the slightest warning . . . just as Esteban was beginning to carve the roast." In order to settle any doubts, the narrator invokes the "very important" testimony of the English-educated twins Jaime and Nicolás "because they were the only members of the family who lived completely removed from the three-legged table, protected from magic and spiritualism by their rigid English boarding school. . . . Esteban Trueba stopped with the carving knife and fork suspended in midair, paralyzed with surprise, and the three children cried, 'Aunt Férula!' almost in unison"(127).[19]

In addition to the accumulation of realistic details around an impossible event, and variations on the naïve or reticent narrator, magical realism employs several other techniques that create a sense of indeterminacy. In *One Hundred Years of Solitude,* both the space of the text and the time of its telling are indeterminate. The scribe Melquíades' presence, which figures the scenes of writing and reading within the novel, in conjunction with the ending that conceptually sweeps world and text away, creates a textual space that is difficult to envision clearly. Most obviously, if the whole world of Macondo and its text has disappeared, how can we be reading it now? If we take Melquíades to be the narrator within the text, he is a mysteriously ubiquitous figure. For many readers, on one hand, since Melquíades narrates and Aureliano reads, and all is swallowed up in the final whirlwind, the novel is enclosed on itself, a self-generating and self-consuming textual world.[20] For Edwin Williamson, on the other hand, who symbolically links the bookseller Gabriel Márquez with García Márquez, making it possible for him to exit Macondo before its destruction and hence to write a different chronicle from that of Melquíades, one that includes the reality of history that we inhabit, the text remains open to historical reality.[21] To me Melquíades stands paradoxically both within and outside the apocalypse he chronicles, a mise-en-abyme in a mirror, perhaps; he is its author and he is not.[22] Whatever the interpretation, an all-encompassing and logically consistent narrative authority is virtually impossible to establish, a circumstance that contributes to the novel's defocalization. With regard to time, the voice that narrates in "the future perfect of Macondo" is indeterminate, situating us in a temporal realm like the physical realm of ice, where all is ended but all is also possible. And this temporal texture is persistent: the future perfect tense appears here twelve times more often than in ordinary speech.[23] Recall the novel's first sentence in the future perfect: "Many years later, as he faced the firing squad, Colonel Aureliano Buendía was to remember that distant afternoon when his father took him to discover ice." As if to acknowledge this tradition of temporal magic, Castillo explicitly mentions tense in *So Far from God:* "Loca was not sure if she was a present nun or a past nun or maybe hasta una future subjunctive nun" (245).

The presence of the slate that can be seen as an analogue for the novel that contains it in *That Voice* endows the text with a similar spatial and temporal indeterminacy. The narrative repeatedly refers to itself as a slate on which many voices have written but also have disappeared and reappeared: "As for those illocalizable people or rustling sounds, voices from all around, from before, from tonight, from after, a pointless distinction, I am their effacement, their spokesman, effacement, write the word again."[24] What is more, this is a magic slate, because at one point we are told, "Getting up at about eight o'clock as usual, I go to the kitchen to get my slate and I see that everything I had noted down and then effaced the previous days had returned, as if freshly traced in my own hand" (75). In addition to this spooky activation of individual memory, the slate also transmits the textual voices of recently deceased ancestors. In both instances, it bridges past and present, confounding our sense of the space of the text and the times of its construction.

By duplicating some of the dynamics of time in *One Hundred Years of Solitude,* Allende's *The House of the Spirits* confirms the magical efficacy of this García Márquezian mode. The proleptic future perfect characterizes the adult describing her child self and contributes to the (artificially) childlike tone of wonder in magical realism. Clara, for example, is shown "never suspecting that fifty years later I *would use* her notebooks to reclaim the past and overcome terrors of my own" (3; my emphasis). Something like the curlicue of the pig's tail that appears at the beginning and the end of *One Hundred Years of Solitude* and embodies its cyclical mode, the magically circular narrative space of this novel-as-manuscript opens its curve with the child Clara writing, "Barrabás came to us by sea" and closes with her granddaughter opening the first notebook after having repeated for us, "Clara wrote them so that they would help me to reclaim the past and overcome terrors of my own," and reading, "Barrabás came to us by sea." The circular structure of the novel, together with the future perfect tense, detaches the reader from the concrete time of linear progress and the literary realism that frequently utilizes it.

In *The Famished Road,* a mythopoetic framework frequently disrupts temporal progression, and time is often indeterminate. The novel opens with a seemingly biblical phrase—"In the beginning there was a river"—and vague time references, such as "that night," "the next morning," "during that time," appear throughout.[25] Madame Koto's bar, like the many roads in the novel, which collectively serve as a mise-en-abyme for the novel itself, is a staging ground for encounters between modern inventions and ancient traditions, figuring an indeterminate space and time. Sometimes Azaro voices that for us, saying, for example, "I felt on the edge of reality. Madame Koto's bar seemed like a strange fairyland in the real world, a fairyland that no one could see" (298). But the sense of this indeterminate realm is evoked even more powerfully when we simply experience it through the events that happen there: "cables connected to her rooftop now brought electricity" (373) at the same time that she has her car baptized by a "great herbalist, . . . a stern man with a face so battered and eyes so daunting that even mirrors would recoil and crack at his glance" (380). It is a relentlessly hybrid place, which confounds our sense of space and time, and in which Azaro meets both scheming politicians and "a massive chicken without feathers [which] strode into the bar, sat next to me, and ordered palm-wine and peppersoup," before being chased out of the bar by Madame Koto, at which point "Dad laughed. The chicken laughed. Madame Koto tripped, fell, and got up" (59–60). And the bar is spatially unstable, its location indeterminate, because it seems to change:

"The bar had moved deep into the forest and all her customers were animals and birds. I sat on a bench which was really the back of a goat and I drank off the back of a bull" (59) before the chicken starts his antics.[26]

Like numerous other modern and contemporary narratives, several magical realist fictions, including *The Famished Road* and *Palace of the Peacock,* like *That Voice, Distant Relations,* and, less clearly, *The White Hotel,* belong to a kind of hallucinatory magical realism, which is more often characterized by fragmentary invocations and creates difficulties in ascertaining which events have happened, which are imagined, and which are dreamed, than other examples such as *One Hundred Years of Solitude, Midnight's Children,* and *Perfume,* in which the distinction between story and discourse is more clearly drawn. In other words, in the former novels, it is difficult to decide which events are irreducible elements and which are visions, either waking or sleeping. This fictional magic seems almost to activate a narrative dreamwork, as it were, conflating and multiplying figures and scenarios, constituting what Gaston Bachelard calls an oneiric optic, closer to reverie than to dream but partaking of many dreamlike qualities.[27] And metafictional statements imply that such confusion reflects our experience of the world and its texts.

The hallucinatory and dreamlike quality of Wilson Harris's writing is of course facilitated by the fact that Harris writes an unusually poetic and metaphorical prose in which lyrical descriptions often figure correspondences between different realms, like the one that images the dying of a fire and the coming of dawn: "the white fur greyed to hourly ash as the night aged in the trees and the fugitive fiery green of dreaming leaves turned faintly silver and grey in anticipation of the pale shadow of dawn."[28] As we follow the narrative, phenomena are brought forth from the unconscious to consciousness, from mental image to actual event, but these images still retain patterns of desire and imagination satisfied in dreams or reveries and not in reality. Like dreams, which conflate and multiply figures and embody potential wishes and desires, they concern paths not taken, people not encountered, events not repeated, all of them existing in "the enormous dreaming forest." The men who travel by boat in *Palace of the Peacock* carry on two voyages at once: their own search for the folk that Donne needs to work his land, and a reenactment of an earlier trip of jungle explorers. During this double life/death trip in which we participate, Harris persistently disorients us by a continual duality of vision. Carroll, for example, "was one burning memory and substance for his mother and another dimmer incestuous substance and myth for his uncertain and unknown father folk. He had become a relative ghost for all as all ultimately became a ghost for everyone" (82).

The narrator sings to us in the voice of the peacock at the very end of the novel: "I felt the faces before me begin to fade and part company from me and from themselves as if our need of one another was now fulfilled, and our distance from each other was the distance of a sacrament, the sacrament and embrace we knew in one muse and one undying soul. Each of us now held at last in his arms what he had been for ever seeking and what he had eternally possessed." By the time we hear this inspiring and consoling vision of assuaged desire, the magical hallucinatory narrative has sufficiently detached us from concrete reality so that we can participate in what seems to be a mystically rising spirit, affirming the soul's always sought and yet miraculously always already present fulfillment. Difficult as it is to interpret definitively, this paradoxical sense of simultaneous quest and arrival is one meaning of the narrator's musing, "How could I surrender myself to be drawn two ways at once? Indeed what a phenomenon it was to have pulled me, even in the slightest degree, away from nature's end and wish, and towards the eternal desire and spirit that charged the selfsame wish of death with shades of mediation, precept upon precept in the light of my consciousness which was in itself but another glimmering shadow hedging the vision and the glory and the light" (48). Even if he cannot surrender to this vision completely, he is continually drawn two ways at once; his consciousness, like ours as we read, becomes a liminal and indeterminate space, a hedge made of shadow on the edge of light.

Like Harris, Fuentes often employs an oneiric optic to merge past and present. It is not only for Felipe and the reader to "know why Aura is living in this house: to perpetuate the illusion of youth and beauty" in Consuelo but to experience the magical dreamlike conflation of the two women. It is suggested over and over, like a recurring dream or vision. At one point, in one of Felipe's dreams "that face with its empty eye sockets comes close to yours" and then merges into "that other . . . smooth, eager body."[29] At the end of the novella, in what we assume is no longer a dream but actuality that resembles one, "Aura's long black hair" becomes "Consuelo's silver-white hair." In *Distant Relations,* hallucinatory magic creates a living past for Branly in the form of a woman who appears and reappears in various guises. At one point, for example, Branly "dreamed about a woman he had loved in the past," and soon a woman "trailing the white satin shreds of a high-waisted ballgown" approaches his bed with a breakfast tray.[30]

Azaro, the child narrator of *The Famished Road,* who exists between the real and the spirit worlds, tells the most hallucinatory tales of his adventures. He travels into magically real dreamlike scenarios where the quotients of irreducible magic and visionary trance are difficult to differentiate. (His hallucinatory mode is tenacious; he is almost impossible to cite briefly.)

> I stayed still. The wind rose again and hurled a fine spray of rain at us. After a while, I felt myself moving. Something in me moved. I resisted. But the wind was stronger. The blind old man laughed as I struggled. I discovered that the wind had divided me, and separated me from myself. I felt an inner self floating towards the blind old man. Or was it that the blind old man was floating into me, invading my consciousness? I wasn't sure.
>
> The wind stopped. The rain fell in silence. Everything went dark. I tried to blink, but couldn't. As if I had woken into a nightmare, thick green substances passed over my eyes. They settled. Gradually, my eyes cleared. When I looked out at the world again, what I saw made me scream. Everything was upside-down. The world was small. Trees were like slow-moving giants. The rain was a perpetual nightfall, and night a perpetual rain. . . . The spaces between things were populated with the most horrifying spirits I had ever seen. . . . My eyes caught fire. (313–14)

Like Gregor Samsa who wakes up as an insect, telling himself and the reader that "it was no dream," Azaro uses the analogy of nightmare to describe the spirited reality he experiences, soliciting our imaginative participation. Since we hear of these phenomena mainly from Azaro, the magic is often not strictly irreducible. Thus Okri's novel remains largely in the nonmagic hallucinatory mode. But occasionally, when Azaro converses with others, hallucinatory magic turns irreducible. Here, for example, Azaro's friend Ade is telling Azaro and his family the story of his blue sunglasses. They were given to him by a white man to whom Ade sells all his fishes and who returns as "a strange Yoruba man" who one day in the marketplace "bought all my fishes. When his hands touched them they all came alive and began to twist in my basin." The man then tells Ade that the sunglasses incident occurred five hundred years previously; since then, he had had a heart attack and died and had now come back. When Ade asks him what he is doing there, alive, the man replies, " 'Time is not what you think it is.' " " 'Strange story' says Azaro. 'It's true,' Mum replied" (482–84). At other times, however, Azaro's mother denies his visions.

> One moment I was in the room and the next moment I found myself wandering the night roads. . . . I was following a beautiful woman with a blue head. She moved in cadenzas of golden light. She floated on the wind of a royal serenity. . . .
> "Where are you going, Azaro?"
> It was Mum.
> "That woman told me to follow her."
> "What woman?"
> I pointed at the woman whose smile was forever in bloom, whose hair was blue, and who was disappearing amongst the pomegranate trees and the chorale of roses. Her head became a solitary cloud.
> "There is no one there," Mum said.
> "Yes there is."
> "I'm taking you home." (307)

It is even easier here than in the previous example to classify this scenario as a soul's vision of a redemptive goddess who functions as a kind of spiritual mother, compensating for the real earthly one, since she "floated on the wind of a royal serenity," is "superimposed on distant plangency of Mum praying in the dark," and "drew my spirit on to fountains of light and lilac music" (307). The alternations that we see here and in other examples between confirmation and doubt, between magical reality and hallucination, contribute to the defocalization that characterizes these texts, to a deconstruction of empirically based authority, and hence to the creation of a narrative that encodes the ineffable.

More generally, because the irreducible elements in magical realism resemble the fantastic scenarios in dreams or hallucinations or reveries, which nevertheless are rooted in actual psyches and events, magical realism is often described as having a dreamlike quality, but one that merges with the objective world through the text. According to Michel Dupuis and Albert Mingelgrün, "in magical realism if it is true that dream keeps its psychological (individual or collective) and metaphysical purposes, it will nevertheless tend to free itself and to distance itself—totally or partially, definitively or provisionally—from the psyche that nevertheless continues to nourish it. It will seem to root itself fraudulently in the sensory reality surrounding the being that engenders it. The genetic link between the imagination and the imagined is thus more or less erased, hidden from view. Without any break in continuity, the interior subjective universe and the exterior objective universe are suspended in the same hybrid environment, half-visible, half-imagined." This type of textual "dreamwork" is part of magical realism's characteristic tendency we noted earlier, to confound individual spaces and identities: "magical realism introduces a confusion between what exists outside the subject and what only exists as a function of it, or, to put it better, between what is truly objective, 'empirical,' and what is, under the appearances of the sensory world, only pseudo-matter, endowed with a purely mental truth." [31] And here again, we can observe how magical realism begins in but departs from modernist practice. In magical realism dreams free themselves from total immersion in individual psyches, often to manifest themselves in the outer world, whereas in modernism dreams tend to remain rooted in individuality and interiority. In a modernist text, Tamina would most likely (as Aschenbach in *Death in Venice* dreams of bacchic rites) dream or hallucinate or imagine her trip to the distopic island of children, and Saleem might dream or have delusions that he could hear multiple voices. But in these texts those dream-like scenarios are actualized.

Bridges

The poetics of magical realism involves various bridging techniques that enable the narrative to conflate different physical and discursive worlds. In *One Hundred Years of Solitude,* for example, when Melquíades arrives with a band of gypsies and the people of Macondo experience a flying carpet, the narrative has incorporated the literary past that includes the tales of the *Thousand and One Nights,* a different discursive space. When the massacre by the banana company occurs in Macondo several hundred pages later, however, the narrative has assimilated another space, that of the United Fruit Company's actual treatment of Colombian workers and of repressed historical fact. Because it detaches itself from a clear origin in the material world, the defocalized narrative facilitates such conflations. It thus functions analogously to the imagery of connectedness—pillars, sacred mountains, ziggurats, trees, poles, bridges, stairs, and so on—in the ideology of shamanism, which pictures the shaman's journey to a different realm.

Frequently, as in some shamanistic curing ceremonies, the narrative bridge magically conflates the worlds of the living and the dead, joining the worlds of the present and the past.[32] As Gloria Anzaldúa has said, speaking in general terms about the writer as shaman, "the role of the shaman is, as it was then, preserving and creating cultural or group identity by mediating between the cultural heritage of the past and the present everyday situations people find themselves in."[33] In still other examples, such as *Midnight's Children,* where a brain is used as a radio transmitter, or Francine Prose's *Bigfoot Dreams,* where a fictional fountain of eternal youth gushes from a front yard, the bridge joins the worlds of physical objects and imaginations.

A text that is particularly rich in examples of this bridging function is Juan Rulfo's *Pedro Páramo,* which merges the worlds of the living and the dead. The lyrical narrative voice seems to embody the qualities of a spirit that moves fluidly from one mind and body to another in the town of Comala, a power of speech that comes from taking on the strength of the dead there. The principal owner of this voice, Juan Preciado, travels "as if time had turned backward," hears his "footsteps on the stones," and sleeps on an adobe pillow.[34] Just before this voice narrates what seems to be its passage between living and dead communities, he hears his dead mother's voice, which "seemed to embrace everything. And then it was lost beyond the earth." Soon, he says (as we have heard in part before),

> I went out into the street for a little air, but the heat followed me out and wouldn't go away. There wasn't any air. Only the silent, stupified night, scorched by the August dog days.
>
> There wasn't any air. I had to swallow the same air I breathed out, holding it back with my hands so it wouldn't escape. I could feel it coming and going, and each time it was less and less, until it got so thin it slipped through my fingers forever.
>
> Forever.
>
> I remember seeing something like a cloud of foam, and washing myself in the foam, and losing myself in the cloud. That was the last thing I saw. (55–56)

The potential for the communication of indefinable currents of feeling and the creation of different discursive worlds in modernist texts such as *As I Lay Dying* and *The Death of Artemio Cruz* is activated with the extraterrestrial voices in *Pedro Páramo, That Voice,* and *Palace of the Peacock,* and the revenants in *Ironweed, So Far from God,* and Cristina García's *Dreaming in Cuban.*

Striking similarities between *As I Lay Dying* and *Pedro Páramo* confirm that literary heritage. Very briefly, they include poetic evocations of personalities in interconnected monologues and connections with chthonic and scriptural forces. For example, both Dewey Dell, whose name evokes the land where her hot wet seed is symbolically planted, and the more ethereal Susana San Juan are American earth goddesses and they are juxtaposed with Rulfo's apocalyptic horseman Miguel and Faulkner's patient Carpenter Cash, both of whom deal with death, but in opposite modes, the first destroying, the second building.

Even more interesting for our scrutiny of narrative techniques is that both books contain a special kind of defocalization, which enhances the narrative's ability to bridge different realms. This is the circumvention of recognizable pronouns. When one character in *As I Lay Dying* refers to another within a given monologue, often the reference is unclear, and the identity of the character is questioned. When we first hear of Addie, for example, we do not know just who the woman whose "face is wasted away so that the bones draw just under the skin in white lines" is, as we are told that "the everlasting salvation and grace is not upon her." And when Darl begins to describe Jewel outlined against the fire in the barn, we wonder who the "he" is who "seems to materialize out of darkness" "against the dark doorway."[35] In this context, recall what Samuel Beckett's the Unnameable says, "you don't know why, you don't know whose, you don't know against whom, someone says you, it's the fault of the pronouns, there is no name for me, no pronoun for me, all the trouble [but also much of the communal magic] comes from that, that, it's a kind of pronoun too."[36] To erase clear distinctions between persons, creating pronominal narrative bridges, as it were, makes it easier to pass between individual people and between living and dead voices, eroding the demarcation between them.[37]

As in *As I Lay Dying,* the voices in *Pedro Páramo* are often unidentified, frequently leaving the reader wondering who is speaking.[38] In Pedro Páramo's first monologue about water, breezes, and Susana, for example, we never hear his name (9). Nor do we hear his name or Susana's in the final words between them; he calls her simply "Chona" (43). Pedro Páramo and his weeping mother are never identified in the scene that recounts his father's death. Juan Preciado calls out "You" to a man in the street, and then, " 'You!' he called back. In my own voice" (41). That circulation of narrative voices is imaged as well as enacted here: " 'The village is full of echoes,' " the echoes we hear throughout the text, recounting the story: " 'Perhaps they got trapped in the hollows of the walls, or under the stones. When you walk in the street you can hear other footsteps, and rustling noises, and laughter. Old laughter, as if it were tired of laughing by now. And voices worn out with use' " (39). When Dorotea says, "I almost was your mother," the narrator's identity is symbolically questioned as well (13). By the time we read this (immediately following Susana's and Pedro's nameless goodbye), the narrative voice is completely unanchored from any single authority at the same time that it also reflects upon its own status: "Noises. Voices. Murmurs. Faraway Songs. / My love gave me a handkerchief / With a border of tears. . . . In falsetto, as if those who sang them were women" (44).

That Voice negotiates personal and temporal realms in a similar fashion, scrambling pronominal references, and increasing the metafictional dimension of that strategy. Set on All Saints' Day, to underline the communication between living and dead souls, Pinget's text embodies an extreme form of defocalization in its virtual erasure of narrative origin and authority. Thus, like *Aura* and *Ironweed,* this seems to be a Day of the Dead book, in which the idea behind that occasion when dead souls are honored is actualized by their magically coming forth and making their presence felt to the living in tangible ways. The text begins by invoking "that voice," which is "cutting in from time immemorial," then shifts from the second person to the third to the first and back again, all of them of indeterminate identity, although some are identified as having died. The narrative thread thus weaves in and out of living and dead voices until any ordinary sense of its origin is destroyed. This same kind of interwoven narrative stream also characterizes *Beloved,* in which the reader is occasionally unsure of who exactly is speaking; one chapter even presents a joint incantation in which the three voices of Sethe, Denver, and Beloved are sometimes indistinguishable, as in the line "Will we smile at me?"[39] And it appears in *Aura* in the way in which the narrative is told in the second person, so that, to repeat, the "you" in the text refers both to Felipe as he speaks to himself and to the reader—and, also, perhaps, in the end, to

Felipe as he is transformed into something other than his original self, into the general re-embodied.[40]

Partly because of its vocal fluidity, the plot of *That Voice* is impossible to describe: the narrative constantly repeats events, merges people and places and voices, the recording of events becoming a part of those events themselves. Thus, as often occurs in the *nouveau roman,* distinctions between repeated actions and retellings are blurred. The novel seems to put into fiction a dreamlike rumination of several voices, among them a man living in a house and communicating with its principal ghost—his uncle—but also voices of dead souls in a nearby cemetery, one of whom seems to be that uncle. Early on, speaking from the cemetery, one voice reminds itself—repeatedly—"repeat, I am dead" (8, 12, 17), and by the end sounds almost resurrected, a topic brought up with the words "between two lines effaced, between two words that have become inaudible, that of resurrection" (111). Is that what his muttering about getting "back into harness again, with other aims" (12, 113) suggests? The narrative often seems to be talking to itself: "This ridiculous attempt at anamnesis will have been necessary to discover where the immemorial resides. . . . See about linking this episode to the rest. . . . A different voice which must take over" (109, 111, 112). And so on. Earlier, "that voice" tells us:

> I went back into my tomb, where I'm awaiting the resurrection of the dead.
>
> To pass the time, and to earn two or three sous, I'm guarding a herd of pigs near the cemetery.
>
> In the evenings I go back into my hole where believe it or not I reflect on unheard-of things, I who thought myself dedicated to perpetual repetition.
>
> The smell of my livestock never leaves me and it's given me a new soul, the miracle has occurred.
>
> I have found my slate again, I no longer note down regrets on it, but other . . .
>
> And then immediately efface them. (108)

The voice moves from one persona to another, from death to life to writing, from remembering to imagining, blurring boundaries between them: "Imagination in place of memory. / Memory in place of imagination" (57). He (if we can even use such a substantial pronoun) uses his imagination to articulate a fable—a tale that takes the place of the past, the place of memory—but then he also uses memory in place of his imagination, living and breathing through his memories and his notes about the past.

Although it does not change pronouns in quite the same way, Cortázar's story "Axolotl" achieves a similar dynamic of pronominal shifting as we experience the narrator become an amphibian and shift from one side of the aquarium glass to the other.

> My face was pressed against the glass of the aquarium, my eyes were attempting once more to penetrate the mystery of those eyes of gold without iris, without pupil. I saw from very close up the face of an axolotl immobile next to the glass. No transition and no surprise. I saw my face against the glass, I saw it on the outside of the tank, I saw it on the other side of the glass. Then my face drew back and I understood.
>
> Only one thing was strange, to go on thinking as usual, to know. To realize that was, for the first moment, like the horror of a man buried alive awaking to his fate. Outside, my face came close to the glass again, I saw my mouth, the lips compressed with the effort of understanding the axolotls.[41]

As we read, the textual shift of the narrator's identity confuses our sense of the narrative's diegesis. From telling about the axolotl the narrator becomes an axolotl, so what we have been experiencing as a heterodiegetic narrative, with a narrator who tells a story in which he is not involved, becomes an autodiegetic narrative, with a narrator involved in the story he tells.[42] The use of the first person possessive to describe something outside of the narrator's self is confusing. Who or what is the "I" that sees "my" face against the glass, and who or what is the "it" on the outside of the tank and the "it" on the other side of the glass? Those two "it"s somehow help to stage the transition without specifying exactly how it takes place. And following that, which face is drawing back, from which side of the glass? Furthermore, in addition to this spatial dislocation, we experience a temporal disorientation as well, because the exact moment of the transformation eludes us. Does it happen in the sentence about no transition and no surprise? Or during the pronominal reign of the two "it"s? Or between the two paragraphs? By the next (and final) paragraph, when we hear that "he returned many times, but he comes less often now," we understand the transition to have taken place. But by the very end of the story when we hear the axolotl say that "perhaps he is going to write a story about us, that, believing he's making up a story, he's going to write all this about axolotls," again things become less clear, and again we are led to wonder about the nature of the narrative itself and its origin, to question the status of the "I" at its inception.[43] And also to wonder whether perhaps the story will begin all over again, with the narrator identifying with the axolotl because it "really" has human characteristics and really was he at one point—or not.[44]

The language in *Midnight's Children* does not generally include what we have been examining under the rubric of pronominal shifting. However, at one point Saleem comes close to it by insisting on using both "I" and "he" when describing himself as the Buddha, in his Pakistani tracking adventures with the Indian army—a kind of jokey version of reincarnation: "I must doggedly insist that I, he, had begun again; that after years of yearning for importance, he (or I) had been cleansed of the whole business, . . . I (or he) accepted the fate" (419). And from then on Saleem describes his activities in the third person using the name of buddha (with a lowercase *b*). This little device linguistically activates in a minor way a reconfiguration of identities that constitutes something of a merging of times, places, and personalities. And it enacts it from both sides, because it is not only Saleem who changes through his identification with the Buddha but also the Buddha who becomes different in our eyes when he is described in an active mode.

A different and micro-textual instance of the bridging function we have been discussing occurs when the reader is induced to participate in a particular kind of verbal magic whereby the metaphorical is imagined to be literal, connecting words and the world.[45] As Tzvetan Todorov has described it, this device enacts a "collapse (which is also to say the illumination) of the limit between matter and mind" and implicitly suggests the linguistically determined nature of experience.[46] Such literalization usually relies on the reader to supply the words. For example, the saying "blood is thicker than water," to convey the idea that family ties are strong, is magically literalized when José Arcadio's blood travels to his mother's kitchen. Sometimes the text itself provides the words: shortly before Remedios' levitation we hear that "Remedios the Beauty was not a creature of this world" (188). And shortly before this miracle happens, Ursula "abandoned her [daughter] to her fate, trusting that sooner or later a miracle would take place and that in this world of everything there would also be a man with enough sloth to put up with her" (221). Miracle there is, but not the one Ursula imagined. García Márquez's story "Light Is Like Water" is based on the conscious use of this linguistic magic.

> On Wednesday night, as they did every Wednesday, the parents went to the movies. The boys, lords and masters of the house, closed the doors and windows and broke the glowing bulb in one of the living room lamps. A jet of golden light as cool as water began to pour out of the broken bulb, and they let it run to a depth of almost three feet. Then they turned off the electricity, took out the rowboat, and navigated at will among the islands in the house.
> This fabulous adventure was the result of a frivolous remark I made while taking part in a seminar on the poetry of household objects. Toto asked me why the light went on with just the touch of a switch, and I did not have the courage to think about it twice.
> "Light is like water," I answered. "You turn the tap and out it comes."[47]

If it is true, on one hand, that, as Bill Ashcroft, Gareth Griffiths, and Helen Tiffin claim, "one characteristic of the world-views of oral cultures is the assumption that words, uttered under appropriate circumstances have the power to bring into being the events or states they stand for, to embody rather than to represent reality," then this feature of magical realism may represent echoes of earlier oral culture, more or less distant depending on historical circumstances.[48] On the other hand, it also seems to partake of and hence to reflect the world-making capacities of the all-encompassing textual worlds (such as complex and interactive video games and IMAX theaters) of contemporary media-oriented culture in which virtual realities nearly eclipse actual environments. Furthermore, it is relevant to my contention that magical realism can be seen as projecting an implicit aura of the sacred, to note, as Irlemar Chiampi does, that, from the Bible to the Popul Vuh, the linguistic magic of incarnated words is often of divine origin.[49]

This kind of linguistic magic pervades *Midnight's Children;* many instances concern the literalizing of the metaphorical ways in which Saleem, born as India becomes independent, is joined to his country, most centrally by his literally hearing all the different voices of the other children who were also born with independence. Near the start of the novel, Saleem describes to us how the metaphor of his identification with all of his countrymen becomes magically real:

Please believe that I am falling apart.

I am not speaking metaphorically; nor is this the opening gambit of some melodramatic, riddling, grubby appeal for pity. I mean quite simply that I have begun to crack all over like an old jug. . . . In short, I am literally disintegrating. . . . I ask you only to accept (as I have accepted) that I shall eventually crumble into (approximately) six hundred and thirty million particles of anonymous, and necessarily oblivious dust. (37)

This process continues at the end of the novel as he joins an Indian "crowd without boundaries" into which he literally disappears, as "they throng around me pushing shoving crushing, and the cracks are widening, pieces of my body are falling off" (551).[50] (Note the narrative distance in that first quotation. The text is aware of the metaphorical literalizing process; such an awareness contrasts with other magical realist narratives in which marvels are reported without commentary. That metafictional awareness may be the result of Rushdie's position as a later magical realist, more self-conscious about its characteristic techniques than his predecessors.) And Saleem is not the only one to undergo literal identification. "It seems [he reports] that the gargantuan (even heroic) efforts involved in taking over from the British and becoming masters of their own destinies had drained the color from their cheeks. . . . The businessmen of India were turning white" (212). In *Pig Tales,* also, Darrieussecq continually plays with literalizing common expressions regarding piggishness, beginning with the title. Once again, this technique that actualizes the magic of metaphor updates a surrealist idea, one presented by Breton in his *Letter to Seers:* "What is will be, by virtue of language alone."[51]

Such literalizing verbal magic also appears frequently in *The Famished Road,* whose title becomes a metaphor for the process of interweaving different worlds because the narrator repeatedly travels along a road between the forest of the spirits and the village of his family. In those journeys the distinction between real and fantastic events tends to be clearer than in most magical realist texts, but Azaro's movement between them is dizzyingly frequent. At one point, metaphors seem to conjure up reality, the magic of which is suggested by the appearance of a group of green men sweating animal blood.

That night I was listening in my childhood hour of darkness. I was listening to Mum's voice and Dad's songs, listening to stories of recurrence told down

through generations of defiant mouths. In that hour laced with ancient moonlight, I was listening to tales of inscrutable heroes who turned into hard gods of
chaos and thunder—when dread paid us a visit. The night brought the dread.
It announced itself through piercing voices from the street, crying out in lam-
entation at the repetition of an old cycle of ascending powers.

We rushed out into the blue memory of a street crowded with shadows. . . .
The green bodies bristling with antimony sweated animal blood from their
naked chests. They were a river of gold jaguars. (177–78)

The tragically recurring story here is the political violence that wracks the
compound again and again. The metaphors enacted are those of dread paying them a visit, and materializing in the form of green bodies with animal
blood, of night literally bringing the dreaded violence in the form of piercing
voices and green bodies, of metaphorical colors that describe the emotions
they felt becoming real men and animals.

The magical elements are clearer in two other scenes that result from
literalization, although as we noted earlier, since the narrator is our sole
witness, we have the option of considering his accounts to be visions rather
than irreducibly magical events. First the metaphors: the narrator says, "I
felt I was again among spirits. One world contains glimpses of others." Then
the words that explain them: certain women ran "as if they were shadows
or visitors from another realm." After that, we experience the realization of
those metaphorical spirits and their world: the women "ran through pitch
darkness, through silence and mists, and into another reality in which the
gigantic Masquerade was riding a white horse. The horse had jagged teeth and
its eyes were diamond bright. . . . the forest swarmed with unearthly beings.
It was like an overcrowded marketplace. Many of them had red lights in their
eyes, wisps of saffron smoke came out of their ears, and gentle green fires
burned on their heads"(12). That description of spirit beings with red lighted
eyes and saffron smoke emerging from their ears literalizes the idea that
Azaro is among spirits. As a complement to this glimpse of another realm,
the notion that spirits take on the form of human beings is also actualized.
This time the literalization comes before the verbal metaphor, which Azaro
understands as the desire of spirits to experience the realities of flesh: sitting
in Madame Koto's bar, watching some people, Azaro "realized for the first
time that many of the customers were not human beings. . . . They seemed
a confused assortment of different human parts. It occurred to me that they

were spirits who had borrowed bits of human beings to partake of human reality. . . . They want to taste human things, pain, drunkenness, laughter, and sex. . . . As I watched them, they began to transform, breaking out of their moulds. Their shoulders seemed momentarily hunchbacked. Their eyes blazed through their glasses and their teeth resembled fangs" (136).

A particular version of this linguistic magic uses a magic feature to question a reigning ideology through literalizing a metaphor implicit in it. The metaphorically high spirits induced by optimistic Communist Party propaganda is literalized as people actually rise into the air in *The Book of Laughter and Forgetting.* García Márquez's old man with enormous wings and the levitation of Remedios the Beauty literalize and hence question the ascents of holy beings as representing the only officially recognized ones that are sanctioned by official Roman Catholic doctrine. In *Perfume,* Grenouille with his scientifically accurate nose is a literal manifestation of the reigning ideology of eighteenth century scientific experimentalism. In *The White Hotel,* Freud, speaking metaphorically, tells Frau Anna that the characters in her drama are interchangeable, an idea that is actualized when we subsequently read in her diary that his son stands in for her fantasy lover. In *Imagining Argentina* the political atrocity of the disappeared, a metaphor for political abductions in Argentina, is actualized in reverse, as it were—countered, ironically mimicked, and critiqued by Carlos Rueda's skill in achieving literal magical reappearances.

Linguistic magic in these fictions sometimes thrives on the presence of intertextual bricolage in postmodern writing; allusion provides a special variety of literalization—making the verbal real—when it makes already created characters into new ones. Such is the case of Rachel Ingalls's novel *Mrs. Caliban,* which actualizes and implicitly reinterprets Shakespeare's character from *The Tempest* and has him interact with a Dorothy who recalls the heroine in *The Wizard of Oz.*[52] Such encounters with ghosts of texts past are metatextual equivalents of the commerce between worlds of the living and the dead that characterizes many magical realist fictions. Near the end of *One Hundred Years of Solitude,* just as Aureliano and Amaranta Ursula "were awakened by the traffic of the dead . . .—Ursula fighting against the laws of creation to maintain the line . . . Fernanda praying, and Colonel Aureliano Buendía stupefying himself with the deception of war and the little gold fishes" (378), we readers are mentally awakened by references to the death of Rocamadour (374) (from Cortázar's *Rayuela)* and the "heroism" (278) of

Artemio Cruz (from Fuentes's *The Death of Artemio Cruz*). *Distant Relations* is created in large part out of the texts of French-Caribbean writers, which provide scenes and characters for the novel: the ghost of Lucie Heredia, for example, and the way in which she appears in a room next to Branly's is an actualization of images in Jules Supervielle's poem "La Chambre voisine." *The Book of Laughter and Forgetting*, closer to reality and history, features Paul Eluard dancing and other literary figures, such as Petrarch, Goethe, and Lermontov, arguing. *Midnight's Children* reactivates events and objects from the *Thousand and One Nights* and Indian epics. In *The Famished Road*, Azaro's Dad as the boxer the Black Tyger reactivates both Ogun and Shango essences derived from Yoruba mythologies. During this literary Day of the Dead, the anxiety of influence is addressed and perhaps partially assuaged; threatening precursors are transformed, as the narratives make free with these ancestors and dance with them on their textual surfaces. This intertextual play also questions narrative's authority to represent the world directly. Rushdie acknowledges this shifting process specifically: after anticipating how his childhood home in Bombay will be destroyed by the wrecker's ball following his family's departure, and after giving that departure a real date, Saleem overturns the historical specificity he has just created and (dis)claims, "I may have got all this from an old film called *Lost Horizon*, in which beautiful women shrivelled and died when they departed from Shangri La" (366).

All of this linguistic magic celebrates the solidity of invention and takes us beyond representation conceived primarily as mimesis to re-presentation. The play of language in these texts, often in the form of literalized metaphors, thus ultimately embodies a central problem of language theory, the question whether words reflect or create the world. It is a question that allies magical realism with much postmodern fiction.

Two-Way Streets

The interchange in magical realism between different worlds and kinds of discourse is embodied on a larger scale than that of linguistic magic in what we might call a two-way-street phenomenon. This verbal traffic maneuver arranges events or objects in the text along an imaginary spectrum running from the improbable to the impossible, or, in other words, from the uncanny to the marvelous, and back again, concentrating its energies near the mid-point. The spectrum ranges from events that are not impossible but so improbable as to be nearly magic to magical occurrences that are nearly real, so that the effect is to blend those two worlds; in some instances near the middle it is virtually impossible to decide to which end of the spectrum an event belongs. The title image in Louise Erdrich's *Tracks* both pictures and illustrates this magically real continuum: the line of tracks leads from the human to the animal, both of which are real, but the transformation of one into the other is magical, so that the line of the discourse leads from metaphoric realism to magical realism. At one point, Fleur

> laid the heart of an owl on her tongue so she could see at night, and went out, hunting, not even in her own body. We know for sure because the next morning, in the snow or dust, we followed the tracks of her bare feet and saw where they changed, where the claws sprang out, the pad broadened and pressed into the dirt. By night we heard her chuffing cough, the bear cough.[53]

In *One Hundred Years of Solitude,* the improbable yet real end of this two-way spectrum is exemplified by José Arcadio Buendía's living—and dying—for years "tied to the trunk of the chestnut tree, huddled on a wooden stool underneath the palm shelter, the enormous old man, discolored by the sun and rain," and the impossible end by the moment when little Aureliano, at the age of three, goes into the kitchen at the moment Ursula is putting a pot of boiling soup on the table (84). "The child, perplexed, said from the doorway, 'It's going to spill.' The pot was firmly placed in the center of the table, but just as soon as the child made his announcement, it began an unmistakable movement toward the edge, as if impelled by some inner dynamism, and it fell and broke on the floor" (23). The magnets on the first page of the novel are difficult to place. On one hand, they simply act as magnets do, attracting metals, but on the other, they go beyond the normal activity of actual magnets in making house beams creak as the nails struggle to emerge: Melquíades "went from house to house dragging two metal ingots and everybody was amazed to see pots, pans, tongs, and braziers tumble down from their places and beams creak from the desperation of nails and screws trying to emerge, and even objects that had been lost for a long time appeared from where they had been searched for most and went dragging along in turbulent confusion behind Melquíades' magical irons. 'Things have a life of their own,' the gypsy proclaimed with a harsh accent. 'It's simply a matter of waking up their souls'" (11). And what of the report of the original José

Arcadio Buendía that "during his prolonged stay under the chestnut tree he had developed the faculty of being able to increase his weight at will" (136)? Or Barrabás in *The House of the Spirits,* a dog who grows to the size of a colt, and sleeps "by Clara's side with his head on her feather pillow and a quilt up to his neck" (19) or Clara, who suddenly speaks after nine years of silence? Our inability to decide just where an event belongs on the spectrum from actual to impossible contributes to a central component of much magical realism, and of García Márquez's especially—the revelation of the wondrous in ordinary events and objects. And to underline that idea there are many instances of nearly incredible but entirely natural and hence just believable events, such as the rain of golden flowers that falls on the occasion of José Arcadio's funeral: "a light rain of tiny yellow flowers . . . fell on the town all through the night in a silent storm, and they covered the roofs and blocked the doors and smothered the animals who slept outdoors. So many flowers fell from the sky that in the morning the streets were carpeted with a compact cushion and they had to clear them away with shovels and rakes so that the funeral procession could pass by" (137).

In these examples, García Márquez (in Tommaso Scarano's terms) "operates hypertrophically" to construct a spectrum spanning the amazing and the magical. In other words, García Márquez frequently "uses the procedure of exaggeration in order to shift an object or event from the plane of the real to that of the supernatural, without it being necessary to give them properties different from their own." In that way, he "increases the quantity in order to obtain a change in quality, thus projecting the object or event into an unreal dimension," creating a "supernaturalized natural."[54] García Márquez then intertwines that "supernaturalized natural" with the kind of "naturalized supernatural" that results from techniques such as the "naïve" narration discussed above (which renders the magical familiar) in order to create the particular tone of his texts, a chiastic procedure that, as Scarano notes, characterizes much of magical realism as it spans different worlds and discourses.

Perfume also provides good examples of the "hypertrophic" phenomenon of exaggeration transforming the real into the unreal. Take, for example, the episode in which Grenouille extracts Laure Richis's scent. Here the sense of wonder is also mixed with horror. After Grenouille killed Laure, he wrapped her in his waxed impregnating cloth, "as a baker rolls strudel, tucking in the corners," and "flipped it over the shaved skull, smoothed down the overlapping ends, gently pressed it tight with a finger." (Note the characteristic admixture of the outrageous with the quotidian here.) Six hours later, he removes it, noting that "the fat peeled off nicely from her skin. Little scraps of it were left hanging only in the smallest crannies, and these he had to scrape off with his spatula." He uses "her undershirt . . . to rub down her body from head to foot one last time, so thoroughly that even the oil in her own pores pearled from her skin."[55] This scene at first appears to be rather nearer the realistic pole of magical realism than most of the others we have examined. The technique for extracting a smell from a body is meticulously described and just barely probable. However, moving beyond that realistic procedure and probability, one must ask what the nature of such a scent would be and whether one could actually capture a person's scent after killing her and then work with it to concoct a perfume that would enhance one's own power. Probably most readers doubt that this is possible, and much else in Grenouille's story as well. For example, earlier in the novel, the way in which Grenouille can make his way to his first red-haired virgin through her scent, across a whole quarter of Paris, is not humanly possible, and therefore already situates us in the realm of the magical and the ineffable even before we read the meticulous description of Grenouille's masterful extracting technique. Grenouille's perfuming abilities, his extreme skill in recalling and duplicating any scent, are just possible, if nearly incredible; perhaps he is simply an uncannily masterful artist. But his success in extracting the scent of a young woman and combining it with many others to create a perfume that drives an entire city crazy is a marvel. Similarly, that Oskar starts to grow again after his fall downstairs had caused him to stop is extremely unlikely but arguably possible; his claims, however, that he willed himself to grow again and that a stone's blow to the back of his head began the process seem much less likely.

The transformations of Tristão and Isabel by a jungle shaman and his tribe in John Updike's *Brazil* are similarly linked along this magically real spectrum: that Isabel becomes black through the primitive art of tattooing is just possible, if unlikely, but that Tristão, seventeen days' walk away, simultaneously becomes white, is not, although the similarity of the results and their passionate exchanges tend to conflate the two processes. In this piece of love magic, whereby Isabel becomes black so that Tristão can become white, Tristão and Isabel seem like sexual axolotls, and Updike's language highlights the interchange: "Being a white woman fucked by a black man is more delicious, she had sadly to conclude, than a black woman being fucked

by a white man."[56] The miracle of love engenders this magic, but the ending
of the novel implies a sobering difference between the miracles of myth and
the grounding of history. In this magical realism, as often before, "the spirit
is strong, but blind matter is stronger." When this Tristan dies, his Isolde
does not: "There would be no miracle today" (260).

Like the snakes and ladders that embody the progressions and reversals of
fortune, in *Midnight's Children* these two-way streets run everywhere, from
the uncanny yet possible dream of Saleem's mother, foretelling that "washing
will hide him, voices will guide him" (195) through his Aunt Amina's culi-
nary magic, feeding "us the birianis of dissension and the nargisi koftas of
discord; [so that] little by little, even the harmonies of my parents' autumnal
love went out of tune" (395), defeated by the disharmony cooked into her
food (possible if it was simply indigestible, magical if it was actual emotions
that they imbibed by eating it), to the impossible though almost believable
death of the gynecologist, "gleaming fiercely in his rage," of whom it was said
that "when Dr. Narliker fell and was crushed to death by the weight of his
beloved obsession, nobody had any trouble locating the body because it sent
light glowing upwards through the waters like a fire" (210). And what about
the Indian businessmen turning pale? It seems like linguistic magic, but it
might just be possible, if they spend generations indoors and marry British
women. In this particular instance, Rushdie almost seems to acknowledge
the spectrum we have been examining, providing alternate explanations of a
phenomenon, as if we might find one more plausible than another. Before he
tells us about the idea of the businessmen fading into British-like paleness,
he first tells us that it is as a result of the shock of Dr. Narliker's death that
his father "began, literally, to fade . . . gradually his skin paled, his hair lost
its colour, until within a few months he had become entirely white except
for the darkness of his eyes." And then he offers his other explanation for
the paling of his father, preceding it by saying that "circumstantial evidence
indicates that the shock of Narliker's death was responsible for giving me a
snow-white father . . . but (although I don't know how much you're prepared
to swallow) I shall risk giving an alternative explanation" (212). Shortly before
this, we have an instance of linguistic magic that is nearer the magical end
of this spectrum: after the Indian government freezes the assets of Muslims,
Saleem's mother discovers that her husband's genitals are literally freezing
cold: " 'Broke,' Ahmed [the father] is saying [with reference to his financial
status], 'Frozen, like water.' " And the mother: " 'I thought you were just

talking dirty but it's true! So cold, Allah, so coooold, like little round cubes of ice!' " And the narrator confirms the event: "Such things happen; after the State froze my father's assets, my mother began to feel them growing colder and colder" (158). In addition, as usual, to underline the idea that actuality is as amazing as magic, we are told many amazing tales, such as the nonmagical but fantastical story that William Methwold, the departing Englishman, who sold the Indians Methwold's Estate, where Saleem lives in Bombay, required that "the entire contents be retained by the new owners"; Saleem's mother asks, "I can't even throw away a spoon? Allah, that lampshade . . . I can't get rid of one *comb*?" (109). No. Methwold explains that his idea is to "stage my own transfer of assets" (111) at the exact moment of independence. Like a shamanic performance that brings a sense of the presence of spirits into a real community, the frequent repetition of such narrative traffic maneuvers weaves a textual fabric of connections between the real and the unreal.

Do these two-way streets weave a seamless web of connections between the real and the magical realms, and between realism and fantasy? Stephen Slemon claims not, because

> in the language of narration in a magic realist text, a battle between two op-
> positional systems takes place, each working toward the creation of a different
> kind of fictional world from the other. Since the ground rules of these two
> worlds are incompatible, neither one can fully come into being, and each
> remains suspended, locked in a continuous dialectic with the "other," a situa-
> tion which creates disjunction within each of the separate discursive systems,
> rending them with gaps, absences, and silences.[57]

As Slemon suggests, if these two-way streets weave a complex fabric connect-ing the material and the nonmaterial, the very fact that they weave it out of those different yarns means that they are constantly recalling the disjunc-tions between them. Azaro, who passes back and forth between different worlds, sometimes keeps their divisions clearly demarcated as he does so. In one chapter, we hear, "I emerged in another reality, a strange world," "I had emerged into another world," "when I looked out through the mask I saw a different world. There were beings everywhere in the darkness and the spirits were each of them a sun," "the wind sounded strange. . . . I had begun to lose my sense of reality," and "from the back of the tree I saw a completely different world to what I had been seeing. I saw a different reality" (241–46).

However, even though magical realism maintains a sense of the demarcation of realms, it also, through the techniques we have just examined, weaves them together. Furthermore, if magical realism questions basic Western beliefs about time, space, and identity, the ground rules of the interacting fictional worlds that compose it will tend to shift as well and cause the separate systems to resemble one another. So we can have it both ways: the verbal texture of magical realism is both disjunctive and conjoined, a seamless fabric woven of diversely colored strands.

This type of interworldly weaving also recalls the deliberate nature of shamanic practice as described by Michael Harner in which "the shaman moves back and forth between the two realities deliberately and with serious intention," because he is aware of the differences between them, but often without noting such movement explicitly in conversation, so that his speech resembles the magical realist technique of presenting magical events with no commentary. According to Harner, for example, a shaman "might tell you of splitting a large tree at a distance with his shamanic power, or that he saw an inverted rainbow inside the chest of a neighbor. In the same breath, he might tell you that he is making a new blowgun, or that he went hunting the previous morning." Furthermore, a shaman's listeners know which reality is being referred to: "your audience, composed of persons of knowledge, will know."[58] While the combination of discursive worlds is similar in magical realist texts, its readers are less likely to "know" for certain which realm is being referred to, with the result that they hesitate.

In a strategy that resembles these two-way streets of narrative invention, rather than investing one or more characters with a clearly recognizable magical power, magical realist fictions tend to diffuse their magic among different figures, so that the magic circulates through ordinary activities. This is true even in *Beloved*, which concentrates the magic mainly in one figure, because Beloved's ghostly presence pervades Sethe's house, sensed by Sethe, by Denver, by Paul D, and by the women who come to help Sethe, who thought "the devil-child was clever" (261). In *One Hundred Years of Solitude*, Macondoans ride on magic carpets, Remedios the Beauty rises up to the heavens, a pot in Ursula's kitchen spontaneously creeps to the edge of a table and falls, José Arcadio and Amaranta give birth to an infant with a pig's tail, Melquíades foretells the family history. In *Midnight's Children*, Saleem hears the children's voices in his head, Parvati the Witch makes him invisible so he can travel undetected from Pakistan to India in a basket, Picture

Singh knows what has happened to him, and approves, and his grandfather's drops of blood turn to rubies. Furthermore, just as the magic may circulate between figures, so it may shift among different discursive registers: the plot may chronicle an impossible event (Beloved's return, Saleem's invisibility); a voice may shift personas or places (in *Distant Relations* we hear stories from Hugo Heredia, through Branly, through Fuentes, but also through a series of French Caribbean poems, a French song, a painting; in *The White Hotel* we hear about events from Lisa, from Anna, from Freud's analysis; in *Pedro Páramo* in addition to Pedro, many of Comala's ghosts narrate); an image may return with uncanny frequency, conflating the scenes in which it figures (the throbbing red heart in *Beloved,* the tick in *Perfume,* the spittoon in *Midnight's Children,* the outstretched hands in *Distant Relations*), and to momentarily usurp the textual foreground of the story. Because they achieve more blurring of boundaries, reorienting our habitual notions of times, places, and persons, such diffusing and shifting contribute to the indeterminate aura of the defocalized narrative.

Narrative Distances and Chinese Boxes

The two-way streets that run between the uncanny and the marvelous in magical realism, together with its juxtaposition of different worlds, encourage frequent—and diverse kinds of—play with narrative distances. At the end of *Palace of the Peacock,* the narrator describes a space he feels widening between him and the faces that fade from him as if "our distance from each other was the distance of a sacrament, the sacrament and embrace we knew in one muse and one undying soul" (152). That ending bears repeating because in addition to enacting a general sacralization of narrative desire, it focalizes the narrative through a multiple persona, which projects the sense that the words have been spoken by and for all of us. And because it grows out of the narrator's journey with his companions and yet reaches beyond those specific people to a muse and a communal undying soul that includes those travelers, the reader, and—beyond them—all of humanity, it is both concrete and ethereal. The final word of *Beloved* achieves a similar narrative slipperiness. The word "Beloved" remains as a ghostly breath, evoking not just that individual being but also other beloveds lost to slavery and its aftermath, hovering in the air, coming from an indefinite place, a place that we now realize the narrative has created through interwoven stories. In these instances, and most ingeniously at the end of *One Hundred Years of Solitude*, in which the text is presumably consumed by the "fearful whirlwind of dust and rubble" that is engulfing all of Macondo, a kind of textual magic conjures the words we read from an uncertain source. Their existence is literally impossible because no actual narrator could have written and preserved them. We might say the same for the letters at the start and the utopia at the end of *The White Hotel*, and for the interlocking stories in *Distant Relations*, and for the story of the axolotl.

Like the pronominal shifting in *Pedro Páramo* and *That Voice*, variation in point of view in magical realist texts problematizes narrative distance in various ways, sometimes through use of the second person. If the future perfect is the symbolic tense of magical realist narrative, then perhaps the second person is its symbolic point of view. Speaking directly to the reader draws the reader into its narrative space, so that he or she experiences at close range the different domains the narrative conflates. In *Aura*, the second person direct address situates the reader at the heart of the novel's final metamorphosis, which he or she thereby virtually enacts. Thus the reader experiences vicariously, from the inside, as it were, through the direct form of address, the strange transformation of Felipe into the General and Consuelo into Aura, as well as the possibility that that transformation will also reverse itself/has been reversing itself *ad infinitum*, a process that constitutes a double reincarnation of sorts.

For just a moment in Toni Morrison's *Song of Solomon*, when Macon Dead the third is entering Circe's house, he speaks one sentence in the second person.

> So when he saw the woman at the top of the stairs there was no way for him to resist climbing up toward her outstretched hands, her fingers spread wide for him, her mouth gaping open for him, her eyes devouring him. In a dream you climb the stairs. She grabbed him, grabbed his shoulders and pulled him right up against her and tightened her arms around him. Her head came to his chest and the feel of that hair under his chin, the dry bony hands like steel springs rubbing his back, her floppy mouth babbling into his vest, made him dizzy.[59]

On one hand, Macon's second person simply indicates either a habitual action or him speaking to himself. On the other hand, the brief intrusion of that voice disorients us, if only for a moment. Furthermore, this happens as Macon is about to encounter a modern witch. Thus, as he speaks this sentence, Macon might almost be in a trance, obeying a will not his own and of uncertain origin. In similar fashion, when we hear Sethe and Beloved speak directly to each other near the end of *Beloved,* in the communal poem that seems to be a trio composed of Sethe's, Denver's, and Beloved's voices, a moment toward which the narrative builds, they speak in the second person familiar. Since English has no formal viewpoint for that voice, Morrison adopts the space of poetry, where it frequently appears, for this semi-ghostly dialogue whose precise space of origin is thereby obscured: "You are my sister / You are my daughter / You are my face; you are me." And finally, "I waited for you / You are mine / You are mine / You are mine" (217). And as with *Aura,* the second person form of address melds the reader into the dialogue as well.

The White Hotel plays with narrative distance and plural viewpoints not through a relentless series of dualities like *Aura*'s but through embedded stories. Fictionalized letters between and about Freud and several of his colleagues precede a poem, memoirs, and reports about Freud's patient Anna G, sometimes called Lisa Erdman. But the boxes operate here with a twist. This embedding leads us from semi-historical reality to the magical, from actual scientists placed within a fiction to an imaginary realm produced by historical events. The text eschews the traditional "Once upon a time," which de-specifies historical time, and imbues its initial words with historical reality. In the end, however, it tricks us back into a fictional realm with a "happily ever after" ending, but one that is highly ironized by history itself. Thomas's Chinese boxing of narrative plays a spatial textual game with the reader. The subjectivity of each textual world is put into question, we might even say bought, colonized, overpowered, by the next. Finally, and perhaps most radically, once we feel as though we have understood this game and have comfortably settled into our role as increasingly informed readers within a Chinese-boxed fiction, we must abandon that game and that role and re-orient ourselves not once but twice, first into the terrifying and real history of the exterminations at Babi Yar and then, in the final chapter, in which, magically, Anna/Lisa and her mother are reanimated, into the utopian space of an imaginary Israel. But *The White Hotel* is a profoundly historiographical fiction, because, as Linda Hutcheon argues, the force behind these disruptions is history, or the real.[60] And so, once again, we see that while magical realism is a radical contestation of realism, it is also ultimately an extension of it, but a much revised extension.

Maxine Hong Kingston provides an instance of a kind of Chinese boxing that achieves narrative indeterminacy at the center of *The Woman Warrior* in a sequence in which the narrator's mother, Brave Orchid, is telling her about an encounter with a ghost in her Chinese medical school. Hong Kingston tells some of this story in her own voice focalized through her mother's consciousness and some of it with quotation marks in her mother's words. First the narrator recounts that "cringes of fear seized her soles as something alive, rumbling, climbed the foot of the bed. It rolled over her and landed bodily on her chest. There it sat." Then, the mother recalls how she recounted her experience of the sitting ghost to her classmates: "Mounds of hair hid its claws and teeth. No true head, no eyes, no face, so low in its level of incarnation it did not have the shape of a recognizable animal. It knocked me down and began to strangle me. It was bigger than a wolf, bigger than an ape, and growing."[61] The mother continues, telling her roommates about her experience:

> "Altogether I was gone for twelve years, but in this room only an hour had passed. The moon barely moved. By silver light I saw the black thing pulling shadows into itself, setting up magnetic whorls. Soon it would suck in the room and begin on the rest of the dormitory. It would eat us up. It threw boulders at me. And there was a sound like mountain wind, a sound so high it could drive you crazy. Didn't you hear it?"
>
> Yes, they had. Wasn't it like the electric wires that one sometimes heard in the city? Yes, it was the sound of energy amassing.
>
> "You were lucky you slept because the sound tears the heart. I could hear babies crying in it. I could hear tortured people screaming, and the cries of their relatives who had to watch."(73)

The origin of the narrative voice is virtually obscured by the removal of quotation marks in the central paragraph, which thereby becomes a kind of communal utterance made up of Brave Orchid and her fellow students. The next paragraph is presumably the voice of one of those women, or of Brave Orchid herself, but we hesitate before assigning it an origin. It therefore constitutes a more specific instance of the defocalization I have been claiming magical realism usually effects by inserting magical irreducible elements into realistic narrative. It is difficult to establish a definite source for what happens. The voice is indeterminate and yet it is forceful. It transmits some of the strength of the ghost itself "that pounced on top of me," rather an unattached ghost, "mysterious, not merely a copy of ourselves" (72), but a powerful one nonetheless, "a serious ghost, not at all playful" (74). The narrative is defocalized, but the tone is affirmative—four yeses resounding in the three short paragraphs. It is enhanced by the description of the noise of the ghost, "the sound of energy amassing." The episode in which that energy amasses is ended by the text's point of greatest indeterminacy: the narrator relates that "when the smoke cleared, I think my mother said that under the foot of the bed the students found a piece of wood dripping with blood" (75). We are much removed from the event by the time, the second-hand knowledge, and the doubt cast on the narrator's recall of her mother's reporting. That "I think my mother said" is a kind of narrative Chinese box that makes a definite authority difficult to establish.

Like the ending of *Beloved,* in which Morrison toys with our rational desires to recuperate the magic in her text, this main irreducible element is thus hedged around with doubts, creating an undefinable and yet powerful narrative magic. And here, as in *Midnight's Children,* mundane magicians appear as implicit foils to that magic, which is closer to reality and more unpredictable; they embody the kind of magic the author rejects (though does not despise), programmatic, commercialized magic. Immediately following this episode, the narrator's mother tells how when she went to market she saw "between the booths and stores, whoever could squeeze a space—a magician who could turn dirt into gold, twenty-five acrobats on one unicycle, a man who could swim—displayed his or her newest feat for money." Much more intriguingly magical are the things the villagers bring from the country: "strange purple textiles, dolls with big feet, geese with brown tufts on their heads, chickens with white feathers and black skin, gambling games and puppet shows, intricate ways to fold pastry and ancestors' money, a new boxing stance" (78). Once again, as in *One Hundred Years of Solitude,* where mirrors, magnets, and movies are made to seem as miraculous as flying carpets, trails of blood, and levitations, the magic in a magical realist text highlights the wondrousness of everyday objects and events.

Mirroring

Within magical realist texts, repetition as a narrative principle, in conjunction with mirrors or their analogues used structurally or symbolically, often creates a play of shifting references.[62] These magical realist mirrors conjure the reader into their shifting world by creating the sense of an "involuntary repetition which evokes the feeling of the uncanny."[63] More generally, these mirroring structures imply a revision of linear time, as they do in their modernist precursors. Repeated elements of various kinds, both intertextual and intratextual, create a narrative hall of mirrors. The road in the title of *The Famished Road* is many roads, actual and imaginary, along which Azaro and others travel: one road Azaro sees is the freshly laid tarmac that is swept away by a storm; another one is evoked by the king of the spirit world who "sometimes appeared in the form of a great cat. He had a red beard and eyes of greenish sapphire. He had been born uncountable times and was a legend in all worlds" (3). It is he who tells Azaro immediately before he is born that "you have to travel many roads before you find the river of your destiny" (76). And there are more.[64] Saleem and his rival, Shiva, duplicate mythical acts associated with the gods Ganesh and Shiva over and over again, repeatedly displaying the skills of Ganesh's sensitive nose and Shiva's active knees. Saleem's mother, Amina, duplicates, or, in the novel's words, "fell under the spell of," "the perforated sheet of her own parents," through which her father, Dr. Aziz, fell in love piece by piece with his patient, her mother, for Amina "resolved to fall in love with her husband bit by bit. / Each day she selected one fragment of Ahmed Sinai, and concentrated her entire being upon it until it became wholly familiar; until she felt fondness rising up within her and becoming affection and, finally, love" (a handy technique in a culture of arranged marriages) (75). At the end of *Brazil,* accompanied by the prosaic strains—two "wrack"s and "five meters"—of a Tempest redivivus, Tristão is killed by a contemporary equivalent of his youthful self, complete with a T-shirt that is virtually identical to the one he wore when he was young. This repeat performance takes place on the beach where Tristão first met Isabel and where she now encounters his body while a boy similar to Tristão returns Tristão's stolen wallet with "a photograph of teen-aged Isabel and Tristão with their heads together." The event recalls "a story she had once read . . . of a woman, long ago, who, her lover dead, lay down beside him and willed herself to die, and did" (255–60).[65] Such repetitions, like magical realism generally, which plays between history and myth, mediates between the two poles of activity and passivity, as Saleem himself says, between whether we control history or it controls us. It encourages readers to question their assumptions about agency and identity.

In *Distant Relations* as well, doubling of characters and stories constitutes a mirror principle of narrative structure. As in *That Voice,* a coherent story line is impossible to establish, and the repetitions of snatches of conversations and scenes, together with the presence of what seem to be ghosts, suggest the existence of parallel and converging realities. Throughout the text, hands extended over and over again structure personal interactions; words of a song and poems reappear many times; through the repetition of selected images, such as thrown balls, turned backs, and extended hands, it is suggested that the young André Heredia may be to old Victor Heredia as young Victor Heredia is to Count Branly, a younger self. This identification between Branly and Victor, and also, through him, to André as well, which at times appears to be actual, at others metaphorical, may motivate Branly's reception of the Heredias in his home, an act that he explains as amends for having snubbed a boy in a park in his own youth: "If the boy to whom I did not offer my hand in the Parc Monceau was named André, that child now, thanks to me, through my mediation—because I invited the Heredias to my home in Paris . . . because I drove Victor to the Clos des Renards . . .—that boy, I say, will never be alone" (202).

A different kind of doubling, the repetition of stories, is enacted as the narrator listens to Branly relate to him "word for word what Hugo Heredia told him late one October afternoon" (162) in Xochicalco, a scene mirrored by the present autumn narration in Paris, in which "the words did not sound his own, it was as if Hugo Heredia were still speaking through the voice of my friend" (197) creating reverberations from the past in the present. Those reverberations continue, as the narrator recounts that after they have returned home, "I left his room bearing an impression of eyes that were both near and faraway, which is perhaps another way of saying that his eyes saw something I could not see," an impression that projects a sense of different and contiguous realities that the many repetitions have suggested throughout the novel (206–7). Several days later, Branly tells the narrator, "There is a second, a contiguous, parallel, invisible narration for every work we think unique. Who has written the novel about the Heredias? Hugo Heredia amid the ruins of Xochicalco, or the boorish owner of the Clos des Renards? I, who have told you the story? You, who someday will tell what I have told you? Or some-one unknown?" (216). Appropriately enough, he then encounters another repetition that hints at the existence of parallel narratives in different times and places: "I can dimly discern a pale hand in the shadows, moving from candle to candle. I remember how once young Victor in broad daylight, but behind drawn drapes, had lighted these same candelabra in this same house, but now, to my sudden awe, the room is transformed, transported to a dif-ferent space, its axis equivocal, its symmetry questionable" (216–17). Soon we encounter yet another repetition, a mysterious woman covering her face with her hands, a posture that replicates a picture of a woman we have seen much earlier, an image, either actual or painted, that reappears from time to time during the story, associated both with Branly and the Heredias. Af-ter asking himself whether we all have a parallel specter, someone who "has lived constantly alongside us, always" the narrator decides that this phantom woman, whom he calls Lucie, is the specter who will come to life as Branly dies, at which point, in an eerie merging of self and other, "My Lucie says, in a fetid voice as dank as fungus: You are growing old, Carlos. . . . Do you know your phantom? It will take your place at the moment of your death, and you will be the phantom of what in your life was your specter" continu-ing the play of repetitions throughout time and in this text (218–20).

All of these structural mirrorings are reinforced by reflecting surfaces within the novel, especially windows. Another scene provides an additional example of the way in which reflections, both structural and visual—words, dreams, stories, actions, and actual reflections—proliferate in this novel, and suggest the existence of contiguous and interpenetrating worlds. Here the narrator tells us of listening to his friend Branly and then passes us into Branly's consciousness, where we encounter both the repeated scene of the turned back (the negative reflection of the extended hand), along with the reflective gleam of windowpanes and eyes.

I had first the sensation, then immediately the certainty, that Branly was speaking words I was thinking an instant before he uttered them, the words of Supervielle's poem. They could only be, I knew then, the words of his last dream at the Clos des Renards. How strange they had all been said before, by the poet, or by his reader, my friend Branly.

[Chapter break] . . . I refuse to walk away from that boy who is observing me from behind the beveled windowpanes. I do not walk away, although I turn my back. I am not sure whether the barbarity I feel in my eyes is my own or a reflection of his gaze and of his baroque stories in which passion and vengeance are raised on a revolving altar of gold leaf and moon mist. (127–8)

The conceptual repetition of texts with which this passage begins confuses words that characters say with words that are said of them or around them by other characters, thought by themselves or others, dreamed, or written. Thus this repetition and trading of texts intratextually, like the intertextual commerce this novel also practices, mixes up levels of discourse. A passage like this one also destabilizes the identities of the characters: do the repetitions of images imply that Branly and the narrator may be the same person, or that they merely share images from a poem they have read or tales and images they have heard spoken?

The repetitions of images and lines from poems and songs that reverberate throughout the text also question the ontological status of the beings it creates. Are they actual persons in an actual world who read and cite poetry, or are they emanations of that poetry, created out of its words? Later on, the narrator tells Branly, "You have made me the new narrator of everything you have told me" (161). That notion is repeated implicitly for us at the end of the novel when we read, "You are Heredia" and "No one remembers the whole story." As we have been told earlier by the narrator, "I didn't want to be the one who knew, the last to know, the one who receives the devil's gift and then cannot rid himself of it. I didn't want to be the one who receives and then must spend the rest of his life seeking another victim to whom to give the gift, the knowing, I did not want to be the narrator" (199). He has wanted to put an end to the story so he will not be condemned to keep on narrating it in order to find an ending, but now we are in that unenviable position. We have in a way become the narrator; we are Heredia, the original narrator who wanted to get rid of this story; we are condemned to keep retelling the story because so many loose narrative ends remain for us to tie up. We will then repeat—mirror—the narrator's many repetitions as we search for plausible connections within his text. Through those repetitions, Fuentes's text transfers the storyteller's task to the reader, thereby alleviating the teller's anxiety but increasing the reader's and effectively altering the status of the reader to that of creator of the text—another kind of mirroring, in effect. This last maneuver is not unique to magical realism; it is found in other modern and, especially, postmodern readerly texts. (Note the second-person form of address, which is concurrently the narrator speaking to both himself and the reader as inheritors of Heredia's story, and which draws us into its magical textual tangle.)

As we have seen, a different and more clearly comprehensible kind of narrative mirroring structures *The White Hotel,* where the same story is retold through reflected personalities. Like reflections in actual mirrors, the reflected narratives are and are not the same as the "original" ones. Moreover, such repetitions undercut the very notions of origin and difference. The clinical prose in Freud's account of Frau Anna's case differs markedly from her erotic fantasy poem and casts doubt on both narrators. Which is the primary document for understanding Anna/Lisa's case? Do the poem in the first section and the images in the second reflect or generate Lisa's experiences in the rest of the novel? Nonetheless, both texts contrast with the horrifying account of her death at Babi Yar, which can be seen to negate the hermetically enclosed atmosphere of her analysis, but all contribute to our engagement with her culture and psychology.[66] Though the structure of the text is very different, a similar erasure of clear vocal origin by repetition occurs in *That Voice* when we hear several times, "Repeat, I am dead" (8, 12, 17, 96), or hear reports about "the murder in the cemetery, a different version every time" in which some elements are repeated and others altered: "you remember, that old man found dead at the bottom of his bed, his nose in his chamber pot, a butcher's knife planted in his back" (27); "the horrible episode in the cemetery, Mortin's body found dead one November evening on the stone of their family vault, a butcher's knife planted in his back" (41); "stabbed him in the back while the old man was stooping to straighten up a pot of chrysanthemums" (42). And, characteristically, the text provides a gloss for its techniques, commenting on "the repetition of facts from one age to the next, only a few years' interval and everything starts again," telling us that "the voices are no longer the same but the words are, and hence the events as they unfold" (46). Again here, events and memories, past and present voices and words are repeated and a clear sense of origin is erased.

A variation on this phenomenon of repetition and mirroring is the occurrence of reversals—a special kind of plot-mirroring. This is a common feature in all literature, but in these texts it occurs with particular frequency and highlights the metaphysically revisionist agenda of magical realism. Reversals are often achieved by characters' changing places. A central element in *Midnight's Children* (a parody of the literary tradition of the foundling) is the switching of babies by a nurse in the nursing home in which Saleem and Shiva were born, so that Saleem is in one sense "really" the son of Shiva's parents and vice versa, a circumstance that achieves a kind of reversal of this original reversal when Saleem adopts the child of Parvati and Shiva's union, so that this bastard son of his is the grandson of his "original" parents. Feeling "trapped in the web of these interweaving geneaologies" Saleem describes his about-to-be-born son as "born to a father who was not his father, although by a terrible irony the child would be the true grandchild of his father's parents" (495). The narrator and the axolotl change places and repeat each other's actions on different sides of the glass in Cortázar's story. Similarly, in his "The Night Face-Up," the experiences of the man in the hospital are repeated, albeit in slightly different fashion, in the actions of the warrior in an Aztec sacrificial rite. In *The White Hotel,* Freud the analyst is analyzed, or placed, through Anna/Lisa's poetic narratives, which repeat her life's events from different perspectives, some of them including Freud. Ultimately he is also analyzed in a slightly different way by historical events themselves: those events deconstruct his analytical system because the personal past is ultimately not the origin of Lisa's suffering and hence a Freudian analysis cannot cure her. In *Distant Relations* Branly and Lucie Heredia change places as haunter and haunted. And in the similar reversal at the end of the novel, when we read, "You are Heredia," we inherit from the character Fuentes a narrative confusion that we feel compelled to try to untangle in the same way that Fuentes the narrator inherited it from Branly. The roles of narrator and listener or writer and reader are reversed. After the double metamorphoses of Tristão and Isabel, Updike describes their lovemaking as "up, down, aggressive, passive, dominant, submissive, hostile, tender—Tristão and Isabel oscillated luxuriously among contrarieties" (210). He plays repeatedly and increasingly with the reversals such a change permits, as Tristão and Isabel retrace the steps of their pasts: Isabel recalls, "You are in no danger from me, he had assured her on the beach. . . . But had he been in danger from her?" (236–37). Like the theme of unpredictability, these patterns of reversal implicitly figure a lack of human control over events and erode distinctions between discrete events and individuals.[67]

4 🕉

"Along the Knife-Edge of Change"

*Magical Realism and the
Postcolonial Dynamics of Alterity*

Decolonization

The irreducible elements and narrative techniques we have been observing, which compose the defocalized narrative of magical realism, question the perceived reliability of realism, as well as the assumptions of empirical thinking on which realism is based, and hence weaken the connection between world and text that it seems to embody. As Irlemar Chiampi points out in a discussion of marvelous realism in Latin America, "being a distortion of habitual logic, the ideology of marvelous realism seeks to break the rational-positivist conception of the constitution of reality and therefore coincides with what [Jurij M.] Lotman calls an 'esthetic of opposition.'"[1] Magical realism therefore undermines the right to represent the world, with which Western readers and their communities have typically invested realism and which constitutes a kind of narrative authority. As a result, that questioning of realism makes way for other forms of representation. Furthermore, when readers of magical realism try to construct the implied author of a text, an entity that is not a person but that represents the norms expressed in that text, they find a complexity and recurring contradictions that produce a polyvocal implied author.[2] It is one that encompasses additional belief systems and forms of knowledge with respect to those normally accommodated in realistic fiction. In other words, through this questioning of realism's right to the function of representation and the mixed messages of a polyvocal implied author, magical realism creates a space in which emergent literatures that reflect non-European traditions mature and replenish dominant forms.[3] Thus, magical realism deconstructs some of realism's narrative authority while also employing its representational power. Such a radical revision and transformation of realism strengthens movements toward cultural decolonization with its consequent production of new forms.[4] Early on, Jaime Alazraki recognized this decolonizing cultural work of magical realism as an answer "from litera-ture to the mutilation and cultural negation of Latin American society."[5]

Although not all of magical realism originates in formerly colonized re-gions, much of it does, and it is that portion of the genre that I am discuss-ing here. As Stephen Slemon has said, "magical realism, at least in a literary context, seems most visibly operative in cultures situated at the fringes of mainstream literary traditions."[6] However, the internationalized—cosmo-politan—climate of contemporary culture means that such a decolonizing imperative and its literary styles expand beyond the borders of postcolonial societies to influence the cultural productions of the entire world. Ute Dap-prich-Barrett in her discussion of magical realism in the novels of Angela Carter and Irmtrud Morgner (from England and Germany) confirms this vitality and suggests that magical realism is often but not only a postcolonial mode. She proposes an intriguing variation on the traditional magical real-ist incorporation of indigenous or pre-industrial tropes into the European form of the realistic novel, claiming that "by using Western literature, and in particular German literature, as though it was the kind of folklore on which the Latin-American magical realists base their fiction, [Carter and Morgner] take over the dominant discourses of the privileged centers of the Brothers Grimm, Goethe, Buchner and Hoffman and re-write them in a way that re-defines the future of humanity from a feminist point of view. Such a rewrite, however, only proves possible with the help of magical realist devices."[7] That a sense of cultural loss and recovery often generates magical realist fiction, whether or not the social situation is postcolonial, is attested to by Günter Grass's statement in connection with *The Tin Drum,* "By losing the war I lost my home town, Danzig, . . . and I tried to bring something back to write about, to win it again by writing."[8]

Magical realism has participated in transculturation processes that have resulted from encounters between different cultures throughout the world for several reasons. First, magical realism has developed in what Homi Bhabha and others have theorized as the indeterminate zone of the colonial encoun-ter, a "place of hybridity."[9] More explicitly, as Slemon formulates it, the hybrid nature of magical realism reveals a particularly intense dynamics of alterity. It does this through the "sustained opposition" of its "two opposing discursive systems" of realism and fantasy, "which are locked in a continuous dialectic with [each] other."[10] Therefore the text suspended between those two discursive systems corresponds to the postcolonial subject suspended between two or more cultural systems, and so it is an appropriate mode in which to represent that situation.[11]

Second, as we have just seen, magical realism creates a new decolonized space for narrative, one not already occupied by the assumptions and techniques of European realism. What narrative authority there is, is elusive, virtually unlocatable, what we might term unanchored. These texts are also often decentered culturally, split between European and indigenous or ancient and modern traditions, exemplifying the very process of transculturation.[12] Thus through its incursions into other—foreign—cultural and discursive traditions, magical realism has a certain anthropological aura; it partakes of the (dubious) anthropological advantage of fieldwork (as expressed by Michael Taussig), whereby "being a stranger conferred certain powers."[13] A third reason for magical realism's imbrication in transculturation processes is that the elements of surprise and unpredictability occasioned by the irreducible elements in its texts tend to destabilize habitual structures of order and authority, a destabilization that makes room for new voices to emerge as transculturation proceeds.

A final, more speculative reason is that a component of spirit in magical realism undermines many colonial paradigms, since it often operates toward the past and belief rather than toward the future and material progress. Magical realism would thus exemplify the idea, as expressed by Michel Foucault, that battles for control over territories (whether actual or textual) are often motivated by a "hidden presence of the sacred," hidden, that is, within the defocalized narrative of magical realism.[14] Or, as Timothy Brennan has phrased it in discussing contemporary cosmopolitanism in a way that might almost be describing magical realism with its mixture of the miraculous and the mundane, "all this wonder at the 'miracle' of the 'mixing and blending of cultures' appears at once religious and strangely utilitarian." In support of this idea, Brennan cites Vlaclav Havel's notion that "we are an integral part of higher, mysterious entities against whom it is not advisable to blaspheme."[15] The way in which Brennan, with Havel's aid, joins the mixing of cultures to the alliance of the religious and the utilitarian corroborates my speculation about the way in which the spirit-based aura of magical realism as it combines the miraculous and the quotidian may contribute to its decolonizing function. From this perspective, magical realism can be seen as participating in the aspect of decolonization described by Gareth Griffiths: "Regaining effective agency and political power in postcolonial space begins and ends now in the recovery of a sense of the immediate and the material. . . . Yet such a material recovery may involve a re-forging of links with the oldest and most spiritual category of local events, the sense of the numinous and the sacred which is resident in indigenous, precolonial religious practices, and which insists on our looking outwards to a wider concept of the natural world, of spiritual space, preserved in ritual practice and cultural narrative."[16]

In this context of postcolonial narrative liberation, one might measure the distance between *Uncle Tom's Cabin* and *Beloved* by the magic in Morrison's novel, which serves as a decolonizing agent, and in some mysterious way, because it highlights the suffering involved, while simultaneously pointing beyond strictly material reality, seems to sanctify Sethe's action of killing her child to keep her from slavery. The magic in these fictions distinguishes them from their immediate nonmagical self-conscious predecessors (and contemporaries), which, in Ralph Flores's terms, "question the question of authority" by largely narcissistic means.[17] They move beyond the self-conscious individual and counter that preceding narrative narcissism. Having absorbed what Flores calls the Cartesian gestures that question narrative authority, they inscribe not authority but possibility. In a recently decolonized society, such a narrative inscription begins to transfer discursive power from colonizer to colonized, to provide a fictional ground in which to imagine alternative narrative visions of agency and history.[18]

Writing early on of magical realism as a "way out of negritude," J. Michael Dash confirms that magical realism can serve a decolonizing function. Dash admires what he terms the Caribbean culture of survival in Jacques Stéphen Alexis (from Haiti) and Wilson Harris (from Guyana). That culture involves an attempt not to inscribe in Caribbean literature a universally conceived negritude with African origins but rather to affirm the contingencies and particularities of Caribbean identity. Alexis himself argues that "the myth, the marvelous can, if they are understood in a materialist sense, become powerful *leavenings* for a realistic art and literature, for the transformation of the world" (my emphasis).[19] Alexis metafictionalizes the image of rising we examined earlier and allies it to the development of autonomous literary identity. The way in which magical realism has served the transformative decolonizing project of imagining alternate histories is also suggested by Kenneth Ramchand in his discussion of Harris's ideas and practices. Harris distinguishes his own type of lyrical and magical realism from mainstream European realism, which he calls "the novel of persuasion," and which, according to him, "rests on grounds of common sense." According to Ramchand, then, "through imaginative fictions it is possible to remember that no social order is inevitable and ultimate, and that the 'individual span of life' need not be identified with the most oppressive of its possibilities."[20]

In this context, the fact that the cultural pasts and beliefs present in magical realism often include encounters with the dead takes on additional significance. In a process analogous to initiation rites that enact ritual experiences of symbolic death and rebirth, readers and their societies strengthen themselves through narratives that bridge the worlds of living and eclipsed or dying cultures. Thus colonized societies may undergo an experience that approximates a kind of symbolic death and reconstruction of their cultural bodies through these narratives, which rediscover and affirm extinct or vanishing indigenous beliefs in the face of colonial ones. *Palace of the Peacock* can be seen as enacting this process. The visionary journey up the waterfall in Harris's novel, similar to that of Juan Preciado to Comala in *Pedro Páramo,* although in a more positive visionary mode that culminates in a vision of personal and perhaps even collective fulfillment, seems to take place after the travelers have died. And even before that, the men on the initial river journey from which this visionary one takes off are said to replicate a journey years ago when men with their same identities made the same trip and perished. So that the replenishing vision of cultural rebirth emerges after an encounter with death.

The social stress such a process of cultural rebirth represents has changed since the origins of realism, however. Ian Watt in his study of those origins ties the development of the novel to the rise of the middle class with its investment in individual experience and achievement.[21] That entrepreneurial individualism has now ceded to international corporate systems, of capital and information, so that the individual's achievement seems increasingly diminished. The destabilization of narrative authority in magical realism may reflect that decrease in individual control and autonomy.

Furthermore, in addition to textual defocalization and polyvocality and to the decentering of narrative authority in texts with irreducible elements of magic and pronominal shifting, thematic destruction of personal authority often appears as well. The heroes of magical realist novels tend to rise, fall, and transform literally and magically in response to cosmic forces beyond their control. We might almost say that they do this in symbolic subservi-ence to natural events, company transfers, or computer programs. The literal metamorphoses and magical bodily movements in magical realism contrast with the way characters in realistic novels rise, fall, or transform metaphori-cally in response to social and psychological forces. Compare in this respect the Buendías who repeat names and characteristics for several generations, Saladin Chamcha (in Salman Rushdie's *The Satanic Verses*) who falls out of the sky as a result of an airplane crash, Saleem Sinai who travels invisibly in a basket to avoid detection by the authorities, Madame Rosa and her stu-dents (in *The Book of Laughter and Forgetting*) who rise into the air, Azaro and his parents for whom "shifts from one experiential plane to another are no longer within [their] control," or Tristão and Isabel in *Brazil,* who actually change skin colors, with Moll Flanders, Eugène de Rastignac, or David Cop-perfield, who, like many of their fictional companions, travel, earthbound, from country to city, from boarding house or poorhouse to elegant lodging, and between lower, middle, and upper classes, and also to Isabel Archer, Gustav Aschenbach, or Conrad's Marlow, who explore new regions of their own minds in foreign settings.[22]

Historical Realities

Magical realism not only reflects history. As we began to see in connection with our initial discussion of defocalization at the end of Chapter 2, it may also seek to change it, by addressing historical issues critically and thereby attempting to heal historical wounds. A number of magical realist texts ex-emplify this magical historicity. Although Beloved is clearly a projection of those she haunts—for Denver, Beloved "held for her all the anger, love and fear she didn't know what to do with"—it is as if Beloved, like Saleem, is born (again) of history.[23] Through the name on her tombstone, which Sethe buys with her own flesh by allowing the engraver ten minutes of intercourse in exchange for seven letters, her verbal existence as a product of slavery, of black enslaved to white, female to male, constitutes a radical critique of his-tory. And her magical existence revises it. That Beloved, around whom cluster the irreducible elements in the novel, leaves at its end, confirms the idea of magical realism as a decolonizing mode. To adopt a metaphor from the novel (the same one Dash invokes), the magic leavening of Beloved's presence is kneaded into the realistic narrative of 124 Bluestone Road, together with the rememories of past events and the emotions they generate, and when the loaf that they form has been cooked in the heat of pain, atonement, and reconciliation, that leavening is no longer needed, and it evaporates, but—in the last line of the novel—its echo remains as a reminder of the history in which it has participated. Even in less specifically motivated situations, magical realist texts frequently assume antibureaucratic positions, using their magic against the established social order. They resemble the "mystical rhetoric charged with oxymora and metaphors," that Victor Turner claims often characterizes popular protest movements as they question long-standing economic and intellectual structures.[24] Oskar drums a rhythm specifically differentiated from the bourgeois one he hears around him. When he shatters the light bulbs in his family's dining room, for example, the married couples "had paired off strangely," everyone fondling someone other than his or her spouse.[25] More generally, that this defocalized narrative includes both historical and magical events infuses it with an uncanny power to criticize the events that he witnesses. Many commentaries have understood Grass's use of magical and extraordinary phenomena to reflect and condemn the extraordinary times of Nazism that he chronicles in *The Tin Drum*.[26]

In *Midnight's Children,* Saleem's midnight conference can be seen as an alternative to the Congress Party, which the narrator seems to believe maintains a death grip on Indian political life; he uses his magic explicitly against the "black widow" Indira Gandhi's. However, as Josna Rege points out, Saleem's multivocal receivership can alternatively be seen as romanticizing the Congress Party's ideal of "unity in diversity," and so Saleem's dispersal into the multitudes at the end of the novel is an even better image of nonauthoritarianism.[27] And, characteristically in this relentlessly satirical novel, Saleem also has his own despotic side, enjoying control over the voices, manipulating them, translating them into English. In both interpretations, though, a univocal authority of one voice from above is questioned by the cacophony of many voices from all over.[28] Thus the reason that Rushdie chooses the exact midnight moment of Indian independence for the birth of the children who constitute the multivocal phenomenon of Saleem's inner voices is to highlight his critique of the way in which that democratic potential has not been realized by subsequent Congress Party politics. And that midnight's children each possess a different magical gift emphasizes the multiplicity of the voices that need to be heard: "a boy who had the ability of stepping into mirrors and re-emerging through any reflective surface in the land—through lakes and (with greater difficulty) the polished metal bodies of automobiles . . . [,] a Goanese girl with the gift of multiplying fish . . . [and] a sharp-tongued girl whose words already had the power of inflicting physical wounds."[29]

To consider these texts, different as they are, together, is to see how the use of magic often ultimately highlights the historical atrocities narrated in them, albeit in very different ways. Beloved's magical return is motivated by the intensity of her own and of Sethe's suffering, a commentary on slavery. Again, because it calls attention to the pain involved, the extra-ordinary magical foreknowledge of Lisa's pains implicitly critiques the extra-ordinary suffering of the massacre that she experiences at Babi Yar. Grenouille's perfuming abilities are less clearly magical, although his prowess in divining scents that humans do not normally perceive and constructing perfumes out of them do seem to me to be miraculous. And his feats such as constructing one odor that makes him virtually invisible, then another that turns an entire population from extreme hatred to extreme love for him goes beyond the humanly possible. As in *Beloved* and *The White Hotel,* that impossibility underscores the extra-ordinary atrocity of a figure such as Hitler, whom Grenouille resembles in various ways (he comes from nowhere and is heartless where human life is concerned and enormously charismatic, and he undertakes programs of experimentation on human subjects). Similarly, the ability of magic to highlight historical atrocity is suggested in passing in *One Hundred Years of Solitude* when the "decrepit lawyers" "controlled by the banana company" are described as dismissing the demands of the workers "with decisions that seemed like acts of magic."[30] The "swinish" treatment of the transforming narrator in *Pig Tales* implicitly critiques the contemporary commodification of women, and Darrieussecq has said that she wrote the novel "in a state of anger" because she "didn't like the society in which [she] was living."[31]

The official recording of history is questioned from the start of *The Book of Laughter and Forgetting* with the airbrushing of Clementis from an official party photograph, so that all that remains of him is the hat he had lent to his comrade Gottwald. The magical levitation of party members as they dance in a ring takes that questioning one step further; like the spiral motion of the schoolgirls who rise with their teacher through the classroom ceiling, this magic has a sinister air about it, suggesting that, in addition to figuring the specific political overtones of forced conformity to a reigning ideology, such a nonempirically based representation may be as authentic a record of the extraordinary cultural atmosphere of those times as an airbrushed photograph. The schoolroom scene begins during an analysis of Ionesco's *Rhinoceros* when a young Israeli girl named Sarah kicks her two co-analysts in their behinds. The girls cry and the class breaks into "unrestrained laughter," but Madame Raphael co-opts both Sarah's rebellion and the girls' tears into her own system, claiming that "Sarah's little misdemeanor had been a prearranged part of a carefully prepared student joke in the interest of getting closer to the work."[32] Soon, after Madame Raphael has taken "her darlings' " tearful writhings of humiliation for a dance, she

> went up to the writhing girls and took Michelle by the hand. . . . took the requisite steps and lifted first one leg, then the other. . . . Still crying, the girls made a timid attempt at following her. . . . [Soon] imperceptibly their faces distorted with weeping turned into faces distorted with laughter, [and] the dancing women were paying no attention to anyone else. . . . All at once Madame Raphael stamped a little harder than before and rose a few inches above the classroom floor. (74)

As the meaning is erased from the girls' actions, their tears changed to laughter by their teacher, the magic of their levitation alerts us to the dangers of conformity, of riding the unbearably light wings of coherent doctrine rather than grounding ourselves in the inconveniently heavy earth of chaotic reality. As we have seen in examples of pronominal shifting and linguistic magic, these texts often respond to heavy doses of political ideology by being poetically subversive, embodying the non-co-optable nature of people, events, objects, and languages. Like the hat at the funeral in *The Book of Laughter and Forgetting* that floats comically from mourner's head to open grave, and Sabina's hat in Kundera's *The Unbearable Lightness of Being*, which signals the subversive nature of her desire, this kind of language is linguistically unruly, whatever its political thematics.

Magical realist texts are frequently written not only against a bureaucratic mentality but in reaction to specific repressive regimes. Grass publishes *The Tin Drum* and Süskind *Perfume* well after World War II but partly in response to the Nazi period in Germany; García Márquez and Fuentes attack North American continental dominance; Kundera opposes the power of Soviet Communism, Rushdie Mrs. Gandhi's autocratic rule. These texts, which are receptive to more than one point of view, to realistic and magical, or material- and spirit-based forms of perception, and which open the door to other worlds, help to deconstruct the univocal narrative authority that characterizes much realistic fiction.[33] As in much postmodern writing, which, as described by Jean-François Lyotard, "wage[s] a war on totality," this deconstruction can be seen as implicitly criticizing totalitarian discourses of all kinds, including that of much modern historical narrative.[34]

Distant Relations, like *Midnight's Children,* seems both to exemplify and address that idea. The sense of contiguous worlds and proliferating narratives that Fuentes's text creates is allied to a theme of communication and friendship, which is contrasted with an exclusive attitude that opposes proliferation and democracy. This is the meaning of the many hands extended or not extended or damaged in the text. Branly mentions several times that he wishes to make amends for the hand that he did not extend to a potential playmate in his youth, claims proudly with respect to Victor and André, "I offered them my hand," and touches the narrator's hand "with affection."[35] An atmosphere of friendship, of literally extended and mutually touching hands, characterizes the scene where Branly tells the narrator his story, which is interrupted many times, as they reconstruct the past together, cooperatively, listening to different voices. At the end of that session, the narrator, progressively enmeshed in the play of hands across the years, saves Branly from drowning by cupping "his chin in my hand," and on their parting, Branly "held out his hand. I took it. I was surprised by its warmth," a surprise that suggests the otherworldly aura of the scene and its reverberations into the past. Significantly, then, it is Branly who tells the narrator, "There is a second, a contiguous, parallel, invisible narration for every work we think unique" (216). At the same time, this text extends narrative hands to its readers, inviting them to weave their own interpretations out of the loose ends of story that remain untied, just as he and Branly have been attempting to piece together the story that Hugo Heredia told Branly, and also the many other stories and histories that Fuentes weaves—incompletely—into his novel. That kind of unfinished, nonexclusive discourse, in conjunction with the contiguous worlds of the past, of literature, of dreams and imagination that course through the text, models a fruitful interchange of stories and worlds, a nontotalitarian kind of discourse.[36]

Hugo Heredia, in contrast, does not tend to extend hands, talking exclusively with his son, to the exclusion of Branly. His attitude is not communal but exclusive. He sees in the ruins he studies "the throne" "of a kind of honor regained." In them, "I, . . . a great lord without a fiefdom, a tyrant without slaves, I took refuge." He admits that his Spanish ancestors could "be what we had been unable to be in Spain. Hidalgos with a vengeance." And that "I, a Creole in search of lost grandeur, could find it only among the monuments of my victims' past." In contrast to the spirit of collective narration in this text, Hugo, given to exclusive possessions, does not want his story shared, telling Branly that he (Hugo) will die if he repeats it (167–69). His son Victor continues that nonbenevolent aristocratic attitude by "beating Jean's Indian servant" and eventually slamming Branly's chauffeur's hand in the car door (17). That injured hand (contrasting with the other extended ones) symbolizes the damage done to the spirit of friendship and community by the autocratic attitude that Victor inherited from his father, with whom he shares "scorn for men, respect for stones" (171).

Branly recognizes Hugo's ideology, telling the narrator that Hugo's "lesson was one of a false colonial aristocracy that equates nobility with a power of corruption and cruelty beyond punishment" (154). Even though Branly himself comes from an aristocratic family in Europe, he is on the other side. And so is the narrator, who, as we have seen earlier, allies himself with an idea that resembles Lyotard's concerning the avoidance of the terror of univocal discourses: near the end of the novel, as he forces Lucie's hands away from her face, he reproaches himself, and says, "I told myself that my conclusions were too facile, too capricious, born of my need to tie up loose ends to conform with the laws of symmetry, but that in truth—*in truth*—I did not have, I would never have, the right or power to interpret or vary the facts, to in any way intrude in the labyrinths of this story so imperiously different to my own" (220). To wish to tie up all the loose ends would be to wish to master this narrative once and for all, and not to leave room for other listeners to continue it; likewise, to conform to the laws of symmetry would be to align himself with the formalistically oriented and ruthless Hugo, who values ruins over relationships. And at this point he glimpses his own phantom, indicating that he is not master of but simply a part of the endlessly interconnected lives and stories in the world. As he leaves the room, he has his own phantom clinging to his arm; it is "merely an illusion, a new illusion, my own," a contiguous presence that touches his own, as the phantoms of other poems and novels have provided material for his text, a text that in both theme and mode contests totalitarian forms of discourse (221).

Realism itself is not inherently authoritarian, although recent commentaries (by Fredric Jameson, Dominick LaCapra, and others) suggest how it has served bourgeois political agendas.[37] Nevertheless, the fact that realism is a European, or First World, export, in conjunction with its claim to portray the world accurately, has tended to ally it with imperialism—Spanish, English, French, Russian, U.S. Writers in colonized situations have therefore frequently experienced it as a hegemonic discourse.[38] Harris's idea that the traditional realistic novel narrates the tension between individuals "on an accepted plane of society we are persuaded has an inevitable existence," so that it is difficult to imagine other social scenarios, and his statement that "conquest is a kind of running amok—a berserk and cannibal realism" expresses that experience (and reconquers by reversing the habitual accusation of cannibalism).[39] For Harris, in contrast to that realism, "the concept of 'marvelous realism' constitutes for me an alchemical pilgrimage, a ceaseless adventure within the self and without the self in nature and beings that are undervalued or that have been eclipsed or imprisoned by models of conquest."[40] Given its attention to social issues, magical realism continues the social analysis in much of realism, but it uses different, postsurrealistic, resources. Rushdie evaluates realism in a similar way, claiming that "the fiction of the Victorian age, which was realist, has to my way of thinking been inadequate as a description of the world for some time now, and nobody has noticed the fact until quite recently. . . . For realism to convince, there must be a fairly broad agreement between the author and the reader about the nature of the world that is being described. . . . But now we don't have that kind of consensus about the world."[41] Magical realism thus registers a discourse of plurality, of disagreement. Furthermore, as Amaryll Chanady points out, magical realism deconstructs the dichotomy Bakhtin articulated between Menippean satire in which dominant systems lead to polyphonic discourses and the epic, which was a foundational narrative affirming official values, because it is one of those postcolonial forms whose foundational fictions are often "critical of dominant paradigms."[42]

As with other historically engaged fictions, magical realism's cultural and psychological pluralism may have political consequences. Like the furor surrounding *The Tin Drum*'s publication, the controversy over Rushdie's *Satanic Verses* is a grisly manifestation of the collapse of a distinction between words and the world, as well as an illustration of the political and social realities Rushdie's books describe. The Rushdie character in the short drama entitled *Iranian Nights,* which was presented at the Royal Court Theatre in London in response to the crisis, laments, "What madness have my verses unleashed?

A fiction greater than any poet's imagination. Now jokes become daggers and rhymes become bullets."[43] The linguistic magic in which words seem to engender events expands to alarming proportions. As one of the authors of *Iranian Nights* writes in an afterword, "Reality, as we know, is stranger than most fiction. The scenes we are observing could easily be excerpts from a Rushdie novel," a reality engendered by a fiction.

At the end of *The Postmodern Condition*, Jean-François Lyotard argues against our expecting a reconciliation among different language games, against hoping that a transcendental illusion will "totalize them into a real unity," because for him, "the price to pay for such an illusion is terror."[44] As I have suggested, several of these novels, most notably *The Book of Laughter and Forgetting, Midnight's Children, The White Hotel,* and *Distant Relations,* suggest that the price to pay for a comforting univocality may be terror. The unreconcilable dialogue between different worlds and discourses in the magical realism of these novels is a textual form of working against its reign.[45]

Ventriloquism

Because the narrative mode of magical realism often encompasses different cultural worlds, irrespective of its engagement with history, it frequently approximates a primitivist aesthetic, attempting to represent elements of a vanishing or emergent culture, to speak, in part, in its voice. That attempt at using, or appropriating, another voice means that this ventriloquism in magical realism reveals, as does the narrative perspective in the earlier novels of Joseph Conrad, E. M. Forster, and Virginia Woolf, which Bette London studies in her analysis of "the appropriated voice," "the text's often unwilling participation in the very ideologies it critiques."[46] It is magical realism's contemporary version of modernist primitivism, and it prompts us to consider the dangers of hubris Wilson Harris invokes in the following passage:

> With the mutilation and decline of the conquered tribe a new shaman or artist struggles to emerge who finds himself moving along the knife-edge of change. He has been, as it were, cross-fertilized by victor and victim and a powerful need arises to invoke the lost generations, in a new creative, visionary light. It is a task which is profoundly personal (and archetypal) and, therefore, accompanying an enormous potency for change—for vision into resources—runs the danger of self-enchantment or hubris.[47]

The difficulty of locating a narrative authority in these texts, their programmatic perversity, which refuses to ground us completely in rationally organized empiricism, may represent the static caused by the silenced and marginalized voices of oral cultures that are now disrupting the European traditions of the printed word. Thus we see that as in any cultural dialogue, this construction of a narrative technique is not "a neutral communication situation of free dialogue," because, as Gyatri Spivak has noted, "there is no such thing."[48] *That Voice* addresses this problem in a general way: "As for those illocalizable people or rustling sounds, voices from all around, from before, from tonight, from after, a pointless distinction, I am their effacement, their spokesman, effacement, write the word again, unaware of what it means for the other people whom my solitude revels in."[49] By referring over and over again to the slate on which his narrator writes and which carries traces of voices effaced, Pinget hints that to speak for someone may also be to efface that person's voice.

These problems of voice are confronted by Roberto González Echevarría as he discusses an anthropological "masterstory" for twentieth-century Latin American literature. He believes that the anthropological discourse in regional novels that nostalgically seek to recover a traditional past remains fragmented myth criticism rather than genuinely mythic. In these "regional novels the language of the narrator is about magic, but it is not magical." They exemplify the same kind of dual voice that characterizes the fantastic literature that appeared in Europe in the nineteenth century, for, as José Monleón points out, "not until nature became objectified, and not until the supernatural was equated with the unnatural, could fantastic literature emerge."[50] González Echevarría calls these novels "mock anthropology that unmasks the conventionality of ethnography, its being a willful imposition on the material studied as an act of appropriation" and maintains that the solution to the problem of recovering indigenous discourse that includes a belief in what Western observers call magic was to write novels that imitated sacred texts, such as those of Miguel Angel Asturias and Carpentier's *The Kingdom of This World*.[51] This complex quality of "mock," of artfully constructed voice, however, is what makes magical realism the sophisticated contemporary—and sometimes primitivist—narrative that it is. Thus magical realism is an enabling mockery that is also authentic.[52]

As I have already suggested, magical realism often speaks for marginalized voices, which it partially separates from their original contexts, drawing them into the mainstream. Sometimes, especially as the mode moves north in the Americas, these voices are demarginalized and as a result their political tone softens. It is as if the raw materials from the colonies were manufactured into consumer goods. Such mainstream films as *The Witches of Eastwick, Seventh Heaven, Shoeless Joe, Ghost, Wolf, Like Water for Chocolate,* and *Chocolat,* and such novels as *Thinner, Bigfoot Dreams, Ironweed,* and *Brazil,* mentioned earlier as examples of the increasing popularity of magical realism, constitute less explicitly political discourses than do *One Hundred Years of Solitude, Midnight's Children, The Book of Laughter and Forgetting, The House of the Spirits, Beloved,* and *The Famished Road.*

In this context, Lawrence Thornton's novel *Imagining Argentina* raises complex questions of cultural politics. It is written by a North American but is set in Argentina, and it uses narrative magic motivated by political event. The political scene as provocateur of magical narrative remains safely in the foreign domain. On one hand, it is simply a well-orchestrated, exciting, emotionally satisfying, and politically empathetic story of love in times of terror. Ingeniously, the visionary magic Carlos Rueda commands, and that allows him clairvoyant-like contact with the disappeared, seems born out of the suffering he undergoes when his wife unexpectedly vanishes and becomes one of the disappeared. On the other hand, given this intradiegetic phenomenon of the magic growing from the terror, one might wonder whether the same should obtain extra-diegetically as well. Should the right to a magical narrative voice born of terror and suffering only belong to its victims? Should this kind of narrative power be shared? Is the excitement of terror artificially induced literary voyeurism and therefore morally unsound?[53] I think not, although it is worth raising the issue. Within a terrorized society the terrorized and silenced can rarely speak; they must always in some sense be spoken for, and often by writers in the safety of exile, and so their sacred power of suffering, except in a few rare cases, is almost always ventriloquized.

In fictions such as these, then, in which a narrative voice that seems to be associated with a more technologically advanced society transmits a shifting focalization that is sometimes more "primitive," undercutting the power of a univocal worldview, the narrative achieves a kind of imaginative, enabling, and troubling power reversal. In considering the link between magical realism and postcolonial society, it is useful to consider Michael Taussig's discussion of magical realism in the context of shamanism because he also raises these troubling questions about the voice appropriation that the mode can be seen to embody. In his study of Latin American shamanism and its relation to colonialism, Taussig suggests that the shamanic healing power of wildness stems from the strange reversal that causes "the conquered to redeem their conquerers," from "the peculiar paradox that endows the figure of the powerless Indian with power to create miraculously empowered Christian saints and virgins," from a "colonial fetishization and reification of savagery," from, finally, the "division of labor into those who rule and those who supply them with magic."[54] Taussig is exposing what he sees as a colonial dynamic in which colonists "steal" magic from native shamans by associating with them and absorbing some of their mysterious power, which they then use for their own purposes. Taussig thus explains, through Walter Benjamin's ideas, what I have been arguing is part of the cultural force of magical realism, as "reappropriating the power bestowed on the objects of mass culture as utopian dream symbols."[55] In Taussig's view of cultural politics, the church in Latin America has used magically real images for reactionary social purposes. Thus Carpentier's sensitivity to myth is very important in the development of a revolutionary and decolonizing culture and literature; that culture and literature developed from "the magical realism of popular culture as the only counter-hegemonic force capable of confronting the reactionary usage to which the Church puts that same magical realism in order to mystify it."[56]

In this same discussion, Taussig addresses the problems inherent in magical realism as a cultural hybrid. He argues that despite Carpentier's seminal position in creating a Creole culture, he succumbed in part to the "fantasia" of "the fantastic presence of the Indian and the Negro," "the very fantasia through which class domination permeates the political unconscious." And also that, in building "a one-way bridge with oral literature," magical realism in modern Latin American literature "finds it hard to evade the heavy handedness Carpentier reacted against in Parisian surrealism."[57] However, I would argue, in the development of Latin American literature, the hybrid nature of magical realism, even with its attendant artificiality or heavy handedness, and its doses of bad faith in texts with pretensions to speaking for the primitive other—what I have been calling its ventriloquism—has served the process of ongoing transculturation. In effect, it constructs a two-way bridge over which different modes of discourse pass.[58] The coexistence of magical indigenous and European realist voices, which, like the Dionysian and Apollonian poles that Nietzsche believed were essential to the excellence of Greek tragedy, has been producing an extraordinary set of texts. It has done this because it has operated between different cultural systems, creating a fertile narrative borderland. Even if magical realism has grown from European realism's exploitation of the indigenous fantastic, its hybrid nature has opened up possibilities for new projects.[59] In other words, realism has not only cannibalized but also replenished the indigenous fantastic. Just as shamanic healing is not a one-way street, and the healer himself or herself may benefit from the healing process, the magical realist cultural bridge is wide enough for two-way traffic.

The problem of a discrepancy between anthropological admiration for the primitive and the embodiment of it appears in a text such as Jacques Stéphen Alexis's *The Musical Trees.*[60] In that novel a certain woodenness characterizes the admiring accounts of indigenous life. Even so, despite this primitivizing gaze, a mysterious power also transfuses the text and confers dignity on that way of life. At the culmination of a meeting where priests speak in favor of indigenous cults, a native music of the spheres moves us upward, as the multiple nouns, verbs, and adjectives mime a shamanic ascension: "In the calm night, at the summit of a neighboring tree, a bird musician sang in the shadow. Its voice was suddenly born from the silence, then rolled on, swelled slowly. . . . The melody was dew, flowers, gems, light. Sounds in scales flowed, rose, merged, sparkled."[61] The "mock" anthropological narrative transmits remnants of a genuine indigenous tradition—postmodern fragments it has shored against its ruin? Thus magical realism may co-opt and hence distort or misrepresent a people's indigenous mythologies and traditions, but it also preserves them for use by their descendants.[62] Similarly, Carpentier's portrait of Ti Nöel reveals a certain disturbing condescension, in part because we rarely hear Ti Nöel himself speak, and so the force of an indigenous personality such as his suffers from being transmitted through the narrator's primitivizing voice; but that force is also housed in this fiction and its healing powers transmitted to Ti Nöel's successors and to us. Thus a decolonizing narrative power develops within these texts, despite their doubtful "anthropological" status, a power that has frequently spearheaded the growth of developing literatures. This process is demonstrated again by the fact that *Beloved,* which draws on buried African indigenous traditions such as crop fertility dances involving antelopes, contains, as Trudier Harris points out, the most empowered women in Morrison's oeuvre.[63]

In his sociological approach to magical realism, Serge Govaert distinguishes Latin American antitotalitarian magical realists from their nonpolitical European counterparts. According to Govaert, even though the Latin Americans are intellectuals distanced from the indigenous peoples whose myths they use and thus are only partial dissidents, they nearly always oppose totalitarian regimes. Their agenda of "reestablishing an identity lost through colonization and neocolonialism," together with the use of popular myths for those ends, gives their writing an obvious political meaning. The Europeans, however, Govaert claims, ultimately serve the status-quo because their idealism causes them to reject a historicist point of view in favor of a "conservative European paradise."[64] While this distinction may be true for the authors Govaert studies (Dino Buzzati, Ernst Jünger, Mircea Eliade, Jorge Luis Borges, Hubert Lampo, Johan Daisne, and Franz Hellens—the last three from Belgium), it seems less clear with the addition of more recent works such as *The Tin Drum, The White Hotel, The Book of Laughter and Forgetting, Perfume,* and *Pig Tales,* which are more historically confrontational.

Perhaps because Fuentes is a transnational who as a child traveled and lived in North and South America and Europe, his stories and novels serve well to illustrate the problems of voice appropriation that magical realism raises. Like Rushdie and García Márquez, among others, Fuentes is an intermittent magical realist and a persistently marginal inhabitant, suggesting the interdependence of magical realism and marginality. Fuentes also embodies the trajectory of contemporary magical realism: roots in Latin America, branches throughout the world. In his story "Constancia," as in other magical realist fictions, such as *The White Hotel, Palace of the Peacock,* and *The Famished Road,* hallucinatory memory and magical event are conflated, so that irreducible elements are difficult to locate. At one point, for example, it seems that the narrator has opened the door to a mysterious magically real region of death in life, where a baroque coffin rests on a circle of red earth in the middle of a floor of "black earth, silt, river mud."[65] The space may actualize the details of a painting described earlier or it may simply be a vision—or, possibly, by extrapolation, even a postmodern gallery exhibit. But even with the possibilities for realistic interpretation of this scene as vision or ekphrasis, the magical events in the story, like the appearance of this realm within a realistically described house in Savannah, classify it as magical realism. The mysterious room of earth and mud contains a wooden box "fashioned to pick up and reflect the pearly light of this region—every surface is cut, angled, opposed to another surface, the infinite surfaces shattering light as if to carry it to some mysterious dimension, the edge of the light of death itself" (45). Note the room's metafictional charge; like Harris's palace of the peacock, Saleem's pickle factory, or Allende's house of spirits, its liminality figures the space of magical realism itself, between art and reality, dream and memory, life and death.

In this story, Fuentes conflates several revolutionary scenarios through the persona of the aristocratic Southerner Gospodin Hull. (Hull's surname suggests that he is a negatively capable shell ready to receive the projections of both Fuentes's writing self and the disadvantaged refugees in the story.) On a trip to Spain, Hull discovers evidence that his recently deceased wife had previously died in the Spanish Civil War years before she met him. Thus somehow, magically, she had survived that first death. Or were the records he consulted simply wrong, and her American life was a reconstruction of her archival history? We do not know. As if this were not enough, on returning home from Spain, Hull finds a family of Salvadorean refugees in the basement of his Savannah house. Composed of father, mother, and son, that family seems to constitute a second survival of his wife's first family, including her former husband and son. Hull expresses solidarity with all of these people, positing the survival of his wife and her family through the Salvadoreans, seeing all of them "finally" "as part of something greater," presumably the general struggle for political asylum and eventual justice.

As the narrator explains his acquisition of solidarity, he consciously mediates between two worlds.

> I don't know why I hesitated, discomposed and irresolute, thinking confusedly that I was no more than a mediator between all these stories, a point between one sorrow and another, between one hope and the next, between two languages, two memories, two ages, and two deaths, and if for a moment this minor role—my role as an intermediary—had upset me, now it no longer did, now I accepted and welcomed it, I was honored to be the intermediary between realities that I could not comprehend, much less control. (61)

Accepting the intermediary's role, Hull proclaims, "Now I devote myself to the family that asked me for asylum, I reach out to them and hold them tight, don't worry, stay here, we will do woodworking together." In addition to the gestures of mediation and solidarity, the icons of the literary profession also appear here, associated with valiant struggle: "Take these pencils, some paper, pens; if they come for you, remember that these things cannot be confiscated, so you can communicate with me if they put you in jail, so you can demand legal aid; pencils, paper, pens: carry them with you always" (63–64). This Salvadorean family exemplifies the underclass motor of such fictions, as well as their moving from marginalized regions toward traditional centers of culture.

What are we to make of this? We are seeing, I think, that there still exists a distinction within the genre between, as Taussig formulates it, those who rule and those who supply them with magic, a distinction maintained in the division between the Hull/Fuentes narrator and the Salvadorean refugees in his cellar, symbolic descendants of the Russian and Spanish refugees of the previous generation. In keeping with their colonized yet subliminally glorified status, they are out of sight of the political majority yet symbolically at the narrative's core, driving the storyteller's pen. Hull hopes to validate that pen through the pens and pencils he offers them. The offer appropriates the moral seriousness of suffering, with which Hull wishes to invest his life, and Fuentes his text, but it also aids political refugees. In this particular instance, then, the dynamics of rulers and empowering magicians are difficult to disentangle. On the conscious surface of the text, Fuentes, through Hull, expresses solidarity with the oppressed. The problem of appropriation appears when Hull feels himself to be renewed through his mysterious connections to the Russian and Spanish refugees, to the "current of emigrants, fleeing persecution, seeking refuge" (56). Have the oppressed here supplied him with magic? As Hull flies home from his trip to Spain, which, like a shamanic curing ceremony, "had been a thorough exorcism," he thinks of his wife, Constancia, and is "grateful to her" because "perhaps she had assumed all the sins of the world so that I would not have to suffer for them." Does the problem disappear because Hull acknowledges his debt? Yes and no. He finds the Salvadoreans in his cellar, and they permit him to satisfy his desire to suffer and affirm his solidarity with them. But his suffering is largely vicarious; pottery and gardening at home hardly equal war and exile. Thus the text reveals a submerged politics of cultural appropriation, together with an overt politics of personal solidarity.

I find "Constancia" less successful than *Aura,* where Consuelo's magical powers of love witchery rule the text. Is that because the story lacks urgency, because Fuentes no longer needs magic to decolonize himself? It is really very difficult to say. In social terms, of course, Fuentes was never in a subaltern position, but in terms of Western literary culture, he, as a Mexican, may have been.[66] The politics of gender are complicated here as well (as I show in more detail in Chapter 5). In *Aura* a narrator participates in eternal life through a magical encounter with the female body; here a narrator uses a similar kind of gendered magic for an encounter with the political subaltern. We should note, however, that the political dimension was already present in *Aura*, for General Llorente is allied with the reactionary forces of Maximilian, and that association, together with Felipe's profession of historian, allows us to draw the conclusion that reactionary politics combined with a narrowly archival view of history can be dangerous. The warning: live your history yourself or it will live you. Hull heeds the warning consciously, even meticulously, integrating the historically atrocious past and its present survivors. Felipe's fate is less clear because of his magically double identity as himself and General Llorente, but his final position as fuel for Consuelo's rejuvenation (and hers for him) can ultimately be seen to achieve a greater symbolic revision of gender and power—though other interpretations disagree.

Issues of appropriation similar to those we nave noted in "Constancia" also trouble André Schwarz-Bart's novel *A Woman Named Solitude*. Speaking with eloquent sympathy, Schwarz-Bart's narrator focalizes through Solitude and her mulatto community. In the vision that ends the novel, Solitude triumphs over her cruel and unjust fate with the dignity of spiritual strength.

> Then throwing back her head and opening wide the magnificent globes of her eyes—made by the Lord, says a legend, to reflect the stars—she burst out laughing. It was a strange laugh, deep in her throat, a gentle cooing, gay and barely tempered with sadness. All the stories, all the legends and fireside tales about Solitude of Guadeloupe end with that laugh, which some likened to a song.[67]

One might ask, however, whether that vision—of a laughter "barely tempered with sadness"—sugarcoats even while condemning the historical atrocity it narrates. As with Fuentes's "Constancia," it is very difficult to say. And are those "magnificent globes" descendants of the "orbs" with which Joseph Conrad either dignifies or dehumanizes (depending on one's point of view) the eyes of one of the "moribund shapes" of native workers in *Heart of Darkness*? If so, they inherit the problematic cultural politics of Conrad's text, consciously critical of but in some ways perhaps unwittingly compliant with the colonial project. The final vision of *A Woman Named Solitude* is preceded by a reverent description of Solitude's *via crucis*, in which her suffering seems almost to be spiritualized out of existence: "Unaccustomed to the daylight, she marveled at the red sun, so bright and gay, that was rising over the last moments of her life. . . . The things of this world were shrouded in a luminous veil, as fragile and beautiful as the reflections in the waters of the Goyave" (171). It is followed by an epilogue in which the narrator associates the ghosts of the massacre in Guadeloupe with those of the Warsaw ghetto. Does that association represent a solidarity of suffering or a contemporary recolonizing, validating new world experience by reference to European history? Once again, it is very hard to say.

Transculturation

Despite these complex issues of voice appropriation and commodification of indigenous culture, I have argued that the defocalized narrative and bridging techniques of magical realism subvert the colonial authority of European realism by disengaging it from the empirical basis on which that authority seems to be built. When we consider the possibility that the irreducible elements of magical realism suggest the presence of a realm of spirits within ordinary reality, we must also note that those techniques also link it to sacred space and time. The narrative thus resembles the vision of a modern shaman whom Taussig describes as enacting the "journey of the soul through sacred space and time," but "disengag[ing] it from its beautifully contrived scaffolding of orderly time and orderly space bound to great authorities, church and state."[68] Here again, then, the comparison with shamanic performance, and in particular, Taussig's analysis of shamanic activity in a postcolonial context, can provide further insight into magical realism's cultural work. Taussig links the shamanic performance of contact with a realm of the spirits to the process of decolonization, as we have been doing here with respect to the defocalized narrative mode of magical realism. Taussig is describing an example of sociocultural exchange, which he labels a cultural conversation; I am extending that exchange to magical realist writing. While it is true that all magical realism embodies a mode of discourse that suggests the integration of a world of the spirits into ordinary reality, this interchange is especially important in postcolonial societies, which suffer from the imposition of a dominant culture on a subordinated one in the realm of ordinary reality, so that an enactment of contact with a different realm serves as an efficacious form of counterdiscourse. And it is a counterdiscourse that transforms not only the discourse of the colonized but that of the colonizer as well. In postcolonial situations such as the ones described by Taussig and in much of magical realism, we are dealing with issues of agency, and, as Michael Lambek maintains in his discussion of shamanic spirit possession, "the invocation of spirits raises questions of agency."[69]

Furthermore, in addition to its decolonizing properties, the implicit cultural exchange this hybrid form represents contributes to the process of transculturation. The hybrid qualities of magical realism are thus analogous to the performances of "a modern kind of shaman, who knows more about fixing a car than he does of his own language and history and so acts as a mediator between cultures."[70] To follow Taussig's analysis of the way in which a modern shaman and a colonist achieve a mutually empowering exchange helps to confirm the idea that magical realism performs the connection between ordinary and extraordinary realities that was traditionally accomplished by a shamanic performance (here a kind of double one) and also allows us to proceed beyond that idea to see how in contemporary times both magical realism and shamanism are involved in transculturation processes. Since that involvement is more explicit in Taussig's analysis than it is with regard to the narrative mode of magical realism, Taussig's account illuminates this aspect of magical realism's cultural work.[71]

After a society achieves a partial disengagement from colonial authority, as Taussig describes it, a cultural conversation that heals "through the hallucinogenic creation of the antiself" can take place. I understand that creation to involve the conversationalists each imagining his counterpart as a kind of alter ego with qualities and powers different from and complementary to his own. After that creation of antiselves has taken place, each conversationalist gets power to act from his appropriation of the powers contained in his image of the other. Taussig's two conversationalists are a lowland Indian shaman who takes inspiration to heal his patients from the splendor of the Colombian army and a white colonist who, using his idea of the power of indigenous magic, imagines "the shaman as devil" and thereby "undergoes his transformative experience." Taussig sees the process as one whereby "colonization [paradoxically] becomes a replenishing of grace through immersion in the wild evil apportioned to the people of the forest." That grace allows the colonizer to gain "release from the civilization that so assails him."[72]

This account of a kind of dual shamanic performance pictures the way in which the mode of magical realism has been articulating a generic conversation between European realism and indigenous and pre-Enlightenment beliefs and narrative practices to achieve a textualized cultural conversation. I am speaking here not of any particular examples that treat this issue thematically but rather of the mode of magical realism generally. In more specific terms, paralleling those of Taussig's analysis, the magical "grace" of the irreducible elements coming from indigenous myths, beliefs, or narrative traditions allows realism to escape from the confines of its mimetic program, and the solid "grace" of that program's realistic description allows the colonized and therefore currently disembodied myths, beliefs, and traditions to shape their own bodies, to escape from the confines of ethereal sacred space and marginalized indigenous culture and emerge into modernity. According to Taussig, the two visions, of the shaman who uses the image of the resplendent army, and the colonist who uses the image of the devilish shaman, are "uncannily complementary," and form a " colonial dream dialogue" (328–29). These two healers dream of or hallucinate their opposites and gain power from those dreams or hallucinations, and the implicit interchangeability of their visions forms the dialogue. The process is analogous to the way in which the disparate elements of fantasy and realism in magical realism constitute a dialogical mode in which they strangely complement each other in a way that is often difficult to explain in rational terms. The notion of a "hallucinogenic creation" of an "antiself" (327) seems especially appropriate for magical realism since the magical images often appear "dreamlike" and yet, like the dreams of these two conversationalists, they are also integrated into everyday reality as represented in realism. In both instances, a hybrid cultural product constructs itself from two radically different modes of authority and systems of production. Thus that magical realist narrative imagined as analogous to shamanic performance depends on otherness is a phenomenon that is especially crucial in the cultural self-definition of postcolonial societies.

Perhaps the mode of magical realism is now beginning to pass beyond the dialogue as Taussig articulates it in political life, where it is an unequal conversation. According to Taussig, in that interchange the odds are "tilted," in favor of the ruling class colonist, who robs the poor shaman of his magic in the same way that Spain robbed the New World of its gold. "The colonist's relation to the shaman is not to give voice to the pinta [the magical healing picture] that the shaman passes on, but to use the shaman himself as an image and, in a way that merges the literal with the metaphoric, climb to heaven on his back" (329). But when the exchange is textual rather than economic, it can achieve a more balanced equilibrium. As we have just noted above, in connection with narrative ventriloquism, magical realism is a two-way cultural bridge. Even though the empirical worldview precariously predominates, the magical elements are also validated through realistic description within the textual fabric. Therefore, the narrative takes advantage of both realism and magic to achieve at least a partial transfer of narrative power from Eurocentric to native voices, and the resulting text passes on some of the pinta or magical healing image, rather than using the shaman and his techniques only as an image on whose back it rides to salvation. We might also go so far as to say that magical realist narrative's "hallucinogenic creation of the antiself"—its generic pinta—is the creation of a mysterious presence of spirit within the body of realist fiction. That spirit, with its occasional literalizing of metaphor, helps to decolonize mimesis, even though it may occasionally appropriate indigenous magic. The fact that the colonized are continuing to use magical realism suggests that this is so. According to Elleke Boehmer in her appraisal of postcolonial literature, magical realism "represents the take-over of a colonial style. By mingling the bizarre and the plausible so that they become indistinguishable, postcolonial writers mimic the colonial explorer's reliance on fantasy and exaggeration to describe new worlds. They now demand the prerogative of 'redreaming' their own lands."[73]

Writing in a similar vein, Timothy Brennan signals a seminal moment for the history of magical realism as a postcolonial style in discussing what Rushdie borrows from García Márquez. Citing García Márquez's reference (in his Nobel Prize speech) to the influence of the Italian explorer Antonio Pigafetta (who, according to García Márquez, wrote "a strictly factual account that nonetheless seemed like a work of fantasy") on his own writing, Brennan claims that, like García Márquez, Rushdie "theorizes his own use of fantasy and does so by referring to colonialism."[74] According to Brennan, García Márquez's statement implies that "his novels have a greater claim to truth than" the "nonfiction" of the colonial explorers, "for their fantasies are the result of the strangeness of a world to which they are alien, while his reports to the metropolis are authoritative because native."[75] (We need to note here that from an indigeno-centric point of view, the status of García Márquez as "native" is questionable, although in relation to Europe it is—just—possible to consider him so.) Part of the power of this mode thus derives from the fact that in accepting the influence of explorers' tales, García Márquez confirms the overwhelming influence of Latin American reality on its colonizers, who are powerless to describe it in language other than that of fantasy. Once again, the empire writes back—by adopting, parodying, and thereby subverting the imperial gaze. The language of the colonizers is willfully assumed, and transformed to construct another kind of discourse, but also occasionally used as a form of simultaneous anticolonial critique and self-parody—a postcolonial mimicry of what thereby is posthumously (and aggressively postcolonially) defined as the earlier explorers' proto-magical realist style.

A similarly decolonizing strategy is discussed by Margaret Cezair-Thompson in relation to *The Famished Road,* which she terms a "decolonized fiction" because the road in question is no longer primarily the colonial way of appropriation that it is in many colonial and even postcolonial novels. Instead, "the origin of the 'famished road' lies in myth, not history. And so the fate of colonialism in *The Famished Road* is that, not only is it disqualified in its claim to be a devouring force, colonialism itself becomes devoured, as mythopoeia overwrites history." Okri's use of the colloquial and familiar forms "Mum" and "Dad" throughout the novel is intriguing in this context; on one hand it familiarizes the strange occurrences this Mum and Dad undergo, and on the other, we are continually surprised by the cultural disjunction that the juxtaposition represents. These vestiges of colonial discourse absorb and are absorbed by the indigenous mythical beings that swirl around them. It is also important to note, as Cezair-Thompson does, that the decolonized quality of the novel stems in part from the fact that its alternation between actual and spirit worlds does not result from the fractures of colonization but can be related to Yoruba myths that tell of a famished road with a "dualistic nature" that includes "both god-like and human qualities."[76]

Given these cultural dynamics, magical realism's transculturation project thus distinguishes it from romance and the fantastic as described by Jameson and Monleón. Jameson argues that "the gradual reification of realism in late capitalism" means that romance once again becomes a "place of narrative heterogeneity and of freedom from that reality principle to which a now oppressive realistic representation is the hostage."[77] It is that "now oppressive realistic representation" that magical realism as a descendent of romance disrupts. Jameson claims that in the nineteenth century, for the most part, the reinvention of romance depends on a transitional moment when two different modes of production or of socioeconomic development coexist.[78] Since the conflict of these two modes may not yet socially manifest itself as such, that conflict is merely imagined in a fictional form that permits its resolution to be projected as a nostalgic or a utopian harmony. This scenario co-opts the impulse toward rebellion and hence is ultimately not politically progressive.

This is where magical realism differs, because since the text is situated more clearly in reality, that harmonic world of romance, in either the past or the future, is not constituted, and the conflicts of political systems are more evident.[79] According to Jameson, romance can make class conflict fade into bad dreams or fantastic scenarios.[80] The combination of irreducible and documentary elements in magical realism work against such fading. Lisa's pains in *The White Hotel,* for example, are not just a bad dream but rather the magical premonition of a terrible and unmistakably real historical nightmare.[81] The same is true of the magical and not magical atrocities of the aftermath of partition in *Midnight's Children* or the banana company massacre in *One Hundred Years of Solitude* or, to a lesser extent, the mass hysteria that devours Grenouille at the end of *Perfume.* In *The Famished Road,* magical events and images merge into and highlight and question the terror of the political strife that continually disrupts Azaro's family. Here Azaro's journey into the nighttime spirit world is rudely terminated by violence in the streets:

> One night I managed to lift myself out through the roof. I went up at breathtaking speed and stars fell from me. . . . I was beginning to learn how to control my motion that night when something happened and a great flash, which was like a sudden noise, exploded all through me. I seemed to scatter in all directions. . . . And when I regained myself I heard, for a moment, the rats chewing, my parents snoring, and someone banging relentlessly on the door. . . . The photographer . . . was bleeding from the head. He sat on my mat, blood dripping down his forehead, past his eyes, and soaking his yellow shirt [having been wounded by the fighting in the street outside].[82]

Just as Azaro is learning to control his motion, that progress is disrupted by the violence, which seems to scatter him in all directions. Scenes such as this, in which the magical is combined with the terrifyingly political, illustrate the way in which, as Jean-Pierre Durix points out with regard to the way Rushdie endows his characters with faith in their magical powers but also with an awareness of their limits, "through magic realism, the writer pretends to play with major issues only to encourage the reader to face them."[83]

Rather than containing and ultimately dissolving impulses toward social disruption, or skirting political issues, magical realism often provides a narrative space that both models and questions them. Furthermore, in Rushdie as in Kundera and Fuentes, the dangerous attraction of an escape into fantasy often seems an already refused option. Saleem says that the "overdose of reality" he and his companions encounter in the Indo-Pakistani war, "gave birth to a miasmic longing for flight into the safety of dreams," so they retreat to the forest regions "south south south" (431). However, neither they nor the narrative remains there, and on their way back from the jungle they re-encounter even more horrible results of war, almost as if their attempted retreat from reality had exacerbated the conflict.[84]

Through such combinations of history and selective magical details (which are not isolated in a separate realm), magical realism moves beyond high realism and naturalism, in which, as Jameson formulates it, time seems sealed off in its "perfected narrative apparatus." Because in magical realist texts the techniques of that apparatus, "the threefold imperatives of authorial depersonalization, unity of point of view, and restriction to scenic representation," are often disrupted, the validity of the social systems they portray in many if not in all cases is challenged.[85] Given this disruptive tendency, together with its magical rewritings of history, magical realism resembles contemporaneous theories of history that move it closer to fiction, allotting a greater place to the consciousness of the historian and his or her own milieu as a necessarily distorting lens through which to view a never entirely accessible past and hence to question existing representations of it.

Monleón also argues that the fantastic has played a defensive role, validating the status quo, modifying "hegemonic discourse in order to justify the survival of bourgeois society."[86] It did this by locating unreason in confined spaces where it represented the cultural metaphor of marginality. Some of magical realism perpetuates this trope, particularly, as in Gothic fiction, in the phenomenon of the haunted house—in *Aura, The House of the Spirits,* "Journey to the Seed," and *Beloved.* But not so much. Beloved is seen by members of the community outside of 124 Bluestone Road; Grenouille is not confined to the inside of perfume factories but operates throughout France; magical events happen not only in old Victor Heredia's Clos des Renards but also in Branly's house in Paris, in Xochicalco, and in the Automobile Club in

Paris; the magical events in *One Hundred Years of Solitude* are not limited to the Buendía household: the insomnia plague, for example, infects the whole town of Macondo. As the magic permeates settings and events and texts, as it marks the intrusion of the marvelous into the everyday, magical realism also signals the breaking down of this configuration, and it often achieves this breakdown from a marginal position, upsetting the spatial politics Monleón charts in nineteenth-century Gothic fiction.

Later, in a discussion of Goya, who departs from the conservative Gothic, Monleón uncovers a sensibility close to that of contemporary magical realism. "Perhaps Goya," Monleón suggests, "situated on Europe's periphery, but embracing the principles of the Enlightenment, had trouble establishing an imagery of differentiation," which kept unreason in its place and instead articulated "that line of suture in which dream and reality coincide." Magical realism occupies and thickens that line. The progression Monleón charts whereby the forces of unreason in the eighteenth century that were isolated in Gothic houses or suburbs move into nineteenth-century cities is similar to two phenomena: first, to the urbanization of magical realist fiction (from the largely rural Hawthorne, Asturias, the early Carpentier, Rulfo, and some aspects of the texts of García Márquez to the more urban Grass, Rushdie, Ingalls, Kennedy, Fuentes, Prose, and Darrieussecq) and, second, to the contemporary migration of magical realism from Latin America to North America and Europe, as well as the increasing global use of the mode. Its hybridity resembles the "internalization of monstrosity by the dominant culture" Monleón chronicles in the last century, when reason and unreason faced off as equals, and which culminates in *The Metamorphosis*.[87] In this context of magical realism as postcolonial discourse, recall that Gregor Samsa's magical outbreak occurs from within Kafka's doubly marginal Jewish German-Czech position.[88] However, moving beyond strictly postcolonial and political concerns, now the internalized category may not be monstrosity but rather immateriality, or the ineffable—a fearful specter for materialist culture. *The Metamorphosis* is such a central text in the development of modern fantastic narrative because in it the monster explicitly moves within; the monster is us, the human psyche, with its internalizations of social evils and its captivation by individual ones.[89] As Georg Lukács argues, in *The Metamorphosis,* Kafka shows us that irrational anguish has taken over.[90]

In this context, the existence of magical realism suggests a complementary possibility. With its often more appealing appearances of the fantastic, does magical realism attempt to tame the monstrous fantastic of irrational anguish? On one hand, perhaps it does partially tame it by endowing it with a liberating dose of spirit rather than with a materially horrifying appearance and thereby integrating it into reality. Such an integration lessens our terror of the deviant. And Gregor, with his dwindling appetite for milk and bread and his decaying body, combined with his continuing hunger for music to nourish his soul, may foreshadow this development. On the other hand, magical realism's fantastic elements are not all appealing, the social and political atrocities it chronicles are untamable, and these texts usually portray them as horrifying. Rejecting Rosemary Jackson's Freudian thesis that the monstrous fantastic represents the repressed "unseen and unsaid of culture," Monleón associates the monsters of unreason with the lower classes.[91] Whether cultural unconscious or social underclass, magical realism's encounter with those monsters may sometimes be irreducible, but it is certainly not intangible, for it is both seen and said. Unreason, for so long the specter, the horror, may have been transformed by these texts into a possible angel—a very old man with enormous wings, a sorcerer called Mackandal, a narrator who inhabits a peacock palace or a white hotel, a beauty who ascends to heaven, or one called Beloved. However, as with the very old man whose exploitation García Márquez makes clear, the political and social teeth and nails of those monsters usually remain undisguised, accusatory presences that have not faded into bad dreams.[92]

Recent Literary History and Cultural Politics

That magical realism has been a commercial success problematizes but does not invalidate its status as a decolonizing style. The anthology McOndo, with its real-life frame tale by editors Alberto Fuguet and Sergio Gómez, which recounts the experiences of two young Latin American writers whose stories were rejected by an American journal editor for not being magical realist, and which therefore implicitly protests against the commercial imposition of magical realism on a new generation of writers, confirms the shifting of the cultural terrain that Fuentes's statement about the too-ubiquitous label of magical realism applied to Latin American texts represents.[93] Fuguet and Gómez seem to favor pop over folk, and the real over the mythological, claiming, "We don't ignore the exoticism and the cultural diversity of the culture and customs of our countries, but it is not possible to accept reductionist essentialisms, and to think that everyone here wears a sombrero and lives in trees."[94] They cite the introduction to another anthology of short stories by the Chilean poet Oscar Hahn as indicative of the commodifying impulse of the international literary marketplace that wants to continue to buy and enjoy magical realism from Spanish American writers.

> When in 1492 Christopher Columbus disembarked on American soil he was received with great excitement and veneration by the islanders, who believed him to be a celestial messenger. After having celebrated the rites of possession in the name of God and of the Spanish crown, he proceeded to ingratiate himself with the indigenous inhabitants by distributing colored glass for their pleasure and astonishment. Nearly five hundred years later, the descendents of those remote Americans decided to pay back the kindness of the Admiral and distributed to the international [reading] public other bits of colored glass for their pleasure and enjoyment: magical realism. In other words, the kind of story that transforms prodigies and marvels into ordinary events and which puts levitation and toothbrushes, afterlife journeys and outings to the country on the same level.[95]

In the stories in *McOndo,* by contrast to what they see as a commodified magical realism, Fuguet and Gómez assert, if people fly it is because they take planes or drugs. This is not the only viewpoint, however; recall Rushdie's conflation of the virtual and the magical in his description of the Moor's growth rate in *The Moor's Last Sigh.* Hahn's statement represents a cultural moment of retrospection rather than an accurate account of reception, and the size, the longevity, and enthusiasm of local audiences (from *One Hundred Years of Solitude* to *Like Water for Chocolate* and beyond) suggest that we are dealing with more than the distribution of shiny exported trinkets. But it does bear witness to a demystifying impulse that produced the later more historically oriented Latin American fictions noted in Chapter 1.[96] Through a broader focus on narrative techniques and types of cultural work, however, a comparative discussion of magical realism as an international mode, while it risks a universalizing homogenization, avoids such specific cultural constructions as wearing sombreros and living in trees.

In contrast to the editors of *McOndo,* Erik Camayd-Freixas suggests that magical realism, despite its co-option by critics into international postmodernism, might serve as an alternative to the still competing claims of nativist and imported mythologies, including, most recently, postmodernism, in Latin America's continuing search for its cultural identity.[97] According to Chiampi, Latin American magical realists poeticized the idea of a magical America through a "non-disjunctive relationship between realist codes (from the Western novelistic tradition) and marvelous ones (from indigenous mythologies)."[98] With the continued presence of magical realism worldwide, it seems that the Latin American trajectory of magical realism heralds its similar role throughout much of the postcolonial world. Brenda Cooper enlists a statement about African artists from V. Y. Mudimbe to characterize the way in which magical realist writers such as Ben Okri, Syl Cheney-Coker, and B. Kojo Laing achieve a fruitful cultural interchange between contemporaneity and tradition: "the artists of the present generation are the children of two traditions, two worlds, both of which they challenge, merging mechanics and masks, machines and the memories of gods."[99] Similarly, Jean-Pierre Durix ends his consideration of magical realism by asserting that "art need not choose between consecrated versions of metropolitan forms and reified representations of revolutionary alternatives. The most powerful novels to have come out of the New Literatures hint at the possibility of a profound dialogue between different conceptions of reality."[100]

In the face of such critiques as we have examined above, then, it seems important to note again here that recent articles concerning post-apartheid South African literature seem to confirm the continuing vitality of magical realism as a decolonizing style. In her analysis of *Missing Persons* by the South African Ivan Vladislavic, Valeria Guidotti proposes that "thanks to its subversive stance, at once therapeutic and re-creative but by no means escapist, magical realism represents a literary discourse which has an important role to play in the dismantling of worn-out, simplistic dichotomies and in the indictment of Eurocentric stereotypes, as well as of political and social obsessions," one that will be used by all cultures in the area.[101] Similarly, Roland Walter stresses the cultural survival work of magical realism in contemporary Chicano fiction, claiming that "through magical realism the act of writing becomes an act of survival and liberation," asserting the vitality of Chicano culture, and proposing "imaginary solutions to existing conflicts."[102] One might counter these arguments with the idea that these emerging voices are using the now-widespread and popular mode of magical realism to gain access to the financial and other benefits of the international literary marketplace. For it is virtually impossible to disengage expressivity from marketability, since both are elements of literary creation, especially in situations of cultural decolonization. But that practical concern does not vitiate the fiction itself.

If we continue to examine literary chronology, it would seem that the side of magical realism that emerges from modernism often operates according to mythic time, using magic as a partial escape from a history from which we are trying to awake. However, as magical realism exists within postmodernism, which is, according to Linda Hutcheon, relentlessly historical in various "un-innocent" ways, it functions in historical time.[103] In Latin America, these two modes have tended to follow each other. The modernist, emergent stage provides the imaginative independence and mythically oriented narrative powers needed to break disabling ties with European realism, and then the historical postmodernist phase re-establishes referential functions at home. Other areas, where magical realism has been less prevalent, seem to lack such temporal progression. In most instances, however, it seems as though the magic frees the discourse, the history grounds the story, and the vitality of the text depends on keeping the lines open between them. Thus magical realism courts the fear of history of which Philip Rahv accused mythologically inclined writers and critics during the 1950s when magical realism was developing. But because it also addresses historical issues, it overcomes that fear and prevents an escape into the mythic time of modernist spatial form.[104] In considering the way that Okri retells colonial history "as part of a larger, timeless, indigenous discourse which acknowledges but does not stagger under the weight of Europe's colonization of Africa," Cezair-Thompson maintains that Okri's mythic vision, "while ahistorical in perspective, is not . . . intended to 'comfort,' sentimentalize or diffuse historic-social conditions."[105] Morrison implicitly addresses such issues concerning possible fictional escapes from the realities of history at the end of *Beloved*. There, the narrator's repetition of the ambiguous words "this is not a story to pass on" forces the reader to consider it not only as fiction but also as history, to examine its social significance as testimony to past injustice.[106] It also suggests the paradoxical "untellability of the story that has just been told, for the attempt to 'pass on' this story is to occupy the shifting boundary between what can and cannot be said," a boundary that the ambiguities of a magical realist presentation with its defocalized narrative mode is especially well-equipped to negotiate.[107]

Whether we consider the appropriation of indigenous Amerindian mythologies by upper-class Latin Americans writing in Spanish, the use of ancient Hindu traditions by the ethnically Muslim, apparently largely atheistic, and Western-educated Rushdie, or the adoption of Latin American–inspired magical realism by mainstream U.S. writers, a troubling flavor of cultural colonialism permeates the mode as it writes itself from the margins toward the centers of contemporary culture and destabilizes those spatial categories. In concluding this discussion, then, it is illuminating to recall Taussig's ideas about what he sees as a primitivist appropriation and commodification of shamans in Latin America. From this perspective, like the colonists Taussig describes, the ventriloquistic narrative voices of magical realism have assimilated "the unsuspected power of the powerless."[108] Taussig claims that the colonists' attempts to appropriate "the power of the primitive," which includes the ability to heal illness, divine the future, and maintain wealth, caused them to project that power onto the beings of Indians, especially shamans. Their projections reified their myth of the pagan savage, subjecting them to its power; during this process, they "sought salvation from the civilization that tormented them as much as the primitive onto whom they projected their antiselves."[109] In this system, the magic in magical realism might be seen to have been bought in the Banana Republic stores as Paul Smith describes them, a purchase that implies, in Smith's words, that "in postcolonial times such nations [i.e., "Banana Republics"] are still the loci of the production of surplus for the capitalist economies of the North."[110] But I would not go as far as that. For one thing, in postcolonial situations, the generic alteration that magical realism effects on European realism differentiates it from a common situation in postcolonial nationalist politics as described by Leila Gandhi (working from the formulations of D. Lloyd and Partha Chatterjee) in which during "the project of State formation" "nationalist discourse surrendered its 'meaning' to a European etymology," mimicking the ideology of nationhood with its concomitant homogenization of the cultural imaginary and in which "nationalist revolutionaries simply come to inhabit the bureaucratic machinery created for the implementation of colonial rule."[111] In other words, postcolonial governmental structures remain virtually the same as the colonial ones. That is not true for magical realism, which alters the form of the discourse; the verbal equivalent of the bureaucratic machinery is changed.

With regard to magical realism, Taussig complains that "too often the wonder that sustains" the stories of Carpentier, Arguedas, Asturias, and García Márquez "is represented in accord with a long-standing tradition of folklore, the exotic, and indigenismo that in oscillating between the cute and the romantic is little more than the standard ruling class appropriation of what is held to be the sensual vitality of the common people and their fantasy life."[112] He contrasts this spirit with the surrealists' irreverent comedy because it avoids this danger, disagreeing with Carpentier, who considered the surrealists' techniques for inducing the marvelous to be too artificial. Given the many appropriations of indigenous cultures in magical realism, his point is partly valid, although, to repeat, those fictions also preserve and provide a vehicle for the strengthening of those cultures. Furthermore, Taussig's own later description of shamanic practices as more tentative and incomplete than Eliade's formulations of shamanic activity seems to me to allow us to align them with the hybrid and defocalized fictions of magical realism, which do not present a unified perspective on indigenous culture. His description of shamanic ordeals, for example, "in which parts are only loosely connected one to another, [in which] there is no centralizing cathartic force, [and] an array exists of distancing techniques involving and disinvolving the reader or spectator and thus, potentially at least, dismantling all fixed and fixing notions of identity," resembles the "array" of magical realist techniques we have discussed, some of them effectuating a narrative "distancing," an "involving and disinvolving [of] the reader," and many of which dismantle "fixed and fixing notions of identity."[113] Taussig might still argue that the force I am claiming for magical realist narrative belongs only to shamans themselves, not to these "shamanistic" magical realist fictions. But I think that the continuing vitality of magical realism as a force of cultural decolonization throughout the world suggests that in transmitting a defocalized narrative that questions the hegemony of realism, it progresses beyond the cute and the romantic, although it does court those dangers.[114] In other words, if this is primitivism, it is a progressive, increasingly self-affirming, and radically hybrid literary primitivism.

Taussig concludes a section of his study by positing that "before there can be a science of man there has to be the long-awaited demythification and re-enchantment of Western man in a quite different confluence of self and otherness. Our way lies upstream, against the current, upriver near the foothills of the Andes where Indian healers are busy healing colonists of the phantoms assailing them."[115] I would propose that such a space of reenchantment and the healing of phantoms is the space of magical realism, and, in Taussig's words, it is migrating metaphorically upriver. It is a welcome migration; its texts are texts of reenchantment or remystification. When writers like

John Updike and John Barth embrace magical realism as elixir and replenishment, and when they and others incorporate its techniques into their texts, magical realist fictions are analogous to foreign princes who rejuvenate the verbal realms of ailing fisher kings.[116] And conversely, when writers such as Isabel Allende and Toni Morrison celebrate and are celebrated for their use of magical realism to conjure healing spirits, they resemble female shamans who are consulted rather than marginalized by missionaries. This is the cultural work of the mode. However, as we have been seeing, the specter of a primitivist colonial appropriation of voices and traditions looms over these dialogues. What is the status, for example, of Harris's "nameless unflinching folk," glorified but also perhaps commodified and almost romanticized out of actual existence, to whom the narrator and his companions near the end of *Palace of the Peacock* are said to have "all come home at last"?[117]

A discussion of the cultural politics of magical realism is necessarily tentative, because it is growing and changing rapidly. Many of its early texts have been milestones in decolonizing the literary imagination and implicitly criticizing repressive regimes. So that on the whole, it, like the literary establishment generally, has a liberal political coloring. Among the notable exceptions are the apolitical stance of Borges and the near-regressive treatment of women by García Márquez and Kundera. It is tempting to regard magical realism's culturally heterogeneous texts as harbingers of improved literary and social relations.[118] And the texts themselves often seem to justify a guarded optimism because listening to their polyvocal textual voices will presumably teach us to listen to many points of view. This is the opinion of Lloyd Davies in his discussion of *The House of the Spirits:* "The instability of style and perspective has positive social implications. If no single reality exists, then no world view is definitively correct, no society can be deemed permanent or stable," and "fantasy disturbs what has been taken to be real, tracing a space within society's cognitive frame"[119] Similarly, M. Keith Booker relates the erosion of individual identities in Rushdie's work, as I do, to his desire for greater pluralism in society, applying this idea specifically to Islamic religion: "Rushdie's fiction, viewed narrowly within the Western tradition, is innovative and provocative, but does not appear to be especially radical or subversive. But, viewed from the Islamic perspective of Iran or Pakistan, the deconstruction of dualities and concomitant questioning of authority inherent in Rushdie's fiction are so powerfully subversive that Khomeini has declared that Rushdie must die."[120] Such a statement implies the radical questioning of authoritarian discourses that Rushdie's fiction represents. Furthermore, the spread of magical realism throughout the world, together with the fact that its magic is now often inspired not only by "primitive" myth but also by technology, means that its modification of realism, which may encourage toleration of the dissonance caused by radically different voices, is being integrated into cultural consciousness, and not only in postcolonial situations.

There is another interpretive scenario, however, a less happy ending to this literary historical story. Even though magical realism is still claimed as a decolonizing force by some writers, as it becomes more and more popular as a style in the international literary marketplace, it is also described as primitivist commodification by others, so that the decolonizing impetus of the mode may be decreasing in some regions even as it participates in a dynamics of change in others. Either scenario is possible. Likewise, the apocalyptic finales of some of these same texts caution us against the optimistic view of the social potential for this hybrid narrative genre that I have posited above. Saleem, Melquíades, Lisa, and Tamina all witness and recount, and their texts incorporate different voices, but they also all disappear, their suffering not only witnessed but also in some sense appropriated by the texts that contain them. Here again, either scenario is possible.[121]

5 ⅔

"Women and Women and Women"

A Feminine Element in Magical Realism

The issue of gender is as problematic in magical realist narrative as it is in modern and postmodern discourses of all kinds. The dialogical, polyphonic, decentered forms that characterize postmodernism as it grows out of modernism correspond to what are often imagined to be female ways of being and knowing.[1] From this perspective, magical realism participates in that female component of postmodernism.[2] According to Christine Buci-Glucksmann, "in the labour of writing, the metaphor of the feminine then rises up as an element in the break with a certain discredited rationality based upon the idea of a historical and symbolic continuum. It does this by designating a new heterogeneity, a new otherness."[3] Although the narrative mode of magical realism belongs, in a sense, to both genders, it may be possible to locate a female spirit characterized by structures of diffusion, polyvocality, and attention to issues of embodiment, to an earth-centered spirit world, and to collectivity, among other things, that is active in magical realism generally, regardless of authorship.[4]

The answer to whether we can discern a feminine thread in magical realism as a whole, whether or not the author is a woman, is a qualified yes.[5] To propose such a connection between magical realism and a female sensibility is not to deny differences among women and their texts but rather to suggest that magical realism has affinities with and exemplifies certain aspects of the experience of women that have been delineated by certain strains of feminist thought. Because of its general narrative properties, that it is a hybrid mode, combining realism and the fantastic, magical realism can be seen to embody (largely French) feminist ideas about women's discourse as reflecting women's experience of belonging to a sex that is, in Luce Irigaray's words, "not one," and to begin to erode a dualistic mode of thinking that draws clear boundaries between self and others, an erosion that has been associated with some strains of female writing.[6] One example of this erosion of distinctions is the pronominal scrambling that we noted in Chapter 3. Similarly, the way that the irreducible elements often exist within the otherwise largely realistic text without any explanation resembles the account of a feminist—and I would say also a postmodernist—relation to otherness given by Drusilla Cornell, in which "the subject does not seek to identify or categorize the object, but rather to let the object be in its difference."[7] As we speculate in more detail at the end of this chapter, if I am correct in discerning in magical realism's defocalized narrative the inherent suggestion of the ineffable, then it might be aligned more with what Julia Kristeva terms a semiotic or hidden and unconscious form of discourse that relates back to a connection to the maternal, and the spiritual, than with the symbolic kind of speech, which is allied with the father, patriarchal society, and rational thought.[8] That it is frequently culturally hybrid connects magical realism to postcolonial and border feminism, which such theorists as Chela Sandoval and Gloria Anzaldúa see as articulating new strategies for negotiating borders between cultures and individuals. Beyond those formal and cultural properties, certain tropes that appear in magical realism, especially in texts by women, also align it with older ideas about female spheres of influence, including houses and cooking, and newer ones concerning attention to the body.

In the end, however, categories and boundaries are especially problematic in this area, and textual modes that we may associate with a particular gender are not necessarily correlated with the corresponding sex of the author. As Shari Benstock has asked, "Isn't it precisely 'the feminine' in Joyce's writings and Derrida's that carries me along?"[9] But there are many points of convergence between postmodernism, postcolonialism, and much feminist thought: all of them have been concerned with investigating possibilities for transgressing boundaries and limits, including, especially, the opposition between selves and others, and with questioning dualistic modes of thought. Kate Rigby, working with the formulations of Val Plumwood, suggests that because it "establishes 'a relation of separation and domination naturalized in culture and characterized by radical exclusion, distancing and opposition between orders constructed as systematically higher and lower,' dualism is therefore the paradigmatic logic of colonization, whereby the other is feigned only in relation to the self as lack or negativity and thereby 'incorporated into the self and its systems of desires and needs'; objectified . . . instrumentalized . . . and stereotyped or homogenized."[10] Finally, then, although we can discern certain common strategies between feminist issues and magical realist practices, magical realism is not a feminist genre, and while works by women authors such as Isabel Allende, Toni Morrison, Laura Esquivel, Ana Castillo, and Marie Darrieussecq have used magical realism in novels that are centered on women's experience and women's problems, there is no single definable feminist ideology that joins them.

In considering the possible female strain in magical realism, the anthropological perspective of Victor Turner is helpful. If we agree to regard realism for the moment as a canonical, patrilineal form, because realism has dominated fiction in the West for the past three centuries, and since the large majority of its writers—until quite recently—have been male, then the global erosion of some of its authority by magical realism resembles the mechanism Turner sees in many kinship patterns. Turner claims that an individual's link to the wider ethical community often depends on his relation to women: "where patrilineality is the basis of social structure, an individual's link to other members of his society through the mother, and hence by extension and abstraction 'women' and 'femininity' tends to symbolize that wider community and its ethical system that encompasses and pervades the politico-legal system. Fascinating correlations can be shown in many societies to exist between this conversion to the perspective of communitas and the assertion of individuality as against status incumbency."[11] Just as the women in a society encourage the individual to develop as an individual in relation to the community at large rather than as a member of a group with an assigned status, so the female-subaltern voice in magical realist texts encourages the development of individual ethnic literatures that serve a decolonizing function within their own societies and that are also linked to each other within a multicultural world.

To align this principle of community development within contemporary literature generally and magical realism in particular solely with the female imagination seems unjust, though statements by feminist writers and critics tend toward such an alignment. Doris Meyer, writing of *The House of the Spirits,* states, "By structuring *La casa de los espíritus* as a double-voiced discourse in which the grandfather represents the internalized patriarchal culture and the granddaughter the newly born feminist, Allende embodies this emergence of a polyvocal feminist text which expresses the hope of an ethically transformed community."[12] Meyer is speaking of different entities within Allende's text than I am, but she views the inclusion of two voices as a female strategy and associates it with the "parented" female text Elaine Showalter defines with the aid of Virginia Woolf's idea that a woman writing thinks back through both her mothers and her fathers. Showalter's idea (following M. M. Bakhtin) that female discourse is double-voiced because it encodes both the "dominant" mode and the "muted" group within it aligns it with the polyvocal nature of magical realism.[13] Here again, this strategy seems to characterize many subaltern forms, not only female ones.

Continuing this line of thought, and allying it with Irigaray's idea of a sex that is not one, we might wonder whether the irreducible elements in magical realism as they disrupt the mimetic program of realism while not dismantling it entirely constitute a discourse that resembles the position of ludic feminism as it develops from and with postmodern deconstruction. It can then be seen to partake of their celebration of the difference within, or *différance,* which undermines the notion of discrete individual identity. The ways in which the protagonist in *Pig Tales* experiences the waxing and waning of her human and porcine characteristics pictures the difference within as a fluid and dynamic entity. Her skin, for example, is sometimes pale, sometimes pink, sometimes smooth and ripe, sometimes sprouting hairs, her face sometimes more and sometimes less snoutish. That she continues farther and farther along the porcine path is also a commentary on the fine line between appreciation and commodification, and on the transformative power of the male gaze, which seems to literally convert her into the animal that will satisfy its animalistic desires, but she never becomes wholly a pig, always keeping some human traits, including, presumably, the ability to write. She claims that she must hurry to finish before her transformation is complete, but we do not experience that within the text, which thus remains a document of mixed sensibilities.

In a different way, that sense of the difference within as it can be magically enacted characterizes Consuelo's conjuring of Aura as her ever-present younger self. Once that interior ideal has been actualized, she uses it to enrapture Felipe, causing him to remain with her, creating an eternal return of their love. Furthermore, the story seems to be a living argument for the necessity of acknowledging gender difference in the reading experience. In that context, we need to ask whether the final scene is creepy or romantic, frightening or empowering.[14]

You bring your lips close to the head that's lying next to yours. You stroke Aura's long black hair. You grasp that fragile woman by the shoulders, ignoring her sharp complaint. You tear off her taffeta robe, embrace her, feel her small and lost and naked in your arms, despite her moaning resistance, her feeble protests, kissing her face without thinking, without distinguishing, and you're touching her withered breasts when a ray of moonlight shines in and surprises you, shines in through a chink in the wall that the rats have chewed open, an eye that lets in a beam of silvery moonlight. It falls on Aura's eroded face, as brittle and yellowed as the memoirs, as creased with wrinkles as the photographs. You stop kissing those fleshless lips, those toothless gums: the ray of moonlight shows you the naked body of the old lady, of Señora Consuelo, limp, spent, tiny, ancient, trembling because you touch her. You love her, you too have come back . . .

You plunge your face, your open eyes, into Consuelo's silver-white hair, and you'll embrace her again when the clouds cover the moon, when you're both hidden again, when the memory of youth, of youth re-embodied, rules the darkness.

"She'll come back, Felipe. We'll bring her back together. Let me recover my strength and I'll bring her back . . ."[15]

From one kind of male-oriented perspective, especially, Aura/Consuelo with her withered breasts, her eroded face, her fleshless lips and toothless gums, her silver-white hair can look like death, and Felipe's co-option into her amorous program like a virtual rape of a young male by an old hag, the symbolic usurpation of the present by the past.[16] And this idea is supported by numerous details in the text, such as Felipe's experiencing Consuelo as a tyrant, against whom he rebels. For Susan Frenck, for example, Felipe is blind to being caught in a kind of eternal return of Aztec myth, which makes him, like the progressive historical forces he can be seen to represent, a sacrificial victim, ascending Consuelo's stairs as sacrificial victims ascended pyramids before their deaths, not the possibly liberatory figure of Quetzalcoatl that he might have seemed at the start but "the mirror image and support of Tezcatlipoca's sacrificial regime."[17]

From one of the more female-centered perspectives in which it is possible to view the novel, however, Consuelo's transformation into Aura and back again, together with Felipe's metamorphosis into the general, can seem like a magical reversal of the *carpe diem* motif, one in which a strong female uses mind and body to overturn the age-old tradition whereby a woman is made to succumb to male pleasure because if she waits too long old age with its attendant decay will make her undesirable, a reversal that achieves instead a realm in which "youth re-embodied" and the love that it represents conquers the darkness. (The novel's final ellipsis suggests that the transformations between youth and age and back again are repeated in such a realm.) And it is a realm that Consuelo, with her female witchly powers, controls. Such a paradigm reversal needs magic to impose itself on our collective imagination. That differential, gendered reading keeps alive one kind of difference between male and female, but it is a problematical kind, which perpetuates stereotypes of women as more at home in the dark, the unconscious and the irrational, desire, and the sexual than men. But I would argue that the text also accommodates another, more androgynous interpretation, also radical, also in need of magical narrative aid. That one would stress the idea that, as Felipe says, speaking in the second person to himself, "you love her, you too have come back," so that the desired realm of eternal love is not only the realm of Consuelo's female fantasy but also of Felipe's emotional need.[18] This is a realm, in which, as Aura says to him earlier in the novel, we'll be loved forever, even when we are old, a desire shared by both sexes.

> You murmur her name in her ear. You feel the woman's full arms against your back. You hear her warm voice in your ear: "Will you love me forever?"
> "Forever, Aura, I'll love you forever."
> "Forever? Do you swear it?"
> "I swear it."
> "Even though I grow old? Even though I lose my beauty? Even though my hair turns white?"
> "Forever, My love, forever."
> "Even if I die, Felipe? Will you love me forever, even if I die?"
> "Forever, forever. I swear it. Nothing can separate us."
> "Come, Felipe, come." (111)

The formalized nature of the dialogue moves it toward the realm of myth and poetic drama rather than that of realistic fiction, making it possible to imagine that both Felipe and Aura are engaged in creating that eternal realm of romantic love celebrated so often before.[19] Frightening and enticing, it is a realm that both women and men can enter. In this interpretation it might even resemble and give body to the space imagined by Virginia Woolf as the "androgynous mind," which she illustrates with her well-known description of the young woman and young man coming from opposite sides of the street to enter a London taxi, which thereby symbolically becomes the space of that androgynous mind, composed of both female and male personae.

That it is Felipe's realm as well as Aura's is suggested by another image earlier in the novel, as Felipe sees Aura for the first time.

> Finally you can see that those eyes are sea green and that they surge, break to foam, grow calm again, then surge again like a wave. You look into them and tell yourself it isn't true, because they're beautiful green eyes just like all the beautiful green eyes you've ever known. But you can't deceive yourself: those eyes do surge, do change, as if offering you a landscape that only you can see and desire. (27)

On one hand, only Felipe can see and desire this landscape that Consuelo has conjured up in the flesh of Aura to entrap him. It is the landscape of their mutual past. Here again, I would argue, despite this plausible idea (that this is yet another of Consuelo's witchly—and therefore creepy—wiles), that the landscape that only he can see and desire can also be imagined as the landscape of his own desire and of their eternally renewed love, in which he also will be loved even when he is old, a landscape that we all covet.[20] Seen in that way, the beauty of the language and the way that Felipe responds to the feeling of youthful love it conjures up suggest that this realm of eternal desire is a positive engagement and not simply an entrapment for Felipe. And even if it is a foolishly desired realm, it is not uncommon and not one-gendered.

The first wave of magical realist fiction, including *Aura,* was written largely by men, but the female voice has been rapidly surfacing, as it has in all domains. The increase in female magical realist texts reflects the decolonizing potential of the mode. If women writers have felt like a colony, telling their own stories provides an exit from that position, and the magical elements that disrupt realism's domination of representation lend them the strength to travel. The consciously female, home-centered novels *The House of the Spirits, Beloved, Like Water for Chocolate, So Far from God,* and *Licorice,* among others, attest to this strength.[21] Isabel Allende sees a link between her magical realism and that of minority women writers in the United States: "Today, great writers from minority groups in the US are finding their voice in the wonderful, rich imagery of magic realism. Writers such as Louise Erdrich, Toni Morrison, Alice Walker and Amy Tan all have a unique, rich way of writing that can be described as magic realism."[22] In linking herself to these minority women writers under the banner of magical realism, Allende enlists magical realism as a kind of support system for feminine writing, confirming its decolonizing potential for women.[23] A popular fiction on the fantastical edge of magical realism, Marion Engel's *Bear,* which chronicles a woman's love affair with the animal of its title, illustrates this idea in that it uses the magic of that encounter to accomplish the difficult discursive task of recuperating pornography for women. In a different domain, *So Far from God* orchestrates another such reconfiguration of power. On her miraculous return to life, when Father Jerome tries to get La Loca to come down from the roof, telling her "let's just go in together, we'll all pray for you," La Loca, sailing down to the ground "with the delicate and effortless motion of a monarch butterfly," retorts "No, padre, . . . Remember, it is *I* who am here to pray for *you,"* reversing the habitual gender of the channel for divine interces-sion.[24] Similarly, through her transformation, the narrator of *Pig Tales* finally becomes a kind of powerful and terrible but desentimentalized avenging goddess in the scene near the end of the novel when she rises up and shoots her former employer and her mother. This potential for the development of female narrative is in part an effect of defocalization, in which the authority of strictly mimetic realism is dissolved, so that alternative possibilities can be imagined. However, this is not a simple matter, because here we confront the same problems in dealing with women and their representation that we did in Chapter 4 dealing with colonized cultures.[25]

Following Allende's lead, however, recall the scene in Maxine Hong King-ston's *The Woman Warrior* in which the narrator's mother recounts her experi-ences of a sitting ghost. The "energy amassing" connected with that ghost that the story records, detached from a clear narrative origin but associated with a communal female voice, is ostensibly frightening but ultimately enabling both at first-hand for the medical students who are learning to integrate sci-ence and images of ghostly magic in the transcultural process of their medi-cal educations and at one remove for Hong Kingston's narrator. That strong and yet delicate sound, not polite or soft, is the sound of the energy needed to free the narrative voice, the sound that appears very faintly later on in the "little squeaks" that come out of the narrator's throat in the American school she attends, vocal sounds that miraculously, after sounding like "splinters" and "bones rubbing jagged against one another," ultimately flower into this story.[26] So the ghost clears out of the medical school in the story, as the students order it to, but remains embedded at the center of the discourse, wrapped in that "I think my mother said"; it is a valuable amulet complete with a protective covering that in turn protects the narrator as she struggles to develop a female Chinese American voice in the last chapter of her text.[27] And as if to confirm that a communal narrative power has been passed on to her through this process, at the end of the novel the narrative focalizes in a way that deconstructs individualized narrative authority, so that the text transmits ancient communal voices through the old family tale that ends the book. With respect to that communal voice, as we have seen in the various bridging techniques in Chapter 3, magical realist texts tend to merge rather than separate different realms, thus implicitly emphasizing relationship more strongly than individuation, a mode often associated with a female sensibility. Its ghosts propose (in Lois Zamora's words in her comparative analysis of Allende's *The House of the Spirits* and the paintings of Remedios Varo) "a model of the self that is collective," so that "subjectivity is not singular but several."[28]

In articulating her program of differential oppositional consciousness as a feminist strategy of cultural survival, Chela Sandoval provides material that suggests why many Chicana authors have adopted magical realism. Like magical realism, oppositional consciousness contains "seeming contradictions and difference"; it is a mode that was "once relegated to the province of intuition and psychic phenomena, but which now must be recognized as a specific practice"; it has "constantly shifting boundaries" and involves a "violent shattering of the unitary sense of self."[29] In this context, we might say that irreducible elements operate like oppositional guerrilla attacks on mimetic territories. Rather than constituting a total aesthetic program, they resemble the ad hoc tactical positions made to confront individual situations that characterize the programs of marginal groups. Like magical realist poetics, those programs are rarely codified into a system. In this context, women, like subalterns generally, can be understood to act through magic because other routes may be closed to them.[30] In addition, a female voice may be able to transmit the ineffable because of its marginal position within the discourses of reason and realism that have tended to mute that mystical sound. According to Laurie Finke, "perhaps because of their oppressive social situation," women in the Middle Ages were especially drawn to radical forms of religious experience. And like magical realist narrative, which resembles a kind of ventriloquism, transmitting a sense of belief in extrasensory phenomena that contrasts with the assumptions behind its own prevailing mode of realism, "the female mystic of the middle ages did not claim to speak in her own voice" because she lacked authority within the church. Nevertheless, in attempting to represent the unrepresentable, she did claim the power to shape her experience.[31]

In contrast to Allende, Toni Morrison has resisted the label of magical realist as disturbingly hegemonic. She claims, "My own use of enchantment simply comes because that's the way the world was for me and for the black people that I knew."[32] (Her declaration virtually duplicates García Márquez's statements that his magical realism results simply from his reporting what he observes or is told, and Alejo Carpentier's claims that "marvelous American reality" simply reflects actual American phenomena and events.) Our focus on the global importance of magical realism does not negate Morrison's specifically cultural orientation; it is "simply" a different topic—although such issues are never simple. In any case, the common concerns and techniques that unite Morrison with other magical realist writers, together with her assertion that her use of "enchantment" reflects her minority cultural tradition, suggest that magical realism is an enabling strategy for diverse postcolonial traditions.[33]

That a writer may dislike the label of magical realism while using its techniques does not erase its presence from a text or prevent the inclusion of a text in the mode. Given the intense political awareness of much magical realism, Morrison is mistaken in considering it "just another evasive label," "another one of those words that covered up what was going on," "a convenient way [for literary critics] to skip again what was the truth in the art of certain writers." Morrison speaks in the past tense about her original attitude toward magical realism, so perhaps that attitude has been changing, and, besides, her animosity is leveled at the critical use of the term that subsumes writers from different traditions rather than at the literature it attempts to categorize. Shortly after the publication of *Beloved* in 1988, she ends the interview in which she makes these statements by saying, "I have become indifferent, I suppose, to the phrase 'magical realism.'"[34] Indifferent—even mildly hostile—to the term, she masterfully employs the techniques.

Adopting a literary historical perspective for a moment, magical realism, in general, and, especially, magical realism within women's writing may in-

herit the subversive element, the disruptive female desire, that Susan Suleiman sees as central in surrealism. From a position of female empowerment,
then, the beginning of magical realism in surrealism signals the beginning of
the end of the patriarchal age. Contemporary female defocalized narratives
metaphorically activate the voices of André Breton's female seers (*voyantes*),
whom he imagines to passively "accuse themselves of sometimes adorably
moral sins." They take back the voices of those seers whose suffering he has
appropriated.[35] In this context, explicit connections to the cosmos in much
magical realism suggest that its practitioners are "worshippers of the goddess"
rather than "celebrants of the cyborg," though that may be changing.[36] Taking surrealist female energies into account, perhaps the magical realist voice
symbolically inhabits the apartment in Cortázar's "Letter to a Young Lady in
Paris," where tiny rabbits appear at the back of the narrator's tongue. The title
of the story mysteriously invokes the absent female owner of this narrative
space, who thus mysteriously and absently enables that voice. Or it may echo
through the room near the end of Harris's *Palace of the Peacock* that "breathed
all burning tranquility and passion together," in which the narrator sees the
last figure before he has his culminating ecstatic vision, a woman who heralds
the merging of all into all that that vision achieves: "Not a grain of her dress
but shone with her hair, clothing her threadbare limbs in the melting plaits
of herself. Her ancient dress was her hair after all, falling to the ground and
glistening and waving until it grew so frail and loose and endless, the straw
in the cradle entered and joined it and the whole room was enveloped in it
as a melting essence yields itself and spreads itself from the topmost pinnacle
and star into the roots of self and space."[37] But how are we to interpret this
image—as strong and commanding cosmic female power or luscious but
essentially passive (melting, yielding) and sensual bodily backdrop for the
male traveler's mental vision? Either way, it clearly enables that vision.[38]

Housekeeping

Within this fiction that frequently figures cosmic connection, Virginia
Woolf's "angel in the house," "intensely sympathetic," "endlessly charm-
ing," "utterly unselfish"—"if there was chicken, she took the leg; if there was
a draught she sat in it"—has become something of a witch, a female shaman,
a goddess.[39] She is Consuelo, for example, who sacrifices the man she entices
inside her house for her own ends. In that instance, they may also be his

ends, the communal desires not for duty but for passionate and everlasting love. From the angel with her soft dust mop, the sexually and imaginatively weakened woman, and in part out of Woolf's warning about the loss of vital energy such a figure represents, grows the powerful, imaginative, and even witchly shamanistic narrator. She is endowed with chthonic powers, and her broomstick is finialized with a pen. This is the metafictional dimention (I retain that typo) represented by Sethe's outrageous act of murder in *Beloved:* she wields a knife to kill her own baby. Even the wicked witch in *Hansel and Gretel* seems tame in comparison. That earlier witch's house was made of gingerbread; her magic erupted from the enclosed space of frustrated domesticity rather than emerging from the shaman's powerhouse connected to the cosmos.

From this perspective of shamanistic magic, the disfigurement of female bodies in surrealism, and the continuation of that tradition in magical realist texts such as Octavio Paz's "My Life with the Wave" and *Aura,* can be seen to represent a subterranean desire for the female power of relational magic, and it often ends in perversity. It is magic wand or muse envy, so to speak.[40] In Paz's story, a female wave eventually disrupts the life of her male lover to such a degree that he allows her to freeze and takes her to a café to be chipped up for drinks. He gets his revenge for the discomfort she has caused him, but one might regard the violence of the disfigurement as signaling a certain desperation, an eagerness to appropriate or annihilate her oceanic emotional power. The mutilated bodies in Frida Kahlo's paintings, having become icons of female suffering transformed into artistic empowerment, represent the next stage in the growth of postsurrealist female art and prefigure the fiction of female magical realists.[41] Following that destructive phase, the female body as a bridge to the beyond is imaginatively reconstructed in magical realist texts by both men and women.[42] Those texts provide that world-spanning body with a dwelling place, a magical realist home of fiction, and the witch becomes a female shaman. Furthermore, in magical realist texts, a fictional house often metafictionally figures as well as metaphorically contains the narrative.

A house is central in *Beloved,* and, by the end of the novel, Sethe's house has been transformed by its ghostly habitation, a form of female intergenerational speech. Even the owner of 124 Bluestone Road "felt something sweeter and deeper about the house."[43] The house is where the magical elements appear early on in Morrison's novel, but delicately, barely perceptibly. We hesitate out of ignorance, if nothing else, and a second reading recognizes more magic: "124 was spiteful. Full of a baby's venom. The women in the house knew it and so did the children. . . . The sons, Howard and Buglar, had run away . . . as soon as merely looking in a mirror shattered it . . . as soon as two tiny hand prints appeared in the cake" (1–2). On the next page, Sethe and Denver hold hands and encourage Beloved (as yet unnamed), " 'Come on. Come on. You may as well just come on.' " Soon, not just the house, but its furniture is affected: "the sideboard took a step forward but nothing else did." And if we doubted that, a few sentences later, "together they pushed the sideboard back against the wall" (4). Beloved tyrannizes 124, until, through a complex process, her spirit is exorcized. But before that process is completed, the magic in the novel transmits her power, usually from within the house: at one point, for example, the whole house shakes and Paul D grabs a table that is whirling around the kitchen.

This magically real American house is a female verbal analogue for Ojib-way shamans' lodges and adds some flesh to those dematerialized spirit houses of poles without walls. Both of them resemble Gaston Bachelard's descriptions of poetic houses of breath and wind and voice, because they are open to the universe, in contact with cosmic forces. As such, they embody the female "wild zone" described by Edwin Ardener, which, in relation to dominant male-centered culture, and like the spirit dimension hidden within the narrative mode of magical realism, is publicly unseen and yet powerful.[44]

Both the cosmic openness and the wildness are important in these female texts. Unlike Gothic fictional dwellings, magical realist houses do not isolate their magic but instead provide focal points for its dispersal. They are openings from which it spreads into the world around it and receivers through which it welcomes cosmic forces, which may either terrorize before ultimately refreshing it, as in *Beloved*, or destroy it, as in *One Hundred Years of Solitude*.[45] But most important for women's narratives, the domestic sphere in these magically real houses is usually not closed in on itself in isolation but opened outward into communal and cosmic life, as proven by the ghosts from other times and places that wander through some of them. In *One Hundred Years of Solitude*, Colonel Aureliano attempts to close himself off from the rest of humanity by drawing an isolationist magic circle around himself. But from within her female magical domestic space, Ursula, who keeps and tirelessly refurbishes the Buendía house, steps over his line and effectively breaks his circle. That circle symbolizes the lonely tyranny enacted in public spaces, usually by men. It contrasts with the house as Ursula maintains it: "Ursula had rejuvenated the house again. . . . There won't be a better, more *open* house in all the world than this madhouse" (my emphasis).[46]

Like *Beloved*, Allende's *The House of the Spirits* opens up female domestic space in several directions, toward the political, toward the passionately sexual, toward the sacred, and (through narrative powers) toward the imaginary.[47] And sometimes these openings include magic. As Lois Zamora has pointed out, the table through which Clara contacts her spirits "serves as the iconic link between spirituality and domesticity: the four-legged family dining table, locus of physical and familiar nourishment, set and presided over by the matriarch, is closely associated with (and sometimes magically transformed into) Clara's three-legged table. So, Allende suggests, the cosmic and the quotidian are interwoven in this house of spirits."[48] And so, too, does she suggest that the ability to see beyond the actual can also promote political awareness, as Deborah Cohn's analysis suggests: Clara's "power to 'see what was invisible' . . . points out to her the hatred and resentment seething at Las Tres Marías."[49] In addition, even more specifically, the house is a place of feminist struggle against the patriarchal Esteban Trueba, and part of that struggle is to keep it open to outside influences, even if sometimes Clara has to achieve this openness by the way (as Ronie-Richelle García-Johnson has expressed it) she "existed spiritually, in another space or dimension, and brought the outside world inside the space of the house to her."[50] This interconnectedness of the domestic, magic, and the outer world seems to me to remain true, irrespective of whether the novel moves increasingly toward a more political orientation. Similarly, magic is generally an empowering strategy if not a pragmatic one; thus it diminishes in frequency as political activity increases but it is also a precursor of that activity because it has helped Clara to survive and pass on her strength to her granddaughter. As Caroline Bennett maintains, "through her magic Clara resists being 'controlled and mastered' and, therefore avoids being merely a possession of her husband," and for her daughter and granddaughter, "magic will continue to exist in their matrilineal memory."[51]

Like Allende's house of spirits, the white hotel is a female space open to the universe. Besides being, in the highly ironized psychoanalytic discourse of the text, "the body of our mother" that as such contains the flowing milk of the maternal breasts Liza displays in its dining room, it is also an imaginative space that embraces the surrounding mountains; the young couple makes love both within the hotel and outside on the hillside; they admire the sunset from their window; a storm flings a stone and a maple leaf into their room in which they feel "the snowy mountain peaks very close"; flood waters rise to the pockets of the billiard table.[52] The same is true of the house in *So Far from God,* which, through the activities of Caridad and La Loca (such as the time when the latter claims that La Llorona, the mythical wandering woman of Mexican legend—in Castillo's words, "Chicana international astral traveler," "who may have been nothing short of a loving mother goddess" [162] comes to tell her of her sister's death in Saudi Arabia), is a cosmically connected space. None of the people in the town "realized just how aware Loca was of her surroundings and of all the things that went on outside and away from Sofi's house" (152).

These fictional houses lend their female narrative spaces for the task of shamanistic healing that frequently forms part of magical realism's program. Both *The White Hotel* and *The House of the Spirits* end with similar regenerative scenarios. At the end of the first novel the white hotel turns into a refugee camp in a promised land where the dead are revived. There, Lisa, whole once again, though with a "very tender" breast that recalls her wounding at Babi Yar, meets her mother, who says that "wonderful healing goes on over here" (266), and soon they suckle each other and are much comforted by it. The end of *The House of the Spirits* is more confrontational, although Allende, like Thomas, partially defuses the horrors of history into the patterns of a fate who weaves "an unending tale of sorrow, blood, and love." In that design, "the grandson of the woman who was raped repeats the gesture with the granddaughter of the rapist." The repetition achieves a kind of poetic justice that seems to be turning the narrator's anger into an unembittered resignation, but it also perpetuates the act of rape, which revives the reader's sense of gendered injustice. Even so, Alba's idea that Clara wrote her notebooks, "so they would help me now to reclaim the past and overcome terrors of my own" suggests the beginning of an end to the cycles of injustice the text chronicles, even as it attests to their regrettable persistence.[53]

Perhaps these disturbingly complicit scenarios are best understood as emotional survival strategies, countering public terror with private faith in the face of otherwise hopeless situations.[54] Allende has confirmed this idea: "It is the spiritual and emotional aspect that in literature is called magical realism; it appears with different forms of expression, in all the underdeveloped world. When we live in permanent contact with all forms of violence and misery, we have to look for explanations and find hope in the supernatural. Reality is so brutal that we need the protection of a magical or spiritual world."[55] The novel ends with a magic circle of regenerative storytelling because otherwise it would end (as *The Odyssey* would have had not Athena intervened to halt that earlier epic cycle of revenge) with a tragic line of death and an endless pattern of revenge: "It would be very difficult for me to avenge all those who should be avenged, because my revenge would be just another part of the same inexorable rite. I have to break that terrible chain" (368). Thus this narrator overwrites—explicitly?—and hence takes her distance from the apocalyptic ending of *One Hundred Years of Solitude*. In so doing she achieves a narrative healing and associates it with a world of spirits and a matriarchal line of descent: "My grandmother wrote in her notebooks that bore witness to life for fifty years. Smuggled out by certain friendly spirits, they miraculously escaped the infamous pyre in which so many other family papers perished. I have them here at my feet, bound with colored ribbons, divided according to events and not in chronological order, just as she arranged them before she left" (368). But the chain of revenge that Alba feels compelled to break is so strong that she needs magic in order to achieve it. Potential healings like those in Thomas's and Allende's texts are made possible by the alternative spaces of the imagination opened up by magical realist narratives. Like the pale sun that rises at the end of Fuentes's *Terra Nostra*, they dare to dream a second chance for the revision of historical disaster, a hope that is only partly destroyed by irony. Because of its partial detachment from empirical evidence, combined with the recording of historical atrocities, magical realism reconfigures the escape from history into fantasy and moves it toward both confrontation and healing.

A collusion between history and magic haunts Abby Frucht's novel *Licorice*, which, like *Beloved*, merges the domestic and the historical. The chapter titles, including "Danka's Soup," and "Stewing," invoke comforting domestic spaces and activities that are progressively eroded. Danka's allusion to her experiences in a concentration camp, her strangely compulsive behavior, and the narrator's oblique references to people disappearing from the small, extremely peaceful town where she now lives, generate an eerie feeling. It is as if the two diametrically opposed times and places of World War II Germany and 1980s upstate New York had leaked into each other, and the text existed at their intersection. The two times mesh in a kind of historical domesticity just as the spaces of camp and kitchen merge when Danka makes a watery

"Skarzysko soup" of turnips for which she seeks a particular "flavor, a hint
of sweetness I can't get, what's that word—pootrid."[56]

That eerie process whereby female domestic space opens out into the
realm of historical atrocity, which leaks into it, continues throughout the
novel through telling images: dismembered dolls used as makeshift flower
vases, teeth appearing in a beautiful pottery bowl, women showering together
after swimming in the college pool (dismembered bodies, extracted teeth, and
communal showers being well-known emblems of concentration camp life).
In this process the domestic peace and happiness where "our lovemaking is
familiar as breathing: gentle and soothing, moist, uncomplicated, lengthy"
disintegrates into a situation where "I couldn't feel anything at all" because "it
feels as if the love itself were lifted away."[57] One day, instead of a missing person, there is a missing house, and then another and another, and the narrator
finally sees the post office in which she is a TLC, a "temporary letter carrier,"
close. She is transformed from the traditionally female caretaker, a giver of
"tender loving care," into a displaced person, although she transforms back
again at the end. On one hand, this may just be a story about one woman's
anxieties concerning pregnancy and dependence, its boundary a timeless
circle; on the other hand, because that domestic circle opens through the
eerie disappearances to a wider historical space of linear time, the magic of
the disappearances registers the shock of the intersection, and the possibility of contented insularity is consequently denied. The revival of heightened
domesticity (that benefits from the doubt into which it has been cast) with
which the book ends does not include a resolution of Danka's fate, which
remains disturbingly and appropriately incomplete. Her psychic wounds bear
witness to the teeth and nails of a modern historical monster.

It is difficult to generalize, but it seems that the male tone within magical realism is often more visionary, the female more curative, these roles
corresponding more to the sexes of characters than to that of authors.[58] In
One Hundred Years of Solitude, Melquíades foresees all and writes it down;
Pilar Ternera lives to be 155 and serves as a comforting figure for Aureliano,
who "took refuge in the compassionate tenderness and understanding of his
unknown great-great-grandmother" (363). Ana Castillo's *So Far from God*
and Laura Esquivel's *Like Water for Chocolate,* both *bildungsromans* of female
shamans, we might say, illustrate this curative trend.[59] The recipes and remedies they include suggest a practical and communal relation to the world

of the spirit. Perhaps *So Far from God* even sets out to symbolically cure its
own title, and it needs magic to accomplish that.[60] Castillo's title comes from
her epigraph, Porfirio Díaz's well-known phrase about Mexico: "So far from
God—So near the United States." In locating her novel in New Mexico, and
including magically real miracles, Castillo begins to heal the split between
God, or, more generally, a world of the spirits, and the pragmatically oriented United States that Díaz's statement implies. Other references to healing
appear throughout the novel. See, for example, the next to the last chapter
title, which introduces a series of curing strategies: "Doña Felicia Calls in
the Troops Who Herein Reveal a Handful of Their Own Tried and Proven
Remedios." And a central element in the story is Caridad's development into
a curandera, a healer (230). Resembling Chela Sandoval's idea about a differential oppositional consciousness, which adopts ad hoc tactical strategies that
change with different situations, Doña Felicia's cures are "remedies born of
sheer ingenuity." Take, for example, the remedy of the "estampas de tabaco,"
in which "the revenue stamps used to seal tobacco can lids—the canceled
ones, naturally—placed at the temples were a sure cure for severe headaches"
(233–34). Similarly, as we have seen, the ending of Allende's novel, in which
history is recorded and preserved to help contemporary lives, and emotions
are partially soothed, is more expressly a cure for social and political ills than
García Márquez's apocalyptic finale. Whether the magical sacred space Ben
Jelloun's narrator enters at the end of *The Sacred Night* soothes her sexual
wound is unclear, but it does seem to afford her some consolation. In *The
White Hotel,* a male author who focalizes through a woman creates a radically
divided text, which largely denies the curative powers of Freudian analysis
and imagines an alternative utopia. Following these gender lines, the ghosts
of personal history are somewhat more constructively laid to rest in *Beloved*
than in *Ironweed,* and the healing process is more central to Morrison's novel
than to Kennedy's. The division between male seers and female healers is not
universally true, however. Sethe sees Beloved because of her guilt, whereas
Paul D protects 124 Bluestone Road, holds down its whirling furniture, and
helps Sethe to heal herself, among other things, by telling her she is her own
"best thing." Carlos Rueda in *Imagining Argentina* acts as a channeler to heal
the wounds of the relatives of Argentina's disappeared (although one might
argue that he uses the traditional patriarchal route into the magical realm:
a woman's body—that of his disappeared wife). And while Vera's narrative

conjuring in Francine Prose's *Bigfoot Dreams* does produce a fountain of youth, it cures no one; on the contrary, it seriously disrupts the life of the family on whose lawn it appears.

"Virgin Paper"; or, Inhabiting Female Bodies

Many of the magically real bodies we have encountered in magical realism are literally inscribed with their social, political, cultural, and geographical coordinates.[61] We have seen how the magically resurrected Beloved still bears the scar of slavery around her neck. The chokecherry tree on Sethe's back that resulted from a whipping is not magical but it is another such cultural inscription. To compare that scarred pattern with the voluntarily inscribed designs on the bodies of African women and men endows it with added pathos. Similarly, the female bodies in *Midnight's Children* are (not surprisingly), as Nalini Natarajan has pointed out, often metaphors for the imagining of the nation. An especially good example is the way in which Saleem's putative grandfather views his grandmother, piecemeal, through a hole in a sheet, a method of female partition that corresponds to the fate of the nation and that is re-enacted on the body of Saleem's famous singer sister.[62] The issue is not confined to female bodies, however, as such examples as Saleem's face that is a virtual map of India, incarnating the idea that he is tied inextricably to his country, Grenouille's artificial manufacture of a perfume for himself, and Felipe's transformation into General Llorente suggest. But because women have traditionally been the inferior "body" side of the mind-body duality, these particular embodiments can be seen as part of what I am claiming is a female strain within magical realism, regardless of the sex of the character.

In a highlighting of bodily inscriptions similar to those we have just examined, throughout *Pig Tales,* several social issues magically transform the flesh of the protagonist. At the start of her slow, partial, and perennially reversing metamorphosis into a sow, which, significantly, coincides with her being out of a job and getting nowhere in her search for a new one until she applies to a "big perfume and cosmetics chain," "at that point in my life, men in general had begun finding me marvelously elastic. . . . My flesh had become firmer, smoother, plumper than before."[63] As if in response to that male desire, her skin also becomes extremely rosy. And interestingly enough, it is not only men who find her more attractive. As she describes herself, comments about how men find her are interspersed with how she finds herself: "I daydreamed about these beauty preparations, about how good I was going to smell, about the glowing complexion I'd have. Honoré would undoubtedly find me even more alluring. . . . I thought I looked—forgive me for saying so—incredibly gorgeous, like a fashion model, but more voluptuous" (4–5). Is she looking at herself as a man would look at her ("Honoré would undoubtedly find me even more alluring"), having absorbed society's predominantly male sexualized gazing at female flesh? Or is she "simply" enjoying her own body ("I thought I looked—*forgive me for saying so*—incredibly gorgeous"), the request for forgiveness suggesting a self-involved pleasure not totally allied to male desire? (my emphasis). It is really very difficult to tell. One form of enjoyment seems to merge into the other.[64] Living out the complex nature of a female person with her desires, aspirations, and social constraints has made her into a hybrid being. By the end, even though she has just told us, "now I'm a sow most of the time," she says in the words that end the book that she tries to do what her lover "Yvan taught me, but for the opposite reason: when I crane my neck toward the Moon, it's to show, once again, a human face." And she extends this embodiment beyond the female. Yvan also finds comfort and expression for his sensual desires through his nightly transformation into a wolf, which affords him a way out of his confining role as a businessman where he had to put up with "audience-pandering stuff" (131).[65]

In *Midnight's Children* both Saleem's and Mrs. Gandhi's physical features are embodiments of their connections to their country. In addition to his magical radio receiver head-full of the voices born at partition and his face modeling the map, by the end of the novel he is literally falling into pieces, once more an embodiment of the multifariousness and fragmentation of India. And his son is also "mysteriously handcuffed to history," for "at the precise instant of India's arrival at Emergency, he emerged." Soon, he falls ill, and Saleem tells us, "I suspected, from the first, something darkly metaphorical in this illness, . . . [and] I insisted then, 'while the Emergency lasts, he will never become well.' "[66] Similarly, according to Saleem, Mrs. Gandhi, embodying the popular phrase "*India is Indira and Indira is India*, . . . had white hair on one side and black on the other; the Emergency, too, had a white part—public, visible, documented, a matter for historians—and a black part which, being secret macabre untold, must be a matter for us" (501).

These magical bodies are instances of the process by which, as Elisabeth Grosz expresses it, following Freud, "the once-clear boundary between the mind and the body, nature and culture, becomes increasingly eroded." That these marked bodies are magically inscribed with ideas may mean that perhaps they constitute the kind of "embodied subjectivity" and "psychical corporality" that Grosz calls for in getting beyond "accounts of the person which divide the subject into the mutually exclusive categories of mind and body." In other words, the linguistic magic that is enacted on bodies in some of these magical realist fictions in which flesh is literally inscribed with or transformed by an idea (in many instances being literally marked by history, as in the phenomenon of "felt history") may partially undermine the distinction between mind and body, idea and corporality. That these bodies are magically transformed by histories, technologies, psychologies, past and present mythologies thus may, like the Mobius strip model that Grosz imagines as the model for relations between body and mind, one twisting into the other, enable "subjectivity to be understood not as fully material and for materiality to be extended and to include and explain the operations of language, desire, and significance."[67] We might note at this point that these questions regarding embodiment are a particular variation on the idea that magical realist texts often question our notions of spatiality and identity.

This attention to the body also has epistemological resonances, bringing up the idea of "feminist epistemologies of embodied knowledges," as Stacy Alaimo has formulated it in her investigation of women and nature, because to experience something in one's body is to know it in a particular way, and even more significantly, to identify with an object of knowledge such as a historical process or another person by interacting with it bodily rather than observing it from a position of objective detachment changes one's knowledge of that object.[68] Thus instances of magical embodiments also illustrate the kind of model for knowledge Sandra Harding proposes of "strong objectivity" that strives for a "reciprocal relationship," often centered in the body, "between the agent and the object of knowledge."[69]

This is the way that Sethe and Beloved come to know each other. Beloved must be embodied and she and Sethe must interact in a bodily way for the knowledge of the love and forgiveness to be communicated and understood and for reconciliation to be achieved.[70] Scenes where they touch, such as the one in which Sethe, Denver, and Beloved hold each other up on ice skates and afterward drink warm milk with cane syrup and vanilla together in front of a roaring stove fire, convey the importance of this kind of bodily communication. Beloved and Sethe "changed beds and exchanged clothes" and dressed themselves in "bright clothes—with blue stripes and sassy prints." Beloved "filled basket after basket with the first things warmer weather let loose in the ground—dandelions, violets, forsythia—presenting them to Sethe, who arranged them, stuck them, wound them all over the house. Dressed in Sethe's dresses, she stroked her skin with the palm of her hand" (240–41). The mood changes, and Beloved breaks things, but her presence is still very much an embodied one: Beloved "was getting bigger" while Denver is "listless and sleepy with hunger and saw the flesh between her mother's forefinger and thumb fade. Saw Sethe's eyes bright but dead" (242–43). As if to portray a kind of communal bodily feeling, both the initial appearances of the baby ghost (handprints on a cake and a sideboard whirling around) are tied to intimate touching, first Denver and Sethe holding hands and then Paul D holding Sethe's breasts.

But this knowledge through the body does not preclude verbal communication, because Beloved also seems to generate stories, asking Sethe repeatedly to "tell me your diamonds," and seems to produce narratives in Sethe's mind. Thus the knowledge that she receives from her mother comprises both bodily and verbal components.[71] Sethe says at one point, "Thank God I don't have to rememory or say a thing because you know it. All" (191), but shortly thereafter she also says, "I'll explain to her even though I don't have to" (200). The stories and the bodily events combine into their joint lived experience, which Sethe imagines creating in Beloved's presence: "Think what spring will be for us! I'll plant carrots just so she can see them, and turnips. Have you ever seen one, baby? A prettier thing God never made. White and purple with a tender tail and a hard head. Feels good when you hold it in your hand and smells like the creek when it floods, bitter but Happy. We'll smell them together, Beloved, Beloved" (201). Does the description of the turnip imagine an inclusive, perhaps androgynous, sensuality from a female point of view? The tender tail and hard head would figure a newly imagined woman that includes both delicate sexuality and hard-headedness, and the thing that feels good to hold in your hand and smells like the creek when it floods, while sexually unspecific, seems rather like a penis physically felt from a woman's side, its fluid associated with the waters that elsewhere in the novel are associated with birth. In any case, the reality of dealing with Beloved is less idyllic than Sethe's fantasy, but it is bodily real. The identification that it involves must have its end, however, or Sethe will be entirely consumed.[72]

Likewise, in *The White Hotel,* Lisa's magical premonitory bodily pains can also be seen as a symbol for a body-related knowledge, but Thomas also shows her writing a poem and a journal in which they have analogues, so the bodily and the verbal are intertwined in her story. Magical images in the journal seem to be embodiments of repressions, bodies returning to assert the knowledge of what has happened to them, except that they are communally rather than individually experienced. As a form of historical knowledge, the way in which we share the experience of Lisa's bodily pains causes us to "know" history in a horrifyingly new and different way.[73] Two hotel guests see an impossible school of whales in the mountain lake, a phenomenon that is then "explained" by the fact that Madame Cottin "is a corsetière. And part of every corset is—to speak bluntly—dead whale." Another of these "odd things [that] have been happening," as one of them puts it, reported by the baker, who "barely audible, said he had seen a womb gliding across the lake," is later associated by an elderly nurse, who waits until she is alone with the baker to tell him, to the fact that her grand niece "had only a month ago undergone an operation for the removal of her womb. . . . I didn't want to say it in public because it would upset her to have it known." A Lutheran pastor "said hesitantly that he had seen a breast flying through the yew trees" and "a heavily busted woman with graying hair said that she had recently had a breast removed." Immediately, "Vogel, looking distinctly yellow, said he *thought* he had seen a petrified embryo floating in the lake shallows, but it could just as easily have been a piece of fossilized tree. His sister, beginning to weep, confessed to an abortion, ten years ago" (52–58). Characteristically, in this novel, these images seem like a simultaneous homage to and spoof of Freudian ideas. This is a male writer focalizing through a female protagonist, so the psychically motivated images of the body can be seen as perpetuating Freudian stereotypes of female hysterical symptoms, but since they are also later shown to relate to Lisa's actual wounds at Babi Yar they can also be interpreted as critiquing that perspective.[74]

In *Perfume*, horrible as it is, Grenouille's wildly successful manufacture of a scent for himself out of the bodies of his opposite numbers, beautiful virgins, the essence of desirability and purity, is an instance of artificial embodiment that radically questions the boundaries between selves and others and fictionalizes debates over the essential or constructed nature of gender. That he can become so desirable through the mask of his perfume, obtained by distilling the odor of lovable virgins, causes us to ask in what does such lovableness reside. The distilling process in which he captures the scent of an entity, human, animal, vegetable, or mineral, by draping them for several hours in a waxed cloth also fictionalizes issues of embodiment and knowledge. His inability to discriminate between his diverse raw materials, treating flowers and pieces of wood in essentially the same way as animals and humans, points to his outrageous lack of empathy. It also therefore constitutes a critique of distanced and instrumental ways of knowing, using the bodies of others with no sense of connection to them, perhaps even an implicit argument for "an epistemology arising out of an experience of continuity and relation."[75]

More generally, if it can be said that (in Stacy Alaimo's words) "the openness of the 'subject' to transformation by the 'object' of knowledge discourages the presumption of mastery and domination," and that "by emphasizing the subject in the object, feminist epistemologies radically reconceptualize the very category of nature," then magically real images that endow normally inanimate objects with movement or other magical properties can be said to share in that revisionist agenda, although they are not necessarily overtly feminist in orientation.[76] Recall in this context Melquíades's idea that things have a life of their own, and the various images that actualize that idea: flying carpets, trails of blood, and a pot that moves across a table in *One Hundred Years of Solitude;* the water that responds to the light switch in García Márquez's story "Light Is Like Water"; glass that breaks in response to Oskar's voice in *The Tin Drum;* a womb and a breast that traverse a lake and the sky in *The White Hotel;* a spiritualist table that moves in *The House of the Spirits;* a mirror and a cake that bear the image of a dead baby's hands in *Beloved;* a mysterious shiny artifact that fuses and unfuses in *Distant Relations;* Saleem's grandfather's blood that freezes into rubies in *Midnight's Children.*

Images of volitional objects such as these, as well as the extraordinary bodies in magical realism, engage some of the issues involved in recent feminist investigations of corporality and the production of meaning. Vicki Kirby's idea about "an inseparability between representation and substance that rewrites causality" seems to describe not only the way in which objects take on active properties, their substance representing an idea or an entity, but also the way in which the irreducible elements in magical realism often disrupt our habitual notions of cause and effect, many of them associated with bodies or objects that behave in surprising ways. With respect to the notion of representation and substance, recall how Grenouille is able to represent himself in stunningly different ways with his efficacious and varying scents, or how

Tita's body "represents" her love for Pedro by spontaneously generating breast milk for his—but not her—daughter. For Caridad, in *So Far from God,* as she is beginning to learn to be a curandera from doña Felicia, her power to cure, which joins with her magical powers of clairvoyance, to confirm her vocation as sage and healer, is centered in her own body: "Life became a rhythm of scented baths, tea remedies, rubdowns, and general good feeling for Caridad. Her body, already externally repaired from the mutilation it had undergone, now was slowly restored internally by the psychic attentiveness she received from her teacher and which she learned to give to herself" (63). With regard to the issue of causality, recall how Colonel Aureliano predicts his father's death, and Melquíades miraculously prewrites the history of Macondo from within it, how the numerous revenants of various kinds (in *Beloved, Pedro Páramo, Ironweed,* and *So Far from God,* among others) rewrite linear chronology, and, most especially, how Lisa's pains magically prefigure the manner of her death.

Likewise, Vicki Kirby's related proposition that "the body is unstable—a shifting scene of inscription that both writes and is written—a scenario where the subject takes itself as its own object, and where, for example, an image could be said to rewrite the image-maker in a movement of production that disrupts the temporal determination of what comes first" recalls a number of magical realist scenarios that destabilize the division between subject and object and disrupt our habitual sense of temporal progression.[77] Consuelo and Aura are unstable bodies that both write their own desires and are rewritten by their past and Mexico's history. Felipe depicts Aura's image for us and is in turn reconfigured by that vision. Experiencing her first as a body, subsequently through that body his ideas about what came first are changed: he thinks he is simply answering an advertisement, a first, when he is really returning to another kind of first in the distant past, his love for the young Consuelo. Thus Felipe as subject takes himself as his own object and the image rewrites the image maker. (His use of the second-person form of address when speaking of himself can be seen as a linguistic encoding of this scenario.) That sense is actualized again in *Distant Relations* when the anonymous narrator who has just witnessed Branly's parallel ghost seems to acquire one of his own; he becomes a subject who now takes himself as his own object, and to underline that switch, Branly calls him Fuentes and Lucie calls him Carlos. The way in which the image of Beloved Sethe has carried around in her mind for years materializes and becomes active, changing

Sethe and reinscribing the past on the present is another example of an image rewriting the image maker and disrupting the temporal determination of what comes first. The malleability of magical realist bodies, together with their historical inscriptibility, and the way that objects can take on a life of their own, calls into question the "common understanding of materiality as a rock-solid 'something'" that is a grounding against which representational practices are measured, eroding the traditional separation between objects and subjects.[78]

The Female Body of Writing

In magical realism as in much earlier literature, the use of the female body as a muse persists: in other words, literary powers are often associated with that body, and the association is frequently underlined by magical occurrences. This kind of inspiration resembles the voice appropriation that we examined in Chapter 4 in connection with "primitive" or traditional cultures and narrative traditions as they appear in both the subjects and the defocalized narrative mode of magical realism. Gérard de Nerval's *Aurélia,* among countless other tales, prefigures these contemporary examples of the female narrative enabler. The narrator describes his journey to a realm of ancient inhabitants who seem to him "like a primitive and celestial family," and as "an expansion of dreams into real life" ("l'épanchement du songe dans la vie réelle").[79] This journey is preceded and implicitly fueled by a deep frustrated love and a doubling of the female body. Before he sets out, the two women in his life benevolently cooperate with each other, the second one softening the original beloved's heart toward him, so that he "thought to see the past pardoned; the divine accent of pity gave an inexpressible value to the simple words that she addressed to me" (294). In addition to the Petrarchan and Dantesque figures of Laura and Beatrice, the magical figure of a talking bird in whom the narrator sees the soul of an ancestor ("mon aïeul") also presides over the text. Both female spirit and magical cosmic power guide this precursor of magical realist journeys.

Moving closer to the present, *The Tin Drum* again provides a metafictional image that anticipates the practice of its successors. Oskar asks his friend Bruno to buy him "a ream of virgin paper." Bruno asks if he means "white" paper, but Oskar tells us, "I stuck to 'virgin,'" and when Bruno returns he reports, "That was the right word you told me. I asked for virgin paper and the salesgirl blushed like mad before getting it.' "[80] That mad blush tints the paper on which Oskar writes and we read.[81] Perhaps the progression in magical realism's female mode could be measured in the distance between this virgin paper inscribed with a male pen and the copies of *The House of the Spirits* a young mother reportedly smuggled into Chile among her newborn baby's diapers.[82] That distance between virgin paper and proximity to diapers encompasses the development of a female strain in magical realism that is often grounded in domestic and curative magic.

The Tin Drum contains another striking and even more empowered metafictional image of female magically real narrative: a female marine shaman whose magic survives transplantation from the ocean. Oskar first sees this woman, a ship's figurehead, which is the pride of the museum's collection, when he accompanies his friend Herbert on his job as museum guard, and he ends up witnessing its magical powers. The sirenlike sculpture, which used to lure mariners to their deaths, is an emblem of magical art, and her sculptor was suitably punished for his audacity: like Paz's wave who is finally chopped up into ice, his model was burned as a witch, and "they chopped off both his gifted hands to prevent him from ever again transforming witches into figureheads" (187).

The epithets of "Niobe" and "the green kitten" that the figurehead attracts are verbal equivalents of the actual attempts to defuse her magic, for they both castrate the powerful female, softening and weakening her. The image of the kitten acts directly, that of Niobe allusively. (Niobe is usually portrayed weeping, because her beloved children have been killed as a result of her boasting about them.) But the strategy is ineffectual. As if she were affirming a magical female power, the figurehead continues to slay men, even from her marginalized post in the maritime museum. The official news media cast doubt on this magical narrative tradition: "The newspapers devoted special columns to their readers' opinions on the 'Niobe case.' The city government spoke of untimely superstition and said it had no intention whatsoever of taking precipitate action before definite proof was provided that something sinister and supernatural had actually occurred" (189). But Grass's narrative, taking off from all of the previous ones, recasts and continues the legend, incorporating both the realism of the news media and the magic of the superstitions, so that the integrity of each discourse is at once preserved and undermined. Oskar has inherited something akin to the figurehead's magical skills in his drumming ability, and the one time Oskar is not with Herbert, protecting him by providing a link to this powerful female magic with that drumming, Herbert, who had been badmouthing Niobe's proportions, is found hanging dead from her breast, the most recent victim of her magical powers.

Fuentes's career is instructive again in this context. Fuentes, whose writings have frequently transmitted female narrative powers, invokes a female precursor in an essay on Jane Austen and Emily Brontë in which he associates the decolonizing force of female and Third World writing. Fuentes claims that "it is hard for a Mexican macho to admit that he was led into the knowledge of literature and society by two women. But the fact is that the kidnapping of the logos by Western culture first became apparent to me when, in my early teens, I read Jane Austen." For Fuentes, however, Austen herself is "an example of a writer in harmony with the predominant values of her society, . . . the novelist of means in a society of means." (A feminist reading might argue with that assumption of harmony, but from a socioeconomic point of view Fuentes is not entirely incorrect.) It is Brontë, however, the other woman in Fuentes's literary past, who helps him to discover his "own complicated experience as a writer from a marginal culture traveling the paths of the central culture." Through this "outcast within the center, the visionary writer," he understood "the other possibility of that Western culture," which was the possibility of "a literature not of linear progression but of circles and simultaneities, capable of receiving the eccentric contributions of our total humanity," including, I would suggest, an openness to the alternative realities of magical realism.[83]

This search for a female narrative power continues into *Constancia and Other Stories for Virgins,* as the narrator ends the title story urging the Salvadorean family in his basement to garden and make pottery with him, both often women's occupations, and especially so in the milieu in which the story is set. With his title in mind, we might ask why Fuentes is still writing stories for virgins; there are hardly any left. In addition to noting the continuing association of writing and virgins that Bruno encountered on his paper buying errand, we can also wonder what writerly fantasy it fulfills for Fuentes as a prominent magical realist. Is it the one the Brooke Shields character in Louis Malle's film *Pretty Baby* represents: the prepubescent prostitute who commands a high price in the bordello because she is a virgin? Perhaps. Or perhaps it is a general nostalgia for an earlier era, part of Fuentes's continuing fascination with history. But there may also be a metatextual "aura" here, because in these stories Fuentes seems to reconstitute his more virginal writing self from *Aura* and *Where the Air Is Clear,* the one who needs the aid of a female narrative power to break through the realistic tradition. So the stories may be dedicated to that virgin as well.

In surveying Fuentes's career, starting from the powerful and destructive witches in *Where the Air Is Clear, Aura,* and *Holy Place,* we arrive at the female body in "La Desdichada" (another of the stories in *Constancia*), which is emptied of life but still serving male fantasies. Imagine this shop window dummy as the paradigmatic body through which surrealist and early magical realist texts are focalized, a female as a bridge to the beyond. She functions as the other that permits male writers to reach the world of the second reality, the subaltern whose liminal power and wisdom they wish to appropriate. In Taussig's terms, she is the poor shaman that provides the rulers with magic. Her masters dress her (more or less), but they cannot seem to invest her with a life, a destiny. Her powers have been used up. She is a surrealistic dummy that has outlived its time, a mannequin that should remain in the shop. For Fuentes, perhaps, she has become an empty shell, because he has long ago reached the world of the second reality in his earlier fiction and has more recently entered the historically oriented realm of the fathers in which he has no need of a magical female muse. In his next novel, *The Campaign,* he enters the male domain of colonial revolutionaries and creates a major confrontation between father and son in the Argentine pampas.

Shortly before this gender shift, Fuentes assumes the powers of Joycean verbal display in *Christopher Unborn,* a historical fantasy with a hybrid gender. The narrator lives in the womb, encompassed by the female body, but he begins to tell his interuterine story as a sperm, locating his origin in the company of "my true grandfathers and great-greats."[84] So that although the novel as a whole combines male and female narrative spaces, the narrative voice is male. That voice encompasses the imaginary country of Pacifica: "come with us to the New World of Pacifica, . . . end your foolish fallacious fascistic fascination with the Atlantic world."[85] Both referent and sign are global American villages, newly constructed mestizo Yoknapatawpha counties of which Carlos Fuentes, like Faulkner before him, is sole owner and proprietor. And like the linguistic magic that causes words to become things, the imaginative pyrotechnical Spanglish that constructs the hybrid metropoli of "Kafkapulco" and "Makesicko Seedy" with its "Car Answer" (Carranza) and "Frank Wood" (Francisco Madero) Streets, endows the idea of Pacifica with verbal flesh.

The imaginary inter-American cooperation that Fuentes envisions in *Christopher Unborn* is actualized when a scene from Morrison's *Song of Solomon* virtually duplicates one in *Aura*. Both novels belong to a tradition with a past that stretches back to Homer, in which the female strain in magical realism is a recent arrival; it includes a witchly seductress who may also be a narrator or a muse with animal familiars, and who inhabits a mysterious house, draws men into her domain, and suffers or effects bodily transformations or mutilations.[86] (It is of course possible that, given the dates of the two novels, 1962 and 1977, *Aura* influenced *Song of Solomon;* but I think it far more likely that their affinities belong to tradition rather than influence.) Milkman Dead entering Circe's house in *Song of Solomon* recalls Felipe entering Consuelo's on the appropriately named Donceles Street—a magical Maiden Lane: the door that "swings open with a sigh" at his touch, the "golden-eyed" dogs he sees at first, the stairs, the old woman, "so old she was colorless," who tells him almost in Consuelo's words, " 'I knew one day you would come back,' " to whom "there was no way for him to resist climbing," who "tightened her arms around him," her "dry bony hands like steel springs rubbing his back," her "floppy mouth babbling into his vest," all correspond closely to Felipe's experiences of Consuelo and her house.[87] In very similar fashion, Felipe enters Consuelo's house when the door with its "knocker, that copper head of a dog . . . opens at the first light push of your fingers," where, after "touching her withered breasts," he stops "kissing those fleshless lips," and finally plunges his face, his "open eyes, into Consuelo's silver-white hair" (*Aura*, 145), hair that, like Circe's "nose, chin, cheekbones, forehead, neck," which had "surrendered their identity to the pleats and crochetwork of skin committed to constant change" (*Song of Solomon*, 245), seems to grow out of and be ready to change back into Aura's black hair—both women's bodies involved in a continual process of magical aging and regeneration.

A brief comparison of *Distant Relations* and *Beloved* further characterizes this aspect of magical realism, which enlists traditionally female narrative power—woman as muse—even in texts by men. It imagines part of the "bold cultural conversation" that José David Saldívar claims Morrison had with the Caribbean and Latin American tradition of magical realism.[88] But first we must note Fuentes's and Morrison's very different voices and modes. They demonstrate the diversity within magical realism.[89] In Fuentes, if we listen carefully, we can discern a female communal spirit occasionally transfiguring a male voice, in a conceptual and symbolic text, in which people serve largely to illustrate cultural patterns. In Morrison, we detect a strength traditionally associated with maleness integrated into a strong female voice, in a text where feeling predominates, and people are valued first as individuals but also as symbols of historical processes.

An initial similarity between *Distant Relations* and *Beloved* concerns time and history. Both Fuentes and Morrison re-envision established historical patterns: Fuentes reverses the traditional direction of literary influence by locating Caribbean writers who wrote in French at the heart of his Parisian story; Morrison endows a former slave woman with the right to violent action. In *Distant Relations* the "angel" old Heredia attempts to make, and which ends up as two joined fetuses floating dead in a pool, represents the danger of ignoring history. Heredia's monstrous angel suggests that live beings must exist in time, not in a perfect circle of eternity. *Beloved*'s return as a ghost who disturbs Sethe's present life also asserts the need to exist within temporal flow by confronting the personal and historical past rather than escaping from it within the comforting walled off space of an eternal present, as 124 Bluestone Road had nearly become for her. The woman in white who appears and disconcerts Branly at the Clos de Renards refuses to stay comfortably in the painting that depicts her or in Branly's nostalgic memories and stories about her, and Lucie haunts the Fuentes narrator at the end of the novel, refusing to stay reassuringly in the text he has co-created about her. Thus both texts contain circulating ghosts that make the past present and force the central characters to deal with it. Each novel comprises three generations and underlines the idea of meaningful inheritance, but with some gender differences: Fuentes's male hierarchical power is transmitted from Old Heredia, through Hugo Heredia, to Hugo's son Victor, who mistreats the servants of the more benevolent Branly and becomes friends with Heredia's son André. This kind of power is symbolized negatively by the remains of theocratic Aztec and aristocratic French culture, the Pyramids at Xochicalco, and the Clos des Renards on the outskirts of Paris. More benevolent alternatives are Branly's outstretched hand and this text that joins poetic fragments and invented stories. Morrison's female line of descent runs from Baby Suggs through Sethe to Denver and Beloved, who, like Victor and André, also fight and befriend each other. It is characterized by both rage and desperate love: by Sethe's estrangement from and subsequent reunion with Baby Suggs, and, especially, by her murder of and ultimate reconciliation with Beloved, as well as by the stories and songs they all share.

The ethereal intellectual connections in *Distant Relations* contrast with the more fleshly blood and birth lines of *Beloved,* symbolized by a reappearing red heart and birthing water.[90] For example, Morrison's novel is less intertextually constructed than *Distant Relations.* It relies more on strong feeling in the vernacular and on "just that eternal, private conversation that takes place between women and their tasks" than on overt references to publicly printed images in delicate and erudite poetic language (172). Fuentes's narrator inherits those kinds of images: he muses as he strolls around Paris, "I know that on this balcony Musset took the sun as a respite from the paleness of the secluded Princess Belgiojoso, and that an anguished, tormented Gérard de Nerval hurried along this wet alleyway, and that from that bridge, at the very moment Nerval was writing 'El desdichado,' Cesar Vallejo was gazing at his reflection in the rushing waters; on the Boulevard La Tour-Maubourg I will hear the voice of Pablo Neruda; on the Rue de Longchamp, that of Octavio Paz."[91] Even so, *Beloved* is built with stones from the ruins of the literary past, though usually less specifically invoked; the most striking allusion is to *Uncle Tom's Cabin,* given the central murderous act of Sethe, which recalls Eliza's escape with Harry, and there are others as well, including church services ("Denver could not hear the lead prayer—only the earnest syllables of agreement that backed it: Yes, yes, yes, oh yes. Hear me. Hear me. Do it, Maker, do it. Yes" [358]—also, perhaps, an overwriting of Molly Bloom's famous last word?), the Bible (Romans 9:25), from which the epigraph is taken ("I will call them my people, which were not my people; and her beloved, which was not beloved"), and folk tales of succubi, among other things.[92] Along these lines, both *Distant Relations* and *Beloved* include songs from childhood. In Fuentes there are the words of an actual French folk ballad about a clear fountain, in Morrison the song Sethe made up for her children; Beloved's recognition of that song proves she is Sethe's daughter because "Nobody knows that song but me and my children" (176). In order for it to remain their secret, we do not hear its words, a fact that confirms once again the difference between Fuentes's more public male discourse and Morrison's more private female mode.

Like the images of flight we examined in *The Kingdom of This World, The Satanic Verses,* and *The Book of Laughter and Forgetting,* as if to symbolize the defocalized narrative program of magical realism, water images (which are frequently associated with a female sensibility) circulate through both novels.[93] In *Distant Relations,* we reread the ballad about the clear fountain, we hear about the section of Mexico City where the streets are named for rivers, and "the dark quiet ocean along the sandy shores of Veracruz, where the exhausted Mediterranean flings itself on the beach" (103); we see the Seine in Paris and a bubbling stream in Xochicalco; and we watch the Automobile Club's pool in Paris turn into a tropical jungle. Each different narrator's story is characterized as "one more river in this hydrograph we have been tracing" (163). In *Beloved,* we witness "a fully dressed woman [who] walked out of the water"—instead of the miracle of a man who walked on top of it (50); we watch Sethe urinate profusely on seeing Beloved approach her house; we see the stream in back of that house where Beloved's footprints "come and go, come and go" (275); we hear about a slave ship in which "if we had more to drink we could make tears," where "storms rock us and mix the men into the women and the women into the men" (210–11). Finally, in the moment when women's voices save Sethe from herself, "the voices of women searched for the right combination, . . . building voice upon voice until they found it, and when they did it was a wave of sound wide enough to sound deep water and knock the pods off chestnut trees. It broke over Sethe and she trembled like the baptized in its wash" (261). Fuentes's waters represent the currents of literary tradition and verbal intertwining that his novel navigates, as well as congress between old and new worlds, while Morrison's waters symbolize a woman's heritage, the life of birthing and nursing that enables the flesh and spirit to survive, and the female verbal stream that portrays and protects it.

A final contrast turns into another connecting link. Perhaps because of the feminocentric orientation of *Beloved,* or perhaps because of more general cultural differences, overt references to spiritual power are more positive in *Beloved* than in *Distant Relations:* Old Heredia is a black witch, with the Satanic individual project of creating a self-sufficient angel by combining two boys in the city; in *Beloved,* Baby Suggs is a white one, as it were, a benevolent priestess who undertakes the God-fearing communal project of saving souls by preaching in the forest. Beyond those magicians in the stories, both novels strike a metafictional chord, celebrating the magic of stories. In *Distant*

Relations we have seen how the emotionally warm scene of the narration between Branly and Fuentes is associated with the imagery of extended hands, whose verbal equivalents are both the poems from the past Fuentes uses in the text and the loose narrative ends he leaves as handles for readers to grasp the story and imagine its endings. And in *Beloved* as well, the healing power of narration is celebrated in the lyrical passages where Sethe and Denver and Beloved speak their own histories, and, as in *Distant Relations,* the confusingly intertwined stories invite the reader's active participation. In both novels, voices come from the margins to the center. Fuentes (who appears in his own persona at the end of the novel) is the Latin American narrator in Paris, revealing the voices of Latin American poets echoing through Paris and changing its literary traditions, just as the Latin American rain forest takes over the French automobile club. Morrison symbolically moves the strong voice of Baby Suggs, holy, who preached in the marginalized forest, into town, if only for a moment, when the voices of the women save Sethe from another murder and another incarceration.

Finally, Miguel Angel Asturias's novel *Mulata* occupies an interesting and pivotal position in this context of female magically real bodies. In portraying the Mulata as sexually powerful and able to literally possess men, it confirms the idea that the female body and magic are allied, and in so doing also perpetuates the tradition of male fantasies and fears regarding female sexuality; according to Diane Marting, "in this novel sexual woman's power destroys rather than nourishes."[94] Asturias wrote that in portraying this woman he was imbuing her with a cosmically mysterious dimension: "behind an ordinary woman, a married mulatto woman, a 'Mrs. Jane Doe,' is hidden a force belonging to the lunar woman, a woman who in her conjugal relations acts like the moon with the sun."[95] Such a statement of course, and a myriad others like it, commodifies and worships in one gesture. However, despite the various stereotypes of powerful and dangerous women he creates, Marting points out, Asturias does not present a rejection of women in the figure of the Mulata: for "the death and destruction she causes . . . were sacred in Mayan culture and thus are respected in Asturias' text." Despite her cruel hedonism, the Mulata "should also be read as a heroic, culture-saving figure because she destroys life," in order to make way for new life in the endless cycles of transformation sacred to the Mayas.[96] While Marting does not deal with magical realism specifically, her argument about Asturias's respect for the forces that he has portrayed women as magically embodying confirms the presence of a strong female element in this early, seminal magical realist text. Although there is a great distance between Asturias and Morrison, Esquivel, Darrieussecq, and other contemporary women authors, the cosmically powerful and magical aura associated with the female body, and, often, with writing itself in magical realism, unites them.

Cooking

In *Midnight's Children,* the repeated comparisons of Saleem's narration to the process of cooking connect the narrative process in Rushdie's novel to a traditionally female domain. Even more specifically, Saleem's powers of narrative invention are rooted in the cooking skills he inherits from the women in his household. The power of this active female creativity magically transforms and literally preserves raw personal and historical events: "Mary Pereira took the time to prepare, for the benefit of their visitors, some of the finest and most delicate mango pickles, lime chutneys, and cucumber kasundies in the world. . . . Amina began to feel the emotions of other people's food seeping into her—because Reverend Mother doled out the curries and meatballs of intransigence, dishes imbued with the personality of their creator" (164).[97] Saleem's Aunt Alia took a particular pleasure in cooking, which "she had, during the lonely madness of the years, raised to the level of an art-form: the impregnation of food with emotions. . . . While we lived in her Guru Mandir mansion, she fed us the birianis of dissension and the nargisi koftas of discord; and little by little, even the harmonies of my parents' autumnal love went out of tune" (395). Like Reverend Mother's curries, Saleem's narrative preservation, his "chutnification" of history (which follows in its specific form that of his teacher, Mary Pereira) is imbued with the intransigence of his particular personality and emotions, creating anything but an objective account of the events he witnesses (again achieving the rapprochement of subject and object that characterizes recent theories of female epistemology). So much so that when he makes an occasional historical error, he lets it stand: "Rereading my work, I have discovered an error in chronology. The assassination of Mahatma Gandhi occurs, in these pages, on the wrong date. But I cannot say, now, what the actual sequence of events might have been; in my India, Gandhi will continue to die at the wrong time" (198). That analogy of cooking with the fictionalizing of history, like the cosmic connections present in magically real houses, imbricates female domesticity into the wider world.

In her enormously popular film and novel, *Like Water for Chocolate,* Laura Esquivel sets this same female magic of emotionally flavored food at the heart of the story. Here it is clear that the irreducible elements in this explicitly feminist novel are enlisted in the service of female desire and power. Forbidden to marry her beloved, Pedro, because of the tradition that dictates that the youngest daughter must remain unmarried (and hence childless) in order to care for her aging mother, Tita weeps as she bakes her sister and Pedro's wedding cake. Her tears, which overflow into the cake, seem likely to be the cause when all the wedding guests cry and regurgitate the cake. And soon, Tita cooks quail in a sauce made from the rose petals of a bouquet that Pedro has given her. The dish communicates her forbidden feelings of love to Pedro, to whom it tastes like "the pleasure of the gods."[98]

This particular magic is not just individual but also, as in the wedding cake episode, communal. Tita's rebellious sister Gertrudis, who eventually becomes a revolutionary general, on eating the rose petal dish, experiences a sympathetic erotic upheaval: "it seemed that the food that she was eating produced in her an aphrodisiac effect since she began to feel an intense heat invade her thighs."[99] She is so hot that when she tries to take a shower her body evaporates the water and in an instance of magical spontaneous combustion her literally smoldering passion causes the wooden bath house to catch on fire. As she exits, nude, a soldier whose path she has crossed earlier in town (and whom she will marry) smells the odor of roses, arrives on his horse, and carries her off nude, as they make passionate love.

Once again, magic is instrumental in achieving the expression of suppressed female desire and power. Near the end of the novel, when Tita cooks *chiles en nogada* joyfully for her niece's wedding (which she explicitly contrasts with the earlier sad occasion of her sister's wedding to Pedro), they provoke positive erotic upheavals in all the wedding guests. One might say that Tita, heretofore silenced by her mother's adherence to a stifling tradition, has found her voice. The magic associated with that discovery underlines the difficulty involved in such a breakthrough. With reference to the rose-petal sauce incident, the narrator comments that "it seemed they had discovered a new system of communication in which Tita was the transmitter, Pedro the receiver, and Gertrudis the fortunate one through which the singular sexual

message was passed, by way of the food."[100] Because it discursively transforms idea into object, Tita's cooking magic constitutes a variation on the
linguistic magic that blurs the limit between words and the world. Interestingly enough, in this context of the magical properties of food, in addition
to her clairvoyance and healing powers, La Loca in *So Far from God* also has
a reputation as an excellent cook.

Somewhat similar to Tita, whose recipes precede each chapter of the
book, Padma, within the narrative chutnification in *Midnight's Children,*
achieves her love magic through her cooking. Padma is a muse who is tied
not to celestial inspiration but to the body and eating, "named after the lotus
goddess, whose most common appellation amongst village folk is 'The One
Who Possesses Dung'" (21). Immediately following this characterization,
Saleem's narrating situation is compared to Scheherazade's, an allusion that
begins with a reference to spicing: "In the renewed silence, I return to sheets
of paper which smell just a little of turmeric, ready and willing to put out
of its misery a narrative which I left yesterday hanging in mid-air—just as
Scheherazade, depending for her very survival on leaving Prince Shahryar
eaten up by curiosity, used to do night after night!" (21–22). (Recalling *The
Tin Drum,* we seem to have progressed in thirty years from the virgin to the
spicy page.) The allusion to Scheherazade further confirms the female narrative power on which the novel draws. Even though, as Patrick McGee has
pointed out, "Padma, the dung-lotus who associates writing with shitting,
is the subaltern whom Saleem cannot speak for," Padma's irreverent stance
is encoded in the text and she could be seen as representing something like
a protofeminist critique of patriarchal discourse from within—to the extent
that such a maneuver is possible.[101] Padma presiding over the scene of narrative invention recalls the situation of a Hindu temple as a nexus of power
and authority of all kinds presided over by a particular deity. In that context,
the novel forms a record of the political, economic, and emotional lives of
its devotees, and an offering to the local goddess.

For all her subalternity, Padma is a potent partner; she provides the sexualized side of this narrative impulse, and a skeptical view of the often lionized
powers of verbal invention, for, as Saleem admits, she is sorely tried "by the
futility of her midnight attempts at resuscitating my 'other pencil,' the useless
cucumber hidden in my pants" (141). And she has her ventriloquizing say as
well, for shortly after we hear about her association with dung, she becomes
enraged at Saleem's "remarks about her name," asking him, "What do you

know, city boy," declaring that in her village "there is no shame to being named for the Dung Goddess," and requiring him to "write at once that you are wrong, completely," and so he inserts "a brief paean to Dung" (30). Mrs. Gandhi, the "black widow," is the other, the destructive, side of this female force, which activates Saleem's pen (if not his other pencil). The combination of the two forces, like the two sides of Durga and the two poles of magic and realism, ridden and guided by Saleem, drives the narrative forward.

In *Midnight's Children,* then, the status and stature of women suggest their fertile narrative power, which is encoded obsessively in the text by the number of allusions to Scheherazade—a nervous profusion of flowery offerings, nearly obscuring the image of this goddess of postmodern narrative invention? So numerous are these allusions that Scheherazade becomes almost too good a narrative mother, not only nurturing the novel with stories and images but also nearly smothering it with her presence. But the offerings seem to work, for Saleem begins to receive the miraculous narrative gift of voices in his head as he watches his own mother, Amina, in the bathroom (an entirely sacrilegious image of a mother-goddess in a niche?), first pleasuring herself and then undressing. To make the connection between mother and narrative even more explicit, in a comic enactment of the sexual activity his mother is currently lacking, the pajama cord Saleem stuffs up his nose to stop its dripping causes the sneeze he stifles and its repressed force initiates the explosion of midnight's children's voices in his head. Even before that, Amina's father "seemed to be getting shorter with the passing years; while Reverend Mother [like this rich and copious narrative] had grown so wide that armchairs, though soft, groaned beneath her weight" (163). Soon thereafter, Saleem reluctantly mounts Evie Burns's bike, she gives him a shove, he does not know how to brake, and smash, "circus-ring accident had completed what washing-chest calamity had begun, and they [midnight's children] were there in my head" (223). Without this infusion of the wild energy of a female biker, combined with the erotic aura of maternally centered pleasure, this tale might never have been born: "if Evie had not come to live amongst us, my story might never have progressed beyond tourism-in-a-clocktower and cheating in class" (216). García Márquez has said of Ursula Buendía that "she was supposed to die before the civil war, when she was nearly a hundred years old. But I discovered that if she were to die, the book would crumble. When she does die, the book already has so much steam that it doesn't matter what happens afterwards."[102] A female narrative power has set it on its way.[103]

Territorial Magic

Several magical realist fictions by women, which forge links between bodies, lands, and language, seem to exemplify the new structure of feminist oppositional consciousness Chela Sandoval proposes as a topography (rather than a typology) tied to specific regions, thereby circling back to Carpentier's early territorially oriented idea of the marvelous real.[104] Like Lynn Andrews's popular autobiographical fiction, Louise Erdrich's work unites a sense of spirit-oriented powers, storytelling within native and Christian traditions, and the land.[105] Furthermore, in articulating the mixture of traditions that characterizes her Chippewa novels, Erdrich creates scenes that emphasize the interchange between worlds. One example of strong human-natural connection and the intersection of two worlds is the near-magical scene near the end of *Tracks* in which Fleur's extraordinary powers seem to topple an entire section of forest, crushing loggers and their equipment but leaving what seems like a charmed circle around her cabin. She triumphs over the forces of modernization she wishes to resist temporarily, but only temporarily, and we wonder whether the cause is magical or natural—her magical powers or just an unusually strong gust of wind. We hear about this from Nanapush, who himself has strong magical connections to the land, as evidenced by the time he guides Eli on a snowy hunt from miles away. Each event can be given either a magical or a rational interpretation.

As these examples suggest, the irreducible elements in Erdrich's *Tracks* are few and questionable, so that I would situate the novel on the fringes of magical realism. Perhaps the only clear example is the incident in which Fleur's tracks are described as changing from human to bear as she moves farther into the woods, picturing the merging of human and natural worlds.[106] And even these are reported by the unreliable Pauline, as are most of the other examples.[107] However, Erdrich always adds a physical detail to corroborate Pauline's visions. At one point, a statue of the Virgin unlocks the trance of a sexually traumatized girl. The description of the way "the girl's face tipped up, slack, less human than the small statue, who offered Her blooded palm" suggests the presence of the extraordinary within the ordinary, which it highlights as strange.[108] The narrator, Pauline, reports of herself and the statue "our gazes were locked now," a statement that, although not a strictly magical event, again suggests the interchange between ordinary human and extraordinary realms, as does Pauline's statement that "the hardened tears that lay scattered at Her feet" resembled "ordinary pebbles of frozen quartz, the kind that children collect and save." That interchange continues to build strength, when we hear how Pauline put the tears in her pocket, so that by the time she reaches her destination "the only proof [of the miraculous encounter] was the damp cloth that soon dried, and my memory, which sharpened on the knowledge" (95). Even though Pauline's deluded state compromises her reliability, her report of the damp cloth and the realistic detail of how it dried argues in favor of the miracle. Similarly, Pauline's claim that she flew into a tree—"twirling dizzily, my wings raked the air, and I rose in three powerful beats and saw what lay below"—gains credibility by the fact that she reports that Bernadette told her that everyone "was amazed that I could climb there, as the trunk was smooth for seven feet and there were no hand-or footholds of any sort" (68).[109]

The importation of Catholicism to the New World, in conjunction with a sensitivity to the land, also structures the magic in Cristina García's *Dreaming in Cuban.* Near the beginning of the novel Celia del Pino's dead husband, Jorge, is described as coming toward her: "At the far end of the sky, where daylight begins, a dense radiance like a shooting star breaks forth. It weakens as it advances, as its outline takes shape in the ether. Her husband emerges from the light and comes toward her, taller than the palms, walking on water in his white summer suit and Panama hat. . . . His blue eyes are like lasers in the night. The beams bounce off his fingernails, five hard blue shields."[110] Just before Jorge appears, Celia has perceived three fishing boats on the horizon, which are named the Niña, the Pinta, and the Santa María. It is almost as if the miracle has been engendered by combining the discourses of history embodied in those three boats and the searchlights (scanning for illegal emigrants) with the visual language of popular religious and commercial culture represented by the blue light and hard colored fingernails. As in other instances, the narrative magic highlights amazing or horrific historical realities—in this instance the discovery and subsequent conquest of America and the desperate attempts at immigration that have eventually resulted from it. But because it can be imagined as a hyperrealistically enhanced video image, it also uses and therefore underlines the extraordinary qualities of contemporary virtual reality.

So Far from God also uses the resources of narrative magic to endow women with extraordinary perceptual powers, which, although they are focused more than Erdrich's on the social world, are undergirded by connections with the land and animals and strongly grounded in a particular locality. Caridad the clairvoyant who "often fell into semiconscious trances and communicated with spirit guides as a way of communicating messages to clients" (119) chooses to live in a trailer house on the outskirts of town, where she keeps a horse named Corazón (heart) who becomes her best friend, and has a dream in which she sees a herd of galloping horses and "felt like I was one of them" (49). In part as a result of her felt affinity with the natural process of sunrise, she stays for a year in a cave kept warm by only a fire and animal skins—a "spartan mountain survival alone" that "seems incredible to everyone": "when she awoke to a delicate scar in the horizon that gradually bled into day and saw the sun then raise itself like a king from its throne over the distant peaks, Caridad only knew that she wanted to stay there and be the lone witness to that miracle every dawn" (89). Caridad finally disappears with a friend (but without a trace) off the edge of the mesa of Acoma Pueblo, and we hear that "there were no morbid remains of splintered bodies tossed to the ground, down, down, like bad pottery or glass. . . . Just the spirit deity Tsichtinako calling loudly with a voice like wind, guiding the two women back, not out toward the sun's rays or up to the clouds but down, deep within the soft moist dark earth" (211).[111] Unlike Caridad, her little sister La Loca mainly stays around the house, but she too has a strong affinity with the natural world. The process of receiving the news of Esperanza's death from La Llorona includes her going outside and circling a cottonwood tree. (Furthermore, "everyone knows, if you want to find La Llorona, go hang out down by the rio, or its nearest equivalent, especially when no one else is around" [165].) Other evidence of Loca's connection to nature include her caring for the family's animals, her ability as a horsewoman ("she had trained all the horses since she was tall enough to climb up and ride on her own"), her understanding of a peacock whom she attempts to teach to talk but about whom she concludes that it "was just not an imitator," and her fondness for the acequia in all its seasonal variety, which was "her own place to be": "she knew its quiet nature in summer, its coolness in spring; and she didn't mind it in winter when the muddy water was frozen most of the time" (151–52).

Like *Woman Warrior, Medicine Woman* by Lynn Andrews is another example of female magical autobiography. And like Erdrich's and Castillo's fiction, it is also strongly territorialized. In narrating her apprenticeship to Agnes Whistling Elk, Andrews is the vehicle for the transfer of power from a female Native American shaman to a white American art dealer and counselor who channels that spirit through a realistic narrative with magical events. Here again, houses are essential carriers of magic spirit. In her "Beverly Hills Wigwam," filled with primitive objects, Andrews begins her inner journey, which ultimately leads her to Agnes's wilderness cabin, where she experiences rituals and emotions that transform her life.[112] Andrews's transition from primitivist collector to shaman, from cultural cannibal to participant in cosmic mysteries resembles magical realism's transitional narrative space in which reason encounters mystery and realism encounters magic. Its primitivism transforms into its participatory narrative magic.[113] In all of these examples, while connections with ancient or traditional lands are essential, modernizing influences are not entirely demonized. Instead, they are sources of fruitful invention, so that, as we noted in the context of magical realism's primitivizing tendencies, these texts are not only examples of nostalgic primitivism. Andrews's "Beverly Hills Wigwam" is both a joke and not a joke.

Medicine Woman thus provides a mainstream female example of an encounter with a goddesslike figure that resembles those that have been created in so many near-magical or magical realist texts written by men: Celestina and the lady of the temple (from *Terra Nostra*), Consuelo and Aura, Anna and Lisa (from *The White Hotel*), Padma, Parvati, Evie, and Jamila Singer (from *Midnight's Children*), Ursula, Pilar, Petra, and Remedios (From *One Hundred Years of Solitude*). And as in many of them, the female figure is doubled, or tripled, a multiplication that augments her embattled powers: Agnes and Lynn, very old and almost young, indigenous and colonist, rural and urban. Her power comes from an intimate relation to the earth as an expression of mana, the interrelation of all things, which is also double, a practical knowledge of the habits of its creatures, which Lynn learns, and the sense of the earth's power, which Agnes explains. Her explanation also exemplifies the magical realist interchange between two worlds.

> Has it ever occurred to you that the human is teetering between two worlds of reflection? Touch the earth, for the mother is awake. The earth is alive and dreaming. Everything the human can think of has substance. There are no holes in your thoughts. The awake ones, the shamaness can wander to the other side of the universe, beyond even the far-away. Here appears the rainbow door to the backward web of substance. If you invade that world, the beings there can give you any power you want. (160)

Just before this, in the dream-vision in which she "had slipped through a crevice between the worlds," Lynn encounters a male spiritual object of desire, Red Dog, "the katchina man [who] was sitting on the altar looking part animal, part bird, part human, winking at me" (156). She uses the power of which Agnes has spoken to resist him, to steal the magical marriage basket of her personal quest, and return to her self and her world. Her text and the adventure it narrates thus bridge the worlds of tradition and modernity, of concrete reality and the spirits, of realism and magic, and they do so by using a female power closely related to the land in which the adventure takes place.

"La Mystérique"

The incorporation of both female and male ghostly spirits into these texts signals the replenishment and integration of narrative powers. To consider these developments from a feminist perspective suggests that if realism commodified the female body and surrealism fragmented it, magical realism reconstructs it as fascinating text, with the aid of both those earlier systems. Its ghosts are reconstructed ghosts, which seem to retain more flesh than usual, and inhabit particular houses and lands.[114] Perhaps magic serves these women as it has postcolonial literature generally, to facilitate the reappropriation of real and imagined territories, whether bodies, lands, spirits, or discourses.

Finally, the idea of a female fluidity and receptivity as espoused by Luce Irigaray, the sense of "a *sensible transcendental* coming into being through us, of which *we would* be the mediators and bridges," is analogous to the way that many magical realist texts mediate and bridge different worlds and discourses, and especially, of the way they may orchestrate a presence of spirit within concrete reality.[115] Signaling the efforts to integrate the concrete and the spirit in many manifestations of the return of the goddess in contemporary culture, Kate Rigby cites Starhawk's advocacy of a "goddess spirituality that is informed by the insights of physics, mathematics, ecology, and biochemistry, while also acknowledging the provisionality and relativity of the knowledge thereby revealed."[116] If we consider the possibility that the combination of the real and the magical enacted in magical realism represents a female kind of "sensible transcendental," then that component of magical realism's spiritual charge may resemble what Irigaray has called "la mystérique": "how one might refer to what, within a still theological onto-logical perspective is called mystic language or discourse," a type of discourse that she associates with a female mode of being.[117]

This question of "la mystérique" takes us in a different direction from attention to corporality, but it is not unrelated to it; the combination of the two suggests the possible re-emergence of the neoplatonic tradition of sexual love open to the sacred.[118] It is probably too visionary to wonder whether magical realism may be playing a small part in forecasting a major reorganization of modern Western spirituality, one that would return us to that ancient tradition. But if we do entertain that vision for a moment, perhaps we might interpret some of magical realism's houses of fiction as the foundations for postpatriarchal temples of love.[119] As such, they would enshrine a body of knowledge achieved through and by and with the body as well as through the mind, a possibility implied by our considerations of feminist epistemologies of embodied knowledges.[120] That form would reverse the *carpe diem* mode in which men use the scientific facts of mortal decay to seduce women. Here women use the imaginary fictions of immortality to seduce men, as demonstrated, for example, in *Aura* and *Song of Solomon.* Expressed positively in the context of an intercultural feminist program, and reflecting the merging of identities characteristic of magical realism, "cross-cultural and cross racial loving" can take place, through the ability of the self to shift its identities in the activity of "world traveling."[121]

The mystical union of body and soul is not a uniquely female issue, but the sense of recovering lost traditions that permeates much of magical realism allies it with recent feminist efforts aimed at recovering lost figures and traditions within which this kind of union can be envisioned as embodied in a female form, with the "ontological shift" in feminist-oriented theology that imagines divinity as female.[122] Recall in this context that the narrator of Harris's *Tumatumari* seeks his atavistic narrative voice by crawling back into the womb, and that the narrator's journey in *Palace of the Peacock* proceeds toward the Mission of Mariella. To invent a tradition of mystic language within a text, these female magical realist fictions often portray several generations, and stories are passed down from one to the next: Clara, Blanca, and Alba in *The House of the Spirits;* Baby Suggs, Sethe, and Denver in *Beloved;* Abuela Celia, Lourdes, and Pilar in *Dreaming in Cuban.* The female line is interrupted in Erdrich's quartet, but the generational sense remains: in *The Bingo Palace* the mother of the incipient shaman Lipsha Morrissey appears to him with a winning bingo card.[123]

Inheriting some fictional magic from the female narrative forces that drove *One Hundred Years of Solitude,* García Márquez's recent *Love and Other Demons* continues to play—magically—both with the commodified female body and the power of female spirituality. The magic is much less clear here than in *One Hundred Years of Solitude*—almost, we might say, "magical realism lite." The novel centers on a mystical spirit housed in a young female body, which contrasts with male church hierarchy. The fact that the bishop has assigned Padre Delaura to deal with Sierva María because he has plenty of the inspiration that most of his brothers lack suggests that she is something more than a bedeviled victim in need of a cure. Delaura is sensitive to Sierva María's mystical charm and negotiates the boundaries between sacred mysteries and misdirected dogmatism. When the abbess in the convent in which she is staying is terrified by the bloodlike marks on Sierva María's cell walls, Father Delaura chides her: "Just because the water was red didn't mean it had to be blood, and even if it were, it didn't have to be the Devil's work. It would be more correct to think that it was a miracle, and that power belongs to God alone."[124] The abbess sarcastically tells Delaura that she knows that the priests own God. But Delaura's relationship to Sierva María suggests that even if they did, he might be speaking to them through her.

Born to a father with a "mystical vocation," the character of Sierva María serves as a bridge to the beyond, an occasion for the involvement of the previously rather dry and static religious community to experience an embodied and unpredictable sense of holiness in the world. The abbess seems to fear this kind of experience and remarks to Delaura as they cross the garden that it contained "flowers of unreal sizes and colors, and some with unbearable smells." That fear, and the idea that "everything ordinary seemed to her to possess something of the supernatural," suggests that she is cut off from the holy spirit rather than in touch with the sacred magic of the ordinary (111). Once again, Delaura warns the abbess not to be too devil-oriented, because "sometimes we blame the devil for things that we don't understand without realizing that they could be incomprehensible things from God" (111). Characteristically pro-miraculous and anticlerical, García Márquez celebrates ordinary incomprehensibility by portraying Sierva María's strange and supposedly bedeviled state as something positively marvelous. At one point, for example, she "seemed to be dead," but her "eyes glowed with the light of the sea" (112).

Like the pervasive light of mystical experience, Sierva María's presence leaks its magic over the rest of the text. She manifests her delicate power, associated with the natural world, when she appears in a vision to place an invisible branch of gardenias in Delaura's study in the monastery. When the priest opens his eyes, the vision has disappeared, but the library was "saturated by the trace of her gardenias" (122). In a negative version of this principle, everything bad that happens in the convent is attributed to her cursed state. Finally, like Grenouille's outrageous and horrifying perfuming feats, the exaggerated nature of these projections onto Sierva María are a simultaneous fulfillment and satire of these male fantasies that pursue spirit in the form of the female body.

The report of an interview with Laura Esquivel, the author of *Like Water for Chocolate,* confirms a general hunger for a female narrative power in touch with a world of the spirits. The tone of the reporter is alternately worshipful and coyly superior, expressing, like the images of Cortázar's "young lady in Paris" and Harris's woman in the room that "breathed all burning tranquility and passion together," fascination and unease, an inextricable mixture of colonized and colonizer. Even though she is described in this minor reportorial fiction as having "the bemused, faintly bewildered look of an innocent abroad," "the Armani sea parted" for Esquivel; furthermore, she "unflinchingly acknowledges the spiritual underpinnings of modern daily life in her every doe-eyed glance," which is "impossible to resist" and charms an "imperious concierge" into providing incense and roses for the altars she constructs in her room at the Los Angeles Westwood Marquis.[125]

A novella contemporaneous with Esquivel's, A. S. Byatt's *The Conjugal Angel,* is of interest in this context, because it provides a sympathetic post-patriarchal view of female mysticism, the initial description of Mrs. Papagay and Sophie Sheeky playing on bird imagery that suggests a birdlike and shamanistic ability to negotiate different realms: "Lilias Papagay, a few steps ahead, wore wine-dark silk with a flounced train and a hat heavy with darkly gleaming plumage, jet-black, emerald-shot, iridescent dragonfly blue on ultramarine, plump shoulders of headless wings with jaunty tail-feathers, like the little wings that fluttered on the hat or the heels of Hermes in old pictures. Sophy Sheeky wore dove-colored wool."[126] Note the brilliance and darkly colored activity of this Lilias bird as Hermes, the messenger god that travels between different worlds. The birds that characterize Sophie tend to be softer, but here and later we "find a kind of flying Sophie, hovering mildly near the ceiling" (282). At one point, as Sophie looks into a mirror and describes her gift for conjuring spirits, we hear that

> behind her the room was full of rustling, as though it was packed with birds. It was fatigue rushing in her ears, it was white wings she would see if she turned to look. She saw in her mind's eye doves with golden eyes, doves all over, doves preening themselves on the bedhead and windowsill. . . . She did not know if she made the doves by expectation, or sensed their presence and brought them with her mind to her vision, or whether the doves were there and she merely happened to be able to see them. . . . Sophie Sheeky combed her hair, and the doves rustled and cooed. (282–84)

Here the hesitation in magical realism that often belongs to the reader permeates Sophie's voice as she questions her vision. Ecstasy of the spirit is transferred to us by an unbelieving narrator, but we feel its force nonetheless.

In passages such as this, the novella can be seen as plumbing the origins of contemporary magical realism in the nineteenth century, in which, as now, the pendulum swinging between the ethereal realm of spirit and the concrete world of matter leans more toward the latter. That direction dictates that, unlike Consuelo, Emily Jesse choose her living husband over the dead Alfred Hallam, choose, that is, the conjugal body over the conjugal angel of the novel's title (the ghost of Hallam, to whom Emily was engaged before his death). That material orientation also motivates the real Captain Papagay's return home from sea to his wife, who "came to rest in his arms, and . . . smelled his live smell, salt, tobacco, his own hair and skin, unlike any other hair and skin in the whole world" (336).

Nevertheless, along with this final opting for the solidly, bodily real, the angelic presence made almost magically real through its recognition by several minds during seances distinguishes this novella from other similar historical evocations. Otherwise the magical congress with the world of the dead is individually experienced and hence not irreducible, though Sophie Sheeky's experience of Arthur Hallam's spirit is narrated as if it were distinctly real. Thus while I would not classify this novella as magical realism, it is a kind of simultaneous pretext. It evokes a historical moment that precedes the flowering of magical realism but it is contemporaneous with it and investigates similar concerns: female shamanistic powers, spirit presences, ghosts, and parallel worlds. Even though the irreducible element is missing, at several points in the novel Byatt stresses the delicate conjunction of spirit and matter that characterizes much magical realism.

That conjunction prompts the conjugal angel's presence to be distinctly felt. The doctrines of Swedenborg provide an intellectual context for that presence. Byatt undercuts Swedenborg's patriarchal moments in which he claims that the lord's union with the divine spirit comes from the father and his state of human humiliation from the mother by putting them in the mouth of the red-faced Mr. Hawkes. And she specifically upholds the female point of view by making the members of the novel's company who contact the divine female. But other aspects of Swedenborg's writings, when he claims to have visited heaven and "to have taught the angels many truths" are less easily dismissed. "Why should this not be so? [Mr. Hawkes asks.] A man who lived in two worlds at once would, by his very doubleness, learn and teach something that no single-world denizen could suspect" (321), as interworldly travelers such as *Pedro Páramo, Beloved,* and *Azaro* demonstrate. In her evocation of the male conjugal angel, Byatt's novel feminizes the Victorian tradition of the fairy bride. Such a creature, who comes from another, more primitive, realm, to join a mortal mate, and who retains some of her supernatural power even as she participates in human life, prefigures the crossover characters and techniques in magical realism.[127]

The final scene of *Like Water for Chocolate* is an appropriate one with which to end this investigation of female magical narrative energies because it figures the space of female mystical discourse, both through the presence of the benevolent and beloved Indian servant Nacha, returned from the dead, and in the nature of Pedro and Tita's lovemaking. In the final scene of the novel, after Pedro carries Tita across the threshold of their little room, fulfilling their fantasies of finally being married, they are "so filled with pleasure that they didn't notice that in a corner of the room Nacha lit the last candle, raised her finger to her lips as if asking for silence, and faded away."[128] A friendly grandmother spirit of female domestic wisdom and love magic arranges the décor and presides over the scene.

Two additional descriptions suggest the spirit-oriented dimension of Pedro and Tita's ecstatic lovemaking. First, that the knocking of the bedhead against the walls and their cries of pleasure are "mixed with the sound of the thousand doves flying free above them" implies that their love is rising from bodily ecstasy to the realms of the spirit (243). Second, Tita's mind during the lovemaking evokes such a realm. In her most intense moment of pleasure Tita recalls the words of her former fiancé, John, who described to her how

> if a strong emotion suddenly lights all the candles we carry inside ourselves, it creates a brightness that shines far beyond our normal vision and then a splendid tunnel appears that shows us the way that we forgot when we were born and calls us to recover our lost divine origin. The soul longs to return to the place it came from, leaving the body lifeless. (243–44)

Compare Irigaray's description of "la mystérique" with its similar evocations of fiery brilliance and female spiritual guidance:

> This is the place where consciousness is no longer master, where, to its extreme confusion, it sinks into a dark night that is also fire and flames. This is the place where "she"—and in some cases he, if he follows "her" lead—speaks about the dazzling glare which comes from the source of light that has been logically repressed, about "abject" and "Other" flowing out into an embrace of fire that mingles one term into another.[129]

Another passage from Irigaray's description of "la mystérique" is also strikingly similar to Pedro and Tita's apocalyptic union, to their experiences of magical togetherness throughout the novel, such as the milk in Tita's breasts for Pedro's child and their communication through the rose-petal sauce, and to the long wait and finality of this last embrace. In both stories, the embrace seems to actualize the sense of fulfillment to be found in such a fluid embrace, and also, in the feeling of finality expressed (together with the future tense in Irigaray and the magical nature of the conflagration in Esquivel), to acknowledge its impossibility in the present. They are enabling but not yet socially enacted visions, blueprints perhaps for future relationships.

> Each becomes the other in consumption, the nothing of the other in consummation. Each will not in fact have known the identity of the other, has thus lost self-identity except for a hint of an imprint that each keeps in order the better to intertwine in a union already, finally at hand. Thus I am to you as you are to me, mine is yours and yours mine, I know you as you know me, you take pleasure with me as with you I take pleasure in the rejoicing of this reciprocal

living—and identifying—together. In this cauldron of identification will melt, mingle, and melt again these reversing matrices of our last embraces.[130]

In a process similar to the one Irigaray describes, during their lovemaking Pedro is shown as undergoing the experience John had described to Tita in which an intense emotion lights all our interior candles and beckons us toward a luminous otherworldly tunnel, leaving our earthly body lifeless. Then in a magical revisioning of *Romeo and Juliet*, perhaps, when Tita realizes what has happened to Pedro and that therefore he is dead, she eats candles while evoking their best moments together in order to duplicate the experience for herself. When the candle that she is chewing unites with the "luminous image" she evokes, her brilliant tunnel containing a "luminous" Pedro appears to her. The tunnel is her long and logically repressed place of nighttime fire and flames, in which consciousness is no longer her master, but Pedro is her lover. And she will lead him out of death into that mystical space. (The original Spanish uses "luminous" twice here rather than replacing one of them with "torrid," as in the translation. The repetition of that word emphasizes the spiritual dimension of their union, but the surrounding text by no means erases its complementary physical ecstasy.) After this vision, Tita lets herself go into a "long embrace," and they leave "together for the lost Eden. Never again would they be apart" (245). In Irigaray's terms, they achieve "an embrace of fire that mingles one term into another."[131] The book ends, however, not on this heavenly note, but in the earthy domain of the kitchen. Tita's great niece, who inherits her cookbook (composed of decidedly spicy rather than virgin pages), tells us that her great aunt Tita "will keep on living as long as there is someone who cooks her recipes" (246) underscoring once again the pragmatic female relation to the mystical, and the necessary coexistence of the worlds of concrete reality and the spirit in magical realist texts.[132]

Notes

Introduction

1. Cf. Jean-Pierre Durix: "such novelists as Gabriel García Márquez, Salman Rushdie, Wole Soyinka and Wilson Harris can perhaps be considered as the founding fathers of a new truly multicultural artistic reality"; *Mimesis, Genres, and Post-Colonial Discourse: Deconstructing Magic Realism* (New York: St. Martin's, 1998), 162.

2. Cf. Carlos Rincón: "recently translated Latin American fictions and texts [including magical realist ones] were incorporated into all aspects of the postmodernism debate, as part of the search for new categorical orientations"; "Posmodernismo, poscolonialismo y los nexos cartográficos del realismo mágico," *Neue Romania* 16 (1995): 199. Theo D'haen goes even farther, proposing an extremely close correlation between the characteristics of postmodernism and magical realism; "Magical Realism and Postmodernism: Decentering Privileged Centers," in *Magical Realism: Theory, History, Community,* ed. Lois Parkinson Zamora and Wendy B. Faris (Durham: Duke University Press, 1995), 191–208.

3. "Magical realism . . . and the concept of the marvelous . . . are included in that decisive bifurcation: postmodernism/postcolonialism"; Rincón, "Posmodernismo, poscolonialismo," 201. See also Dean J. Irvine, "Fables of the Plague Years: Postcolonialism, Postmodernism, and Magic Realism in 'Cien años de soledad' ('One Hundred Years of Solitude')," *Ariel: A Review of International English Literature* 29, 4 (1998): 53–80.

4. In this study of a genre, then, I am shuttling between the two options that Fredric Jameson initially articulates in connection with such an enterprise (before he eventually adds the third necessary element of history into which the other two open out). The first is the semantic tendency, in which "the objective of study is less the individual comic text than some ultimate comic vision," and the aim is "to describe the essence or meaning of a given genre by way of the reconstruction of an imaginary entity—the 'spirit' of comedy or tragedy . . . which is something like the generalized existential experience behind the individual texts." The second approach, the syntactic, "proposes rather to analyze the mechanisms and structure of a genre such as comedy, and to determine its laws and limits." Jameson, *The Political Unconscious: Narrative as a Socially Symbolic Act* (Ithaca: Cornell University Press, 1981), 107–8. While I have not separated these two concerns entirely, I address the first, the investigation of the "spirit" of magical

realism, more intensively in Chapters 2, 4, and 5, and the second, the analysis of how it works, in Chapters 1 and 3.

5. The relative neglect of magical realism as a major postcolonial genre in the theoretical mainstream of postcolonial studies, even though it embodies central concepts within it, is attested to by its absence from Homi Bhabha's *The Location of Culture* (New York: Routledge, 1994) and from Timothy Brennan's formulations of cosmopolitanism in his *At Home in the World: Cosmopolitanism Now* (Cambridge: Harvard University Press) (despite the fact that its final chapter is devoted to the musicology of Alejo Carpentier, a major practitioner and theorist of early magical realism). That lack is beginning to be remedied by various studies, including the book by Durix, *Mimesis,* the recent collection edited by Elsa Linguanti, Francesco Casotti, and Carmen Concilio, *Coterminous Worlds: Magical Realism and Contemporary Post-Colonial Literature in English* (Amsterdam and Atlanta: Rodopi, 1999), and the brief treatment of magical realism in Elleke Boehmer's *Colonial and Postcolonial Literature: Migrant Metaphors* (New York: Oxford University Press, 1995), as well as in studies of magical realism in particular postcolonial regions.

6. Many thanks to Dave Faris for giving me *Perfume, The White Hotel,* and *Beloved,* and to Robert McDowell for encouraging me to read Harris in conjunction with this project.

7. A useful resource is the anthology *Magical Realist Fiction,* ed. Robert Young and Keith Hollaman (New York: Longman, 1984)—not only because of the fiction included but for the good introductory discussion.

8. Cf. Isabel Allende: "What I don't believe is that the literary form often attributed to the works of . . . Latin American writers, that of magic realism, is a uniquely Latin American phenomenon. Magic realism is a literary device or a way of seeing in which there is space for the invisible forces that move the world: dreams, legends, myths, emotion, passion, history. All these forces find a place in the absurd, unexplainable aspects of magic realism. . . . Magic realism is all over the world. It is the capacity to see and to write about all the dimensions of reality." "The Shaman and the Infidel" (interview), *New Perspectives Quarterly* 8, 1 (1991): 54.

9. A beginning in this area has been made by Susan Napier in her article "The Magic of Identity: Magic Realism in Modern Japanese Fiction," in Zamora and Faris, *Magical Realism,* 451–75.

10. Suzi Gablik documents a similar movement toward the search for spirit in modern painting and performance art in her book *The Reenchantment of Art* (New York: Thames and Hudson, 1991).

11. James Clifford, *The Predicament of Culture: Twentieth-Century Ethnography, Literature, and Art* (Cambridge: Harvard University Press, 1988), 224.

Chapter 1

1. Because he deals quite extensively with *One Hundred Years of Solitude,* Seymour Menton would presumably include such elements in his understanding of magical realism.

However, he stresses its surprising nonmagical components and focuses on the way that magical realism "emphasizes the improbable, unexpected, and surprising BUT real elements of the real world"; *Historia verdadera del realismo mágico* (Mexico City: Fondo de Cultura Económica, 1998), 30.

2. Cf. Gabriel García Márquez, "A Very Old Man with Enormous Wings," in Robert Young and Keith Hollaman, *Magical Realist Fiction: An Anthology* (New York: Longman, 1984). I owe the useful term "irreducible element" to Young and Hollaman's introduction to their anthology, from which these initial quotations are taken (4–5). Patricia Hart provides a summary of several studies of magical realism and proposes five similar defining characteristics: "1. the real and the magic are juxtaposed; 2. this juxtaposition is narrated matter-of-factly; 3. the apparently impossible event leads to a deeper truth that holds outside the novel; 4. conventional notions of time, place, matter, and identity are challenged; and 5. the effect of reading the fiction may be to change the reader's prejudices about what reality is"; *Narrative Magic in the Fiction of Isabel Allende* (London: Associated University Presses, 1989), 27.

3. Irlemar Chiampi posits a kind of "enchantment of the reader" in the texts of the marvelous real, resulting from a "diegetic process that doesn't oppose marvels and reality"; *El realismo maravilloso: Forma e ideología en la novela hispanoamericana,* trans. Agustín Martínez and Margara Russotto (Caracas: Monte Avila, 1983), 73.

4. This aspect of magical realism is also reflected in what Timothy Brennan describes as Rushdie's obsessive awareness of "the privileges [and consequently the distance] separating Third-world authors from the realities they describe"; *Salman Rushdie and the Third World* (New York: St. Martin's, 1989), 85.

5. Amaryll Chanady, *Magical Realism and the Fantastic: Resolved Versus Unresolved Antinomy* (New York: Garland, 1985), 25–26. Graciela Ricci della Grisa signals this same tendency toward abolishing discursive contradictions in magical realism. For her, the meaning of magical realist texts is generated through "the dissolution of the principle of non-contradiction that rules Western critical thought"; *Realismo mágico y conciencia mítica en América Latina* (Buenos Aires: Cambeiro, 1985), 189.

6. Brenda Cooper, *Magical Realism in West African Fiction: Seeing with a Third Eye* (New York: Routledge, 1998), 221.

7. Ana Castillo, *So Far from God* (New York: Norton, 1993), 163.

8. Toni Morrison, *Beloved* (New York: Knopf, 1987), 176. Further citations are given in the text.

9. Gabriel García Márquez, *One Hundred Years of Solitude,* trans. Gregory Rabassa (New York: Avon, 1971), 180. Further citations are given in the text.

10. Patrick Süskind, *Perfume: The Story of a Murderer,* trans. John E. Woods (New York: Knopf, 1986), 183. Further citations are given in the text.

11. José Saramago, *The Stone Raft,* trans. Giovanni Pontiero (New York: Harcourt Brace, 1995), 289–90.

12. Ben Okri, *The Famished Road* (New York: Doubleday, 1992), 241–47.

13. In her study of "the unreal," Christine Brooke-Rose notes that "the sense that empirical reality is not as secure as it used to be is now pervasive at all levels of society. Certainly

what used to be called empirical reality, or the world, seems to have become more and more unreal, and what has long been regarded as unreal is more and more turned to or studied as the only 'true' or 'another and equally valid' reality." *A Rhetoric of the Unreal: Studies in Narrative and Structure, Especially of the Fantastic* (Cambridge: Cambridge University Press, 1981), 4. Marguerite Alexander describes this same interaction of real and unreal in Pyncheon's *The Crying of Lot 49* in similar terms: "the 'real' California is defamiliarized, but in such a way as to suggest that California itself outstrips anything that may be imagined about it"; *Flights from Realism: Themes and Strategies in Post-modernist British and American Fiction* (New York: Routledge, 1990), 108. That this is a common notion in modern and contemporary fiction is again confirmed by Idris Parry's statement that as a result of "the modern novel's mania for detail," "the familiar object becomes stranger than a moon crater"; "Aspects of Günter Grass's Narrative Technique," *Forum for Modern Language Studies* 3 (1967): 109.

14.   Erik Camayd-Freixas, *Realismo mágico y primitivismo: Relecturas de Carpentier, Asturias, Rulfo, y García Márquez* (Lanham, Md.: University Press of America, 1998), 318. 15.

15.   Robert K. Anderson, "La realidad y la destrucción de la línea en *Cien años de soledad*," *Explicación de Textos Literarios* 25, 1 (1996–97), 73.

16.   Salman Rushdie, *Midnight's Children* (New York: Avon, 1982), 40. Further citations are given in the text.

17.   Michael Hollington articulates this idea as he discusses the grotesque in *The Tin Drum*: "grotesque representations of distorted forms . . . challenge our conventional notions of 'normal' reality. The world of everyday reality is 'made strange'; the strange and fantastical is presented in a matter-of-fact way as if it were commonplace." *Günter Grass: The Writer in a Pluralist Society* (Boston: Marion Boyars, 1980), 24. And Stephen Hart notes that "by treating the supernatural as if it were a natural occurrence, and by describing natural phenomena such as scientific inventions and political conflicts as if they were supernatural," García Márquez "manages to create a world in which the boundaries between the marvelous and the quotidian, the mythical and the real, are dissolved"; "Magical Realism in Gabriel García Márquez's *Cien años de soledad, INTI* 16–17 (1982–83): 51.

18.   Gabriel García Márquez, "Light Is Like Water," in *Strange Pilgrims,* trans. Edith Grossman (New York: Knopf, 1993), 158.

19.   Salman Rushdie, *The Moor's Last Sigh* (New York: Random House, 1996), 381. Further citations are given in the text.

20.   André Schwarz-Bart, *A Woman Named Solitude,* trans. Ralph Manheim (New York: Atheneum, 1973), 154.

21.   See Roland Barthes, "L'Effet de réel," *Communications* 2 (1968): 19–25.

22.   Franz Roh, preface to "Magic Realism: Post Expressionism," first published (as a book) in German in 1925, translated into Spanish (as a book and also published as an article) in 1927; trans. Wendy B. Faris and reprinted in Lois Parkinson Zamora and Wendy B. Faris, *Magical Realism: Theory, History, Community* (Durham: Duke University Press, 1995), 16. I have included several references to Roh's seminal essay here not to imply a direct influence on the primary texts of magical realism but because the essay provides

insights into the concept of magical realism that help to explain its artistic power.

23. Cooper, *Magical Realism in West African Fiction*, 36.

24. For additional discussion of the historical dimensions of magical realism, see Lois Par-kinson Zamora, "Magic Realism and Fantastic History: Carlos Fuentes's *Terra Nostra* and Giambattista Vico's *The New Science*," *Review of Contemporary Fiction* 8, 2 (1988): 249–56. For analysis of a particular way in which history structures three magical realist novels, see Richard Todd, "Narrative Trickery and Performative Historiography: Fic-tional Representation of National Identity in Graham Swift, Peter Carey, and Mordecai Richler," in Zamore and Faris, *Magical Realism*, 305–28.

25. Erich Auerbach, *Mimesis: The Representation of Reality in Western Literature* (Princeton: Princeton University Press, 1974), 491.

26. Carlos Fuentes, *Distant Relations*, trans. Margaret Sayers Peden (New York: Farrar, Straus & Giroux, 1982), 225.

27. Milan Kundera, *The Book of Laughter and Forgetting*, trans. Michael Henry Heim (New York: Penguin, 1982), 76.

28. Günter Grass, *The Tin Drum*, trans. Ralph Manheim (New York: Random House, 1964), 66.

29. See John Burt Foster, "Magic Realism in *The White Hotel:* Compensatory Vision and the Transformation of Classic Realism," *Southern Humanities Review* 20, 3 (1986): 205–19.

30. See Tzvetan Todorov, *The Fantastic: A Structural Approach to a Literary Genre*, trans. Richard Howard (Ithaca: Cornell University Press, 1975), 41.

31. Thanks to Lois Zamora for this formulation regarding the magic in magical realism.

32. According to Bernard McElroy, Grass "plays deftly with the boundaries of credibility, never allowing us to be quite certain at what point behavior becomes so outlandish that we must conclude that the narrator is no longer sticking to real events"; "Lunatic, Child, Artist, Hero: Grass's Oskar as a Way of Seeing," *Forum for Modern Language Studies* 22, 4 (1986): 310.

33. Gabriel García Márquez, *Del amor y otros demonios* (Mexico City: Editorial Diana, 1994), 11.

34. An interesting treatment of a similar issue is Clayton Koelb's discussion of the particular strategy in the reading of fantasy that he calls "lethetic reading," which concerns what happens when we read a text the literal truth of which we don't believe but to which we attribute meaning nonetheless: it "does not go so far as to deny that a text has 'meaning,' but denies that its 'meaning' could consist of a correspondence between its statements and actual states of affairs in the world." However, the objects of Koelb's scrutiny are fantasy, not magical realism. The "lethetic mode" of fiction is "untruth in its purest form." *The Incredulous Reader: Literature and the Function of Disbelief* (Ithaca: Cornell University Press, 1984), 220. That the fiction he examines is so different from magical realism seems to me to strengthen my contention that some hesitation obtains in the reading of magical realism.

35. See Chanady, *Magical Realism and the Fantastic*, 149, 24, 12.

36. Nancy Gray Díaz avoids confronting this thorny problem of belief or disbelief by using

the concept of mutability to characterize and to discuss the magical metamorphoses in Latin American narrative: "if we call an Indian legend *'fantastic'* we violate it with our arrogance. By talking about stories, novels, myths, and legends as 'mutable worlds,' we are able to remain neutral as to whether we believe or not and yet remain engaged in the meaning of these worlds." *The Radical Self: Metamorphosis to Animal Form and Modern Latin American Narrative* (Columbia: University of Missouri Press, 1989), 99.

37. Camayd-Freixas, *Realismo mágico y primitivismo,* 88.

38. Rawdon Wilson explains how generic characters are born out of this "hybrid" fictional world of two worlds, "bizarre creatures who owe their natures to both worlds at once. . . . At such moments it seems as if two systems of possibility have enfolded each other: two kinds of cause and effect, two kinds of organism, two kinds of consequence." "The Metamorphoses of Space: Magic Realism," in *Magic Realism and Canadian Literature,* ed. Peter Hinchcliffe and Ed Jewinski (Waterloo: University of Waterloo Press, 1986), 75. Like the definition of magical realism I am presenting here, David K. Danow's description of the carnivalesque in literature highlights the merging of different worlds: "the carnivalesque makes the extraordinary or 'magical' as viable a possibility as the ordinary or 'real,' so that no true distinction is perceived or acknowledged between the two"; *The Spirit of Carnival: Magical Realism and the Grotesque* (Lexington, Kentucky: The University Press of Kentucky, 1995), 3.

39. Cited in Catherine Rodgers, "Aucune Evidence: Les Truismes de Marie Darrieussecq," *Romance Studies* 18, 1 (2000): 76.

40. Brian McHale, *Postmodernist Fiction* (New York: Methuen, 1987), 75.

41. Ado Quayson maintains that Okri often blurs the distinction between "the esoteric and the real," and that the narrative in *The Famished Road* "suggests that in its universe of discourse it is difficult to differentiate the one from the other"; *Strategic Transformations in Nigerian Writing: Orality and History in the Work of Rev. Samuel Johnson, Amos Tutuola, Wole Soyinka, and Ben Okri* (Oxford: James Curry, and Bloomington: Indiana University Press, 1997), 136.

42. Hans Peter Duerr, *Dreamtime: Concerning the Boundary Between Wilderness and Civilization,* trans. Felicitas Goodman (New York: Blackwell, 1987), 109.

43. André Breton, "Second Manifesto of Surrealism," in *Manifestoes of Surrealism,* trans. Richard Seaver and Helen R. Lane (Ann Arbor: University of Michigan Press, 1969), 162.

44. William Kennedy, *Ironweed* (New York: Penguin, 1984), 1, 97–98.

45. Isabel Allende, *The House of the Spirits,* trans. Magda Bogin (New York: Knopf, 1985), 246, 367.

46. For an investigation of one variety of this particular aspect of magical realism, see Jon Thiem, "The Textualization of the Reader in Magical Realist Fiction," in Zamora and Faris, *Magical Realism,* 235–47.

47. McHale, *Postmodernist Fiction,* 83. According to Lars Sauerberg, *The White Hotel* is "a web of two different realities: a psychological reality with its origin in a (day) dream world, and a social reality with its origin in individual histories"; "When the Soul Takes Wing: D. M. Thomas's *The White Hotel,*" *Critique* 31 (1989): 3–15.

48. Cited in Rodgers, "Aucune Evidence," 77.

49. The kind of textual and ideological heterogeneity that results from the merging of referential and discursive worlds in magical realism makes it an especially strong example of Bakhtin's dialogical and carnivalesque modes, characteristics that have frequently been noted by critics. See, among other examples, Danow's *Spirit of Carnival;* Brenda Cooper's application of Bakhtin's theories in her *Magical Realism in West African Fiction;* and Lloyd Davies's excellent discussion of the carnivalesque in *The House of the Spirits,* in his *Allende: La casa de los espíritus* (London: Grant and Cutler, 2000), 76–85. However, Bakhtin's emphasis on the low, the physical, within the carnivalesque is only one side of magical realism. My contention—below—that magical realism's defocalized narrative points indirectly to a non-material realm is its other side.

50. Wayne Ude also includes this characteristic in his discussion of North American magical realist fictions, which "distort time, space, and identity, as those elements are understood in conventional realism"; "North American Magical Realism," *Colorado State Review* 8, 11 (1981): 23. More recently, Jean-Pierre Durix defines magical realism in a similar way: "the magic realist aims at a basis of mimetic illusion while destroying it regularly with a strange treatment of time, space, characters, or what many people (in the Western world, at least) take as the basic rules of the physical world"; *Mimesis, Genres, and Post-Colonial Discourse: Deconstructing Magic Realism* (New York: St. Martin's, 1998), 146.

51. Fredric Jameson, "The Realist Floor-Plan," in *On Signs,* ed. Marshall Blonsky (Baltimore: Johns Hopkins University Press, 1985), 374–75.

52. Carlos Fuentes, *Aura,* trans. Lysander Kemp (New York: Farrar, Straus & Giroux, 1975), 11, 124.

53. Michael Minden analyzes the way in which Grass deconstructs the authorial personality who generates images, using images that come from a common stock of emblems, such as cupids and hourglasses, among others: therefore in Oskar's case, "it is the drum, not the drummer from which the ramified narrative springs," implying that "nobody is a character in the traditional Realist sense, if that is taken to imply an unchanging, irreducible essence of personality"; "A Post-Realist Aesthetic: Günter Grass, *Die Blechtrommel,*" in *The German Novel in the Twentieth Century: Beyond Realism,* ed. David Midgley (Edinburgh: Edinburgh University Press, 1993), 154, 157.

54. Michel Dupuis and Albert Mingelgrün also argue that in magical realism "subjectivity always ends up by transforming itself into a kind of objectivity . . . , if only because the latter inevitably opens onto some general truth that transcends the individual circumstances of the hero"; "Pour une poétique du réalisme magique," in *Le Réalisme magique: Roman, peinture et cinéma,* ed. Jean Weisgerber (Brussels: Le Centre des Avant-gardes littéraires de l'Université de Bruxelles, 1987), 221.

55. In investigating the way in which Rushdie deconstructs dualities, including the boundaries between contrasting personalities, M. Keith Booker signals Rushdie's erosion of the boundaries between self and other, questioning ideas about individual identity. According to Booker, Saleem Sinai used as a canine tracking unit in *Midnight's Children* is one of the metamorphoses in Rushdie's texts that "profoundly question the view of

the self as a stable, self-contained entity." "Beauty and the Beast: Dualism as Despotism in the Fiction of Salman Rushdie," *ELH* 57 (1990): 980. Jean M. Kane argues that a number of Saleem's de-individualizing tendencies and experiences reflect ancient Vedic traditions. His ideas regarding his multiplicity, for example, correspond to Vedic ideas about the permeability of the individual body, which is highly interactive with its surroundings via elements common to both." "The Migrant Intellectual and the Body of History: Salman Rushdie's *Midnight's Children*," *Contemporary Literature* 37, 1 (1996): 103.

56.   Kathleen Flanagan discerns a Marxist agenda in Saleem's move from an individual viewpoint beyond the private self to embrace such an ideology of collectivity. Saleem's delusions about his central role in historical events are in this view a parody of the great man theory of history, and Rushdie takes us away from the "self as center of existence" to the "self as a nexus of social relations historically determined." "The Fragmented Self in Salman Rushdie's *Midnight's Children*," *The Commonwealth Novel in English* 5, 1 (1992): 44.

57.   Okri, *Famished Road,* 445–46.

58.   Julio Cortázar, "Axolotl," in *The End of the Game and Other Stories,* trans. Paul Blackburn (New York: Harper and Row, 1967), 9.

59.   John Updike, *Brazil* (New York: Knopf, 1994), 185.

60.   As Linda Hutcheon argues with regard to several other notions, the reality of the subject is also reaffirmed; *A Poetics of Postmodernism: History, Theory, Fiction* (New York: Routledge, 1988), 173.

61.   In contrast to Bruce Kawin's fictional ineffable, which tends to point toward a self beyond the text, these fictions conflate selves within the text, thus tending toward embodying worlds without selves; see Kawin, *The Mind of the Novel: Reflexive Fiction and the Ineffable* (Princeton: Princeton University Press, 1982), 221.

62.   Several recent efforts to define magical realism have been rather more exclusive than this one, aiming at exactitude. See, for example, Seymour Menton, *Magic Realism Rediscovered, 1918–1981* (Philadelphia: Art Alliance Press, 1983), which concentrates on painting; Chanady, *Magical Realism and the Fantastic,* an early and excellent general definition of magical realism; Danow, *Spirit of Carnival,* which concentrates on Latin American and European fiction of the Second World War; Cooper, *Magical Realism in West African Fiction;* Chiampi, *El realismo maravilloso;* and Camayd-Freixas, *Realismo mágico y primitivismo,* which deal with magical realism in Latin Amercia. The general articles in Weisgerber, *Réalisme magique,* represent a more inclusive approach, as do Menton, *Historia verdadera;* Durix, *Mimesis;* and Zamora and Faris, *Magical Realism.* My project here, then, is similarly inclusive, given my wish to argue that magical realism is a central component of contemporary international narrative.

63.   Weisgerber, *Réalisme magique,* 27.

64.   Roberto González Echevarría, "Isla a su vuela fugitiva: Carpentier y el realismo mágico," *Revista Iberoamericana* 40, 86 (1974): 35.

65.   Both Chanady and, following her, Dean J. Irvine, trace the origins of magical realism

in Latin America back to the clash of cultures during the conquest; see Amaryll Chanady, "The Origins and Development of Magic Realism in Latin American Fiction," in Hinchcliffe and Jewinski, *Magic Realism and Canadian Literature;* and Dean J. Irvine, "Fables of the Plague Years: Postcolonialism, Postmodernism, and Magic Realism in 'Cien años de soledad' ('One Hundred Years of Solitude')," *Ariel: A Review of International English Literature* 29, 4 (1998): 58–60.

66. I am echoing here the title of Jo Anna Isaak's study of modernist practices, *The Ruin of Representation in Modernist Art and Texts* (Ann Arbor: UMI Research Press, 1986). See Dupuis and Mingelgrün, "Pour une poétique du réalisme magique," 220. They write that in magical realism, realism is "the tool of an experimental procedure, it integrates itself into a system which surpasses it and uses it for its own ends."

67. Citing Rushdie's statement that he grew up assuming that telling stories including marvelous events was normal narrative procedure, Shaul Bassi argues that this kind of narration is "Indian realism" and therefore to call Rushdie's writing magical realism is misleading, given the divergent definitions of realism. As he also points out, however, Indian novelists have been "traditional realists in the European sense." Thus I would argue that the label is appropriate. Bassi, "Salman Rushdie's Special Effects," in *Coterminous Worlds: Magical Realism and Contemporary Post-colonial Literature in English,* ed. Elsa Linguanti, Francesco Casotti, and Carmen Concilio (Amsterdam and Atlanta: Rodopi, 1999), 49–50.

68. Victor Turner, *The Ritual Process: Structure and Anti-Structure* (Chicago: Aldine, 1969), 95.

69. John Barth, "The Literature of Replenishment," *Atlantic Monthly,* January 1980, 65; John Updike, "Chronicles and Processions" (review of Ismail Kadare's *Chronicle in Stone* and José Saramago's *Baltasar and Blimunda*), *New Yorker,* March 14, 1988, 113.

70. The many and striking similarities between these three giants, which Patricia Merivale documents in her article "Saleem Fathered by Oskar: Intertextual Strategies in *Midnight's Children* and *The Tin Drum,*" *Ariel* 21, 3 (1990): 5–21, confirm the importance of this triumvirate in the development of international magical realism. See also Kenneth Ireland's discussion of what he considers Rushdie's tacit reference to magical realism in his article on *The Tin Drum* and *Midnight's Children:* "as if alluding to this label ['magic realism'], Rushdie himself defined the resemblance between MC and DB in terms of 'magic children projected against history'"; "Doing Very Dangerous Things: *Die Blechtrommel* and *Midnight's Children,*" *Comparative Literature* 42, 4 (1990): 336. In his introduction to a collection of Grass's essays, Rushdie includes the fictions of Borges and *The Tin Drum* in his list of literary passports to authorship. See Günter Grass, *On Writing and Politics, 1967–1983,* trans. Ralph Manheim (New York: Harcourt Brace Jovanovich, 1985).

71. Rushdie in an interview with Ameenta Meer, from *BOMB* 27 (1989), reprinted in Michael R. Reder, *Conversations with Salman Rushdie* (Jackson: University Press of Mississippi, 2000), 111.

72. In the course of reading *Ulysses* as a subaltern text, in which various guerrilla tactics,

such as disjunctive stylistic shifts from chapter to chapter, indicate proximity to rather than covering over of a climate of political terror in Ireland, Enda Duffy argues that what postcolonial writing inherits from modernism is just this proclivity to such "shock tactics" in fiction, in which she would presumably include the strategies of magical realism, which she terms "probably the most striking formal characteristic of postcolonial writing across any number of cultures"; *The Subaltern Ulysses* (Minneapolis: University of Minnesota Press, 1994), 8–10.

73. Irvine argues that *One Hundred Years of Solitude* illustrates McHale's thesis, specifically, that "the shift from questions of knowledge to questions of being is dramatized in the acts of reading embedded" in the text, and especially, at the end, when "the embedded reader, Aureliano Babilonia, and the implied reader of *Cien años de soledad* are thrown, as Robert Alter puts it, into an 'ontological vertigo' "; "Fables of the Plague Years," 61–62; Robert Alter, *Partial Magic: The Novel as a Self-Conscious Genre* (Berkeley: University of California Press, 1975), 6. In associating it with the search for "American man," which he claims was "ontologically conceived" from the start, Adalbert Dessau suggests that magical realism engages ontological issues; "Realismo mágico y nueva novela latinoamericana; Consideraciones metodológicas e históricas," in *Actas del Simposio Internacional de Estudios Hispánicos,* ed. Horányi Mátyás (Budapest: Akademia Kiadó, 1978), 355.

74. All of these techniques, however, constitute the way in which magical realism, as Emil Volek has noted, "bears the marks of experimental technique, the 'international style,' as a mark of its modernity"; "Realismo mágico entre la modernidad y la postmodernidad: Hacia una remodelización cultural y discursiva de la nueva narrativa hispanoamericana," *INTI* 31 (1991): 13.

75. For a more complete discussion of the way magical realism involves a revisioning of space, see Rawdon Wilson, "The Metamorphoses of Fictional Space: Magical Realism," in Zamora and Faris, *Magical Realism,* 209–33.

76. Juan Rulfo, *Pedro Páramo,* trans. Lysander Kemp (New York: Random House, 1959), 55–59.

77. See Suzanne Jill Levine, "A Second Glance at the Spoken Mirror: Gabriel García Márquez and Virginia Woolf," *INTI: Revista de Literatura Hispánica* 16–17 (1982–83): 53–60.

78. That intermediate position is confirmed by Wilson Harris: "The way I diverge from the post-modernists . . . is that the post-modernists have discarded depth, they have discarded the unconscious, thus all they are involved in is a game, . . . whereas . . . I am convinced that there is a tradition in depth which returns, which nourishes us even though it appears to have vanished"; "Literacy and the Imagination," in *The Literate Imagination: Essays on the Novels of Wilson Harris,* ed. Michael Gilkes (London: Macmillan, 1989), 27.

79. In writing of Latin American postmodernism generally, in which he includes *One Hundred Years of Solitude,* Julio Ortega agrees that García Márquez's novel blurs the lines between modernism and postmodernism; "Postmodernism in Latin America,"

in *Postmodern Fiction in Europe and the Americas,* ed. Theo D'haen and Hans Bertens (Amsterdam: Rodopi, 1988), 193–208. Writing of *One Hundred Years of Solitude,* Irvine argues that it constitutes a "discursive enchainment" of both postmodernism and post-colonialism, a concatenation he illustrates by analyzing the insomnia plague and the banana massacre. The former embodies an instance of the postmodernist representation of competing truth claims that corrode semiotic chains of signifier and signified, as well as of postcolonial contestations of the colonial erasure of indigenous culture; "Fables of the Plague Years," 66–67.

80. Liam Connell locates magical realism more solidly in modernism than I do. Citing the theories of Marcel Mauss and Claude Lévi-Strauss, among others, regarding the similarities between mythical beliefs and western rationality, Connell argues that magical realism belongs within modernism, rather than being distinguished from it and relegated to the primitive, since both modernism and magical realism "are active ways of negotiating new situations produced by modernization"; "Discarding Magic Realism: Modernism, Anthropology, and Critical Practice," *Ariel* 29, 2 (1998): 102–4.

81. Camayd-Freixas, *Realismo mágico y primitivismo,* 33–34.

82. In an interview by Joaquín Soler Serrano in Serrano, *Escritores a fondo* (Barcelona: Editorial Planeta, 1986), 156, cited in Theo D'haen, "Magical Realism and Postmodernism: Decentering Privileged Centers," in Zamora and Faris, *Magical Realism,* 203, Carpentier states: "I began to see America via the Surrealist movement. I saw that the Surrealists searched in their daily lives for marvelous things that were very hard for them to find, and that sometimes they used tricks, very often collecting different things in order to create a prefabricated marvelous reality. And there, in Paris, I realized that we really had all those marvelous things in America." Napoleón Sánchez recreates the intellectual milieu in Latin America (as it is presented in essays by Pedro Enríquez Ureña, J. E. Iturriaga, and Juan Larrea) for Carpentier's theorization of the marvelous real. In considering the creation of extraordinary images, Larrea, according to Sánchez, "focuses on the objective synthesis of America[,] contrasting it with the individualistic synthesis of Europe." Sánchez, "Lo real maravilloso americano o la americanización del surrealismo," *Cuadernos Americanos* 219, 4 (1978): 77.

83. The seminal documents here are Carpentier's preface to *The Kingdom of This World* (first published in Spanish in 1949), its expansion into his essay "On the Marvelous Real in America" (first published in Spanish in 1967; trans. Tanya Huntington and Lois Parkinson Zamora and reprinted in Zamora and Faris, *Magical Realism,* 76–88) from which the dissecting-table detail and this quotation come (85–86), and his essay "The Baroque and the Marvelous Real" (first published in Spanish in 1975; trans. Tanya Huntington and Lois Parkinson Zamora and reprinted in Zamora and Faris, *Magical Realism,* 89–108). For further discussion of the ways in which Carpentier was inspired by surrealism's ideas about the marvelous and reacted against them, see Amaryll Chanady, "The Territorialization of the Imaginary in Latin America: Self-Affirmation and Resistance to Metropolitan Paradigms," in Zamora and Faris, *Magical Realism,* 125–44.

84. Chiampi, *El realismo maravilloso,* 158; see also 133–67. For an additional detailed account of these developments, see also Camayd-Freixas, *Realismo mágico y primitivismo,* 5–49.

85. Gabriel García Márquez, *El olor de la guayaba: Conversaciones con Plinio Apuleyo Mendoza* (Bogotá: Oveja Negra, 1982), 50, 55.

86. Rachel Swarns, "South Africa's Black Writers Explore a Free Society's Tensions," *New York Times,* June 24, 2002.

87. For a discussion of the post-boom return to historical grounding, see Doris Sommer, "Irresistible Romance: The Foundational Fictions of Latin America," in *Nation and Narration,* ed. Homi K. Bhabha (New York: Routledge, 1990), 71–98.

88. Kwame Anthony Appiah, "Is the Post—in Postmodernism—the Post in Postcolonial?" *Critical Inquiry* 17 (1991): 353–54.

89. According to Brenda Cooper, "Tutuola's fables may truly be the ancestors of the West African magical realists, but . . . those fables have to undergo crucial mutations, in both their narrative strategies and their politics, before they emerge as contemporary magical realist novels"; *Magical Realism in West African Fiction,* 51. For a more detailed history of the development of African magical realism in the context of other postcolonial African fiction, see ibid., 37–66. Cooper argues that because West African nations were formed so recently, West African magical realists are more nationalistically oriented than those in Latin America. For additional analogies between the development of magical realism in Latin America and in Africa, see Aizenberg, "*The Famished Road:* Magical Realism and the Search for Social Equity," *Yearbook of Comparative and General Literature* 43 (1995): 25–30.

90. Margaret Cezair-Thompson, "Beyond the Postcolonial Novel: Ben Okri's *The Famished Road* and Its 'Abiku' Traveller," *Journal of Commonwealth Literature* 31, 2 (1996): 43. As Cezair-Thompson notes, the phrase "the refusal to be" comes from Soyinka's *The Interpreters,* a novel of greater social and cultural alienation than Okri's.

91. See P. Gabrielle Foreman, "Past-On Stories: History and the Magically Real: Morrison and Allende on Call," *Feminist Studies* 18, 2 (1992): 369–85.

92. Laura Moss sees this as an already historical phenomenon; she distinguishes between *The Moor's Last Sigh,* which she claims parodies magical realism rather than using it for liberatory ends, and *Midnight's Children,* proposing that "with its increasing popularity, magic realism is paradoxically being drained of the potential for multiplicity and perhaps even resistance," because "the extraordinary loses its extraordinariness when it becomes predictable through repetition"; "'Forget those damnfool realists!' Salman Rushdie's Self-Parody as the Magic Realist's 'Last Sigh,'" *Ariel: A Review of International English Literature* 29, 4 (1998): 121, 137. This is an intriguing and difficult issue. Magical realism's resistance value is a volatile compound. But given the continuing vitality of the genre, I am not sure it has come to an end yet. See the brief discussion in Chapter 2 regarding the use of magical realism by new black South African writers.

93. See, for example, Glenn A. Guidry's discussion of this aspect of *The Tin Drum;* "Theoretical Reflections on the Ideological and Social Implications of Mythic Form in Grass'

Die Blechtrommel," *Monatschefte* 83, 2 (1991): 142–44. Similarly, Josna Rege investigates the complexities of this issue in *Midnight's Children*. Saleem's authorial megalomania was enabling for other novelists, Rege points out, but that megalomania is something that must be surpassed for other voices to be heard; "Victim into Protagonist: *Midnight's Children* and the Post-Rushdie National Narratives of the Eighties," in *Critical Essays on Salman Rushdie,* ed. M. Keith Booker (New York: G. K. Hall, 1999), 270.

94. According to Aizenberg, "we might say that Latin Americans helped Okri to release energies already present in Africa and African literature, to move traditions of contemporary African literature ahead by combining a look homeward with a look abroad—albeit an 'abroad' not entirely unfamiliar, just as Africa was not entirely unfamiliar to the Latin Americans"; *"The Famished Road,"* 28.

95. Carlos Fuentes, *La nueva novela hispanoamericana* (Mexico City: Joaquín Mortiz, 1969), 19.

96. Carlos Fuentes, *Valiente mundo nuevo* (Madrid: Mondadori, 1990), 24.

97. This idea is supported by Brenda Cooper's assertion that there exists a group of African novels that are "heir to the cultural traditions of both Africa and the Latin American brand of magical realism"; *Magical Realism in West African Fiction,* 15.

98. Salman Rushdie, *Imaginary Homelands: Essays and Criticism, 1981–1991* (New York: Penguin, 1992), 301.

99. Fredric Jameson, "Modernism and Imperialism," in *Nationalism, Colonialism, and Literature,* ed. Terry Eagleton, Fredric Jameson, and Edward Said (Minneapolis: University of Minnesota Press, 1990), 48–49. In an earlier article Jameson focuses on the economic basis for magical realism, theorizing that "magic realism depends on a content which betrays the overlap of the coexistence of precapitalist with nascent capitalist or technological features"; "On Magic Realism in Film," *Critical Inquiry* 12 (1986), 311. This may be true for the most part, and certainly for the emergence of the mode in Latin America, but its continuance in economically diverse societies requires additional explanation.

100. For documentation of the uses of the term *magical realism,* see Jean Weisgerber, "La Locution et le concept," in Weisgerber, *Le Réalisme magique,* 11–32. Emir Rodríguez Monegal complains that the term *magical realism* paralyzes rather than stimulates critical dialogue ("Realismo mágico versus literatura fantástica: Un diálogo de sordos," in *Otros mundos, otros fuegos: Fantasía y realismo mágico en Iberoamérica,* ed. Donald B. Yates [Michigan State University: Latin American Studies Center, 1975], 33), and Roberto González Echevarría complains that it possesses "neither the specificity nor the theoretical foundation to be . . . useful" (*Alejo Carpentier: The Pilgrim at Home* [Ithaca: Cornell University Press, 1977], 111–12).

101. Chiampi argues—logically enough—for the term *marvelous realism (realismo maravilloso)* in the Latin American context because the marvelous is a specific literary category and therefore more appropriate to the study of literary texts, and also because it recalls how early explorers resolved their difficulties in describing things that "resisted the rationalist code of European culture" by recourse to the literary marvelous; *El realismo*

maravilloso, 56. Perhaps an additional reason that magical realism has prevailed despite such logical arguments to the contrary is precisely because it does confuse the real and the textual, ontological and epistemological forms of reference.

102. Jameson, "On Magic Realism in Film," 302.

103. Carlos Rincón implicitly confirms the central place of magical realism in the contemporary world by briefly documenting the reception of *One Hundred Years of Solitude,* including examples from the former Soviet Union, Japan, China, Islamic-Arabic countries, Europe, and the United States. He notes a number of diverse phenomena, including the specific ways in which García Márquez's narrative coincides with ancient Japanese literary practices, such as "the combination of the marvelous with the everyday." More generally, he notes that the wide referential range of García Márquez's novel provided a model for "articulating the contemporary polarity between globality and local cultures" and that its cultural and textual hybridity promoted "the search with the aid of fiction for identities of class, ethnicity, gender, religion, and culture in the midst of processes of modernization"; "Streams out of Control: The Latin American Plot," in *Streams of Cultural Capital: Transnational Cultural Studies,* ed. David Palumbo-Liu and Hans Ulrich Gumbrecht (Stanford: Stanford University Press, 1997), 187, 191, 187.

104. See Theo D'haen's recent defense of magical realism as an important component of postmodernism with its postcolonial considerations; "Magical Realism and Postmodernism, 191–95.

105. Durix, *Mimesis,* 190.

106. Todorov, *The Fantastic,* 120. Neither does Stephen Slemon speculate about the spiritual charge in magical realism that may enable the revisioning of history he discusses in his excellent article on magical realism as a specifically postcolonial phenomenon; "Magic Realism as Postcolonial Discourse," in Zamora and Faris, *Magical Realism,* 407–26.

107. Slemon, "Magic Realism as Postcolonial Discourse," 408.

108. I am encouraged in this endeavor by Masao Miyoshi's statement: "I am concerned with restoring a sense of totality to the academic and intellectual world. . . . Literary and cultural critics must look out at the world and interconnect all the workings of political economy and artistic and cultural productions: "Turn to the Planet: Literature, Diversity, and Totality," *Comparative Literature* 53, 4 (2001), 295.

109. Aizenberg, *"Famished Road,"* 26.

110. Franco Moretti, *Modern Epic: The World System from Goethe to García Márquez,* trans. Quintin Hoare (New York: Verso, 1996), 233.

111. Meyer Schapiro*, Modern Art, 19th and 20th Centuries: Selected Papers* (New York: G. Braziller, 1978), 200; cited in W.J.T. Mitchell, *"Ut Pictura Theoria:* Abstract Painting and the Repression of Language," *Critical Inquiry* 15 (1989): 367.

Chapter 2

1. According to Prince, working from Gérard Genette's definition, "focalization" is defined as "the perspective in terms of which the narrated situations and events are presented;

the perceptual or conceptual position in terms of which they are rendered"; Prince, *Dictionary of Narratology* (Lincoln: University of Nebraska Press, 1978), 31–32.

2. In analyzing the hybrid nature of Caribbean literature, Joan Miller Powell also asserts the importance of paying attention to focalization in hybrid narratives, because, according to her, focalization is "heterogeneous and multi-structural, essentially hybrid, and as such the focus of struggle and contradiction," concluding that the theory of focalization addresses an intrinsic hybridity and discusses how language and narration replay this hybridity"; "The Conflict of Becoming: Cultural Hybridity and the Representation of Focalization in Caribbean Literature," *Literature and Psychology* 45, 1 and 2 (1999): 68, 90. The indeterminate voice she sees as characteristic of Caribbean literatures refers to cultural hybridity. This indeterminate voice is certainly true of much magical realism, an issue that I address shortly, but my point here concerns the ontological hybridity of real and imagined worlds.

3. That the magical realism of *The White Hotel* is tied to the dissonance between radically different perspectives is attested by D. M. Thomas's statement that the book came from his desire to write about the history of the twentieth century that flows "from that very personal landscape [of Freudian analysis] where people were studied individually with great care . . . into the time when masses were wiped out for no good reason"; Laura de Coppet, *Interview* (June 1982): 32; cited in Lars Sauerberg, "When the Soul Takes Wing: D. M. Thomas's *The White Hotel*," *Critique* 31 (1989): 4.

4. David Herman in his discussion (from within the critical perspective of narratology) of what he calls "hypothetical focalization," which he defines as "the use of hypotheses, framed by the narrator or a character, about what might be or have been seen or perceived—if only there were someone who could have adopted the requisite perspective on the situations and events at issue," approaches something like what I am attempting to describe. Because it takes account of recent developments in narratology, including theories about "possible worlds" (that themselves take account of virtual and nonrealistic narratives), and including such categories as "counter-factual" focalizers, hypothetical focalization seems similar to, though much more specific than, the general narrative situation I call defocalization. And because it addresses various kinds of epistemic stances that can be adopted toward what is being represented in a narrative," it might be useful in distinguishing between realistic and non- or postrealistic fiction, or, at least, as Herman suggests, in analyzing "narrative devices typically exploited by texts that question or resist the norms and presupposition of realistic genres." His analysis however, so far as I can see, remains within the domain of realistic narrative. "Hypothetical Focalization," *Narrative* 2, 3 (1994): 231, 239.

5. Ibid., 32.

6. Alexander Gelley, "Art and Reality in *Die Blechtrommel*," *Forum for Modern Language Studies* 3 (1967): 121.

7. Günter Grass, *The Tin Drum*, trans. Ralph Manheim (New York: Vintage, 1964), 47. Further citations are given in the text.

8. Ato Quayson discusses this quality of Okri's narrative: "because Azaro decides to

stay in the real world while at the same time refusing to break links with that of his spirit companions, both the real world and that of spirits are rendered problematically equivalent in his experience. Since the narration is in the first person, with all events being focalized through the consciousness of Azaro, the universe of action is located simultaneously within both the real world and that of spirits"; *Strategic Transformations in Nigerian Writing: Orality and History in the Work of Rev. Samuel Johnson, Amos Tutuola, Wole Soyinka, and Ben Okri* (Oxford: James Curry, and Bloomington: Indiana University Press, 1997), 124.

9. William Kennedy, *Ironweed* (New York: Penguin, 1984), 17.

10. Irlemar Chiampi articulates a similar pragmatic dynamic in magical realism, foregrounding its metafictional qualities. Working from Roland Barthes's notion that bourgeois realism hid the narrative situation, she argues that magical realism as it belongs to modernity questions that hidden quality, problematizing the narrative act and frequently presenting the reader with an " 'impossible' combination of two kinds of traditionally incompatible registers"—the real and the magical. That combination injects into the reader's experience "a systematic questioning of the narrative process" and problematizes diegesis (the recounting of the story) itself from within, a questioning she illustrates with Jorge Luis Borges's suggestion that "if the characters of a fictional work can be readers or spectators, we its readers or spectators, can be fictitious" (Borges, "Partial Magic in the *Quijote*," in *Labyrinths: Selected Stories and Other Writings*, ed. Donald A. Yates and James E. Irby [New York: New Directions, 1964], 196). This is an idea that forces the reader to deconstruct habits of thought based in the separation of opposites. Chiampi, *El realismo maravilloso: Forma e ideología en la novela hispanoamericana*, trans. Agustín Martínez and Margara Russotto (Caracas: Monte Avila, 1983), 96–101.

11. According to Keith Maillard, "the interweaving of realistic convention with magical elements" is motivated by the desire "to produce that symptomatic eerie shimmer, which must be seen as an attempt to express what is nearly inexpressible"; "*Middlewatch* as Magic Realism," *Canadian Literature* 92 (1982): 12.

12. Bruce Kawin, *The Mind of the Novel: Reflexive Fiction and the Ineffable* (Princeton: Princeton University Press, 1982), xiii.

13, Ludwig Wittgenstein, *Tractatus Logico-Philosophicus*, trans. D. F. Pears and B. F. McGuinness (London: Routledge & Kegan Paul, 1961), 4.1212, quoted in Kawin, *The Mind of the Novel*, 85. After having formulated my notions of the ineffable and defocalized narrative, I came on Kawin's excellent study, in which he uses the terms "ineffable" and "unanchored" to describe similar phenomena. He stresses the limits that discussion of the ineffable encounters in modernist realism, while I investigate the ways in which the conventions of that mode are subverted by magical realism. According to Kawin, "a text's attempts to go beyond its limits—to discuss the ineffable, for instance, or to engage its author or reader in spontaneous conversation—has the effect of foregrounding those limits" (82). It is my contention that magical realism ventures farther than its predecessors in encoding the ineffable. Kawin is correct, however in signaling the limits of a genre, because even magical realism can go only so far in the direction of the ineffable—or the realistic or the fantastic—before becoming something else.

14. Kawin, *Mind of the Novel,* 86.

15. Wilson Harris, *Palace of the Peacock* (London: Faber and Faber, 1968), 151. Further citations are given in the text.

16. André Breton, "Second Manifesto of Surrealism," in *Manifestoes of Surrealism,* trans. Richard Seaver and Helen R. Lane (Ann Arbor: University of Michigan Press, 1969), 158.

17. For a discussion of the various shifts in Oskar's perspective, which contribute to the defocalized nature of his text, see H. E. Beyersdorf, "The Narrator as Artful Deceiver: Aspects of Narrative Perspective in *Die Blechtrommel,*" *Germanic Review* 55 (1980): 129–38.

18. Stephen Slemon, "Magic Realism as Post-Colonial Discourse," in *Magical Realism: Theory, History, Community,* ed. Lois Parkinson Zamora and Wendy B. Faris, (Durham: Duke University Press, 1995), 410.

19. Even if, as Chiampi argues, because they are assimilated so closely to reality in magical realism, marvelous occurrences are "liberated from mystery," I think that some of that mystery nevertheless clings to the text; *El realismo maravilloso,* 70.

20. As Hena Maes-Jellinek notes, this image is "not a transcendental symbol but rather a metaphorical representation of community reconciling the human and the divine"; *Wilson Harris* (Boston: Twayne, 1982), 13.

21. Wilson Harris, *History, Fable, and Myth in the Caribbean and Guyanas,* (Georgetown, 1970), 20; quoted in Maes-Jellinek, "The True Substance of Life: Wilson Harris's *Palace of the Peacock,*" in *Common Wealth,* ed. Anna Rutherford (Aarhus, Denmark: University of Aarhus, n.d.), 158.

22. Alejo Carpentier, *The Kingdom of This World,* trans. Harriet de Onís (New York: Collier, 1970), 41–42.

23. Ibid., 40–41. See also, Alejo Carpentier, *El reino de este mundo* (Mexico City: Compañía General de Ediciones, 1962), 55–56. Hereafter, all page numbers following quotations from this novel are from the English translation; where a second page number appears, it refers to the Spanish edition. Amaryll Chanady analyzes the contradictory focalizations, between which it is not always possible to distinguish clearly, in this novel in general and in this scene in particular, in "La focalización como espejo de contradicciones en *El reino de este mundo,*" *Revista Canadiense de Estudios Hispánicos* 12, 3 (1988): 454–55. She agrees that the phrase "todos sabían" begins to eclipse the educated invisible narrator, permitting the reader to identify with Ti Nöel's viewpoint. As she points out, as the novel progresses, "the primary Europeanized focalizer disappears, and events are presented through Ti Nöel," although he himself occupies an ambiguous position, having identified enough with the Europeanized world to have lost much of his Negro culture.

24. Amaryll Chanady, *Magical Realism and the Fantastic: Resolved Versus Unresolved Antinomy* (New York: Garland, 1985), 39–40.

25. Chiampi explains this narrative event as an occasion for questioning the reader's habitual assumptions: the text presents a "non-conflictive coexistence (for the reader)" of "two pragmatic modalities." As a result of that presentation, "voodoo mythology . . . 'explains' the impossible event, so that the reader is not obliged to opt for either the natural or the supernatural version, but rather to revise [his or her idea about] the separation of those zones of meaning"; *El realismo maravilloso,* 76.

26. Carpentier's 1949 preface was expanded in "On the Marvelous Real in America," first published in Spanish in 1967; trans. Tanya Huntington and Lois Parkinson Zamora and reprinted in *Magical Realism: Theory, History, Community,* ed. Lois Parkinson Zamora and Wendy B. Faris (Durham: Duke University Press, 1995), 87.

27. Alejo Carpentier, "The Baroque and the Marvelous Real," first published in Spanish in 1975; trans. Tanya Huntington and Lois Parkinson Zamora and reprinted in Zamora and Faris, *Magical Realism,* 105.

28. Chanady's requirement that a magical realist text have a consistent focalization, and hence disqualifying *The Kingdom of This World,* seems too limiting to me because it is consistently violated by texts whose other characteristics align them with magical realism. Various other critical studies of magical realism also include the novel within the category of magical realism. See, among others, Jaime Alazraki, "Para una revalidación del concepto realismo mágico en la literatura hispanoamericana," in *Homenaje a Andrés Iduarte* (Clear Creek, In: American Hispanist, 1976), 9–21; Victor Bravo, *Magias y maravillas en el continente literario: Para un deslinde del realismo mágico y lo real maravilloso* (Caracas: La Casa de Bello, 1988); Erik Camayd-Freixas, *Realismo mágico y primitivismo: Relecturas de Carpentier, Asturias, Rulfo, y García Márquez* (Lanham, Md.: University Press of America, 1998) (who asserts that *The Kingdom of This World* is among the texts most frequently classified as magical realism); and Chiampi, *El realismo maravilloso.*

29. Trudier Harris says, "Baby Suggs becomes a communal poet/artist, the gatherer of pieces of her neighbors' experiences and the shaper of those experiences into a communal statement. Her role is in many ways like that of a ritual priestess"; *Fiction and Folklore in the Novels of Toni Morrison* (Knoxville: University of Tennessee Press, 1991), 174.

30. Houston Baker discusses the importance of flight as an index of spirit and traces its importance in the genealogy of the Solomon character in Toni Morrison's *Song of Solomon,* from Ajax's conjuring mother through Pilate (the novel's medium) to Milkman Dead; *The Workings of the Spirit: The Poetics of Afro-American Women's Writing* (Chicago: University of Chicago Press, 1991), 98. Marilyn Sanders Mobley also discusses the ways in which the imagery of flight serves a similarly enabling function in the fiction of Sarah Orne Jewett; "Rituals of Flight and Return: The Cyclical Journeys of Jewett's Female Characters," in *Folk Roots and Mythic Wings in Sarah Orne Jewett and Toni Morrison: The Cultural Function of Narrative* (Baton Rouge: Louisiana State University Press, 1991), 27–62.

31. Isabel Allende, *The House of the Spirits,* trans. Magda Bogin (New York: Knopf, 1985), 6.

32. Ibid., 12. The affinities of angels and magical realism are numerous, since angels exist

in many cultures, within which they bridge the realms of flesh and spirit. Angels, like magical realism, are a cultural hybrid, a result of "an extraordinary Hebrew program of cross-breeding original Egyptian, Sumerian, Babylonian and Persian supernatural beings." Like magical realism, which is a mode of the margins, almost all information about angels comes from outside orthodox scriptures; see Malcolm Godwin, *Angels: An Endangered Species* (New York: Simon and Schuster, 1990), 9, 19, a book that, along with the appearance of numerous others on the same subject, rather disproves its own subtitle. And like magical realist texts, which question received notions of time, space, and identity, in popular belief and "by scriptural tradition, angels pull back the curtain, however briefly, on the realm of the spirit. In offering a glimpse of a larger universe, they issue a challenge to priorities and settled ways" ("The New Age of Angels," *Time,* December 27, 1993, 56). That these angelic texts reflect a contemporary cultural trend is further corroborated by the *Time* article, which calls the recent increase of interest in angels "a grass roots revolution of the spirit." The article also cites a survey conducted by *Time,* according to which 69 percent of Americans believe in angels.

33. See Roberto González Echevarría, *Myth and Archive: A Theory of Latin American Narrative* (Cambridge: Cambridge University Press, 1990). Appropriately enough, then, González Echevarría's analysis focuses on *The Lost Steps* rather than on *The Kingdom of This World*. Carlos Fuentes, in his recent book, *Valiente mundo nuevo* (Madrid: Mondadori, 1990), which emphasizes the historical mode in Latin American fiction, also discusses *The Lost Steps* at length.

34. Jurij M. Lotman, "On the Metalanguage of a Typological Description of Culture," *Semiotica* 14, 2 (1975): 97.

35. For a well-informed discussion of these temporal issues, see Elizabeth Deeds Ermarth, *Sequel to History: Postmodernism and the Crisis of Representational Time* (Princeton: Princeton University Press, 1991), 35.

36. Milan Kundera, *The Book of Laughter and Forgetting,* trans. Michael Henry Heim (New York: Penguin, 1980), 188–90.

37. Patrick Süskind, *Perfume: The Story of a Murderer,* trans. John E. Woods (New York: Knopf, 1986), 254.

38. Franco Moretti also concurs that part of the West's attraction to magical realism results from the desire "of contemporary societies" for [the kind of] " 'meaning,' imagination, *re-enchantment*" that can "find an outlet in stories belonging *to another culture*"; *Modern Epic: The World System from Goethe to García Márquez,* trans. Quintin Hoare (New York: Verso, 1996), 249.

39. Michael Valdez Moses's comparison of magical realism to the historical romances of Sir Walter Scott confirms this primitivist component. For Valdez Moses the cultural function of both is to permit "their readers to indulge in a nostalgic longing for and an imaginary return to a past that is past, or passing away." I would say, however, that magical realism as it continues to develop offers by virtue of its narrative mode more than "purely symbolic or token resistance to the inexorable triumph of modernity"; "Magical Realism at World's End," *Literary Imagination: The Review of the Association of Literary Scholars and Critics* 3, 3 (2001): 106.

40. In borrowing elements from indigenous cultures, magical realism resembles the movement that Daniel C. Noel characterizes as a "new shamanism," led by such anthropologist-practitioners as Joan Halifax, Michael Harner, and others, because it is a similarly educated and appreciative approach to "primitive" culture, a Western construct based on studies of and contact with indigenous cultures, specifically with shamans, in which Western practitioners, through a combination of knowledge, contact, and fantasy reenact and modify traditional shamanic performances; see Noel, *The Soul of Shamanism: Western Fantasies, Imaginal Realities* (New York: Continuum, 1997).

41. Quayson, *Strategic Transformations in Nigerian Writing,* 148–49.

42. James Clifford, *The Predicament of Culture: Twentieth-Century Ethnography, Literature, and Art* (Cambridge: Harvard University Press, 1988), 219.

43. The terms are Susan Stewart's, from her study *On Longing: Narratives of the Miniature, the Gigantic, the Souvenir, the Collection* (Baltimore: Johns Hopkins University Press, 1984), 163.

44. Clifford, *Predicament of Culture,* 229.

45. Adam Phillips expresses this idea about a fetish in connection with Freud's treatment of fetishes in *Kissing, Tickling, and Being Bad: Psychoanalytical Essays on the Unexamined Life* (Cambridge: Harvard University Press, 1993), 88.

46. See Edward Dudley and Maximilian E. Novak, *The Wild Man Within: An Image in Western Thought from the Renaissance to Romanticism* (Pittsburgh: University of Pittsburgh Press, 1972).

47. Edna Aizenberg, " *The Famished Road:* Magical Realism and the Search for Social Equity," *Yearbook of Comparative and General Literature* 43 (1995): 29.

48. Salman Rushdie, *The Moor's Last Sigh* (New York: Random House, 1995), 143.

49. In comparing the magical realism of Carpentier with that of Heinrich Böll, José Miguel Mínguez confirms that magical realism appears in vastly different circumstances: "there has been an effective rapprochement between the existence of the mythifying and exalted variety of the marvelous real of the Franco-Cuban creole and the resignedly bitter brand of the Rheinish writer"; "Günter Grass *(Die Blechtrommel)* y Julio Cortázar *(Rayuela),* Heinrich Böll *(Opiniones de un payaso)* y Alejo Carpentier *(El reino de este mundo):* Notas sobre el realismo mágico y las nuevas actitudes del novelista ante su obra," *Boletín de Estudios Germánicos* 9 (1972): 276.

50. Magical realism thus belongs to the modern and contemporary trajectory, "the movement from the idea of the primitive to spiritual emotions," that Marianna Torgovnik charts in *Primitive Passions: Men, Women, and the Quest for Ecstasy* (Chicago: University of Chicago Press, 1996), 10. Oddly enough, in this context, in her excellent discussion of magical realism as postcolonial writing, Brenda Cooper invokes the extension of magical realism into a realm of the sacred with the title of her chapter taken from Ben Okri's *The Famished Road,* "Sacred names into profane spaces," but she does not develop that idea at length as central to magical realism; *Magical Realism in West African Fiction: Seeing with a Third Eye* (New York: Routledge, 1998).

51. Peter S. Hawkins and Anne Howland Schotter, eds., *Ineffability: Naming the Unnameable from Dante to Beckett* (New York: AMS Press, 1984), 2.

52. Alexander Gelley, "Art and Reality in *Die Blechtrommel,* 124.

53. Because it involves voices of indeterminate origin, magical realism's defocalized narrative constitutes a technique for including a sense of mystery akin to that of late nineteenth- and early twentieth-century texts produced under the influence of spiritualism as practiced by writers such as Victor Hugo and Yeats, who used automatic writing—a narrative text of uncertain origin—to contact a realm beyond the real. But it locates that realm within rather than beyond the real, and it is for the most part an entirely modal strategy rather than a thematic one.

54. Arturo Uslar-Pietri, "Realismo Mágico," in *Godos, insurgentes y visionarios* (Barcelona: Seix Barral, 1986), 34.

55. Fredric Jameson, "The Realist Floor-Plan," in *On Signs,* ed. Marshall Blonsky (Baltimore: Johns Hopkins University Press, 1985), 373.

56. Salman Rushdie and Cécile Wajsbrot, "Utiliser une technique qui permette à Dieu d'exister," *Quinzaine Littéraire* 449 (1985): 22.

57. Chiampi, following Carpentier, moves in a similar direction, but without explicitly referring to the sacred domain, by associating Latin American marvelous realism with a baroque sensibility that uses proliferation to describe the "unnameable" and the "nondesignatable," a process legitimized, according to Carpentier, by the necessity of describing "American objects not inscribed in universal culture"; *El realismo maravilloso,* 104. See Carpentier, "Problemática de la actual novela latinoamericana," in *Tientos y diferencias* (Montevideo: Arca, 1967), 37–38.

58. Bakhtin sees the Rabelesian chronotope of "fantastic realism" in a similar way, as an overturning of existing traditions, but in something of a reverse direction from the one Roh was signaling. He gives among his examples Gargantua's birth out of his mother's ear, carefully explained as a result of a weakening of the uterus, caused by the diarrhea occasioned by a meal of tripe. In such a description, Bakhtin maintains, "grotesque fantasy is combined with the precision of anatomical and physiological analysis"; *The Dialogical Imagination,* trans. Caryl Emerson and Michael Holquist (Austin: University of Texas Press, 1983), 171–72.

59. The collage was shown in an exhibition on the eye in twentieth-century painting in Villa Stuck, Munich, in the summer of 1988.

60. Franz Roh, "Magic Realism: Post-Expressionism," trans. Wendy B Faris, in Zamora and Faris, *Magical Realism,* 24.

61. Ibid., 51.

62. Lawrence Thornton, *Imagining Argentina* (New York: Bantam, 1988), 15.

63. Günter Grass, *On Writing and Politics, 1967–1983,* trans. Ralph Manheim (New York: Harcourt Brace Jovanovich, 1985), 26.

64. See Alejo Carpentier, Prologue to *El reino de este mundo* (Mexico City: Companía General de Ediciones, 1962), 11.

65. Tahar Ben Jelloun. *The Sacred Night,* trans. Alan Sheridan (San Diego: Harcourt Brace, 1989).

66. In all fairness to Gide, however, we should note his acknowledgment of such a perspective in the figure of Oedipus in *Theseus,* who has "found a source of supernatural

light, illuminating the world of the spirit," but it is a luminous source that, unlike Ben Jelloun's, does not transform the realism of his text; Gide, *Two Legends: Oedipus and Theseus,* trans. John Russell (New York: Random House, 1950), 106.

67. David Ellison, *Ethics and Aesthetics in European Modernist Literature: From the Sublime to the Uncanny* (Cambridge: Cambridge University Press, 2001), 212, 224–30.

68. Ibid., 226.

69. See, for example, the statement by Laura Pérez (who is speaking in the context of Chicana discourse, but her words imply a broader application): "beliefs and practices consciously making reference to the s/Spirit as the common life force within and between all beings are largely marginalized from serious intellectual discourse as superstition, folk belief, or New Age delusion, when they are not relegated to the socially controlled spaces of the orientalist study of 'primitive animism' or of 'respectable' religion within dominant culture. . . . Yet the very discomfort that attends talk of the spiritual outside of authorized and institutionalized spaces (i.e. churches, certain disciplines, old and new Eurocentric ideological and theory orthodoxies) alerts us to a tender zone constituted by the (dis)encounters of culturally different and politically significant beliefs and practices"; "Spirit Glyphs: Reimagining Art and Artist in the Work of Chicana *Tlamatinime*," *Modern Fiction Studies* 44, 1 (1998): 37–38.

70. Thornton, *Imagining Argentina,* 13.

71. George B. Hutchinson, *The Ecstatic Whitman: Shamanism and the Crisis of the Union* (Columbus: Ohio State University Press, 1986), 151.

72. The *Time* magazine article "New Age of Angels" confirms this sense: "in their modern incarnation, these mighty messengers and fearless soldiers have been reduced to bite-size beings easily digested. The terrifying cherubim have become Kewpie-doll cherubs. For those who choke too easily on God and his rules, theologians observe, angels are the handy compromise, all fluff and meringue, kind, nonjudgmental. And they are available to everyone, like aspirin." Sophy Burnham writes of angels that their appearances as dreams, comforting presences, pulses of energy, people, is a way that "the mysteries are presented to them [skeptics] in such a flat and factual, everyday, reasonable way so as not to disturb." The rule, she says, is that "people receive only as much information as they can bear, in the form they can stand to hear it"; cited in ibid., 56–65.

73. Walter Burkert, *Ancient Mystery Cults* (Cambridge: Harvard University Press, 1987), 89.

74. Slavoj Zizek, *Looking Awry: An Introduction to Jacques Lacan through Popular Culture* (Cambridge: MIT Press, 1991), 6–9.

75. Roh notes a similar trajectory in painting. He maintains that the avowedly transcendental leanings of expressionism disappeared, making way for a new reverence for daily life, but that those leanings had their effect, for "that daily world is seen through new eyes"; "Magic Realism," 36.

76. Bradley Butterfield agrees that *Perfume* represents not only a manifestation of the mass appeal of horror but also a critique of both enlightenment culture and fascism, through a negative view of their practices; "Enlightenment's Other in Patrick Süskind's

Das Parfum: Adorno and the Ineffable Utopia of Modern Art," *Comparative Literature Studies* 32, 3 (1995): 401–18.

77. Carpentier, Prologue to *El reino de este mundo*, 11.

78. Borges makes this sally in a review of Leslie Weatherhead's book *After Death* that was added in 1942 to the second edition of his collection *Discusión*, originally published in 1932; "*After Death*," trans. Suzanne Jill Levine, in Borges, *Selected Non-Fictions*, ed. Eliot Weinberger (New York: Viking, 1999), 254–55.

79. Susan Frenk provides these possible Aztec resonances in "Rewriting History: Carlos Fuentes' *Aura*," *Forum for Modern Language Studies* 30, 3 (1994): 264, 269. Uncannily enough, in what almost seems like an intrusion of magical realism into historical reality, in the exact part of the city in which *Aura* is set, ostensibly for its colonial echoes, ten years after Fuentes published this story about layers of time in Mexico, subway excavations revealed the ancient ritual center of Tenochtitlán, the Templo Mayor.

80. According to Bernard Terramorsi, "the hidden presence of Xolotl shows that this transmutation is a gift of the self, a sacrifice to the god of doubling": "Le Discours mystique du fantastique dans les contes de Julio Cortázar," in *Lo lúdico y lo fantástico en la obra de Cortázar*, vol. 1 (Madrid: Fundamentos, 1986), 171.

81. Michael Hollington notes that the old Slavonic Casubian folklore is "steeped in stories about dwarfs," so that Oskar's very conception owes much to this tradition; see *Günter Grass: The Writer in a Pluralist Society* (London: Marion Boyars, 1980), 5, 25.

82. Richard T. Gray's article on *Perfume* as a critique of Enlightenment culture confirms this tendency for the attraction to spirit to camouflage itself in critical as well as fictional discourse. Arguing convincingly that Süskind's "imbrication of enlightened reason and aesthetic modernism constitutes the primary critical thrust of *Das Parfum*," Gray confines his analysis to historiographical and thematic concerns, not tying Süskind's critique of the enlightenment to the narrative mode of magical realism with its encoding of the ineffable. That this excellent article does not mention magical realism may also suggest that Süskind, like other contemporary magical realists, is transmitting the radical other of spirit in well-disguised form. Gray, "The Dialectic of 'Enscentment': Patrick Süskind's *Das Parfum* as Critical History of Enlightenment Culture," *PMLA* 108, 3 (1993): 489–505.

83. André Breton, "A Letter to Seers," in *Manifestoes of Surrealism*, 202.

84. According to Edna Aizenberg, "the liminal figure of the abiku organizes the various magical realist dimensions—the 'marvelous real,' the defamiliarization, the social concerns, the postcolonial foregrounding of discontinuities, the archeological impulse, the utopic hope." This in-between status is emblematic of the magical realist text in general: "like the magical realist text, the abiku child remains forever 'in-between,' caught in the interspace of the spirit world and the Living—roughly, the magic and the real." *Famished Road*, 28.

85. Ana Castillo, *So Far from God* (New York: Norton, 1993), 86–87. Further citations are given in the text.

86. Richard K. Cross reports Thomas's idea in his article, "The Soul Is a Far Country: D. M. Thomas and *The White Hotel*," *Journal of Modern Literature* 18, 1 (1992): 43.

87. Just recently (many years after having formulated this connection between magical realism and shamanism) I was encouraged to read the article by Renato Oliva on Okri's "shamanic realism." Oliva maintains (citing my earlier formulation) that "a literature that 'weaves a web of connections between the lands of the living and the dead' " (Wendy B. Faris, "Scheherazade's Children: Magical Realism and Postmodern Fiction," in Zamora and Faris, *Magical Realism,* 172) that crosses, blurs, or dissolves the boundaries between these two lands, may perhaps be termed a shamanic literature, for "the shaman stands on the border between the human realm and the spirit-realm, and can cross it in either direction." Further, "if . . . one of the characteristics of the shaman is his ability to shift his level of consciousness, thus moving between conscious and unconscious, reality and dream, natural and supernatural, this is equally true of magical realism." Oliva, "Re-Dreaming the World: Ben Okri's Shamanic Realism," in *Coterminous Worlds: Magical Realism and Contemporary Post-colonial Literature in English,* ed. Elsa Linguanti, Francesco Casotti, and Carmen Concilio (Amsterdam and Atlanta: Rodopi, 1999), 174, 177.

88. For Gabriel Weisz, "the knowledge/power discourse [of modern ethnology] is transferred to a thematization of shamanism from the vantage point, scale and identity of the thematizer," a practice "designed to extend a cognitive territoriality in order to inhabit space with its own power systems," so that it is necessary to adopt a position of "theoretical relativity," which "willingly accepts otherness in shamanism as largely unthematizable"; "Shamanism and Its Discontents," in *Methods for the Study of Literature as Cultural Memory,* ed. Raymond Vervliet and Annemarie Estor, vol. 6 of *Literature as Cultural Memory* (Amsterdam and Atlanta: Rodopi, 2000), 279–80. Weisz's skepticism regarding the thematic elements observable in shamanic practice confirms my sense of the importance of basing the analogy between magical realism (or any other discursive practice) and shamanism primarily on the mode of the discourse rather than on its thematics.

89. Gabriel Weisz, "Subliminal Body: Shamanism, Ancient Theater, and Ethnodrama," in *Primitivism and Identity in Latin America: Essays on Art, Literature, and Culture,* ed. Erik Camayd-Freixas and Eduardo González (Tucson: University of Arizona press, 2000), 216.

90. Douglas Sharon, *Wizard of the Four Winds: A Shaman's Story* (New York: Macmillan, 1978), 150.

91. Arthur Rimbaud to Georges Izambard (1871), in *Oeuvres de Rimbaud,* ed. Suzanne Bernard (Paris: Garnier, 1960), 344; my translation.

92. Wenceslas Sieroszewski, "Du chamanisme d'après les croyances des Yakoutes," *Revue de l'histoire des religions* 46 (1902): 326; cited in Mircea Eliade, *Shamanism: Archaic Techniques of Ecstasy,* trans. Willard R. Trask (Princeton: Princeton University Press, 1974), 229–36.

93. In his treatment of Okri's texts as "shamanic realism," Oliva stresses that it is only through the "arduous dialectic of reality-dream, only by being both realist and magician, and only by being at one and the same time chronicler of the everyday and seer

or prophet that the magical-realist writer can avoid the danger of psychic inflation, or indeed of literary inflation"; "Re-Dreaming the World," 196.

94. Michel Perrin, "Formas de comunicación chamánica: El ejemplo guajiro (Venezuela y Colombia),"*Abya-Yala, Colección 500 Años* (Quito, Ecuador), no. 1 (1988): 64–65 (my translation); cited in Mario Califano, "Los Rostros del Chamán: Nombres y Estados," in *Chamanismo en latinoamérica: Una revisión conceptual,* ed. Jacques Galinier, Isabel Lagarriga, and Michel Perrin (Mexico City: Plaza y Valdéz, Editores, 1995), 124. Califano does not give the name of the shaman he cites.

95. See Lilian Scheffler, "Especialistas: Pachita," in *Magia y brujería en México* (Mexico City: Panorama Editorial, 1983); discussed in Weisz, "Subliminal Body," 216.

96. Michael Harner, *The Way of the Shaman: A Guide to Power and Healing* (San Francisco: Harper, 1990), 175–76.

97. Michael Lambek, *Human Spirits: A Cultural Account of Trance in Mayotte* (Cambridge: Cambridge University Press, 1981), 183.

98. Gabriel García Márquez, "Light Is Like Water," in *Strange Pilgrims,* trans. Edith Grossman (New York: Knopf, 1993), 158.

99. Roger Walsh, *The Spirit of Shamanism* (Los Angeles: Jeremy P. Tarcher, 1990), 118.

100. Harner, *The Way of the Shaman,* 176. See also, among too many others to cite here, Holger Kalweit, *Dreamtime and Inner Space: The Way of the Shaman* (Boston: Shambhala, 1988); J.M.G. Le Clézio, *The Mexican Dream; or, The Interrupted Thoughts of Amerindian Civilizations,* trans. Teresa Fagan (Chicago: Chicago University Press, 1988); Walsh, *Spirit of Shamanism;* works by Joan Halifax, such as *Shamanic Voices: A Survey of Visionary Narratives* (New York: Penguin, 1991); *The Shaman's Drum* magazine.

101. Wilson Harris, *Tumatumari* (London: Faber and Faber, 1968), 134.

102. Maes-Jellinek, *Wilson Harris,* 10.

103. Fredric Jameson has proposed "the very provisional hypothesis that the possibility of magic realism as a formal mode is constitutively dependent on a type of historical raw material in which disjunction is structurally present," an idea that has subsequently been frequently voiced in studies of magical realism as postcolonial discourse; "On Magic Realism in Film," *Critical Inquiry* 12 (1986): 311.

104. According to Marjorie Mandelstam Balzer following S. Shirogarov's views, shamans often serve as psychological facilitators for communication in stressful stages of deterioration or change; Balzer, ed., *Shamanism: Soviet Studies of Traditional Religion in Siberia and Central Asia* (Armonk, N.Y.: M. E. Sharpe, 1990), ix.

105. Although he does not develop the analogy, Glenn A. Guidry in his discussion of Oskar as a healing culture hero, a trickster with magical powers, refers to his shamanistic drum," implying that Oskar's cultural activities are akin to those of a shaman; "Theoretical Reflections on the Ideological and Social Implications of Mythic Form in Grass' *Die Blechtrommel, Monatshefte* 83, 2 (1991): 131.

106. Gloria Anzaldúa, "Metaphors in the Tradition of the Shaman," in *Conversant Essays: Contemporary Poets on Poetry,* ed. James McCorkle (Detroit: Wayne State University Press, 1990), 100.

107. Juan Rulfo, *Pedro Páramo,* trans. Lysander Kemp (New York: Grove Press, 1978), 123.
108. D. M. Thomas, *The White Hotel* (New York: Viking, 1981), 212–14.
109. Toni Morrison, *Beloved* (New York: Knopf, 1987), 200.
110. Kennedy, *Ironweed,* 19.
111. This movie exists on the fringes of magical realism, because the ghost in question is clearly circumscribed, his activities relatively predictable, so that we are not asked to reorient our conceptions of time, space, and identity as magical realist texts often induce us to, but it is a close cousin to that mode. The adoption of magical realist techniques in films and television series including *Northern Exposure* and *Allie McBeal,* in which a character literally flies, corresponds to a popularization pattern of shamanic healings, in which, paradoxically, "as a shaman becomes more popular, both diagnosis and treatment may become simpler and shorter"; Walsh, *Spirit of Shamanism,* 187.

Chapter 3

1. Salman Rushdie and Cécile Wajsbrot, "Utiliser une technique qui permette à Dieu d'exister," *Quinzaine Littéraire* 449 (1985): 22.
2. I am indebted to Steve Walker for suggesting this connection between Rimbaud and magical realism. Arthur Rimbaud to Georges Izambard (1871), in *Oeuvres de Rimbaud,* ed. Suzanne Bernard (Paris: Garnier, 1960), 344; my translation.
3. Salman Rushdie, *Midnight's Children* (New York: Avon, 1982), 14–15. Further citations are given in the text.
4. Jorge Luis Borges, "The Aleph," in *The Aleph,* trans. Norman Thomas di Giovanni (New York: Dutton, 1969), 19.
5. Ibid., 27–28.
6. I realize that Borges's fictions are more cerebral than much of magical realism, and that here he can be seen primarily to be simply speculating about the difficulty of describing imagined realities in words, rather than creating an irreducible element inserted into the real. But because both Carlos Daneri and Borges are said to have seen the Aleph (although perhaps, as Borges implies, it is not the exact same Aleph), the story seems to me to qualify as early magical realism or a close precursor of it. The imaginative power of Borges's prose, the way in which his descriptions combine the actual and the imaginary, together with its speculative reconfigurations of time, space, and identity were a strong early influence on magical realism and are very similar to magical realist techniques of mixing the marvelous and the ordinary. This therefore seems like an appropriate place to begin.
7. Gabriel García Márquez, *One Hundred Years of Solitude,* trans. Gregory Rabassa (New York: Avon, 1971), 129–30. Further citations are given in the text.
8. William Kennedy, *Ironweed* (New York: Penguin, 1984), 17. Further citations are given in the text.
9. Günter Grass, *The Tin Drum,* trans. Ralph Manheim (New York: Vintage, 1964), 71. Further citations are given in the text.

10. Isabel Allende sees magical realism as breaking away from a "way of facing reality in which the only thing one dares talk about are those things one can control. What cannot be controlled is denied"; "The Shaman and the Infidel" (interview), *New Perspectives Quarterly*, 55.

11. Patrick Süskind, *Perfume: The Story of a Murderer*, trans. John E. Woods (New York: Knopf, 1986), 242.

12. For further discussion of this technique, see Amaryll Chanady's chapter "Authorial Reticence," in her *Magical Realism and the Fantastic: Resolved Versus Unresolved Antinomy* (New York: Garland, 1985), 121–60. There she notes that the absence of an explanation for a supernatural event is an important technique in magical realism.

13. André Breton, "Second Manifesto of Surrealism," in *Manifestoes of Surrealism,* trans. Richard Seaver and Helen R. Lane (Ann Arbor: University of Michigan Press, 1969), 123–24.

14. Cf. Chanady, *Magical Realism and the Fantastic,* 49: "the description of the metamorphosis itself is so matter-of-fact and detailed, that the reader unreservedly accepts the incredible event."

15. Ben Okri, *The Famished Road* (New York: Doubleday, 1992), 45. Further citations are given in the text.

16. Ana Castillo, *So Far from God* (New York: Norton, 1993), 199. Further citations are given in the text.

17. Isabel Allende, *The House of the Spirits,* trans. Magda Bogin (New York: Knopf, 1985), 228. Further citations are given in the text.

18. Christine Brooke-Rose, *A Rhetoric of the Unreal: Studies in Narrative and Structure, Especially of the Fantastic* (Cambridge: Cambridge University Press, 1981), 142.

19. Lloyd Davies discusses what he calls the "oscillating" narrative perspective in *The House of the Spirits,* "which dismisses as well as vindicates magical practice"; *Allende, La casa de los espíritus* (London: Grant and Cutler, 2000), 67.

20. See Emir Rodríguez Monegal, *"One Hundred Years of Solitude:* The Last Three Pages," *Books Abroad* 47, 3 (1973): 485–89; and Roberto González Echevarría, "With Borges in Macondo," *Diacritics* 2, 1 (1972): 57–60. Similarly, for Angel Rama, since Melquíades is the author, Aureliano is the critic of the book; *Edificación de un arte nacional y popular: Gabriel García Márquez* (Bogotá: Colcultura, 1991), 88.

21. Edwin Williamson, "Magical Realism and the Theme of Incest in *One Hundred Years of Solitude,"* in *Gabriel García Márquez: New Readings,* ed. Bernard McGuirk and Richard Cardwell (Cambridge: Cambridge University Press, 1987), 61.

22. For a more extended discussion of this viewpoint, see Lois Parkinson Zamora, *Writing the Apocalypse: Historical Vision in Contemporary U.S. and Latin American Fiction* (Cambridge: Cambridge University Press, 1989), 39.

23. Marta Gallo, "El futuro perfecto de Macondo," *Revista Hispánica Moderna* 38 (1974–75): 115–35.

24. Robert Pinget, *That Voice,* trans. Barbara Wright (New York: Red Dust, 1982), 14. Further references are given in the text.

25. Ato Quayson discusses this temporal indeterminacy as a feature of Okri's narrative

technique. According to Quayson, because of the "lack of definite temporal indices in relation to events, . . . a homogeneous sense of a-temporality, relieved only by the vaguest time indices, is spread throughout the narrative"; *Strategic Transformations in Nigerian Writing: Orality and History in the Work of Rev. Samuel Johnson, Amos Tutuola, Wole Soyinka, and Ben Okri* (Oxford: James Curry, and Bloomington: Indiana University Press, 1997), 127–29.

26. Brenda Cooper has also noted this facet of Madame Koto's bar; *Magical Realism in West African Fiction: Seeing with a Third Eye* (New York: Routledge, 1998), 85–88.

27. Gaston Bachelard, *The Poetics of Space,* trans. Maria Jolas (Boston: Beacon Press, 1968).

28. Wilson Harris, *Palace of the Peacock* (London: Faber and Faber, 1968), 45. Further citations are given in the text.

29. Carlos Fuentes, *Aura,* trans. Lysander Kemp (1962; New York: Farrar, Straus & Giroux, 1975), 76.

30. Carlos Fuentes, *Distant Relations,* trans. Margaret Sayers Peden (New York: Farrar, Straus, & Giroux, 1982), 66–67. Further citations are given in the text.

31. Michel Dupuis and Albert Mingelgrün, "Pour une poétique du réalisme magique," in *Le Réalisme magique: Roman, peinture et cinéma,* ed. Jean Weisgerber (Brussels: Le Centre des Avant-gardes littéraires de l'Université de Bruxelles, 1987), 24.

32. For a discussion of magical realism's elaboration of connections between the worlds of the living and the dead, see Lois Parkinson Zamora, "Magical Romance/Magical Realism: Ghosts in U.S. and Latin American Fiction," in *Magical Realism: Theory, History, Community,* ed. Lois Parkinson Zamora and Wendy B. Faris (Durham: Duke University Press, 1995), 497–550.

33. Gloria Anzaldúa, "Metaphors in the Tradition of the Shaman," in *Conversant Essays: Contemporary Poets on Poetry,* ed. James McCorkle (Detroit: Wayne State University Press, 1990), 99.

34. Juan Rulfo, *Pedro Páramo,* trans. Lysander Kemp (New York: Grove Press, 1978), 53. Further citations are given in the text.

35. William Faulkner, *As I Lay Dying* (New York: Random House, 1957), 208.

36. Samuel Beckett, *The Unnameable,* in *Three Novels by Samuel Beckett: Molloy, Malone Dies, The Unnameable* (New York: Grove Press, 1965), 403–4.

37. Gene Bell-Villada studies a similar phenomenon used to a different end in García Márquez's *Autumn of the Patriarch.* He claims that García Márquez shifts voices and pronouns in that novel "to convey a full sense of despotism and its both systematic and arbitrary network of relationships"; "Pronoun Shifters: Virginia Woolf, Béla Bartók, Plebian Forms, Real-Life Tyrants, and the Shaping of García Márquez's *Patriarch,*" *Contemporary Literature* 28, 4 (1987): 465. Idris Parry associates the occasional confusion of pronouns in *The Tin Drum,* when Oskar refers to himself as both I and Oskar, with the sense in both art and science that "there is a natural order not yet revealed to us"; "Aspects of Günter Grass's Narrative Technique," *Forum for Modern Language Studies* 3 (1967): 109.

38. According to Paul B. Dixon, "the dichotomy between life and death and the incongru-

ous arrangement of textual evidence put the reader in a quandary. Who is dead and who is alive?"; *Reversible Readings: Ambiguity in Four Modern Latin American Novels* (Tuscaloosa: University of Alabama Press, 1985), 66.

39. Toni Morrison, *Beloved* (New York: Knopf, 1987), 215. Further citations are given in the text.

40. Blanca Merino agrees that the "you" points simultaneously at Felipe and the reader. And she also sees the sexual dynamics of the novel embodied in its pronouns: "the opposition between the *you* and the *I,* the future and the past, against the *she* that is eternal, is reproduced throughout the text through other binary opposites—history and myth, science and magic, logic and intuition, the temporal and the eternal, culture and nature, which continue to be associated with the masculine and feminine voices"; "Fantasía y realidad en *Aura* de Carlos Fuentes, *Literatura Mexicana* 2, 1 (1991): 139.

41. Julio Cortázar, "Axolotl," in *The End of the Game and Other Stories,* trans. Paul Blackburn (New York: Harper and Row, 1967), 8.

42. Such pronominal confusion inspires various interpretations. Alfred MacAdam believes that no transformation takes place and that the connection between man and axolotl was only temporary. It enacts an avowedly fictional "what if" scenario in which the axolotl's consciousness momentarily visits the man's mind. Though a sentence near the end of the story supports this interpretation, it seems to me that the details that locate the reader at the heart of the transformation, and actualize it, together with the statement by the narrator "I am an axolotl now" work against it; "La Torre de Danae," *Revista Iberoamericana* 39 (1973): 461–65. Both MacAdam and Nancy Gray Díaz analyze the metafictional implications of this transformation. According to Díaz, in "Axolotl," "the writer investigates it, contemplates it, becomes obsessed with it, becomes it." Furthermore, the trope of metamorphosis itself mimes the poetic act of admiration and appropriation of another being. *The Radical Self: Metamorphosis to Animal Form in Modern Latin American Narrative* (Columbia: University of Missouri Press, 1989), 80.

43. Pamela McNabb analyzes several other techniques that create a mysterious aura in this story, including repeated construction and deconstruction of dualities or multiplicities. She also signals the way in which the narrator enters progressively smaller worlds—from Paris at large to the Jardin des Plantes, to the aquarium, as he approaches his final transformation into the body of an axolotl; "Julio Cortázar's Axolotl: Literary Archeology of the Unreal," *International Fiction Review* 24, 1–2 (1997: 12–22.

44. That regenerative possibility is supported by Daniel Reedy's analysis of the story as a rewriting of the myth of the Aztec god Xolotl, who was a larval twin of Quetzalcoatl, and who is spiritually reborn, though the narrator's dismay at his transformation and the modern setting only suggest that possible rebirth, not confirm it; "Through the Looking-Glass: Aspects of Cortázar's Epiphanies of Reality," *Bulletin of Hispanic Studies* 54 (1976): 125–34.

45. Another bridging technique, perhaps even a variety of the one we are discussing here, another kind of "linguistic magic," as it were, is the use of the expression "as if," which, as Robert K. Anderson demonstrates about *One Hundred Years of Solitude,* tends to

merge the actual with the imagined; "La realidad y la destrucción de la línea en *Cien años de soledad*," *Explicación de Textos Literarios* 25, 1 (1996–97): 82–83.

46. Tzvetan Todorov, *The Fantastic: A Structural Approach to a Literary Genre*, trans. Richard Howard (Ithaca: Cornell University Press, 1975), 116.

47. Gabriel García Márquez, "Light Is Like Water," in *Strange Pilgrims*, trans. Edith Grossman (New York: Knopf, 1993), 158.

48. Bill Ashcroft, Gareth Griffiths, and Helen Tiffin, *The Empire Writes Back: Theory and Practice in Post-Colonial Literatures* (London: Routledge, 1989), 81.

49. Irlemar Chiampi, *El realismo maravilloso: Forma e ideología en la novela hispanoamericana*, trans. Agustín Martínez and Margara Russotto (Caracas: Monte Avila, 1983), 51.

50. Jean-Pierre Durix sees this same phenomenon as typical of Rushdie's novel: "For the children of midnight, magical powers mean that words can create reality, signifiers can trigger off the appearance of what they refer to. Since Saleem never blinks, his mother shuts his eyelids, occasioning the comment that 'I learned: the first lesson of my life: nobody can face the world with his eyes open all the time.' Thus fantasy arises out of verbal creation." *The Writer Written: The Artist and Creation in the New Literatures in English* (New York: Greenwood Press, 1987), 124.

51. André Breton, "Letter to Seers," in *Manifestoes of Surrealism*, 195.

52. In her recent article on *Mrs. Caliban* Rebecca Ann Bach does not classify the novel as magical realism, but she suggests its inclusion in the genre by maintaining that *Mrs. Caliban* is "a late-twentieth century creation that continually questions its own premises. Is its monster real? The novel refuses to answer." Rather, it "deliberately unsettles our wish for a 'real' understanding of its situation." "*Mrs. Caliban:* A Feminist Postmodernist *Tempest?*" in *Critique* 41, 4 (2000): 391–401.

53. Louise Erdrich, *Tracks* (New York: Harper and Row, 1989), 12. Joni Adamson Clarke writes, "Fleur Pillager is human; yet, at times, she is wolf, watermonster, and bear," and her radically ambiguous nature means that "she embodies what Julia Kristeva calls 'the abject,' . . . that which 'disturbs identity, system, order,'" although she considers Fleur's embodiment as a bear to be a vicious rumor. As Clarke notes, Fleur's liminal status embodies the characteristic strategies needed to survive in a culturally hybrid world. Clarke, "Why Bears Are Good to Think, and Theory Doesn't Have to be Murder: Transformation and Oral Tradition in Louise Erdrich's *Tracks*," *S.A.I.L.* 4, 1 (1992): 28, 34. Clarke quotes from Kristeva, *Powers of Horror: An Essay on Abjection*, trans. Leon S. Roudiez (New York: Columbia University Press, 1982), 4.

54. Tommaso Scarano, "Notes on Spanish-American Magical Realism," in *Coterminous Worlds: Magical Realism and Contemporary Post-colonial Literature in English*, ed. Elsa Linguanti, Francesco Casotti, and Carmen Concilio (Amsterdam and Atlanta: Rodopi, 1999), 26–27.

55. Süskind, *Perfume*, 216–20.

56. John Updike, *Brazil* (New York: Knopf, 1994), 204. Further citations are given in the text.

57. Stephen Slemon, "Magic Realism as Postcolonial Discourse," in Zamora and Faris, *Magical Realism,* 409.

58. Michael Harner, *The Way of the Shaman: A Guide to Power and Healing* (San Francisco: Harper, 1990), 46–48.

59. Toni Morrison, *Song of Solomon* (New York: Signet, 1978), 241–42.

60. By the end of the novel, according to Hutcheon, "something is about to intervene that will radically change Lisa's sense of herself, and that something is history"; *A Poetics of Postmodernism: History, Theory, Fiction* (New York: Routledge, 1988), 173.

61. Maxine Hong Kingston, *The Woman Warrior* (New York: Vintage, 1989), 72. Further citations are given in the text.

62. Dupuis and Mingelgrün have also noted this tendency in magical realism: "repetitions, constants, leitmotifs, resemblances, correspondences, conjunctions, mirror effects, symmetries, cyclical structures give the impression of a strange coherence among apparently different elements, spread out horizontally in time and space. Once exploited by the reader, this impression leads him to desubstantiate and to further intellectualize the novelistic world, to lift the veil covering the 'other side' of things, as their 'inner reality' appears." "Pour une poétique du réalisme magique," 226.

63. See the discussion of this idea in John T. Irwin, *Doubling and Incest, Repetition and Revenge: A Speculative Reading of Faulkner* (Baltimore: Johns Hopkins University Press, 1975), 94–97.

64. Brenda Cooper, who also notes this proliferation of roads in Okri's novel, analyzes them in more detail; *Magical Realism in West African Fiction,* 77–80.

65. I think Updike's novel is generally less successful than those of his Latin American models. The images and situations often seem artificial and the events simplistically primitivistic, embodying what Helmbrecht Breinig calls a "tortured metaphoricity" and a "confused exoticism," but *Brazil,* like Barth's and Morrison's avowed readings of García Márquez, signals an important moment in the history of magical realism. Breinig, "Inter-American Internationality: Updike's *Brazil,* Curley's *Mummy,* and the Question of Magical Realism," in *Cases and Problems,* vol. 1 of *The Internationality of National Literatures in Either America: Transfer and Transformation,* ed. Armin Paul Frank and Helga Ehrmann (Göttingen: Wallstein Verlag, 1999), 252.

66. Mary Robertson engages a number of these issues in her study of the novel. She discusses how Thomas dramatizes the incompatibility of historical atrocity and poetic sensibility, including fantasy: "the first part of the novel seems to confirm the often touted idea that every piece of 'fact' is always a fiction," in contrast to the scene at Babi Yar, which changes the direction of the novel entirely, discrediting the psychoanalytic discourse that precedes it. "Thomas seems to be arguing that Freud's larger failure to put himself in dialogue with real history is symptomatic of the failure of prominent analytical languages to make the world better by understanding what happens in history." "Hystery, Herstory, History: 'Imagining the Real' in Thomas's *The White Hotel,*" *Contemporary Literature* 25, 4 (1984): 461–63.

67. It is interesting to note, in connection with my contention that magical realist narrative

operates in similar ways to shamanic performances, that these reversals can also be seen as projecting the sense of a translation from a different register of experience in which the order of the original may have become reversed. In shamanic transformations, that sense of reality in reverse can provide evidence of a different register of experience, an alternative to ordinary reality that confers shamanic power. Such a translation is embodied in the way in which Colombian Tukanos describe the difference between real jaguars and shamans who are men-turned-jaguars: "a common jaguar is like a dog. But a paye[shaman]-turned-jaguar is upside down. Everything is reversed." Like the lovemaking of Tristão and Isabel after their transformations, "what is below, is up, and what is up is below." See the discussion of this issue at the end of the book by G. Reichel-Dolmatoff, *The Shaman and the Jaguar: A Study of Narcotic Drugs Among the Indians of Colombia* (Philadelphia: Temple University Press, 1975), 120.

Chapter 4

1. Irlemar Chiampi, *El realismo maravilloso: Forma e ideología en la novela hispanoamericana,* trans. Agustín Martínez and Margara Russotto (Caracas: Monte Avila, 1983), 199.

2. It is particularly important in the case of magical realism, which tends toward de-individualization of the narrative voice, to understand that the implied author is a "set of norms," an "it" that "instructs us silently, through the design of the whole" text; see Shlomith Rimmon-Kenan, *Narrative Fiction: Contemporary Poetics* (New York: Methuen, 1983), 88; and Seymour Chatman, *Story and Discourse: Narrative Poetics in Fiction and Film* (Ithaca: Cornell University Press, 1978), 148. For a discussion of the connection between focalizers and implied authors, see Patrick O'Neill, "Points of Origin: On Focalization in Narrative," *Canadian Review of Comparative Literature* 19, 3 (1992): 341–45. Thanks to Emma Kafalenos for helping me to clarify these, and other, issues in narratology.

3. One might also propose that because of its disruptive nature within realism, the irreducible element in magical realism is a particular form of what Homi Bhabha analyzes as the slippage, excess, and difference typical of colonial mimicry; *The Location of Culture* (New York: Routledge, 1994), 86.

4. Oliver Lovesey ends his consideration of Ngũgĩ wa Thiong'o's transformation of Christian allegory by proposing that "to suggest a cultural and political metamorphosis of reality, Ngũgĩ had to overcome the problems encoded in Western novelistic representation, by drawing on discourses that could enable a poetics of transformation." Although he is not analyzing magical realism as such, and while he maintains that "Ngũgĩ's work is predicated on a purely materialistic eschatology," that formulation holds true for the way in which magical realism as a decolonizing style draws on non-realistic discourses that model cultural transformation. "The Post-Colonial 'Crisis of Representation' and Ngũgĩ wa Thiong'o's Religious Allegory," in *"And the Birds Began to Sing": Religion and Literature in Post-Colonial Cultures,* ed. Jamie S. Scott (Amsterdam and Atlanta: Rodopi, 1996), 189.

5. Jaime Alazraki, "Para una revalidación del concepto realismo mágico en la literatura hispanoamericana," in *Homenaje a Andrés Iduarte,* ed. Alazraki et al. (Clear Creek, In.: American Hispanist, 1976), 18.

6. Stephen Slemon, "Magic Realism as Postcolonial Discourse," in *Magical Realism: Theory, History, Community,* ed. Lois Parkinson Zamora and Wendy B. Faris (Durham: Duke University Press, 1995), 408.

7. See Ute Dapprich-Barrett, "Magical Realism: Sources and Affinities in Contemporary German and English Writing," in *The Novel in Anglo-German Context,* ed. Susanne Stark (Amsterdam/Atlanta: Rodopi, 2000), 345.

8. Günter Grass, "Fictions Are Lies That Tell the Truth: Salman Rushdie and Günter Grass: In Conversation," in *Conversations with Salman Rushdie,* ed. Michael R. Reder (Jackson: University Press of Mississippi, 2000), 72.

9. Bhabha, *Location of Culture,* 25.

10. The formulations are from the article by Stephen Slemon, "Magic Realism as Postcolonial Discourse," 409, which I discovered as I was developing this argument. According to Bill Ashcroft, Gareth Williams, and Helen Tiffin, hybridity is "the primary characteristic of all post colonial texts"; *The Empire Writes Back: Theory and Practice in Post-Colonial Literatures* (New York: Routledge: 1989), 185.

11. For a discussion of the ways in which in Louise Erdrich's fiction "textual evocation of various conflicting codes . . . produces in the reader an experience of marginality," see Catherine Rainwater, "Reading between Worlds: Narrativity in the Fiction of Louise Erdrich," *American Literature* 62, 3 (September 1990): 406.

12. In his discussion of the transculturation process in Latin American narrative, Angel Rama cites the example of García Márquez, who he believes solves the problem of joining historical realities and fantastic perspectives by recourse to oral and popular narrative structures; *Transculturación narrativa en América latina* (Mexico City: Siglo Veintiuno, 1982), 44–45. As Michael Valdez Moses points out, while the realism in magical realism comes from the European realistic canon, for the most part the magical elements tend to originate in local traditions; "Magical Realism at World's End," *Literary Imagination: The Review of The Association of Literary Scholars and Critics* 3 (2001): 110–11. However, as magical realism expands its geographic range, especially in the developed world, this division tends to be less and less true.

13. Michael Taussig, *The Nervous System* (New York: Routledge, 1992), 149.

14. Michel Foucault, "Of Other Spaces," trans. Jay Miskowiec, *Diacritics* 16 (1986): 23; cited in Jamie S. Scott, "Introduction," in Jamie S. Scott and Paul Simpson-Housley, eds., *Mapping the Sacred: Religion, Geography, and Postcolonial Literatures* (Amsterdam and Atlanta: Rodopi, 2001), xxviii.

15. Timothy Brennan, *At Home in the World: Cosmopolitanism Now* (Cambridge: Harvard University Press, 1997), 189.

16. Gareth Griffiths, "Postcoloniality, Religion, Geography: Keeping Our Feet on the Ground and Our Heads Up," in Scott and Simpson-Housley, *Mapping the Sacred,* 445–46.

17. Ralph Flores, *The Rhetoric of Doubtful Authority: Deconstructive Readings of Self-Questioning Narratives, St. Augustine to Faulkner* (Ithaca: Cornell University Press, 1984).

18. Josna Rege points out how this process is thematized in *Midnight's Children:* "Even though Saleem is supremely the person to whom things have been done, it is Rushdie's magic that 'against all indications to the contrary,' transforms victim to protagonist"; "Victim into Protagonist: *Midnight's Children* and the Post-Rushdie National Narratives of the Eighties," in *Critical Essays on Salman Rushdie,* ed. M. Keith Booker (New York: G. K. Hall, 1999), 261.

19. Jacques Stéphen Alexis, "Lettre à mes amis peintres," *Reflets d'Haïti* 16 (January 21, 1956): 3; cited in J. Michael Dash, "Marvelous Realism: The Way Out of Negritude," *Caribbean Studies* 13, 4 (1973): 69.

20. Wilson Harris, "Tradition and the West Indian Novel," in *Tradition, the Writer and Society* (London: New Beacon Publications, 1967); cited in Kenneth Ramchand, Preface to Wilson Harris, *Palace of the Peacock* (London: Faber and Faber, 1960), no pagination.

21. See Ian Watt, *The Rise of the Novel* (Berkeley and Los Angeles: University of California Press, 1969).

22. Ado Quayson, *Strategic Transformations in Nigerian Writing: Orality and History in the Work of Rev. Samuel Johnson, Amos Tutuola, Wole Soyinka, and Ben Okri* (Oxford: James Curry, and Bloomington: Indiana University Press, 1997), 137.

23. Toni Morrison, *Beloved* (New York: Knopf, 1987), 103.

24. Victor Turner, *Dramas, Fields, and Metaphors: Symbolic Action in Human Society* (Ithaca: Cornell University Press, 1974), 258.

25. Günter Grass, *The Tin Drum,* trans. Ralph Manheim (New York: Random House, 1964), 68.

26. In his discussion of *The Tin Drum,* Alexander Gelley links the magical realist technique in which "inanimate objects seem to be endowed with a compelling power" directly to historical outrage, such as, for example, the death of the toyshop owner Sigismund Markus on Kristallnacht as narrated by Grass, eliminating human agency, because "it is as if no uncorrupted human agent could still be found fit to see and judge"; "Art and Reality in *Die Blechtrommel,*" *Forum for Modern Language Studies* 3 (1967): 117. Bernard McElroy links Grass's technique with the history he is depicting; his playing with the boundaries of credibility, creating "a fluidity of perspective, multiplying the possibilities for bizarre incidents by diminishing the differences between sane and insane, subject and object, history and fantasy [is] a fluidity that proves invaluable in dealing with a period when history was fantastic and behavior insanity on an international scale; "Lunatic, Child, Artist, Hero: Grass's Oskar as a Way of Seeing," *Forum for Modern Language Studies* 22, 4 (1986): 310. Ann L. Mason agrees that Grass's departures from realism derive in part from his experience of Nazism: "for Grass, Mann's view of history [as a logical sequence of events leading to a verifiable result] is not only incommensurate with the absurdity and chaos of the Nazi period, but also smacks somewhat of the romantic tendencies of Nazi rhetoric itself"; *The Skeptical Muse: A Study of Günter Grass' Conception of the Artist* (Bern: Peter Lang, 1974), 72. Alan F. Keele studies the

motif of the seer or visionary with magical powers into which Grass taps in his novel *Hundejahre,* and to which Oskar's extraordinary power can also be related, proposing that a magical kind of extraordinary perception that goes beyond conventional histories is needed to reflect the virtually unbelievable world of the Third Reich; "'. . . Through a (Dark) Glass Clearly': Magic Spectacles and the Motif of the Mimetic Mantic in Postwar German Literature from Borchert to Grass," *Germanic Review* 57, 2 (1982): 49–59.

27. Josna E. Rege, "Victim into Protagonist," 268.

28. According to Marguerite Alexander, "the supernatural gifts of midnight's children, which in the beginning were a magical intrusion into the known facts of history, generating comedy, have acquired meaning as subversive, transformative powers, alien to the processes of government because they suggest alternative possibilities"; *Flights from Realism: Themes and Strategies in Postmodernist British and American Fiction* (New York: Routledge, 1990), 142.

29. Salman Rushdie, *Midnight's Children* (New York: Avon, 1982), 237. Further citations are given in the text.

30. Gabriel García Márquez, *One Hundred Years of Solitude,* trans. Gregory Rabassa (New York: Avon, 1971), 279.

31. Marie Darrieussecq cited in Catherine Rodgers, "Aucune Evidence: Les Truismes de Marie Darrieussecq," *Romance Studies* 18, 1 (2000): 79.

32. Milan Kundera, *The Book of Laughter and Forgetting,* trans. Michael Henry Heim (New York: Penguin, 1982), 73. Further citations are given in the text.

33. Although he does not deal specifically with magical realism, David Horrocks makes a similar point with respect to historical authority and individual agency and change in Grass and Rushdie. He aligns their texts with the ideas of Hayden White, who claims that in attempting to give meaning to history, rather than allowing it to exist as chaos and uncertainty (as Horrocks sees it doing in the novels of Grass and Rushdie), modern historians (in White's words) "deprive history of the kind of meaninglessness that alone can goad human beings to make their lives different, . . . to endow their lives with a meaning for which they alone are responsible." Hayden White, "The Politics of Historical Interpretation: Discipline and De-Sublimation," in White, *The Content of the Form: Narrative Discourse and Historical Representation* (Baltimore: Johns Hopkins University Press, 1990), 72; cited in Horrocks, "The Undisciplined Past: Novel Approaches to History in Grass and Rushdie," in *The Novel in Anglo-German Context: Cultural Cross-Currents and Affinities,* ed. Susanne Stark (Amsterdam and Atlanta: Rodopi, 2000), 349.

34. Jean-François Lyotard, *The Postmodern Condition: A Report on Knowledge,* trans. Geoff Bennington and Brian Massumi (Minneapolis: University of Minnesota Press, 1984), 82.

35. Carlos Fuentes, *Distant Relations,* trans. Margaret Sayers Peden (New York: Farrar, Straus & Giroux, 1982), 203, 215. Further citations are given in the text.

36. There is an entirely different way to interpret Fuentes's narrative strategies here (and in *Terra Nostra* as well), and that is to accuse him of constructing such a confusing

narrative web that only he is in complete control of it and so has executed the ultimate hegemonic power move. But that accusation can be leveled at much modern and postmodern fiction.

37. Arun Mukherjee sees many "similarities between Brecht's epic theatre and what has been termed 'magic realism.'" Both Brecht and Rushdie "wish to break the hold of mimetic forms and their concomitant imperatives of a well-structured plot and life-like characters" who induce an empathy in the reader that camouflages social inequities. Instead, they use distancing devices such as opinionated narrators, exaggeration, mimicry, parody, and allegory to destroy empathy and to politicize readers; "Characterization in Salman Rushdie's *Midnight's Children:* Breaking out of the Hold of Realism and Seeking the 'Alienation Effect,'" in *The New Indian Novel in English: A Study of the 1980's,* ed. Viney Kirpal (New Delhi: Allied Publishers, 1990), 111, 114.

38. This idea is related to the argument for the revolutionary aura of antirealism presented by Gerald Graff, who maintains that "the revolt against realism and representation is closely tied to the revolt against a unitary psychology of the self. [And furthermore,] as Leo Bersani argues in *A Future for Astyanax,* 'the literary myth of a rigidly ordered self,'" a myth perpetuated by realism, "contributes to a pervasive cultural ideology of the self which serves the established social order"; Graff, "The Politics of Anti-Realism," in *The Salmagundi Reader,* ed. Robert Boyers and Peggy Boyers (Bloomington: Indiana University Press, 1983), 397; see also Leo Bersani, *A Future for Astyanax: Character and Desire in Literature* (New York: Little, 1976), 56, cited in Graff, "Politics of Anti-Realism." For an engaging account of the link between literary realism and intellectual authority in the United States, see Phillip Barrish, *American Literary Realism, Critical Theory, and Intellectual Prestige, 1880–1995* (Cambridge: Cambridge University Press, 2001).

39. Wilson Harris, "The Native Phenomenon," in *Common Wealth,* ed. Anna Rutherford (Aarhus, Denmark: University of Aarhus, n.d.), 148.

40. Wilson Harris, cited in Michel Fabre, "Recovering Precious Words: On Wilson Harris and the Language of Imagination," in *The Uncompromising Imagination,* ed. Hena Maes-Jellinek (Mundelstrup and Sydney: Dangaroo, 1991), 48.

41. Rushdie in an interview with David Brooks, from *Helix,* 19/20 (1984): 55–69; reprinted in Reder, *Conversations with Salman Rushdie,* 57.

42. See Chanady, "The Territorialization of the Imaginary: Self-Affirmation and Resistance to Metropolitan Paradigms," in Zamora and Faris, *Magical Realism,* 19.

43. Howard Brenton in Tariq Ali and Howard Brenton, *Iranian Nights* (London: Nick Hern Books, 1989), 7.

44. Lyotard, *Postmodern Condition,* 82.

45. Cf. Timothy Brennan, on the magical realism practiced in postcolonial societies, as "the anti-authoritarian formal logic, not of postmodernism's decentered subject, but of the degraded citizen-victim, wildly associating fact and fiction as if to outwit the censors, or (alternatively) to suggest the impossibility of accepting the perverse dimensions of modern 'totalitarianism'"; "Fantasy, Individuality, and the Politics of Liberation," *Polygraph* 1, 1 (1987): 94.

46. For a good discussion of the issues of voice appropriation as they complicate modernist texts and mediate the intersection of modern and postmodern discourses, see Bette London, *The Appropriated Voice: Narrative Authority in Conrad, Forster, and Woolf* (Ann Arbor: University of Michigan Press, 1990). The passage quoted here is from page 6. As London points out, "it is in appropriation itself that we might locate the site of resistance to political hegemony—in, for example, the discourses of mimicry, parody, and pastiche" (4). A similar argument over authenticity of voice takes place within postcolonial theory between "diasporic" and "resident" voices. See, for example, R. Radhakrishnan, "Postcoloniality and the Boundaries of Identity," *Callaloo* 16, 4 (1993): 750–71. For a discussion of this problematic issue of voice appropriation in the context of the Latin American testimonial novel, see John Beverley and Hugo Achugar, eds., *La voz del otro: Testimonio, subalternidad y verdad narrativa* (Pittsburgh: Latinoamericana Editores, 1992).

47. Wilson Harris, *Explorations,* ed. Hena Maes Jellinek (Aarhus: Dangaroo, 1981), 16–17; cited in Rosemary Jolly, "Rehearsals of Liberation: Contemporary Postcolonial Discourse and the New South Africa," *PMLA* 110, 1 (1995): 17. For a discussion of similar issues of cultural appropriation specifically related to shamanism, see Gabriel Weisz's "ethnodiscursive" reading of Carlos Castañeda's Don Juan tales in which he analyzes how Castañeda appropriates the otherness of exotic shamans. Weisz contrasts that discourse with what I would call a magical realist tale in which a coyote serves as an interlocutor in conversation with an anthropologist. During that tale, according to Weisz, "an invisible world acquires materiality through those elements which are only tangible to Coyote," a phenomenon illustrated by a scene in which Coyote places a cup of coffee on a hair from his tail suspended in the air. "Shamanism and Its Discontents," in *Methods for the Study of Literature as Cultural Memory,* ed. Raymond Vervliet and Annemarie Estor, vol. 6 of *Literature as Cultural Memory* (Amsterdam: Rodopi, 2000), 284.

48. Gayatri Chakravorty Spivak, *The Postcolonial Critic: Interviews, Strategies, Dialogues* (New York: Routledge, 1990), 72.

49. Robert Pinget, *That Voice,* trans. Barbara Wright (New York: Red Dust, 1982), 14.

50. José B. Monleón, *A Specter Is Haunting Europe: A Sociohistorical Approach to the Fantastic* (Princeton: Princeton University Press, 1990), 8. See also Amaryll Chanady, *Magical Realism and the Fantastic: Resolved Versus Unresolved Antinomy* (New York: Garland, 1985).

51. Roberto González Echevarría, *Myth and Archive: A Theory of Latin American Narrative* (Cambridge: Cambridge University Press, 1990), 159.

52. Nicholas Thomas confronts this issue of a commodifying primitivism that is also enabling for indigenous identity formation in his examination of an early exhibition of Maori cultural artifacts. See his *Colonialism's Culture: Anthropology, Travel, and Government* (Princeton: Princeton University Press, 1994), 188.

53. That these questions are fast entering the mainstream is evidenced by a review of a set of compact disks called *Global Meditations—Authentic Music from Meditative Traditions of the World* in *Esquire,* June 1993), 36–37. Under a picture of Ghanaian drummers is the caption: "Whole Lotta Shaman." This review implicitly objects to some of the assump-

tions behind the marketing of this type of music by "never-to-chart-wise primitives who by virtue of their very otherness are assumed to be closer to god/goddess-head than poor soulless us."

54. Michael Taussig, *Shamanism, Colonialism, and the Wild Man: A Study in Terror and Healing* (Chicago: University of Chicago Press, 1987), 190, 168, 216.

55. Ibid., 166. Here Taussig is citing Susan Buck-Morss's formulation of Benjamin's ideas as expressed in his *Passagenwerk;* Buck-Morss, "Benjamin's *Passagenwerk,"New German Critique* 29 (1983): 211–40.

56. Taussig, *Shamanism, Colonialism, and the Wild Man,* 167.

57. Ibid.

58. Patrick Murphy makes a similar argument in favor of men "rendering" women as speaking subjects through the application of feminist theories. He also cites Gary Snyder, who maintains that in cave paintings "the animals were speaking through the people and making their point." Murphy, "Ground, Pivot, Motion: Ecofeminist Theory, Dialogics, and Literary Practice," *Hypatia* 6 (Spring 1991): 152–53.

59. Jean-Pierre Durix would seem to agree with this assessment, stating in his book on magical realism and postcolonial literature that "this new genre may well have provided a new mode of expression whose potential has not been fully explored"; *Mimesis, Genres, and Post-Colonial Discourse: Deconstructing Magic Realism* (New York: St. Martin's, 1998), 159.

60. For an excellent discussion of these complex issues as embodied in Cortázar's story "Axolotl," see R. Lane Kauffmann, "Cortázar's 'Axolotl' as Ethnographic Allegory," in *Primitivism and Identity in Latin America: Essays in Art, Literature, and Culture,* ed. Erik Camayd-Freixas and José Eduardo González (Tucson: University of Arizona Press, 2000), 135–55. According to Kauffmann, "what is remarkable about the story . . . is the way it both sets up a Eurocentric allegory about encountering the Other, and yet seems to invite an ironic deconstruction of that allegory" (148–49). His reading of "Axolotl" thus "suggests how difficult it remains to separate the urge to know cultural others from our deeper need to reinvent them—to explore, through fiction, our imaginary relations (affective, libidinal, or ideological) with those others" (150). Marcy Schwartz also reads "Axolotl" as engaging with postcolonial issues. She maintains that "the exchange of identities only partially works, and thus the fantastic shift coincides with the postcolonial predicament. The protagonist changes form but not substance, trades bodies but not minds. Both man and animal remain locked into the colonial paradigm that their respective estrangement in France glaringly mirrors back to them." *Writing Paris: Topographies of Desire in Contemporary Latin American Fiction* (Buffalo: State University of New York Press, 1999), 39.

61. Jacques Stéphen Alexis, *Les Arbres musiciens* (Paris: Gallimard, 1957), 180.

62. Valdez Moses is more skeptical than I regarding this preservation in his discussion of the issue; "Magical Realism at World's End," 115.

63. Trudier Harris, *Fiction and Folklore in the Novels of Toni Morrison* (Knoxville: University of Tennessee Press, 1991), 9–11. Sethe thinks of Denver in her womb as "the little antelope," though "why she thought of an antelope Sethe could not imagine since

she had never seen one," but Morrison gives us a hint when Sethe recalls that back at Sweet Home "sometimes they danced the antelope," presumably a remnant of the Bambara harvest ritual in Mali that uses the tall and elegant Chi Wara headdresses that are among the most well-known West African sculptures, some of them with a "little antelope" perched on the back of its mother. Morrison, *Beloved*, 30–31. The association also returns that cultural icon to the African American descendants of its creators rather than leaving it in the realm of primitive art galleries largely frequented by other constituencies or to the advertisements for expensive perfume that it adorned in the recent past. Thanks to Steve Walker for reminding me that some of these headdresses have their babies on their backs, carved out of the same piece of wood, a detail that is especially pertinent in the context of Sethe and Beloved.

64. Serge Govaert, "Une Approche sociologique," in *Le Réalisme magique: Roman, peinture et cinéma*, ed. Jean Weisgerber (Brussels: Le Centre des Avant-gardes littéraires de l'Université de Bruxelles, 1987), 243, 238.

65. Carlos Fuentes, *Constancia and Other Stories for Virgins*, trans. Thomas Christensen (New York: Harper, 1991), 45. Further citations are given in the text.

66. See the discussion in Chapter 5 of Fuentes's essay "Central and Eccentric," in which he compares himself to Emily Brontë as cultural subaltern.

67. André Schwarz-Bart, *A Woman Named Solitude*, trans. Ralph Manheim (New York: Atheneum, 1973), 174. Further citations are given in the text.

68. Taussig, *Shamanism, Colonialism, and the Wild Man*, 329.

69. Michael Lambek, Afterword to Jeannette Marie Mageo and Alan Howard, eds., *Spirits in Culture, History, and Mind* (New York: Routledge, 1996), 245.

70. Holger Kalweit, *Dreamtime and Inner Space: The World of the Shaman* (Boston: Shambhala, 1988), 254.

71. I realize that Taussig himself is extremely suspicious of correlations between shamanic activity and narrative, as examples of what he considers Western appropriations, systematizations, and fantasy projections—in short, the reification—of indigenous practices. In deconstructing Mircea Eliade's formulations of shamanism as an erroneous "mystifying of Otherness as a transcendent force," he cites Black Elk's statement regarding the trouble he has reconstituting his own visions, because " 'more was shown me than I can tell,' " and proposes that "it is to that *not knowing,* and to that risk [of having a vision misunderstood] that we must . . . refer shamanic discourse. I would argue that those qualities of incompleteness, of *not knowing,* of uncertainty, and also of fabrication, of civilized reification of indigenous images and traditions, are embodied in magical realism's narrative techniques and its cultural hybridity. Deconstructed in this way, shamanism provides concepts that shed light on magical realism. Because of their location at the site of transculturation, magical realist narratives, like shamanic practice as Taussig describes it, transmit not a unitary voice that reveals an original kernel of truth but rather uncertain visions of varied origin. His description of that practice seems very applicable to magical realist narrative: "a type of modernism in which parts are only loosely connected one to the other, there is no centralizing cathartic force, and there exists an array of distancing techniques involving and disinvolving the reader

or spectator and thus, potentially at least, dismantling all fixed and fixing notions of identity." Taussig, *Nervous System,* 159–60.

72. Taussig, *Shamanism, Colonialism, and the Wild Man,* 327. All quotations in the next two paragraphs are from Taussig's discussion in ibid., 327–29. Page numbers appear in the text.

73. Elleke Boehmer, *Colonial and Postcolonial Literature: Migrant Metaphors* (New York: Oxford University Press, 1995), 242.

74. Gabriel García Márquez, "The Solitude of Latin America," *Granta* 9 (1983): 58. Cited in Timothy Brennan, *Salman Rushdie and the Third World* (New York: St. Martin's, 1989), 66.

75. Brennan, *Salman Rushdie and the Third World,* 66–68.

76. Margaret Cezair-Thompson, "Beyond the Postcolonial Novel: Ben Okri's *The Famished Road* and Its 'Abiku' Traveller," *Journal of Commonwealth Literature* 31, 2 (1996): 35, 37.

77. Fredric Jameson, *The Political Unconscious* (Ithaca: Cornell University Press, 1984), 104.

78. Ibid., 148.

79. Both Marguerite Suárez-Murias and P. Gabrielle Foreman (who cites her) agree with this assessment of magical realism, though the latter would associate it with a female sensibility. According to Suárez-Murias, "the marvelous [or magic realism] presupposes an element of faith on the part of the author or the audience"; further, surrealism and the fantastic require "the total negation of faith and tradition. It is here where magic realism splits away" (brackets added by Foreman). Suárez-Murias, "El Realismo Mágico: Una definición étnica," in *Essays on Hispanic Literature/Ensayos de literatura hispana: A Bilingual Anthology* (Washington, D.C.: University Press of America, 1982), 103; cited in Foreman, "Past-On Stories: History and the Magically Real: Morrison and Allende on Call," *Feminist Studies* 18, 2 (1992): 370.

80. This is the opinion of Carlos Blanco Aguinaga with regard to *One Hundred Years of Solitude.* He believes that the rain that falls for four years, eleven months, and two days fictionally erases any attempts on the part of Macondo or its readers to come to terms with the Banana Company's massacre of workers. *De mitólogos y novelistas* (Madrid: Ediciones Turner, 1975), 478. Brian Conniff disagrees, claiming that García Márquez and magical realism "can depict events strange enough, and oppressive enough, to make apocalypse appear not only credible but inevitable," thereby criticizing the systems that lead us there; "The Dark Side of Magical Realism: Science, Oppression, and Apocalypse in *One Hundred Years of Solitude,*" *Modern Fiction Studies* 36, 2 (1990): 168.

81. Many readers have been uncomfortable with Thomas's combination of psychic fantasy, particularly the utopian ending of the novel, with historical atrocity. Lars Sauerberg believes Thomas is unable to solve the problem of uniting "the individual's wish for an afterlife with the historical certainty of the absolute, irrevocable, and monstrous reality of death." "When the Soul Takes Wing: D. M. Thomas's *The White Hotel,*" *Critique* 31 (1989), 8. In contrast, Laura Tanner takes a different position when she investigates a rhetorical strategy similar to the one for which I argue here. She claims that finally

"violence refuses to be contained in purely metaphorical terms [even though it may have been introduced that way]. The collision of lovemaking and violence—unlike the collision of sex and metaphorical, aestheticized violence—is horrific rather than exciting." Hence she sees Thomas as condemning "Freud's metaphorical perception of Lisa's agony." "Sweet Pain and Charred Bodies: Figuring Violence in *The White Hotel*," *Boundary* 2, 18 (1991): 145.

82.   Ben Okri, *The Famished Road* (New York: Doubleday, 1992), 188–90.

83.   Jean-Pierre Durix, *The Writer Written: The Artist and Creation in the New Literatures in English* (New York: Greenwood, 1987), 127. P. Gabrielle Foreman claims that in García Márquez's text the magical and the historical repel each other, and that in Allende's and Morrison's the reverse is true. While it may be true that, as she points out, Allende does pass from magic to politics, so that she can entrance her international audience before politicizing it, I think that the implicit critique of real history by narrative magic operates in both texts. Foreman, "Past-On Stories," 179–80. Furthermore, Lloyd Davies points out that while politics is more prevalent in the latter part of *The House of the Spirits*, the reference to Barrabás at the end, which recalls the magical beginning of the novel, means that magical realism coexists with testimonial discourse; Allende, *La casa de los espíritus* (London: Grant and Cutler, 2000), 100.

84.   For a discussion of Saleem's escape from and re-entry into history, see Patrick McGee, *Telling the Other: The Question of Value in Modern and Postcolonial Writing* (Ithaca: Cornell University Press, 1992), 141–44.

85.   Jameson, *Political Unconscious*, 104.

86.   Monleón, *Specter Is Haunting Europe*, 14

87.   Ibid., 51, 63.

88.   For a discussion of Kafka's marginal position, see Gilles Deleuze and Félix Guattari, *Kafka: Pour une littérature mineure* (Paris: Minuit, 1975).

89.   In his report of discussions at the Marxist writers' conference on Kafka in 1963, Günter Grass focuses on *The Castle* rather than on *The Metamorphosis*. Nevertheless, the spirit of that conference, concerned with the problem of reconciling a fantastic form of narrative with a progressive social program resembles the agenda of many magical realists, including Grass himself in *The Tin Drum*, published a few years earlier. See Grass, "Kafka and His Executors," in his *On Writing and Politics, 1967–1983*, trans. Ralph Manheim (New York: Harcourt Brace Jovanovich, 1985), 31–50.

90.   Georg Lukács, *Marxism and Human Liberation* (New York: Dell, 1973), 297.

91.   Rosemary Jackson, *Fantasy, the Literature of Subversion* (New York: Methuen, 1981), 4; cited in Monleón, *A Specter Is Haunting Europe*, 14.

92.   Edna Aizenberg argues that "García Márquez manipulates the discourse of the marvelous in order to reproduce, puncture, and overcome the unreality imposed by the colonialist enterprise"; "*The Famished Road*: Magical Realism and the Search for Social Equity," *Yearbook of Comparative and General Literature* 43 (1995): 27. See also her statements in "Historical Subversion and Violence of Representation in García Márquez and Ouloguem," *PMLA* 107 (1992): 1247. Brennan makes a similar point about the political turn in magical realism in regard to Rushdie by claiming that García Márquez's influ-

ence on him "passed through Nicaragua." Visiting that country, Rushdie wrote that in the city of Matagalpa García Márquez's " 'Macondo did not seem very far away.' " For Brennan, "the Anglicization of 'magical realism' and the saleable 'Third-Worldism' it represents, required the adoption of a specific attitude towards the colonial legacy," in which magical realism served "as the imaginative expression of 'freedom.' " And that consequently Rushdie uses "unrealism" to legitimize his political observations. Brennan, *Salman Rushdie and the Third World*, 65–66; Rushdie quoted on p. 65.

93. Valdez Moses stresses the way in which contemporary international magical realism "is both an effect and a vehicle for globalization." Although he does not cite it, the impetus behind this collection supports his point; "Magical Realism at World's End," 105.

94. Alberto Fuguet and Sergio Gómez, eds., *McOndo* (Barcelona: Mondadori, 1996), 14.

95. Ibid., 26.

96. Maarten Van Delden discusses this change in Latin America from the historically liberatory agenda, including magical realism, to the sense of a need for more historical grounding with respect to Fuentes's work: "In *La nueva novela,* Fuentes presented Latin American history as a nightmare from which the new novelist was going to awake the continent. He saw the work of Cortázar, García Márquez, Carpentier, and others, as sharing in 'a magical atmosphere' that presented a deliberate alternative to 'the historical nightmare' . . . of Latin America. The new novel [and, I would add, magical realism] was an escape from 'the monolithic exigencies of history and geography.' By 1993 the problem has become not the excess weight of the past, but rather the loss of a sense of history. And so the novel has a new task: to oppose the process of 'de-historicization and de-socialization of the world we live in.' " Van Delden, *Carlos Fuentes, Mexico, and Modernity* (Nashville: Vanderbilt University Press, 1998), 112. The citations from Fuentes, which I have translated from the Spanish in Van Delden's text, are taken from *La nueva novela* (Mexico City: Joaquín Mortiz, 1969), 67–68; and *La Geografía de la novela* (Mexico City: Fondo de Cultura Económica, 1993), 13.

97. Erik Camayd-Freixas, *Realismo mágico y primitivismo: Relecturas de Carpentier, Asturias, Rulfo, y García Márquez* (Lanham, Md.: University Press of America, 1998), 299–300.

98. Chiampi, *El realismo maravilloso*, 219.

99. V. Y. Mudimbe, *The Idea of Africa* (Bloomington: Indiana University Press, 1994), 207; cited in Cooper, *Magical Realism in West African Fiction*, 225.

100. Durix, *Mimesis*, 189.

101. Valeria Guidotti, "Magical Realism Beyond the Wall of Apartheid?" in *Coterminous Worlds: Magical Realism and Contemporary Post-colonial Literature in English,* ed. Elsa Linguanti, Francesco Casotti, and Carmen Concilio (Amsterdam and Atlanta: Rodopi, 1999), 230. In addition to claiming that because of its culturally hybrid status, the Afrikaaner community will continue to use magical realism, she also reports that "the same seamless interweaving of everyday, sometimes brutal reality with magic and mystery seems to be a distinctive feature in the works of such black writers as Joel Matlou and Zakes Mda" (229). Sandra Chait gives a contrasting evaluation of magical

realism's liberatory potential based on her reading of André Brink's *Cape of Storms: The First Life of Admastor* and Mike Nicol's *Horseman,* which she claims use magical realism in mythopoetic texts that universalize the horrors of apartheid and thus absolve white South Africans of blame; "Mythology, Magic Realism, and White Writing After Apartheid," *Research in African Literatures* 3, 2 (2000): 26.

102. Roland Walter, *Magical Realism in Contemporary Chicano Fiction* (Frankfurt am Main: Vervuert Verlag, 1993), 135–36.

103. See Linda Hutcheon, *A Poetics of Postmodernism: History, Theory, Fiction* (New York: Routledge, 1988).

104. Philip Rahv, "The Myth and the Powerhouse," in *Myth and Literature: Contemporary Theory and Practice,* ed. John B. Vickery (Lincoln: University of Nebraska Press, 1969), 109–18. Michael Hollington says of *The Tin Drum* that "the oscillation between stylization and horror prohibits conventionalized responses that might either mythologize or rationalize away the reality of Treblinka"; *Günter Grass: The Writer in a Pluralist Society* (London: Marion Boyars, 1980), 28.

105. Cezair-Thompson, "Beyond the Postcolonial Novel," 43–44.

106. James Phelan made this point in a paper on *Beloved* at the 1992 conference on Narrative at Vanderbilt University.

107. Barbara Freeman, *The Feminine Sublime: Gender and Excess in Women's Fiction* (Berkeley: University of California Press, 1995), 145.

108. Jean Barstow, quoted in Taussig, *Shamanism, Colonialism, and the Wild Man,* 189.

109. Ibid., 168.

110. Paul Smith, "Visiting the Banana Republic," in *Universal Abandon? The Politics of Postmodernism,* ed. Andrew Ross (Minneapolis: University of Minnesota Press, 1988), 130.

111. Leila Gandhi, *Postcolonial Theory: A Critical Introduction* (New York: Columbia University Press, 1998), 119

112. Taussig, *Shamanism, Colonialism, and the Wild Man,* 201.

113. See Taussig, *Nervous System,* 160.

114. The question is, then, whether we still need to wonder whether "magical realism might in part be seen as an unconscious . . . conspiracy between European or North American critics eager to get away, in their imagination, to the colourful world of Latin America, and certain Latin American writers desperate to take refuge, in their writing, from the injustice and brutality of their continent's unacceptable reality"; Gerald Martin, "On 'Magical' and Social Realism in García Márquez," in *Gabriel García Márquez: New Readings,* ed. Bernard McGuirk and Richard Cardwell (Cambridge: Cambridge University Press, 1987), 103–4. Edna Aizenberg thinks not; specifically addressing Martin's statement, and similar ones by others, she responds that "this is undoubtedly correct, but the equation has . . . a decolonizing side. . . . Magical realism challenges socio-historical verities, punctures 'exoticisms,' projects a future, and forces the metropolis to learn from rather than to feel superior towards the 'periphery'"; "*The Famished Road,*" 30.

115. Taussig, *Shamanism, Colonialism, and the Wild Man,* 135.

116. The initial reception of Updike's *Brazil* confirms that magical realism is increasingly known as moving north, that it represents a replenishing force, but also that it is a voice which is not so easily appropriated. One reviewer claims that the novel is "an exotic tale self-consciously embellished with elements of magical realism," showing "a remove and a condescension to its characters that . . . ultimately undermines its power," another that the novel's switching of identities is achieved "in a spasm of Latin American magic realism," and "the sacred and the profane are part of the same ooze." Thomas Christensen, "A Lusty Tropical Fable: *Brazil* by John Updike," *San Francisco Chronicle,* February 15, 1994; R. Z. Sheppard, "Warning: The Rabbit is Loose," *Time,* February 14, 1994. This migration, as well as the positive view of magical realism by segments of the Hispanic community in the United States is documented by Chon A. Noriega in his article "Chicano Cinema and the Horizon of Expectations: A Discursive Analysis of Film Reviews in the Mainstream, Alternative, and Hispanic Press, 1987–1988," *Aztlán: A Journal of Chicano Studies* 19, 2 (1988–90): 1–32. Noriega reports that in contrast to a negative review by a mainstream Anglo-American, which compared the magical realism in *The Milagro Beanfield War* to that of García Márquez, "seen within the context of Chicano culture, 'magic realism' did not detract from the film, but instead helped it become a poetic 'monumento a la identidad hispana en Norteamérica' ('monument to Hispanic identity in North America'). Thus the film was seen as pivotal in the history of 'magic realism' and its dissemination to North America" (18). Noriega is citing Jorge Luis Rodriguez, "Los santos en el celuloide americano, *La Opinión* 26 (March 1988): 1–2.

117. Harris, *Palace of the Peacock,* 143.

118. Stephen Slemon expresses this viewpoint in "Magic Realism as Postcolonial Discourse."

119. Davies, *Allende,* 59.

120. M. Keith Booker, "Beauty and the Beast: Dualism as Despotism in the Fiction of Salman Rushdie," *ELH* 57 (1990): 995.

121. Jean M. Kane takes up this issue of individual decease and plural discourse in relation to *Midnight's Children,* citing Rushdie's statement, "The story of Saleem does indeed lead him to despair [and death]. . . . But the story is told in a manner designed to echo, as closely as my abilities allowed, the Indian talent for non-stop self-regeneration. . . . The form—multitudinous, hinting at the infinite possibilities of the country—is the optimistic counterweight to Saleem's personal tragedy." Signaling the element of wishful imagination in Rushdie's project, Kane comments that *Midnight's Children* "attempts to compensate for the premature foreclosure of the 'actual' imaginary nation by preserving the text of memory as the 'real' imaginary home. If these dynamics vex the novel's formulation of a postcolonial politics, they also map political realities not easily surmounted." Kane, "The Migrant Intellectual and the Body of History: Salman Rushdie's *Midnight's Children,*" *Contemporary Literature* 37, 1 (1996): 115; Kane cites Rushdie in *Imaginary Homelands: Essays and Criticism, 1981–1991* (London: Granta, 1991), 16.

Chapter 5

1. This idea is not new. See, for example, Alice Jardine, *Gynesis: Configurations of Woman and Modernity* (Ithaca: Cornell University Press, 1985); and Elaine Showalter, "Feminist Criticism in the Wilderness," in *Critical Inquiry: Special Issue: Writing and Sexual Difference* 8 (1981): 179–205. Robert J. Lifton (already in 1970) also sees "a convergence between premodern, non-Western patterns and postmodern tendencies. . . . a *protean style of self-process,* [to which] feminine knowing may make specific contributions." Furthermore, recent thought appears to have "placed special value on those very modes of knowing which had been preciously part of the feminine informal underground"; "Woman as Knower," in *History and Human Survival* (New York: Random House, 1970), 270–72; cited in Mary Robertson, "Hystery, Herstory, History: 'Imagining the Real' in Thomas's *The White Hotel,*" *Contemporary Literature* 25, 4 (1984): 466. As Robertson points out, this claim for the field of thought does not always extend into practice.

2. The rubrics under which Nancy Walker studies the uses of irony and fantasy in contemporary women's novels (problems of finding a voice, multiple narratives that revise the self, dreams and imaginings, and time travel) align them with much contemporary magical realism, but the majority of the narratives she studies are realistic, and the remaining ones, in her final section on "alternate realities," are utopian (or distopian); *Feminist Alternatives: Irony and Fantasy in the Contemporary Novel by Women* (Jackson: University Press of Missouri, 1990).

3. Christine Buci-Glucksmann, *Baroque Reason: The Aesthetics of Modernity,* trans. Patrick Camiller (London: Sage, 1994), 49.

4. Therefore, in addition to discussing novels by women in this chapter, I also analyze novels by men.

5. Wendy Kolmar discusses several features of the writing of these women that I claim are central for much magical realism: the erosion of dualisms, including those of human/ ghostly, known/unknown worlds, the inhabiting of liminal spaces. The narratives Kolmar studies, like magical realism generally, are "narratives of multiplicity and connection," which often contain a metafictional charge. " 'Dialectics of Connectedness': Supernatural Elements in Novels by Bambara, Cisneros, Grahn, and Erdrich," in Lynette Carpenter and Wendy Kolmar, *Haunting the House of Fiction: Feminist Perspectives on Ghost Stories by American Women* (Knoxville: University of Tennessee Press, 1991), 242.

6. Luce Irigaray, "This Sex Which Is Not One," in *This Sex Which Is Not One,.* trans. Catherine Porter with Carolyn Burke (Ithaca: Cornell University Press, 1985), 23–33.

7. Drusilla Cornell, *Beyond Accommodation: Ethical Feminism, Deconstruction, and the Law* (New York: Routledge, 1991), 148.

8. Julia Kristeva, *Revolution in Poetic Language,* trans. Margaret Waller (New York: Columbia University Press, 1984), esp. 21–30.

9. Shari Benstock, *Textualizing the Feminine: On the Limits of Genre* (Norman: University of Oklahoma Press, 1991), 45.

10.   Kate Rigby, "The Goddess Returns: Ecofeminist Reconfigurations of Gender, Nature, and the Sacred," in *Feminist Poetics of the Sacred: Creative Suspicions*, ed. Frances Devlin-Glass and Lyn McCudden (New York: Oxford University Press, 2001), 46.

11.   Victor Turner, *The Ritual Process: Structure and Anti-Structure* (Chicago: Aldine, 1969), 117. Cf. also Raymond Walter's idea that in contemporary Chicano fiction, "the magical aspect of his world view helps the protagonist to redefine his individual identity in relation to his communal one"; *Magical Realism in Contemporary Chicano Fiction* (Frankfurt am Main, Vervuert Verlag, 1993), 136.

12.   Doris Meyer, " 'Parenting the Text': Female Creativity and Dialogic Relationships in Isabel Allende's *La casa de los espíritus*," *Hispania* 73, 2 (1990): 363. Similarly, Patricia Hart argues that Clara's clairvoyance is no real help to her at crucial moments, that it is tied to her passivity and hence implies a critique of female conditioning: "magic fails to prevent life's brutalities"; *Narrative Magic in the Fiction of Isabel Allende* (London: Associated University Presses, 1989), 37–56, 60. Arguing along different lines, but also positing Allende's text as a critique of patriarchal discourse, Ruth Jenkins focuses on "the enabling presence of the supernatural" and considers that both *The House of the Spirits* and Hong Kingston's *Woman Warrior* appropriate "ghosts and spirits to authorize female voice"; "Authorizing Female Voice and Experience: Ghosts and Spirits in Kingston's *The Woman Warrior* and Allende's *The House of the Spirits, MELUS* 19, 3 (1994): 63.

13.   Showalter, "Feminist Criticism in the Wilderness,"185.

14.   I agree with Susan Frenk's assessment that "*Aura* is suspended between a utopian model in which 'romance' with the other could potentially bring about a simultaneous individual and social revolution, a 'happy ending,' and a distopian outcome towards which it finally moves"; except that I would argue for a double-voiced ending rather than a distopic outcome; "Rewriting History: Carlos Fuentes' *Aura*," *Forum for Modern Language Studies* 30, 3 (1994): 265.

15.   Carlos Fuentes, *Aura*, trans. Lysander Kemp (New York: Farrar. Straus, & Giroux, 1975), 143–45. Further citations are given in the text.

16.   Critical opinion has tended to favor this view of the novella. For an overview, and a complementary interpretation, see Lois Marie Jaeck, "The Text and Intimations of Immortality: From Proust's *Recherche* to Fuentes's *Aura*," *Dalhousie French Studies* 38 (1997): 109–17. She argues that, like Proust's narrator, "outside time," "Felipe is able to recognize and love the essence (Aura) common to Consuelo and her past youth; an essence that has the capacity of transcending the passage of time" (116).

17.   Frenk, "Rewriting History," 258, 273.

18.   Marianella Collette's reading of *Aura* supports this view. For her, *Aura* constitutes a "fantasmatic search for the lost other." At the novel's end, "the female and male dualities of the novel unite to form this new being, essentially androgynous, for in it both opposites are fused. . . . The past, present, and future join in dialogue, in order to create, and—why not?—to die and be reborn on a woman's breast"; "La fase del espejo, lo simbólico y lo imaginario en la novela *Aura*, de Carlos Fuentes," *Revista Canadiense de Estudios Hispánicos* 19, 2 (1995): 281, 295–96.

19. Blanca Merino also recognizes that "the dependency is mutual. Consuelo can't triumph alone. To provide *consuelo* [consolation] she needs her opposite, desire. Felipe's *desire* and love are the necessary ingredients for a process of continual creation and recreation, and with each reincarnation the hope for eternal life and love are reinforced; "Fantasía y realidad en *Aura* de Carlos Fuentes," *Literatura Mexicana* 2, 1 (1991): 144.

20. Collette reads this image in a similar way, agreeing that the scenario represented by these eyes "is also a part of [Felipe's] own nature"; "La fase del espejo," 290.

21. Diane Marting's remark in relation to Miguel Angel Asturias's novel *Mulata (Mulata de Tal)* that "powerful male figures dominate the more realistic first half of the novel, but strong female ones play a greater role in the more magical second half" suggests that magical realism is often allied with a female sensibility; *The Sexual Woman in Latin American Literature: Dangerous Desires* (Gainesville: University of Florida Press, 2001), 137.

22. Isabel Allende, "The Shaman and the Infidel" (interview), *New Perspectives Quarterly* 8, 1 (1991): 55.

23. Cf. Deborah Cohn: "*The House of the Spirits* suggests that prevailing discourses for constructing and depicting reality are . . . handmaidens of a patriarchal system whose pseudo-objective voice . . . reproduces only that which affirms and perpetuates its own norms. Accordingly, magic realism is refigured here from a feminist perspective to describe women's experiences and strengths within a male-dominated system." *History and Memory in the Two Souths: Recent Southern and Spanish American Fiction* (Nashville: Vanderbilt University Press, 1999).

24. Ana Castillo, *So Far from God* (New York: Norton, 1993), 24. Further citations are given in the text. According to Michelle Sauer, "Castillo gives women permission to claim spiritual authority by creating a space in which every woman can be defined as a saint," a strategy she sees as returning "to a time before the saint-making process became a formal procedure and reincorporates the community voice, and more importantly, the female voice, in bestowing sainthood"; "Saint-Making in Ana Castillo's *So Far from God:* Medieval Mysticism as Precedent for an Authoritative Chicana Spirituality," *Mester* 29 (2000): 72.

25. For a discussion of the problems of representation, in the context of the female and the subaltern, which do not vanish even when one is dealing with self-representation, see Rey Chow, "Gender and Representation," in *Feminist Consequences: Theory for the New Century*, ed. Elisabeth Bronfen and Misha Kavka (New York: Columbia University Press, 2001), 38–57.

26. Maxine Hong Kingston, *The Woman Warrior* (New York: Random House, 1989), 166–69.

27. Ruth Jenkins also recognizes the centrality of this scene in the development of a female narrative sensibility and authority. She reminds us that after Brave Orchid's exorcism of the sitting ghost, rather than chant linear descent lines, the patronymic and patriarchal, "they called out their own [non-patronymic] names, women's pretty names, haphazard names, horizontal names of one generation. They pieced together new directions,

and my mother's spirit followed them instead of the old footprints." Hong Kingston, *Woman Warrior,* 89; cited in Jenkins, "Authorizing Voice and Experience," 69.

28. Lois Parkinson Zamora, "Magical Romance/Magical Realism: Ghosts in U.S. and Latin American Fiction," in *Magical Realism: Theory, History, Community,* ed. Lois Parkinson Zamora and Wendy B. Faris (Durham: Duke University Press, 1995), 498.

29. Chela Sandoval, "U.S.-Third World Feminism: The Theory and Method of Oppositional Consciousness in the Postmodern World," *Genders* 10 (1991): 23.

30. Theo D'haen expresses this same idea in more general terms: "As the privileged center discourse leaves no room for a 'realistic' insertion of those that history—always speaking the language of the victors and rulers—has denied a voice, such an act of recuperation [as the insertion of a subaltern voice] can only happen by magic or fantastic or unrealistic means"; "Magical Realism and Postmodernism: Decentering Privileged Centers," in Zamora and Faris, *Magical Realism,* 197.

31. Laurie A. Finke, "Mystical Bodies and the Dialogics of Vision," in *Maps of Flesh and Light: The Religious Experience of Medieval Women Mystics,* ed. Ulrike Wiethus (Syracuse: Syracuse University Press, 1993), 29, 44. Similarly, Susan Starr Sered claims that "in many cultures women are believed to be particularly skilled at or prone to possession trance" and cites a study by I. M. Lewis that claims that possession trance affords women the opportunity to obtain benefits not ordinarily available to them as members of a subordinate group; Starr, *Priestess, Mother, Sacred Sister: Religions Dominated by Women* (Oxford: Oxford University Press, 1994), 182.

32. See "Interview with Toni Morrison" by Christina Davis, *Présence Africaine* 145 (1988): 141–50.

33. P. Gabrielle Foreman in her comparative treatment of magical realism in Allende and Morrison, states, "Although the term [*magical realism*] has been used primarily to categorize a Latin American genre, I assume its relevance in examining an aspect of African American literature. Gabriel García Márquez . . . often cites the African Caribbean coast of Colombia as the source of his magically real. Allende has asserted that magical realism 'relies on a South American reality: the confluence of races and cultures of the whole world superimposed in the indigenous culture, in a violent climate.' These, too, are the dynamics of Africans in the Americas; they are inscribed, although differently, in both Allende's and Morrison's texts." Foreman, "Past-On Stories: History and the Magically Real, Morrison and Allende on Call," *Feminist Studies* 18, 2 (Summer 1992): 370; the Allende citation is from her "Ventana: Barricada Cultural," *La Barricada* (Nicaragua) 323, 23 (January 1988): 7.

34. Davis interview with Morrison, 149.

35. André Breton, "A Letter to Seers," in *Manifestoes of Surrealism,* trans. Richard Seaver and Helen R. Lane (Ann Arbor: University of Michigan Press, 1969), 197.

36. Susan Rubin Suleiman, *Subversive Intent: Gender, Politics, and the Avant-Garde* (Cambridge: Harvard University Press, 1990), 205. The gameyness, or, more conventionally, gamesmanship, of "the happy cosmopolitan" Suleiman suggests as a strategy for a "feminist postmodernist" extends to magical realist textual practices and locates them in the postmodern camp; but the spiritual seriousness of the genre that I am propos-

ing with respect to the genre runs in a complementary direction, one perhaps more consonant with the modernism it is replenishing, and with Romanticism (ibid.). The sexual politics of such gendered images are extremely complex, to say the least.

37. Wilson Harris, *Palace of the Peacock* (London: Faber and Faber, 1968), 139.

38. Jean-Pierre Durix proposes that Harris transmutes the "subaltern position of women in colonial society" "into a superior sense of vision, which opens on to possible solutions to the deadlock of polarized social structures"; *Mimesis, Genres and Post-Colonial Discourse: Deconstructing Magic Realism* (New York: St. Martin's, 1998), 175. This is Harris's vision, however, not Guyanian reality, and can be anything but politically subversive in the end, for such visionary transmutation can camouflage actual inequity and oppression.

39. Virginia Woolf, "Professions for Women," in *Collected Essays,* ed. Leonard Woolf (London: Chatto and Windus, 1972), 2:285.

40. Fuentes, nearly a generation later than Paz, goes further toward empowering female creativity in *Aura,* but the power can be seen as threatening, and the narrating voice remains decidedly male.

41. For a discussion of Allende in a similar context, see Lois Parkinson Zamora, "The Magical Tables of Isabel Allende and Remedios Varo," *Comparative Literature,* 44, 2 (1992): 113–43. Zamora argues that both these artists depict a female creative energy in their texts, one that is especially transformative. "Varo's female figures routinely move from one state to another" (119). Thus her discussion supports my contention that female surrealist energies significantly inform magical realism.

42. Kahlo's less well-known contemporary, Remedios Varo, is a good visual analogue for that textual reconstruction.

43. Toni Morrison, *Beloved* (New York: Knopf, 1987), 259. Further references are given in the text.

44. See Gaston Bachelard, *The Poetics of Space,* trans. Maria Jolas (Boston: Beacon Press, 1968), esp. 51–61; and Bachelard, *La Terre et les rêveries du repos* (Paris: Corti, 1948), 96. Edwin Ardener, "Belief and the Problem of Women," in *Perceiving Women,* ed. Shirley Ardener (New York: Wiley, 1975), 3. Caroline Bennett, also citing Ardener, through Showalter ("Feminist Criticism in the Wilderness"), agrees that "metaphorically, magic can be seen as a cultural construct, as the 'wild zone,' a form of psychological protection serving a similar function to the bonds or informal networks which women forge between themselves to preserve their sanity in times of repression"; "The Other and the Other-Worldly: The Function of Magic in Isabel Allende's *La casa de los espíritus,*" *Bulletin of Hispanic Studies* 75 (1998): 363.

45. Janet Larson in her discussion of Victorian female spirituality, in some senses a precursor of the female spirit I am treating here, stresses the spirit as a "life-giving plentitude that fills the world—not a separatist, specialized, subjective or merely localized power but an inclusive, relational, and generative force"; "Lady-Wrestling for the Victorian Soul: Discourse, Gender, and Spirituality in Women's Texts," *Religion and Literature* 23, 3 (1993): 45.

46. Gabriel García Márquez, *One Hundred Years of Solitude,* trans. Gregory Rabassa (New

York: Avon, 1971), 173. Further citations are given in the text. Nina M. Scott proposes an alternate and convincing version of the Buendía house, not open to the universe but closed in on itself, like the incestuous passions of the Buendías, who are doomed to destruction, a fate that Ursula is fighting against with her "open house"; "Vital Space in the House of Buendía," *Studies in Twentieth-Century Literature* 8, 11 (1984): 265–72. It seems to me that the Buendía house is both open and closed, in different ways.

47. The female line of descent here encodes both private and public realms. As Mario A. Rojas has said, "the women of the saga receive via their mothers a double inheritance: an overflowing imagination and a clear awareness of social justice"; "*La casa de los espíritus:* Un caleidoscopio de espejos desordenados," *Revista Iberoamericana* 52 (1985): 920. For a more detailed analysis of the way in which the Trueba house functions in regard to magical and political domains (and the critical discussion the topic has generated), see Cohn, *History and Memory in the Two Souths,* 109–14.

48. Zamora, "The Magical Tables of Isabel Allende and Remedios Varo," 122.

49. Cohn, *History and Memory in the Two Souths,* 113. This interdependence between the political and spirit worlds means, according to Cohn, that Clara (typically for a magical realist text) "gradually erases the boundaries between public and private, the spaces between 'masculine' and 'feminine,' and along with those, the distinctions between her earthly and otherworldly enterprises" (ibid.).

50. Ronie-Richelle García-Johnson, "The Struggle for Space: Feminism and Freedom in *The House of the Spirits,*" *Revista Hispánica Moderna* 47, 1 (1994): 185.

51. Bennett, "The Other and the Other-Worldly," 362, 364. For more details on this subject, see Hart, *Narrative Magic in the Fiction of Isabel Allende,* 29–44; and Foreman, "Past-On Stories."

52. D. M. Thomas, *The White Hotel* (New York: Viking, 1981), 46. Further citations are given in the text.

53. Isabel Allende, *The House of the Spirits,* trans. Magda Bogin (New York: Knopf, 1985), 367.

54. According to Peter G. Earle, "the dramatic nucleus [of *The House of the Spirits*] is the struggle between Trueba and the forces he generates, on the one hand, and the female members of his family. He is the blind force of history, its collective unconscious, its somatomic (i.e. aggressive, physical) manifestation. They embody historical awareness and intuitive understanding," their names, Clara, Blanca, and Alba symbolizing freedom and hope. Earle, "Literature as Survival: Allende's *The House of the Spirits,*" *Contemporary Literature* 28, 4 (1987): 550.

55. Allende's statement is included in Gloria Bautista, "El realismo mágico en *La casa de los espíritus,*" *Discurso Literario* 6, 2 (1989): 308. Bautista also constructs a helpful list of the characteristics of magical realism as they appear in Allende's text.

56. Abby Frucht, *Licorice* (New York: Grove Press, 1993), 94.

57. Ibid., 33, 102–3.

58. It is interesting to correlate this possible difference to a difference in shamanic practice discussed by Susan Starr Sered, who draws on evidence that male shamans undertake ecstatic flights much more often than female shamans, who incorporate spirits into

their bodies—serving as channels for supernatural beings—much more often than do men. Sered associates this kind of possession with Linda Rubin's theories, which draw on the ideas of Carol Gilligan and Nancy Chodorow concerning the development of girls as relational and boys as individuating, to claim that a woman's ego boundaries are more fluid than a man's. Sered, *Priestess, Mother, Sacred Sister,* 186–88.

59. The ties to healing and to the land that I discover in magical realism by women is supported by Lynette Carpenter and Wendy Kolmar, who discover an American tradition of female ghost stories that investigate and implicitly seek consolation for images of domestic violence and victimization, often through understanding female history and female bonds, including those with the dead; Introduction to Carpenter and Kolmar, *Haunting the House of Fiction,* 10.

60. Yvonne Yarbro-Bejarano discusses how Ana Castillo's earlier writing works toward the erosion of unitary subjectivity that I am claiming magical realism embodies. Yarbro-Bejarano's article precedes the publication of *So Far from God.* "The Multiple Subject in the Writing of Ana Castillo," *The Americas Review: A Review of Hispanic Literature and Art of the USA* 21, 1 (Spring 1992): 65–72.

61. These magically real embodiments may thus respond to the same need that Elizabeth Grosz addresses when she signals the need in feminist thought for more attention to issues of the body, "regarded as a site of social, political, cultural, and geographical inscriptions," as *"the* cultural product"; *Volatile Bodies: Toward a Corporeal Feminism* (Bloomington: University of Indiana Press, 1994), 23.

62. See Nalini Natarajan, "Woman, Nation, and Narration in *Midnight's Children,*" in *Scattered Hegemonies: Postmodernity and Transnational Feminist Practices,* ed. Inderpal Grewal and Caren Kaplan (Minneapolis: University of Minnesota Press, 1994), 76–89.

63. Marie Darrieussecq, *Pig Tales,* trans. Linda Coverdale (New York: The New Press, 1997), 2–3. Further citations are given in the text.

64. Cf. Catherine Rodgers's statement, "The narrator has for the most part interiorized the values of this society. . . . Continually, she evaluates herself according to the gaze of others; "Aucune Evidence: Les Truismes de Marie Darrieussecq," *Romance Studies* 18, 1 (2000): 72.

65. In the narrator's acceptance of her porcine body, and her enjoyment in it of sexual pleasure with Yvan, Darrieussecq's novel can be seen to put into fiction the kind of chaotic multiplicity of representations that Judith Butler calls for in her contemporaneous discussion of identity and representation throughout her *Gender Trouble: Feminism and the Subversion of Identity* (New York: Routledge, 1990). At the same time, the critique of social constructions of femininity and masculinity, which initially relegate the narrator to the status of (co)modified body and Yvan to that of entrepreneurial mind, and of late twentieth-century capitalist society, which increasingly dispenses with social services such as shelters for the homeless, aligns it with more socially oriented theorists such as Seyla Benhabib and Rosi Braidotti. For discussion of these issues in gender criticism, see Susan Bordo, "Feminist Foucault and the Politics of the Body,"

in *Up Against Foucault: Explorations of Some Tensions Between Foucault and Feminism,*
ed. C. Ramazomoglu (New York: Routledge, 1993), 191–93.

66. Salman Rushdie, *Midnight's Children* (New York: Avon, 1982), 504. Further citations
are given in the text.

67. Grosz, *Volatile Bodies,* 21–22.

68. Stacy Alaimo, *Undomesticated Ground: Recasting Nature as Feminist Space* (Ithaca: Cornell University Press, 2000), 144–72. Alaimo is working from Donna Haraway's idea of
situated knowledges, presented in her *Simians, Cyborgs, and Women: The Reinvention
of Nature* (New York: Routledge, 1991). For a discussion of these issues as they appear
in a popular magical realist text, see Alaimo's discussion of Marian Engel's *Bear.*

69. Sandra Harding, *Whose Science, Whose Knowledge? Thinking from Women's Lives* (Ithaca:
Cornell University Press, 1991), 161.

70. For an excellent discussion of language and the body in *Beloved,* see Jean Wyatt, "Giving
Body to the Word: The Maternal Symbolic in Toni Morrison's *Beloved,*" *PMLA* 108
(1993): 474–88. She maintains that "to make room for the articulation of alternative
desires, Morrison's textual practice flouts basic rules of narrative discourse" (474). She
also notes what we have termed linguistic magic in magical realism: "What at first
appears symbolic becomes actual in a characteristic collapse of metaphor into literal
reality—a slippage that accompanies the central materialization of the novel, Beloved's
embodiment" (480).

71. Cf. Barbara Freeman: "Only when their voices merge can the characters begin to
separate from the past and from each other; only when the past's legacy has been
acknowledged can the process of letting go of it begin." Thus is the work of mourning
accomplished." This is a mourning, as Freeman notes, not of detachment, as Freud
would have it, but of attachment—a more female mode of mourning. Freeman, *The
Feminine Sublime: Gender and Excess in Women's Fiction* (Berkeley: University of California Press, 1995), 143.

72. Thus we could see the novel as fictionalizing the kind of epistemology advocated by
Linda Holler, working through the ideas of Evelyn Fox-Keller and Barbara McClintock,
one that partakes of the Bergsonian identification with the object of knowledge but is
modified with enough of a sense of distance from it that we can hear what the material
has to say to us. See Linda Holler, "Thinking with the Weight of the Earth: Feminist
Contributions to an Epistemology of Concreteness," *Hypatia* 5, 1 (1990): 14–15, who
cites Evelyn Fox-Keller, *A Feeling for the Organism: The Life and Work of Barbara Mc-
Clintock* (New York: Freeman, 1983), esp. 198. Interestingly enough in connection
with my contention that magical realism generically suggests the presence of a world
of spirit within concrete reality, McClintock, whose ideas are central to the discussion
by Holler and Fox-Keller, "calls herself 'a mystic'" (Holler, "Thinking with the Weight
of the Earth," 16).

73. I would categorize these images on the fringes of magical realism since they are so
clearly approaching psychic allegory, but they are presented as real, which they would
not be in a realist novel, and so I include them in this discussion.

74. In having Lisa magically "forefeel," the Holocaust, Mary Robertson believes that Thomas suggests that that "woman has a kind of knowledge the world could use," but in the end finds no way to actualize that suggestion; "Hystery, Herstory, History," 465.

75. This phrase is from Alaimo, *Undomesticated Ground,* 147.

76. Ibid., 155.

77. Vicki Kirby, *Telling Flesh: The Substance of the Corporeal* (New York: Routledge, 1997), 61.

78. Ibid.

79. Gérard de Nerval, *Aurélia,* in *Les Filles du feu, suivi de Aurélia,* ed. Béatrice Didier (Paris: Gallimard, 1972), 305, 296. Further citations are given in the text. All translations are mine.

80. Günter Grass, *The Tin Drum,* trans. Ralph Manheim (New York: Random House, 1964), 16–17. Further citations are given in the text.

81. André Breton reports that "the book of evil Spirits is written on a paper that is commonly referred to as 'virgin parchment' "; "Second Manifesto of Surrealism," in *Manifestoes of Surrealism,* trans. Richard Seaver and Helen R. Lane (Ann Arbor: University of Michigan Press, 1969), 179.

82. Isabel Allende, "La magia de las palabras," *Revista Iberoamericana* 51 (1985): 450.

83. Carlos Fuentes, "Central and Eccentric Writing," in *Lives on the Line: The Testimony of Contemporary Latin American Authors,* ed. Doris Meyer (Berkeley: University of California Press, 1988), 114, 117–18.

84. Carlos Fuentes, *Christopher Unborn,* trans. Alfred Mac Adam and the author (New York: Farrar Straus Giroux, 1989), 9.

85. The splendor of Fuentes's language in this novel is inspired by and inspires his vision for inter-American cooperation. It is an impossible vision and therefore exists now only in the magical realm of his interuterine text, narrated from inside the womb, but that text hopes for its realization: "Angeles, Cristopher, I don't want a world of progress which captures us between North and East and takes away from us the best of the West. . . . We shall arrive at Pacifica one day if we first stop being North or East in order to be ourselves, West and all. That would be Kantinflas's categorical imperative: Mock de Summa! Mere Cortésy won't take Cuautémoc off his bed of roses. All the cold rains of the world come to us from the Escorial! Queen Juana the Mad-der-of-Fact! Isabel the Chaotic" (*Christopher Unborn,* 523).

86. The more habitual example of this connection is Morrison's admiration of García Márquez. See, for example, Gayle Jones, *Liberating Voices: Oral Tradition in African American Literature* (Cambridge: Harvard University Press, 1991), 173.

87. Toni Morrison, *Song of Solomon* (New York: Signet, 1978), 241–43. Further citations are given in the text.

88. See José David Saldívar, *The Dialectics of Our America: Genealogy, Cultural Critique, and Literary History* (Durham: Duke University Press, 1991), 89.

89. Trudier Harris also believes that *Beloved* encodes both male and female energies, com-

paring Beloved's power, which motivates the narrative that contains her, to that of the trickster, who embodies a traditionally male kind of energy; *Fiction and Folklore in the Novels of Toni Morrison* (Knoxville: University of Tennessee Press, 1991), 161.

90. In his reading of *Beloved,* David Lawrence stresses the connection of language and the body: "Fleshly Ghosts and Ghostly Flesh: The Word and the Body in *Beloved,*" *Studies in American Fiction* 19, 2 (1991): 194–202.

91. Carlos Fuentes, *Distant Relations,* trans. Margaret Sayers Peden (New York: Farrar, Straus, & Giroux, 1982), 222. Further citations are given in the text.

92. For a discussion of the connection with *Uncle Tom's Cabin* and its importance in the politics of discourse, see Eileen Bender, "Repossessing Uncle Tom's Cabin: Toni Morrison's *Beloved,*" in *Cultural Power/Cultural Literacy: Selected Papers from the 14th Florida State University Conference on Literature and Film,* ed. Bonnie Braendlin (Gainesville: University Press of Florida, 1989), 129–42. According to Carolyn A. Mitchell, the ministry of Baby Suggs, who "preaches 'liberation spirituality,'" is a "refiguration of Christ's public life"; "'I Love to Tell the Story': Biblical Revisions in *Beloved,*" *Religion and Literature* 23, 3 (Autumn 1991): 27–42.

93. Both Marianne DeKoven and Klaus Theweleit, whom she cites as evidence for her position, see water imagery as "a locus of representation of the feminine"; DeKoven, *Rich and Strange: Gender, History, Modernism* (Princeton: Princeton University Press, 1991), 33; Theweleit, *Women, Floods, Bodies, History,* vol. 1 of *Male Fantasies* (Minneapolis: University of Minnesota Press, 1978).

94. Marting, *Sexual Woman in Latin American Literature,* 63.

95. Miguel Angel Asturias, "Algunos apuntes sobre *Mulata de Tal,*" *Studi di Letteratura Ispanoamericana* [Milan] 5 (1974): 19, cited in Marting, *Sexual Woman in Latin American Literature,* 83.

96. Marting, *Sexual Woman in Latin American Literature,* 64.

97. For a discussion of the process of chutnification as an analogue for Rushdie's narrative, and also of women and cooking generally, see James Harrison, *Salman Rushdie* (New York: Twayne, 1992), 63–67.

98. Laura Esquivel, *Like Water for Chocolate: A Novel in Monthly Installments with Recipes, Romances, and Home Remedies,* trans. Carol Christensen and Thomas Christensen (New York: Doubleday, 1992), 51.

99. Esquivel, *Como agua para chocolate* (Mexico City: Editorial Planeta, 1990), 56 (my translation); for the English version, see Esquivel, *Like Water for Chocolate,* 51. I have translated the Spanish in this and the next quotation because the English version is adequate but different.

100. Esquivel, *Como agua para chocolate,* 57; for the English version see *Like Water for Chocolate,* 52.

101. Patrick McGee, *Telling the Other: The Question of Value in Modern and Postcolonial Writing* (Ithaca: Cornell University Press, 1992), 144.

102. Gabriel García Márquez, *El olor de la guayaba: Conversaciones con Plinio Apuleyo Mendoza* (Bogotá: Oveja Negra, 1982), 112.

103. María Eulalia Montaner Ferrer corroborates this sense of female narrative power in

One Hundred Years of Solitude. She reads the chastity belt Ursula puts on herself as an instance of matriarchal power, speculating that Ursula has made up the genealogy that would lead to the birth of a child with a pig's tail because she feared the vengeance that would follow on the ill-gotten gains of her ancestors; "Falaz Gabriel García Márquez: Ursula Iguarán, narradora de *Cien años de soledad, Hispanic Review* 55, 1 (1987): 77–93.

104. Sandoval, "U.S. Third World Feminism," 2. Because Erdrich's work implicitly advocates attention to issues of territorial despoliation, it is close to concerns about Native American land ownership and use as well as to those of the ecofeminist movement.

105. For additional studies of this conjunction of the literary, the sacred, and the territorial in postcolonial writing, see Jamie S. Scott and Paul Simpson-Housley, eds., *Mapping the Sacred: Religion, Geography and Postcolonial Literatures* (Amsterdam and Atlanta: Rodpi, 2001).

106. Additional evidence that Erdrich's novels exist on the fringe of magical realism and how that fringe is culturally hybrid appears in Hans Bak's analysis of the way Erdrich induces "a sense of epistemological confusion" and "hermeneutical uncertainty" in the reader by "bringing together two incongruent and mutually exclusive concepts of time" in *The Beet Queen;* "Toward a Native American 'Realism': The Amphibious Fiction of Louise Erdrich," in *Neo-Realism in Contemporary American Fiction,* ed. Kristiaan Versluys (Amsterdam and Atlanta: Rodopi, 1992), 153.

107. For a discussion of the novel that advocates taking Pauline's point of view more seriously than it often has been, see Daniel Cornell, "Woman Looking: Revis(ion)ing Pauline's Subject Position in Louise Erdrich's *Tracks," S.A.I.L.* 4, 1 (1992): 49–64.

108. Louise Erdrich, *Tracks* (New York: Harper and Row, 1989), 94. Further citations are given in the text.

109. In considering the magical realism in *Tracks,* Magdalena Delicka focuses on Erdrich's alternation of narrators in order to create a stand-off between the magical and the realistic; "American Magic Realism: Crossing the Borders in Literatures of the Margins," *Journal of American Studies of Turkey* 6 (1997): 26–28.

110. Cristina García, *Dreaming in Cuban* (New York: Ballantine, 1992), 5.

111. Theresa Delgadillo also points to the affinity of Loca and Caridad with nature as an integral element of their spirituality, and, additionally, interprets the death of Caridad as an implicit statement about "the often unconsidered issue of destruction of the living earth"; "Forms of Chicana Feminist Resistance: Hybrid Spirituality in Ana Castillo's *So Far from God," Modern Fiction Studies,* 44, 4 (1998): 901.

112. Lynn V. Andrews, *Medicine Woman* (New York: Harper, 1981), 54. Further citations are given in the text.

113. Andrews's primitivism, however, has been politically problematic. Like D. M. Thomas, Lawrence Thornton, and others, Andrews does not belong to the ethnic community whose magic she invokes, and so her book, like *Mutant Message: Downunder* by Marlo Morgan, has provoked protests of appropriation from within that community. Irrespective of how we may evaluate Andrews's rights to the stories and cultural images within her texts, the popularity of her books attests to the growth and mainstreaming

of spiritual aspirations through magical realism in contemporary society. Very different in cultural context and originality, they nonetheless form part of the same general
cultural shift that energizes the novels of Erdrich, Castillo, García, and Esquivel, and,
indeed, I would argue, of magical realism generally.

114. They demonstrate that, as Zamora has suggested with respect to William Goyen, Juan
Rulfo, and Elena Garro, in American magical realism, ghosts are tied closely to actual
lands and their histories; "Magical Romance/Magical Realism."

115. Luce Irigaray, *The Irigaray Reader*, ed. Margaret Whitford (Oxford: Blackwell, 1991),
144.

116. Starhawk, *The Spiral Dance: A Rebirth of the Ancient Religion of the Great Goddess* (San
Francisco: Harper, 1989), 203; cited in Rigby, "Goddess Returns," 54.

117. Luce Irigaray, "La Mystérique," in *Speculum of the Other Woman*, trans. Gillian C. Gill
(Ithaca: Cornell University Press, 1984), 191–202.

118. As Lloyd Davies notes, the presence of angels in *The House of the Spirits* can be seen to
represent "the otherness of woman and her part-human part-divine status"; *Allende, La
casa de los espíritus* (London: Grant and Cutler, 2000), 100. That status, Davies suggests,
seems to be confirmed by Irigaray's contention that angels "link what has been split by
patriarchy—the flesh and the spirit, nature and gods, the carnal and the divine, and
are a way of conceptualizing a possible overcoming of the deadly and immobilizing
division of the sexes in which women have been allocated body, flesh, nature, earth,
carnality while men have been allocated spirit and transcendence"; Irigaray, *Irigaray
Reader*, 157; cited in Davies, *Allende*, 100.

119. James Mandrell investigates a similar tendency in women's fiction; "The Prophetic
Voice in Garro, Morante, and Allende," *Comparative Literature* 42, 3 (1990): 227–44.

120. According to Michelle Sauer, who discusses medieval mysticism as a precedent for
authentic Chicana spirituality in *So Far from God*, Castillo "expressly illustrates how
Chicana spirituality cannot be disconnected from literal physical and sensual bodies,
and their figurative community bodies"; "Saint-Making in Ana Castillo's *So Far from
God*," 86.

121. María Lugones, "Playfulness, 'World-Travelling,' and Loving Perception," in *Haciendo
Caras/Making Faces, Making Soul*, ed. Gloria Anzaldúa (San Francisco: Aunt Lute,
1990); cited by Sandoval, "U.S.-Third World Feminism," 15.

122. This is of course a whole subject in itself and has taken many forms. See, among others,
the works of Mary Daly, Carol Christ, and Maria Gimbutas.

123. Catherine Rainwater explains that Erdrich de-emphasizes biological ties in favor of
spiritual ties of friendship and love, a phenomenon that is explained by the idea that
the gaps between phases of individual lives are more characteristic of ceremonial time
than of traditional family sagas; "Reading Between Worlds: Narrativity in the Fiction
of Louise Erdrich," *American Literature* 62, 3 (September 1990): 419–20.

124. Gabriel García Márquez, *Of Love and Other Demons*, trans. Edith Grossman (New
York: Knopf, 1995), 113. Further citations are given in the text.

125. Molly O'Neill, "Sensing the Spirit in All Things, Seen and Unseen," *New York Times*,
March 31, 1993.

126. A. S. Byatt, *The Conjugal Angel,* in her *Angels and Insects: Two Novellas* (New York: Random House, 1992), 188. Further citations are given in the text.

127. See Carole Silver, "'East of the Sun and West of the Moon': Victorians and Fairy Brides," *Tulsa Studies in Women's Literature* 6, 2 (Fall 1987): 183–98. Like many magical realist fictions, the narratives Silver discusses have their roots in folklore and yet are created within a realistic tradition. Thus they share the power of survival I am claiming for the female spirit in magical realism.

128. Esquivel, *Like Water for Chocolate,* 243. Further citations are given in the text.

129. Irigaray, "La Mystérique," 191.

130. Ibid., 196.

131. The breaking down of boundaries between selves that this scene and others in magical realist fictions enact allies them with moves of feminist theologists, such as Carol Christ, who attempt to get beyond the sense that, in Julia Kristeva's words, "the one and the other are two aspects, semantic and logical, of the imposition of a strategy of identity, which is in all strictness that of monotheism"; Kristeva, *The Powers of Horror: An Essay on Abjection,* trans. Leon Roudiez (New York: Columbia University Press, 1982), 94.

132. For a reading of *Beloved* that deals thematically with Morrison's sense of a "liberatory plan" based on "the interconnectedness of the spiritual and material," see Mitchell, "'I Love to Tell the Story,'" 28.

Works Consulted

Aizenberg, Edna. "*The Famished Road:* Magical Realism and the Search for Social Equity." *Yearbook of Comparative and General Literature* 43 (1995): 25–30.

———. "Historical Subversion and Violence of Representation in García Márquez and Ouloguem." *PMLA* 107 (1992): 1235–52.

Alaimo, Stacy. *Undomesticated Ground: Recasting Nature as Feminist Space.* Ithaca: Cornell University Press, 2000.

Alazraki, Jaime. "Para una revalidación del concepto realismo mágico en la literatura hispanoamericana." In *Homenaje a Andrés Iduarte.* Clear Creek, IN: American Hispanist, 1976.

Alexander, Marguerite. *Flights from Realism: Themes and Strategies in Postmodernist British and American Fiction.* New York: Routledge, 1990.

Alexis, Jacques Stéphen. *Les Arbres musiciens.* Paris: Gallimard, 1957.

Ali, Tariq, and Howard Brenton. *Iranian Nights.* London: Nick Hern Books, 1989.

Allende, Isabel. *The House of the Spirits.* 1982 (in Spanish). Translated by Magda Bogin. New York: Knopf, 1985.

———. "La magia de las palabras." *Revista Iberoamericana* 51 (1985): 447–52.

———. "The Shaman and the Infidel" (interview with Marilyn Berlin Small). *New Perspectives Quarterly* 8, 1 (1991): 54–58.

Alter, Robert. *Partial Magic: The Novel as a Self-Conscious Genre.* Berkeley: University of California Press, 1975.

Anderson, Robert K. "La realidad y la destrucción de la línea en *Cien años de soledad.*" *Explicación de Textos Literarios* 25, 1 (1996–97): 71–85.

Anderson Imbert, Enrique. "El 'realismo mágico' en la ficción hispanoamericana." *Far-Western Forum* 1, 1 (1984): 175–86.

Andrews, Lynn V. *Medicine Woman.* New York: Harper, 1981.

Angulo, María-Elena. *Magic Realism: Social Context and Discourse.* New York: Garland, 1995.

Antoni, Robert. "Parody or Piracy: The Relationship of *The House of the Spirits* to *One Hundred Years of Solitude.*" *Latin American Literary Review* 16, 32 (1988): 16–28.

Anzaldúa, Gloria. "Metaphors in the Tradition of the Shaman." In *Conversant Essays: Con-*

temporary Poets on Poetry, edited by James McCorkle, 99–100. Detroit: Wayne State University Press, 1990.

Appadurai, Arjun. "Consumption, Duration, and History." In *Streams of Cultural Capital: Transnational Cultural Studies,* edited by David Palumbo-Liu and Hans Ulrich Gumbrecht, 23–45. Stanford: Stanford University Press, 1997.

———. *Modernity at Large: Cultural Dimensions of Globalization.* Minneapolis: University of Minnesota Press, 1996.

Appiah, Kwame Anthony. "Cosmopolitan Reading." In *Cosmopolitan Geographies: New Locations in Literature and Culture,* edited by Vinay Dharwadker, 197–227. New York: Routledge, 2001.

———. "Is the Post—in Postmodernism—the Post in Postcolonial?" *Critical Inquiry* 17 (1991): 336–57.

Ardener, Edwin. "Belief and the Problem of Women." In *Perceiving Women,* edited by Shirley Ardener, 1–17. New York: Wiley, 1975.

Ashcroft, Bill, Gareth Griffiths, and Helen Tiffin. *The Empire Writes Back: Theory and Practice in Post-Colonial Literatures.* London: Routledge, 1989.

Auerbach, Erich. *Mimesis: The Representation of Reality in Western Literature.* Princeton: Princeton University Press, 1974.

Bach, Rebecca Ann. "*Mrs. Caliban:* A Feminist Postmodernist *Tempest?*" *Critique* 41 (2000): 391–401.

Bachelard, Gaston. *The Poetics of Space.* Translated by Maria Jolas. Boston: Beacon Press, 1968.

———. *La Terre et les rêveries du repos.* Paris: Corti, 1948.

Bak, Hans. "Toward a Native American 'Realism': The Amphibious Fiction of Louise Erdrich." In *Neo-Realism in Contemporary American Fiction,* edited by Kristiaan Versluys, 145–70. Amsterdam and Atlanta: Rodopi, 1992.

Baker, Houston. *The Workings of the Spirit: The Poetics of Afro-American Women's Writing.* Chicago: University of Chicago Press, 1991.

Bakhtin, M. M. *The Dialogical Imagination.* Translated by Caryl Emerson and Michael Holquist. Austin: University of Texas Press, 1983.

Balzer, Marjorie Mandelstam, ed. *Shamanism: Soviet Studies of Traditional Religion in Siberia and Central Asia.* Armonk, N.Y.: M. E. Sharpe, 1990.

Barrish, Phillip. *American Literary Realism, Critical Theory, and Intellectual Prestige, 1880–1995.* Cambridge: Cambridge University Press, 2001.

Barth, John. "The Literature of Replenishment." *Atlantic Monthly,* January 1980, 65–71.

Barthes, Roland. "L'Effet de réel." *Communications* 2 (1968): 19–25.

Bassi, Shaul. "Salman Rushdie's Special Effects." In *Coterminous Worlds: Magical Realism and Contemporary Post-colonial Literature in English,* edited by Elsa Linguanti, Francesco Casotti, and Carmen Concilio, 47–60. Amsterdam and Atlanta: Rodopi, 1999.

Bautista, Gloria. "El realismo mágico en *La casa de los espíritus.*" *Discurso Literario* 6, 2 (1989): 299–309.

Beckett, Samuel. *The Unnameable.* 1958. Reprinted in *Three Novels by Samuel Beckett: Molloy, Malone Dies, The Unnameable.* New York: Grove Press, 1965.

Bell-Villada, Gene. "Pronoun Shifters: Virginia Woolf, Béla Bartók, Plebian Forms, Real-Life Tyrants, and the Shaping of García Márquez's *Patriarch.*" *Contemporary Literature* 28, 4 (1987): 460–82.

Bender, Eileen. "Repossessing Uncle Tom's Cabin: Toni Morrison's *Beloved.*" *Cultural Power/ Cultural Literacy: Selected Papers from the 14th Florida State University Conference on Literature and Film,* edited by Bonnie Braendlin, 129–42. Gainesville: University Press of Florida, 1989.

Ben Jelloun, Tahar. *The Sacred Night.* 1987 (in French). Translated by Alan Sheridan. San Diego: Harcourt Brace, 1989.

Bennett, Caroline. "The Other and the Other-Worldly: The Function of Magic in Isabel Allende's *La casa de los espíritus.*" *Bulletin of Hispanic Studies* 75 (1998): 357–65.

Benstock, Shari. *Textualizing the Feminine: On the Limits of Genre.* Norman: University of Oklahoma Press, 1991.

Bersani, Leo. *A Future for Astyanax: Character and Desire in Literature.* New York: Little, 1976.

Beverley, John, and Hugo Achugar, eds. *La voz del otro: Testimonio, subalternidad y verdad narrativa.* Pittsburgh: Latinoamericana Editores, 1992.

Beyersdorf, H. E. "The Narrator as Artful Deceiver: Aspects of Narrative Perspective in *Die Blechtrommel.*" *Germanic Review* 55 (1980): 129–38.

Bhabha, Homi. *The Location of Culture.* New York: Routledge, 1994.

Bidney, Martin. "Creating a Feminist-Communitarian Romanticism in *Beloved:* Toni Morrison's New Uses for Blake, Keats, and Wordsworth." *Papers on Language and Literature* 36, 2 (2000): 271–301.

Blanco Aguinaga, Carlos. *De mitólogos y novelistas.* Madrid: Ediciones Turner, 1975.

Boehmer, Elleke. *Colonial and Postcolonial Literature: Migrant Metaphors.* New York: Oxford University Press, 1995.

Bontempelli, Massimo. *L'avventura novecentista.* Florence: Vallechi, 1974.

Booker, M. Keith. "Beauty and the Beast: Dualism as Despotism in the Fiction of Salman Rushdie." *ELH* 57 (1990): 970–97.

Bordo, Susan. "Feminist Foucault and the Politics of the Body." In *Up Against Foucault: Explorations of Some Tensions Between Foucault and Feminism,* edited by C. Ramazomoglu, 179–202. New York: Routledge, 1993.

Borges, Jorge Luis. "The Aleph." 1949 (in Spanish). Translated by Norman Thomas di Giovanni. In *The Aleph,* 15–30. New York: Dutton, 1969.

———. "Partial Magic in the *Quijote.*" 1949 (in Spanish). In *Labyrinths: Selected Stories and Other Writings,* edited by Donald A. Yates and James E. Irby, 193–96. New York: New Directions, 1964.

———. Review of *After Death,* by Leslie Weatherhead. 1943 (in Spanish). Translated by Suzanne Jill Levine. In Borges, *Selected Non-Fictions,* edited by Eliot Weinberger, 254–55. New York: Viking, 1999.

Bravo, Victor. *Magias y maravillas en el continente literario: Para un deslinde del realismo mágico y lo real maravilloso.* Caracas: La Casa de Bello, 1988.

Breinig, Helmbrecht. "Inter-American Internationality: Updike's *Brazil,* Curley's *Mummy,* and the Question of Magical Realism." In *Cases and Problems*, vol. 1 of *The Internationality of National Literatures in Either America: Transfer and Transformation*, edited by Armin Paul Frank and Helga Essmann, 245–60. Göttingen: Wallstein Verlag, 1999.

Brennan, Timothy. *At Home in the World: Cosmopolitanism Now.* Cambridge: Harvard University Press, 1997.

———. "Fantasy, Individuality, and the Politics of Liberation." *Polygraph* 1, 1 (1987): 89–99.

———. *Salman Rushdie and the Third World.* New York: St. Martin's, 1989.

Breton, André. "A Letter to Seers." 1925 (in French). In *Manifestoes of Surrealism*, translated by Richard Seaver and Helen R. Lane, 195–203. Ann Arbor: University of Michigan Press, 1969.

———. "Second Manifesto of Surrealism." 1930 (in French). Translated by Richard Seaver and Helen R. Lane. In *Manifestoes of Surrealism*, 117–94. Ann Arbor: University of Michigan Press, 1969.

Brooke-Rose, Christine. *A Rhetoric of the Unreal: Studies in Narrative and Structure, Especially of the Fantastic.* Cambridge: Cambridge University Press, 1981.

Brooks, David. "Interview with Salman Rushdie." *Helix* 19/20 (1984): 55–69. Reprinted in *Conversations with Salman Rushdie*, edited by Michael R. Reder, 57–71. Jackson: University Press of Mississippi, 2000.

Buci-Glucksmann, Christine. *Baroque Reason: The Aesthetics of Modernity.* Translated by Patrick Camiller. London: Sage, 1994.

Burkert, Walter. *Ancient Mystery Cults.* Cambridge: Harvard University Press, 1987.

Butler, Judith. *Gender Trouble: Feminism and the Subversion of Identity.* New York: Routledge, 1990.

Butterfield, Bradley. "Enlightenment's Other in Patrick Süskind's *Das Parfum:* Adorno and the Ineffable Utopia of Modern Art." *Comparative Literature Studies* 32, 3 (1995): 401–18.

Byatt, A. S. *The Conjugal Angel.* In *Angels and Insects: Two Novellas.* New York: Random House, 1992.

Califano, Mario. "Los Rostros del Chamán: Nombres y Estados." In *Chamanismo en latinoamérica: Una revisión conceptual*, edited by Jacques Galinier, Isabel Lagarriga, and Michel Perrin (Mexico City: Plaza y Valdéz, Editores, 1995).

Camayd-Freixas, Erik. *Realismo mágico y primitivismo: Relecturas de Carpentier, Asturias, Rulfo, y García Márquez.* Lanham, Md.: University Press of America, 1998.

de la Campa, Roman. "Magical Realism and World Literature: A Genre for the Times?" *Revista Canadiense de Estudios Hispánicos* 23, 2 (1999): 205–19.

Carpenter, Lynette, and Wendy Kolmar. *Haunting the House of Fiction: Feminist Perspectives on Ghost Stories by American Women.* Knoxville: University of Tennessee Press, 1991.

Carpentier, Alejo. "The Baroque and the Marvelous Real." 1975 (in Spanish). Translated by Tanya Huntington and Lois Parkinson Zamora. In *Magical Realism: Theory, History, Community*, edited by Lois Parkinson Zamora and Wendy B. Faris, 89–108. Durham: Duke University Press, 1995.

————. *The Kingdom of This World.* 1949 (in Spanish). Translated by Harriet de Onís. New York: Collier, 1970.

————. "On the Marvelous Real in America." 1967 (in Spanish). Translated by Tanya Huntington and Lois Parkinson Zamora. In *Magical Realism: Theory, History, Community,* edited by Lois Parkinson Zamora and Wendy B. Faris, 76–88. Durham: Duke University Press, 1995.

————. "Problemática de la actual novela latinoamericana." In *Tientos y diferencias,* 7–35. Montevideo: Arca, 1967.

————. *El reino de este mundo.* 1949. Reprint, Mexico City: Compañía General de Ediciones, 1962.

Castillo, Ana. *So Far from God.* New York: Norton, 1993.

Castle, Terry. *The Freudian Thermometer: Eighteenth-Century Culture and the Invention of the Uncanny.* New York: Oxford University Press, 1995.

Cezair-Thompson, Margaret. "Beyond the Postcolonial Novel: Ben Okri's *The Famished Road* and Its 'Abiku' Traveller." *Journal of Commonwealth Literature* 31, 2 (1996): 33–45.

Chait, Sandra. "Mythology, Magic Realism, and White Writing After Apartheid." *Research in African Literatures* 3, 2 (2000): 17–28.

Chanady, Amaryll. "La focalización como espejo de contradicciones en *El reino de este mundo.*" *Revista Canadiense de Estudios Hispánicos* 12, 3 (1988): 454–55.

————. *Magical Realism and the Fantastic: Resolved Versus Unresolved Antinomy.* New York: Garland, 1985.

————. "The Origins and Development of Magic Realism in Latin American Fiction." In *Magic Realism and Canadian Literature: Essays and Stories,* edited by Peter Hinchcliffe and Ed Jewinski, 49–58. Waterloo: University of Waterloo Press, 1986.

————. "The Territorialization of the Imaginary in Latin America: Self-Affirmation and Resistance to Metropolitan Paradigms." In *Magical Realism: Theory, History, Community,* edited by Lois Parkinson Zamora and Wendy B. Faris, 125–44. Durham: Duke University Press, 1995.

Chatman, Seymour. *Story and Discourse: Narrative Poetics in Fiction and Film.* Ithaca: Cornell University Press, 1978.

Chiampi, Irlemar. *El realismo maravilloso: Forma e ideología en la novela hispanoamericana.* Translated (from Portuguese) by Agustín Martínez and Margara Russotto. Caracas: Monte Avila, 1983.

Chow, Rey. "Gender and Representation." In *Feminist Consequences: Theory for the New Century,* edited by Elisabeth Bronfen and Misha Kavka, 38–57. New York: Columbia University Press, 2001.

Christensen, Thomas. "A Lusty Tropical Fable: *Brazil* by John Updike." *San Francisco Chronicle,* February 15, 1994.

Clarke, Joni Adamson. "Why Bears Are Good to Think, and Theory Doesn't Have to Be Murder: Transformation and Oral Tradition in Louise Erdrich's *Tracks.*" *S.A.I.L.* 4, 1 (1992): 24–48.

Clifford, James. *The Predicament of Culture: Twentieth-Century Ethnography, Literature, and Art.* Cambridge: Harvard University Press, 1988.

Cohn, Deborah. *History and Memory in the Two Souths: Recent Southern and Spanish American Fiction.* Nashville: Vanderbilt University Press, 1999.

Collette, Marianella. "La fase del espejo, lo simbólico y lo imaginario en la novela *Aura,* de Carlos Fuentes." *Revista Canadiense de Estudios Hispánicos* 19, 2 (1995): 281–98.

Colomines, Gabrielle. "Convergencias y divergencias: De Gabriel García Márquez a Isabel Allende." In *La narrativa de Isabel Allende: Claves de una marginalidad,* edited by Adriana Castillo de Berchenko, 39–68. Perpignan, France: Centre de Recherches Ibériques et Latinoaméricaines, Université de Perpignan, 1990.

Connell, Liam. "Discarding Magic Realism: Modernism, Anthropology, and Critical Practice." *Ariel* 29, 2 (1998): 95–110.

Conniff, Brian. "The Dark Side of Magical Realism: Science, Oppression, and Apocalypse in *One Hundred Years of Solitude.*" *Modern Fiction Studies* 36, 2 (1990): 167–79.

Cooper, Brenda. *Magical Realism in West African Fiction: Seeing with a Third Eye.* New York: Routledge, 1998.

Cornell, Daniel. "Woman Looking: Revis(ion)ing Pauline's Subject Position in Louise Erdrich's *Tracks.*" *S.A.I.L.* 4, 1 (1992): 49–64.

Cornell, Drusilla. *Beyond Accommodation: Ethical Feminism, Deconstruction, and the Law.* New York: Routledge, 1991.

Cortázar, Julio. "Axolotl." 1951 (in Spanish). Translated by Paul Blackburn. In *The End of the Game and Other Stories,* 3–9. New York: Harper and Row, 1967.

———. "Para una poética." *La Torre* 2, 7 (1954): 121–38.

Cross, Richard K. "The Soul Is a Far Country: D. M. Thomas and *The White Hotel.*" *Journal of Modern Literature* 18, 1 (1992): 19–47.

Danow, David K. *The Spirit of Carnival: Magical Realism and the Grotesque.* Lexington: University Press of Kentucky, 1995.

Dapprich-Barrett, Ute. "Magical Realism: Sources and Affinities in Contemporary German and English Writing." In *The Novel in Anglo-German Context,* edited by Susanne Stark, 333–45. Amsterdam and Atlanta: Rodopi, 2000.

Darrieussecq, Marie. *Pig Tales.* 1996 (in French). Translated by Linda Coverdale. New York: New Press, 1997.

Dash, J. Michael. "Marvelous Realism: The Way Out of Negritude." *Caribbean Studies* 13, 4 (1973): 57–70.

Davies, Lloyd. *Allende: La casa de los espíritus.* London: Grant and Cutler, 2000.

Debray-Genette, Raymonde. "Profane, Sacred: Disorder of Utterance in *Trois contes.*" In *Flaubert and Postmodernism,* edited by Naomi Schor and Henry F. Majewski, 13–29. Lincoln: University of Nebraska Press, 1984.

DeKoven, Marianne. *Rich and Strange: Gender, History, Modernism.* Princeton: Princeton University Press, 1991.

Deleuze, Gilles, and Félix Guattari, *Kafka: Pour une littérature mineure.* Paris: Minuit, 1975.

Delgadillo, Theresa. "Forms of Chicana Feminist Resistance: Hybrid Spirituality in Ana Castillo's *So Far from God.*" *Modern Fiction Studies* 44, 4 (1998): 888–916.

Delicka, Magdalena. "American Magic Realism: Crossing the Borders in Literatures of the Margins." *Journal of American Studies of Turkey* 6 (1997): 25–33.

Dessau, Adalbert. "Realismo mágico y nueva novela latinoamericana: Consideraciones metodológicas e históricas." In *Actas del Simposio Internacional de Estudios Hispánicos,* edited by Horányi Mátyás, 351–58. Budapest: Akademia Kiadó, 1978.

D'haen, Theo. "Magical Realism and Postmodernism: Decentering Privileged Centers." In *Magical Realism: Theory, History, Community,* edited by Lois Parkinson Zamora and Wendy B. Faris, 191–208. Durham: Duke University Press, 1995.

Dharwadker, Vinay, ed. *Cosmopolitan Geographies: New Locations in Literature and Culture.* New York: Routledge, 2001.

Díaz, Nancy Gray. *The Radical Self: Metamorphosis to Animal Form and Modern Latin American Narrative.* Columbia: University of Missouri Press, 1989.

Dixon, Paul B. *Reversible Readings: Ambiguity in Four Modern Latin American Novels.* Tuscaloosa: University of Alabama Press, 1985.

Dudley, Edward, and Maximilian E. Novak. *The Wild Man Within: An Image in Western Thought from the Renaissance to Romanticism.* Pittsburgh: University of Pittsburgh Press, 1972.

Duerr, Hans Peter. *Dreamtime: Concerning the Boundary Between Wilderness and Civilization.* Translated by Felicitas Goodman. New York: Blackwell, 1987.

Duffy, Enda. *The Subaltern Ulysses.* Minneapolis: University of Minnesota Press, 1994.

Dupuis, Michel, and Albert Mingelgrün. "Pour une poétique du réalisme magique." In *Le Réalisme magique: Roman, peinture et cinéma,* edited by Jean Weisgerber, 24. Brussels: Le Centre des Avant-gardes littéraires de l'Université de Bruxelles, 1987.

Durix, Jean-Pierre. *Mimesis, Genres, and Post-Colonial Discourse: Deconstructing Magic Realism.* New York: St. Martin's, 1998.

———. *The Writer Written: The Artist and Creation in the New Literatures in English.* New York: Greenwood Press, 1987.

Dussel, Enrique. "Beyond Eurocentrism: The World-System and the Limits of Modernity." Translated by Eduardo Mendieta. In *The Cultures of Globalization,* edited by Frederic Jameson and Masao Miyoshi, 3–31. Durham: Duke University Press, 1998.

Earle, Peter G. "Literature as Survival: Allende's *The House of the Spirits.*" *Contemporary Literature* 28, 4 (1987): 543–54.

Eliade, Mircea. *Shamanism: Archaic Techniques of Ecstasy.* Translated by Willard R. Trask. Princeton: Princeton University Press, 1974.

Ellison, David. *Ethics and Aesthetics in European Modernist Literature: From the Sublime to the Uncanny.* Cambridge: Cambridge University Press, 2001.

Erdrich, Louise. *Tracks.* New York: Henry Holt, 1988. Reprint, New York: Harper and Row, 1989.

Erickson, John. "Metoikoi and Magical Realism in the Maghrebian Narratives of Tahar ben Jelloun and Abdelkebir Khatibi." In *Magical Realism: Theory, History, Community,* edited by Lois Parkinson Zamora and Wendy B. Faris, 427–50. Durham: Duke University Press, 1995.

Ermarth, Elizabeth Deeds. *Sequel to History: Postmodernism and the Crisis of Representational Time.* Princeton: Princeton University Press, 1991.

Esquivel, Laura. *Como agua para chocolate: Novela de entregas mensuales con recetas, amores y remedios caseros.* 1989. Reprint, Mexico City: Editorial Planeta, 1990.

———. *Like Water for Chocolate: A Novel in Monthly Installments with Recipes, Romances, and Home Remedies.* Translated by Carol Christensen and Thomas Christensen. New York: Doubleday, 1992.

Fabre, Michel. "Recovering Precious Words: On Wilson Harris and the Language of Imagination." In *The Uncompromising Imagination,* edited by Hena Maes-Jellinek, 42–53. Mundelstrup and Sydney: Dangaroo, 1991.

Faris, Wendy B. "Scheherazade's Children: Magical Realism and Postmodern Fiction." In *Magical Realism: Theory, History, Community,* edited by Lois Parkinson Zamora and Wendy B. Faris, 163–90. Durham: Duke University Press, 1995.

Faulkner, William. *As I Lay Dying.* New York: Jonathan Cape and Harrison Smith, 1930. Reprint, New York: Random House, 1957.

Finke, Laurie A. "Mystical Bodies and the Dialogics of Vision." In *Maps of Flesh and Light: The Religious Experience of Medieval Women Mystics,* edited by Ulrike Wiethus, 28–44. Syracuse: Syracuse University Press, 1993.

Flanagan, Kathleen. "The Fragmented Self in Salman Rushdie's *Midnight's Children.*" *Commonwealth Novel in English* 5, 1 (1992): 38–45.

Flores, Ralph. *The Rhetoric of Doubtful Authority: Deconstructive Readings of Self-Questioning Narratives, St. Augustine to Faulkner.* Ithaca: Cornell University Press, 1984.

Foreman, P. Gabrielle. "Past-On Stories: History and the Magically Real: Morrison and Allende on Call." *Feminist Studies* 18, 2 (1992): 369–85.

Foster, John Burt. "Magic Realism in *The White Hotel:* Compensatory Vision and the Transformation of Classic Realism." *Southern Humanities Review* 20, 3 (1986): 205–19.

Foster, Thomas. "Cyber-Aztecs and Cholo-Punks: Guillermo Gómez-Peña's Five-Worlds Theory." *PMLA* 117 (2002): 43–67.

Foucault, Michel. "Of Other Spaces." Translated by Jay Miskowiec. *Diacritics* 16 (1986): 22–27.

———. *Reflections on Gender and Science.* New Haven: Yale University Press, 1985.

Freeman, Barbara. *The Feminine Sublime: Gender and Excess in Women's Fiction.* Berkeley: University of California Press, 1995.

Frenk, Susan. "Rewriting History: Carlos Fuentes' *Aura.*" *Forum for Modern Language Studies* 30, 3 (1994): 256–76.

Freud, Sigmund. *The Standard Edition of the Complete Psychological Works of Sigmund Freud.* Translated and edited by James Strachey. London: Hogarth Press, 1953–66.

Frucht, Abby. *Licorice.* Saint Paul, Minn.: Graywolf Press, 1990. Reprint, New York: Grove, 1993.

Fuentes, Carlos. *Aura.* 1962 (in Spanish). Translated by Lysander Kemp. New York: Farrar, Straus & Giroux, 1975.

———. "Central and Eccentric Writing." In *Lives on the Line: The Testimony of Contempo-*

rary Latin American Authors, edited by Doris Meyer, 113–25. Berkeley: University of California Press, 1988.

———. *Christopher Unborn.* 1987 (in Spanish). Translated by Alfred Mac Adam and the author. New York: Farrar, Straus & Giroux, 1989.

———. *Constancia and Other Stories for Virgins.* 1989 (in Spanish). Translated by Thomas Christensen. New York: Harper, 1991.

———. *Distant Relations.* 1980 (in Spanish). Translated by Margaret Sayers Peden. New York: Farrar, Straus & Giroux, 1982.

———. *La nueva novela hispanoamericana.* Mexico City: Joaquín Mortiz, 1969.

———. *Valiente mundo nuevo.* Madrid: Mondadori, 1990.

Fuguet, Alberto, and Sergio Gómez, eds. *McOndo.* Barcelona: Mondadori, 1996.

Gablik, Suzi. *The Reenchantment of Art.* New York: Thames and Hudson, 1991.

Gallo, Marta. "El futuro perfecto de Macondo." *Revista Hispánica Moderna* 38 (1974–75): 115–35.

Gandhi, Leila. *Postcolonial Theory: A Critical Introduction.* New York: Columbia University Press, 1998.

García, Cristina. *Dreaming in Cuban.* New York: Ballantine, 1992.

García-Johnson, Ronie-Richelle. "The Struggle for Space: Feminism and Freedom in *The House of the Spirits.*" *Revista Hispánica Moderna* 47, 1 (1994): 184–93.

García Márquez, Gabriel. *Del amor y otros demonios.* 1987. Mexico City: Editorial Diana, 1994.

———. "Light Is Like Water." 1978 (in Spanish). Translated by Edith Grossman. In *Strange Pilgrims,* 157–61. New York: Knopf, 1993.

———. *Of Love and Other Demons.* 1987 (in Spanish). Translated by Edith Grossman. New York: Knopf, 1995.

———. *El olor de la guayaba: Conversaciones con Plinio Apuleyo Mendoza.* Bogotá: Oveja Negra, 1982.

———. *One Hundred Years of Solitude.* 1967 (in Spanish). Translated by Gregory Rabassa. New York: Avon, 1971.

———. "The Solitude of Latin America." *Granta* 9 (1983): 55–59.

———. "A Very Old Man with Enormous Wings." 1968 (in Spanish). Translated by Gregory Rabassa. In *Magical Realist Fiction: An Anthology,* ed. Robert Young and Keith Hollaman, 457–62. New York: Longman, 1984.

Garuba, Harry. "Ben Okri: Animist Realism and the Famished Genre." *The Guardian* (Lagos), March 13, 1993.

Gelley, Alexander. "Art and Reality in *Die Blechtrommel.*" *Forum for Modern Language Studies* 3 (1967): 115–25.

Gide, André. *Two Legends: Oedipus and Theseus.* 1931 (in French). Translated by John Russell. New York: Random House, 1950.

Gilkes, Michael. *Wilson Harris and the Caribbean Novel.* London: Longman, 1975.

Godwin, Malcolm. *Angels: An Endangered Species.* New York: Simon and Schuster, 1990.

Gómez-Peña, Guillermo. *The New World Border.* San Francisco: City Lights, 1996.

González Echevarría, Roberto. *Alejo Carpentier: The Pilgrim at Home.* Ithaca: Cornell University Press, 1977.

———. "Isla a su vuelo fugitiva: Carpentier y el realismo mágico." *Revista Iberoamericana* 40, 86 (1974): 9–64.

———. *Myth and Archive: A Theory of Latin American Narrative.* Cambridge: Cambridge University Press, 1990.

———. "With Borges in Macondo." *Diacritics* 2, 1 (1972): 57–60.

Govaert, Serge. "Une Approche sociologique." In *Le Réalisme magique: Roman, peinture et cinéma,* edited by Jean Weisgerber, 233–44. Brussels: Le Centre des Avant-gardes littéraires de l'Université de Bruxelles, 1987.

Graff, Gerald. "The Politics of Anti-Realism." In *The Salmagundi Reader,* edited by Robert Boyers and Peggy Boyers, 394–420. Bloomington: Indiana University Press, 1983.

Grass, Günter. "Kafka and His Executors." Translated by Ralph Manheim. In *On Writing and Politics, 1967–1983,* 31–50. New York: Harcourt Brace Jovanovich, 1985.

———. *On Writing and Politics, 1967–1983.* Translated by Ralph Mannheim. New York: Harcourt Brace Jovanovich, 1985.

———. *The Tin Drum.* 1959 (in German). Translated by Ralph Manheim. New York: Random House, 1964.

Gray, Richard T. "The Dialectic of 'Enscentment': Patrick Süskind's *Das Parfum* as Critical History of Enlightenment Culture." *PMLA* 108 (1993): 489–505.

Grewal, Inderpal, and Caren Kaplan, eds. *Scattered Hegemonies: Postmodernity and Transnational Feminist Practices.* Minneapolis: University of Minnesota Press, 1994.

Griffiths, Gareth. "Postcoloniality, Religion, Geography: Keeping Our Feet on the Ground and Our Heads Up." In *Mapping the Sacred: Religion, Geography, and Postcolonial Literatures,* edited by Jamie S. Scott and Paul Simpson-Housley, 445–61. Amsterdam and Atlanta: Rodopi, 2001.

della Grisa, Graciela Ricci. *Realismo mágico y conciencia mítica en América Latina.* Buenos Aires: Cambeiro, 1985.

Grosz, Elisabeth. *Volatile Bodies: Toward a Corporeal Feminism.* Bloomington: University of Indiana Press, 1994.

Guenther, Irene. "Magic Realism in the Weimar Republic." In *Magical Realism: Theory, History, Community,* edited by Lois Parkinson Zamora and Wendy B. Faris, 33–73. Durham: Duke University Press, 1995.

Guidotti, Valeria. "Magical Realism Beyond the Wall of Apartheid?" In *Coterminous Worlds: Magical realism and Contemporary Post-colonial Literature in English,* edited by Elsa Linguanti, Francesco Casotti, and Carmen Concilio, 227–43. Amsterdam and Atlanta: Rodopi, 1999.

Guidry, Glenn A. "Theoretical Reflections on the Ideological and Social Implications of Mythic Form in Grass' *Die Blechtrommel.*" *Monatshefte* 83, 2 (1991): 127–46.

Halifax, Joan. *Shamanic Voices: A Survey of Visionary Narratives.* New York: E. P. Dutton, 1979. Reprint, New York: Penguin, 1991.

Harding, Sandra. *Whose Science, Whose Knowledge? Thinking from Women's Lives.* Ithaca: Cornell University Press, 1991.

Harner, Michael. *The Way of the Shaman: A Guide to Power and Healing.* San Francisco: Harper, 1990.

Harris, Trudier. *Fiction and Folklore in the Novels of Toni Morrison.* Knoxville: University of Tennessee Press, 1991.

Harris, Wilson. "Literacy and the Imagination." In *The Literate Imagination: Essays on the Novels of Wilson Harris,* edited by Michael Gilkes, 23–31. London: Macmillan, 1989.

———. "The Native Phenomenon." In *Common Wealth,* edited by Anna Rutherford, 144–50. Aarhus, Denmark: University of Aarhus, n.d.

———. *Palace of the Peacock.* London: Faber and Faber, 1960. Reprint, London: Faber and Faber, 1968.

———. *Tumatumari.* London: Faber and Faber, 1968.

Harrison, James. *Salman Rushdie.* New York: Twayne, 1992.

Hart, Patricia. *Narrative Magic in the Fiction of Isabel Allende.* London: Associated University Presses, 1989.

Hart, Stephen. "Magical Realism in Gabriel García Márquez's *Cien años de soledad.*" *INTI* 16–17 (1982–83): 37–52.

Hawkins, Peter S., and Anne Howland Schotter, eds. *Ineffability: Naming the Unnameable from Dante to Beckett.* New York: AMS Press, 1984.

Herman, David. "Hypothetical Focalization." *Narrative* 2, 3 (1994): 230–53.

Hinchcliffe, Peter, and Ed Jewinski, eds. *Magic Realism and Canadian Literature: Essays and Stories.* Waterloo: University of Waterloo Press, 1986.

Holler, Linda. "Thinking with the Weight of the Earth: Feminist Contributions to an Epistemology of Concreteness." *Hypatia* 5, 1 (1990): 1–23.

Hollington, Michael. *Günter Grass: The Writer in a Pluralist Society.* Boston: Marion Boyars, 1980.

Hong Kingston, Maxine. *The Woman Warrior.* New York: Knopf, 1976. Reprint, New York: Vintage, 1989.

Horrocks, David. "The Undisciplined Past: Novel Approaches to History in Grass and Rushdie." In *The Novel in Anglo-German Context: Cultural Cross-Currents and Affinities,* edited by Susanne Stark, 347–55. Amsterdam and Atlanta: Rodopi, 2000.

Hutcheon, Linda. *A Poetics of Postmodernism: History, Theory, Fiction.* New York: Routledge, 1988.

Hutchinson, George B. *The Ecstatic Whitman: Shamanism and the Crisis of the Union.* Columbus: Ohio State University Press, 1986.

Ireland, Kenneth. "Doing Very Dangerous Things: *Die Blechtrommel* and *Midnight's Children.*" *Comparative Literature* 42, 4 (1990): 335–61.

Irigaray, Luce. *The Irigaray Reader.* Edited by Margaret Whitford. Oxford: Blackwell, 1991.

———. *Speculum of the Other Woman.* 1974 (in French). Translated by Gillian C. Gill. Ithaca: Cornell University Press, 1984.

———. "This Sex Which Is Not One." 1977 (in French). Translated by Catherine Porter with Carolyn Burke, In *This Sex Which Is Not One,* 23–33. Ithaca: Cornell University Press, 1985.

Irvine, Dean J. "Fables of the Plague Years: Postcolonialism, Postmodernism, and Magic

Realism in 'Cien años de soledad' ('One Hundred Years of Solitude')." *Ariel: A Review of International English Literature* 29, 4 (1998): 53–80.

Irwin, John T. *Doubling and Incest, Repetition and Revenge: A Speculative Reading of Faulkner.* Baltimore: Johns Hopkins University Press, 1975.

Isaak, Jo Anna. *The Ruin of Representation in Modernist Art and Texts.* Ann Arbor: UMI Research Press, 1986.

Iser, Wolfgang. *Prospecting: From Reader Response to Literary Anthropology.* Baltimore: Johns Hopkins University Press, 1989.

Jackson, Rosemary. *Fantasy, the Literature of Subversion.* New York: Methuen, 1981.

Jacobson, Mark. "Whole Lotta Shaman." *Esquire,* June 1993, 36–37.

Jaeck, Lois Marie. "The Text and Intimations of Immortality: From Proust's *Recherche* to Fuentes's *Aura.*" *Dalhousie French Studies* 38 (1997): 109–17.

Jameson, Fredric. "Globalization as a Philosophical Issue." In *The Cultures of Globalization,* edited by Jameson and Masao Miyoshi, 54–77. Durham: Duke University Press, 1998.

———. "Modernism and Imperialism." In *Nationalism, Colonialism, and Literature,* edited by Terry Eagleton, Fredric Jameson, and Edward Said, 48–49. Minneapolis: University of Minnesota Press, 1990.

———. "On Magic Realism in Film." *Critical Inquiry* 12 (1986): 301–25.

———. *The Political Unconscious: Narrative as a Socially Symbolic Act.* Ithaca: Cornell University Press, 1981.

———. "The Realist Floor-Plan." In *On Signs,* edited by Marshall Blonsky, 373–83. Baltimore: Johns Hopkins University Press, 1985.

Janmohammed, Abdul R. *Manichean Aesthetics: The Politics of Literature in Colonial Africa.* Amherst: University of Massachusetts Press, 1983.

Jardine, Alice. *Gynesis: Configurations of Woman and Modernity.* Ithaca: Cornell University Press, 1985.

Jenkins, Ruth. "Authorizing Female Voice and Experience: Ghosts and Spirits in Kingston's *The Woman Warrior* and Allende's *The House of the Spirits.*" *MELUS* 19, 3 (1994): 61–73.

Jolly, Rosemary. "Rehearsals of Liberation: Contemporary Postcolonial Discourse and the New South Africa." *PMLA* 110, 1 (1995): 17–29.

Jones, Gayle. *Liberating Voices: Oral Tradition in African American Literature.* Cambridge: Harvard University Press, 1991.

Jung, C. G. "On the Relation of Analytical Psychology to Poetry." 1922 (in German). Translated by R.F.C. Hull. In *The Spirit in Man, Art, and Literature,* 65–83. Princeton: Princeton University Press, 1966.

Kadohata, Cynthia. *The Floating World.* New York: Viking Penguin, 1989. Reprint, New York: Ballantine, 1991.

Kalweit, Holger. *Dreamtime and Inner Space: The Way of the Shaman.* Boston: Shambhala, 1988.

Kane, Jean M. "The Migrant Intellectual and the Body of History: Salman Rushdie's *Midnight's Children.*" *Contemporary Literature* 37, 1 (1996): 94–118.

Kant, Immanuel. *Critique of Judgment*. Translated by J. H. Bernard. London: Collier-Macmillan, 1951

Kauffmann, R. Lane. "Cortázar's 'Axolotl' as Ethnographic Allegory." In *Primitivism and Identity in Latin America: Essays on Art, Literature, and Culture,* edited by Erik Camayd-Freixas and Eduardo González, 135–55. Tucson: University of Arizona Press, 2000.

Kawin, Bruce. *The Mind of the Novel: Reflexive Fiction and the Ineffable*. Princeton: Princeton University Press, 1982.

Keele, Alan F. " ' . . . Through a (Dark) Glass Clearly': Magic Spectacles and the Motif of the Mimetic Mantic in Postwar German Literature from Borchert to Grass." *Germanic Review* 57, 2 (1982): 49–59.

Kennedy, William. "Carlos Fuentes: Dreaming of History." *Review of Contemporary Fiction* 8, 2 (1989): 234–37.

———. *Ironweed*. New York: Viking Penguin, 1983. Reprint, New York: Penguin, 1984.

Kirby, Vicki. *Telling Flesh: The Substance of the Corporeal*. New York: Routledge, 1997.

Kolmar, Wendy. " 'Dialectics of Connectedness': Supernatural Elements in Novels by Bambara, Cisneros, Grahn, and Erdrich." In Lynette Carpenter and Wendy Kolmar, *Haunting the House of Fiction: Feminist Perspectives on Ghost Stories by American Women,* 236–49. Knoxville: University of Tennessee Press, 1991.

Kristeva. Julia. *The Powers of Horror: An Essay on Abjection*. 1980 (in French). Translated by Leon Roudiez. New York: Columbia University Press, 1982.

———. *Revolution in Poetic Language*. 1974 (in French). Translated by Margaret Waller. New York: Columbia University Press, 1984.

Kundera, Milan. *The Book of Laughter and Forgetting*. 1979 (in French). Translated from Czech by Michael Henry Heim. New York: Penguin, 1982.

Lambek, Michael. *Human Spirits: A Cultural Account of Trance in Mayotte*. Cambridge: Cambridge University Press, 1981.

Larson, Janet. "Lady-Wrestling for Victorian Soul: Discourse, Gender, and Spirituality in Women's Texts." *Religion and Literature* 23, 3 (1993): 43–64.

Lawrence, David. "Fleshly Ghosts and Ghostly Flesh: The Word and the Body in *Beloved*." *Studies in American Fiction* 19, 2 (1991): 194–202.

Le Clézio, J. M. G. *The Mexican Dream; or, The Interrupted Thoughts of Amerindian Civilizations*. Translated by Teresa Fagan. Chicago: Chicago University Press, 1988.

Levine, Suzanne Jill. "A Second Glance at the Spoken Mirror: Gabriel García Márquez and Virginia Woolf." *INTI: Revista de Literatura Hispánica* 16–17 (1982–83): 53–60.

Levitt, Morton P. "From Realism to Magic Realism: The Meticulous Modernist Fictions of García Márquez." *Critical Perspectives on Gabriel García Márquez,* edited by Bradley A. Shaw and Nora Vera-Godwin, 73–89. Lincoln: University of Nebraska Press, 1986.

Linguanti, Elsa. "Wilson Harris: A Case Apart." In *Coterminous Worlds: Magical Realism and Contemporary Post-colonial Literature in English,* edited by Elsa Linguanti, Francesco Casotti, and Carmen Concilio, 245–68. Amsterdam and Atlanta: Rodopi, 1999.

Linguanti, Elsa, Francesco Casotti, and Carmen Concilio, eds. *Coterminous Worlds: Magical Realism and Contemporary Post-colonial Literature in English*. Amsterdam and Atlanta: Rodopi, 1999.

London, Bette. *The Appropriated Voice: Narrative Authority in Conrad, Forster, and Woolf.* Ann Arbor: University of Michigan Press, 1990.

Lotman, Jurij M. "On the Metalanguage of a Typological Description of Culture." *Semiotica* 14, 2 (1975): 97–123.

Lovesey, Oliver. "The Post-Colonial 'Crisis of Representation' and Ngũgĩ wa Thiong'o's Religious Allegory." In *"And the Birds Began to Sing": Religion and Literature in Post-Colonial Cultures,* edited by Jamie S. Scott. Amsterdam and Atlanta: Rodopi, 1996.

Lukács, Georg. *Marxism and Human Liberation.* New York: Dell, 1973.

Lyotard, Jean-François. *The Postmodern Condition: A Report on Knowledge.* Translated by Geoff Bennington and Brian Massumi. Minneapolis: University of Minnesota Press, 1984.

MacAdam, Alfred. "La Torre de Danae." *Revista Iberoamericana* 39 (1973): 457–69.

Maes-Jellinek, Hena. "The True Substance of Life: Wilson Harris's *Palace of the Peacock.*" In *Common Wealth,* edited by Anna Rutherford, 151–59. Aarhus, Denmark: University of Aarhus, n.d.

———. *Wilson Harris.* Boston: Twayne, 1982.

Mageo, Jeannette Marie, and Alan Howard, eds. *Spirits in Culture, History, and Mind.* New York: Routledge, 1996.

Maillard, Keith. "*Middlewatch* as Magic Realism." *Canadian Literature* 92 (1982): 10–21.

Mandrell, James. "The Prophetic Voice in Garro, Morante, and Allende." *Comparative Literature* 42, 3 (1990): 227–44.

Martin, Gerald. "On 'Magical' and Social Realism in García Márquez." In *Gabriel García Márquez: New Readings,* edited by Bernard McGuirk and Richard Cardwell, 95–116. Cambridge: Cambridge University Press, 1987.

Marting, Diane. *The Sexual Woman in Latin American Literature: Dangerous Desires.* Gainesville: University of Florida Press, 2001.

Mason, Ann L. *The Skeptical Muse: A Study of Günter Grass' Conception of the Artist.* Bern: Peter Lang, 1974.

McElroy, Bernard. "Lunatic, Child, Artist, Hero: Grass's Oskar as a Way of Seeing." *Forum for Modern Language Studies* 22, 4 (1986): 308–22.

McGee, Patrick. *Telling the Other: The Question of Value in Modern and Postcolonial Writing.* Ithaca: Cornell University Press, 1992.

McHale, Brian. *Postmodernist Fiction.* New York: Methuen, 1987.

McNabb, Pamela. "Julio Cortázar's Axolotl: Literary Archeology of the Unreal." *International Fiction Review* 24, 1–2 (1997): 12–22.

Menton, Seymour. *Historia verdadera del realismo mágico* (Mexico City: Fondo de Cultura Económica, 1998).

———. "Jorge Luis Borges, Magic Realist." *Hispanic Review* 50, 1 (1982): 411–26.

———. *Magic Realism Rediscovered, 1918–1981.* Philadelphia: Art Alliance Press, 1983.

Merino, Blanca. "Fantasía y realidad en *Aura* de Carlos Fuentes." *Literatura Mexicana* 2, 1 (1991): 135–47.

Merivale, Patricia. "Saleem Fathered by Oskar: Intertextual Strategies in *Midnight's Children* and *The Tin Drum.*" *Ariel* 21, 3 (1990): 5–21.

Meyer, Doris. "'Parenting the Text': Female Creativity and Dialogic Relationships in Isabel Allende's *La casa de los espíritus.*" *Hispania* 73, 2 (1990): 360–65.

Minden, Michael. "A Post-Realist Aesthetic: Günter Grass, *Die Blechtrommel.*" In *The German Novel in the Twentieth Century: Beyond Realism,* edited by David Midgley, 149–63. Edinburgh: Edinburgh University Press, 1993.

Mínguez, José Miguel. "Günter Grass *(Die Blechtrommel)* y Julio Cortázar *(Rayuela),* Heinrich Böll *(Opiniones de un payaso)* y Alejo Carpentier *(El reino de este mundo):* Notas sobre el realismo mágico y las nuevas actitudes del novelista ante su obra." *Boletín de Estudios Germánicos* 9 (1972): 273–90.

Mitchell, Carolyn A. "'I Love to Tell the Story': Biblical Revisions in *Beloved.*" *Religion and Literature* 23, 3 (Autumn 1991): 27–42.

Mitchell, W.J.T. "*Ut Pictura Theoria:* Abstract Painting and the Repression of Language." *Critical Inquiry* 15 (1989): 348–71.

Miyoshi, Masao. "Turn to the Planet: Literature, Diversity, and Totality." *Comparative Literature* 53, 4 (2001): 283–97.

Mobley, Marilyn Sanders. *Folk Roots and Mythic Wings in Sarah Orne Jewett and Toni Morrison: The Cultural Function of Narrative.* Baton Rouge: Louisiana State University Press, 1991.

Monleón, José B. *A Specter Is Haunting Europe: A Sociohistorical Approach to the Fantastic.* Princeton: Princeton University Press, 1990.

Montaner Ferrer, María Eulalia. "Falaz Gabriel García Márquez: Ursula Iguarán, narradora de *Cien años de soledad.*" *Hispanic Review* 55, 1 (1987): 77–93.

Moretti, Franco. *Modern Epic: The World System from Goethe to García Márquez.* Translated by Quintin Hoare. New York: Verso, 1996.

Morrison, Toni. *Beloved.* New York: Knopf, 1987.

———. "Interview with Toni Morrison." By Christina Davis. *Présence Africaine* 145 (1988): 141–50.

———. *Song of Solomon.* New York: Knopf, 1977. Reprint, New York: Signet, 1978.

Moss, Laura. "'Forget those damnfool realists!': Salman Rushdie's Self-Parody as the Magic Realist's 'Last Sigh.'" *Ariel: A Review of International English Literature* 29, 4 (1998): 121–39.

Mukherjee, Arun. "Characterization in Salman Rushdie's *Midnight's Children:* Breaking out of the Hold of Realism and Seeking the 'Alienation Effect.'" In *The New Indian Novel in English: A Study of the 1980's,* edited by Viney Kirpal, 109–20. New Delhi: Allied Publishers, 1990.

Murphy, Patrick. "Ground, Pivot, Motion: Ecofeminist Theory, Dialogics, and Literary Practice." *Hypatia* 6 (Spring 1991): 146–61.

Napier, Susan. "The Magic of Identity: Magic Realism in Modern Japanese Fiction." In *Magical Realism: Theory, History, Community,* edited by Lois Parkinson Zamora and Wendy B. Faris, 451–75. Durham: Duke University Press, 1995.

Natarajan, Nalini. "Woman, Nation, and Narration in *Midnight's Children.*" In *Scattered Hegemonies: Postmodernity and Transnational Feminist Practices,* edited by Inderpal Grewal and Caren Kaplan, 76–89. Minneapolis: University of Minnesota Press, 1994.

Nerval, Gérard de. *Aurélia.* 1855. Reprinted in *Les Filles du feu, suivi de Aurélia,* edited by Béatrice Didier, 289–354. Paris: Gallimard, 1972.

"The New Age of Angels." *Time,* December 27, 1993, 56–65.

Noel, Daniel C. *The Soul of Shamanism: Western Fantasies, Imaginal Realities.* New York: Continuum, 1997.

Noriega, Chon A. "Chicano Cinema and the Horizon of Expectations: A Discursive Analysis of Film Reviews in the Mainstream, Alternative, and Hispanic Press 1987–1988." *Aztlán: A Journal of Chicano Studies* 19, 2 (1988–90): 1–32.

Okri, Ben. *The Famished Road.* London: Jonathan Cape, 1991. Reprint, New York: Doubleday, 1992.

———. "Whisperings of the Gods: An Interview with Ben Okri by Delia Falconer." *Island* 71 (1997): 43–51.

Oliva, Renato. "Re-Dreaming the World: Ben Okri's Shamanic Realism." In *Coterminous Worlds: Magical Realism and Contemporary Post-colonial Literature in English,* edited by Elsa Linguanti, Francesco Casotti, and Carmen Concilio, 171–96. Amsterdam and Atlanta: Rodopi, 1999.

O'Neill, Molly. "Sensing the Spirit in All Things, Seen and Unseen." *New York Times,* March 31, 1993.

O'Neill, Patrick. "Points of Origin: On Focalization in Narrative." *Canadian Review of Comparative Literature* 19, 3 (1992): 331–50.

Ortega, Julio. "Postmodernism in Latin America." In *Postmodern Fiction in Europe and the Americas,* edited by Theo D'haen and Hans Bertens, 193–208. Amsterdam: Rodopi, 1988.

Palumbo-Liu, David, and Hans Ulrich Gumbrecht, eds. *Streams of Cultural Capital: Transnational Cultural Studies.* Stanford: Stanford University Press, 1997.

Parry, Idris. "Aspects of Günter Grass's Narrative Technique." *Forum for Modern Language Studies* 3 (1967): 100–114.

Pérez, Laura. "Spirit Glyphs: Reimagining Art and Artist in the Work of Chicana *Tlamatinime.*" *Modern Fiction Studies* 44, 1 (1998): 36–76.

Phillips, Adam. *Kissing, Tickling, and Being Bad: Psychoanalytical Essays on the Unexamined Life.* Cambridge: Harvard University Press, 1993.

Pinget, Robert. *That Voice.* 1975 (in French). Translated by Barbara Wright. New York: Red Dust, 1982.

Powell, Joan Miller. "The Conflict of Becoming: Cultural Hybridity and the Representation of Focalization in Caribbean Literature." *Literature and Psychology* 45, 1 and 2 (1999): 63–93.

Prince, Gerald. *Dictionary of Narratology.* Lincoln: University of Nebraska Press, 1978.

Quayson, Ato. *Strategic Transformations in Nigerian Writing: Orality and History in the Work of Rev. Samuel Johnson, Amos Tutuola, Wole Soyinka, and Ben Okri.* Oxford: James Curry, and Bloomington: Indiana University Press, 1997.

Radhakrishnan, R. "Postcoloniality and the Boundaries of Identity." *Callaloo* 16, 4 (1993): 750–71.

Rahv, Philip. "The Myth and the Powerhouse." In *Myth and Literature: Contemporary Theory and Practice,* edited by John B. Vickery, 109–18. Lincoln: University of Nebraska Press, 1969.

Rainwater, Catherine. "Reading Between Worlds: Narrativity in the Fiction of Louise Erdrich." *American Literature* 62, 3 (September 1990): 406–22.

Rama, Angel. *Edificación de un arte nacional y popular: Gabriel García Márquez.* Bogotá: Colcultura, 1991.

———. *Transculturación narrativa en América latina.* Mexico City: Siglo Veintiuno, 1982.

Ramchand, Kenneth. Introduction to *Palace of the Peacock,* by Wilson Harris. London: Faber and Faber, 1968.

Reder, Michael R., ed. *Conversations with Salman Rushdie.* Jackson: University Press of Mississippi, 2000.

Reedy, Daniel. "Through the Looking-Glass: Aspects of Cortázar's Epiphanies of Reality." *Bulletin of Hispanic Studies* 54 (1976): 125–34.

Rege, Josna. "Victim into Protagonist: *Midnight's Children* and the Post-Rushdie National Narratives of the Eighties." In *Critical Essays on Salman Rushdie,* edited by M. Keith Booker. New York: G. K. Hall, 1999.

Reichel-Dolmatoff, G. *The Shaman and the Jaguar: A Study of Narcotic Drugs Among the Indians of Colombia.* Philadelphia: Temple University Press, 1975.

Rigby, Kate. "The Goddess Returns: Ecofeminist Reconfigurations of Gender, Nature, and the Sacred." In *Feminist Poetics of the Sacred: Creative Suspicions,* edited by Frances Devlin-Glass and Lyn McCudden, 23–54. New York: Oxford University Press, 2001.

Rimmon-Kenan, Shlomith. *Narrative Fiction: Contemporary Poetics.* New York: Methuen, 1983.

Rincón, Carlos. "Posmodernismo, poscolonialismo y los nexos cartográficos del realismo mágico." *Neue Romania* 16 (1995): 193–210.

———. "Streams out of Control: The Latin American Plot." In *Streams of Cultural Capital: Transnational Cultural Studies,* edited by David Palumbo-Liu and Hans Ulrich Gumbrecht, 179–98. Stanford: Stanford University Press, 1997.

Robbins, Bruce. "The Sweatshop Sublime." *PMLA* 117 (2002): 84–97.

Robertson, Mary. "Hystery, Herstory, History: 'Imagining the Real' in Thomas's *The White Hotel.*" *Contemporary Literature* 25, 4 (1984): 452–77.

Rodgers, Catherine. "Aucune Evidence: Les Truismes de Marie Darrieussecq." *Romance Studies* 18, 1 (2000): 69–81.

Rodríguez Monegal, Emir. "Novedad y anacronismo de *Cien Años de Soledad.*" In *Homenaje a Gabriel García Márquez: Variaciones interpretativas en torno a su obra,* edited by Helmy F. Giacoman, 13–42. New York: Las Américas, 1972.

———. "*One Hundred Years of Solitude:* The Last Three Pages." *Books Abroad* 47, 3 (1973): 485–89.

———. "Presentación." In *El realismo maravilloso: Forma e ideología en la novela hispanoamericana,* by Irlemar Chiampi, translated (from Portuguese) by Agustín Martínez and Margara Russotto, 9–16. Caracas: Monte Avila, 1983.

———. "Realismo mágico versus literatura fantástica: Un diálogo de sordos." In *Otros mun-*

dos, otros fuegos: Fantasía y realismo mágico en Iberoamérica, edited by Donald B. Yates, 25–37. Michigan State University: Latin American Studies Center, 1975.

Roh, Franz. *Realismo mágico/post expresionismo: Problemas de la pintura europea mas reciente.* 1925 (in German). Translated by Fernando Vela. Madrid: Revista de Occidente, 1927. Excerpt published in 1927 in the *Revista de Occidente.* Translated by Wendy B. Faris and reprinted under the title "Magic Realism: Post-Expressionism," in *Magical Realism: Theory, History, Community,* edited by Lois Parkinson Zamora and Wendy B. Faris, 15–31. Durham: Duke University Press, 1995.

Rojas, Mario A. *"La casa de los espíritus:* Un caleidoscopio de espejos desordenados." *Revista Iberoamericana* 52 (1985): 917–25.

Ross, Andrew, ed. *Universal Abandon? The Politics of Postmodernism.* Minneapolis: University of Minnesota Press, 1988.

Rulfo, Juan. *Pedro Páramo.* 1955 (in Spanish). Translated by Lysander Kemp. New York: Random House, 1959.

Rushdie, Salman. *Imaginary Homelands: Essays and Criticism, 1981–1991.* New York: Penguin, 1992.

———. Interview by Ameenta Meer. *BOMB* 27 (1989). Reprinted in Michael R. Reder, *Conversations with Salman Rushdie,* 110–22. Jackson: University Press of Mississippi, 2000.

———. Interview by Chandrabhanu Pattanayak. *Literary Criterion* (India) 18, 3 (1983): 19–22.

———. *Midnight's Children.* New York: Knopf, 1980. Reprint, New York: Avon, 1982.

———. *The Moor's Last Sigh.* London: Jonathan Cape, 1995. Reprint, New York: Random House, 1996.

Rushdie, Salman, and Cécile Wajsbrot, "Utiliser une technique qui permette à Dieu d'exister." *Quinzaine Littéraire* 449 (1985): 22.

Saldívar, José David. *The Dialectics of Our America: Genealogy, Cultural Critique, and Literary History.* Durham: Duke University Press, 1991.

Sánchez, Napoleón. "Lo real maravilloso americano o la americanización del surrealismo." *Cuadernos Americanos* 219, 4 (1978): 69–95.

Sandoval, Chela. "U.S. Third World Feminism: The Theory and Method of Oppositional Consciousness in the Postmodern World." *Genders* 10 (1991): 1–24.

Saramago, José. *The Stone Raft.* 1986 (in Portuguese). Translated by Giovanni Pontiero. New York: Harcourt Brace, 1995.

Sauer, Michelle. "Saint-Making in Ana Castillo's *So Far from God:* Medieval Mysticism as Precedent for an Authoritative Chicana Spirituality." *Mester* 29 (2000): 72–91.

Sauerberg, Lars. "When the Soul Takes Wing: D. M. Thomas's *The White Hotel." Critique* 31 (1989): 3–15.

Scarano, Tommaso. "Notes on Spanish-American Magical Realism." In *Coterminous Worlds: Magical Realism and Contemporary Post-colonial Literature in English,* edited by Elsa Linguanti, Francesco Casotti, and Carmen Concilio, 9–28. Amsterdam and Atlanta: Rodopi, 1999.

Schor, Naomi. *Breaking the Chain: Women, Theory, and French Realist Fiction.* New York: Columbia University Press, 1985.

Schwartz, Marcy. *Writing Paris: Topographies of Desire in Contemporary Latin American Fiction.* Buffalo: State University of New York Press, 1999.

Schwarz-Bart, André. *A Woman Named Solitude.* 1972 (in French). Translated by Ralph Manheim. New York: Atheneum, 1973.

Scott, Jamie S., ed. *"And the Birds Began to Sing": Religion and Literature in Post-Colonial Cultures.* Amsterdam and Atlanta: Rodopi, 1996.

Scott, Jamie S., and Paul Simpson-Housley, eds. *Mapping the Sacred: Religion, Geography, and Postcolonial Literatures.* Amsterdam and Atlanta: Rodopi, 2001.

Scott, Nina M. "Vital Space in the House of Buendía." *Studies in Twentieth-Century Literature* 8, 11 (1984): 265–72.

Sered, Susan Starr. *Priestess, Mother, Sacred Sister: Religions Dominated by Women.* Oxford: Oxford University Press, 1994.

Sharon, Douglas. *Wizard of the Four Winds: A Shaman's Story.* New York: Macmillan, 1978.

Sheppard, R. Z. "Warning: The Rabbit Is Loose." *Time,* February 14, 1994.

Showalter, Elaine. "Feminist Criticism in the Wilderness." *Critical Inquiry: Special Issue: Writing and Sexual Difference* 8 (1981): 179–205.

Silver, Carole. "'East of the Sun and West of the Moon': Victorians and Fairy Brides." *Tulsa Studies in Women's Literature* 6, 2 (Fall 1987): 183–98.

Simpkins, Scott. "Magical Strategies: The Supplement of Realism." *Twentieth Century Literature* 34, 2 (1988): 140–54.

Slemon, Stephen. "Magic Realism as Postcolonial Discourse." In *Magical Realism: Theory, History, Community,* edited by Lois Parkinson Zamora and Wendy B. Faris, 407–26. Durham: Duke University Press, 1995.

Smith, Paul. "Visiting the Banana Republic." In *Universal Abandon? The Politics of Postmodernism,* edited by Andrew Ross, 128–48. Minneapolis: University of Minnesota Press, 1988.

Sommer, Doris. "Irresistible Romance: The Foundational Fictions of Latin America." In *Nation and Narration,* edited by Homi K. Bhabha, 71–98. New York: Routledge, 1990.

Spivak, Gayatri Chakravorty. *The Postcolonial Critic: Interviews, Strategies, Dialogues.* New York: Routledge, 1990.

Stewart, Susan. *On Longing: Narratives of the Miniature, the Gigantic, the Souvenir, the Collection.* Baltimore: Johns Hopkins University Press, 1984.

Suárez-Murias, Marguerite. "El Realismo Mágico: Una definición étnica." In *Essays on Hispanic Literature/Ensayos de literatura hispana: A Bilingual Anthology,* 95–114. Washington, D.C.: University Press of America, 1982.

Suleiman, Susan. *Subversive Intent: Gender, Politics, and the Avant-Garde.* Cambridge: Harvard University Press, 1990.

Süskind, Patrick. *Perfume: The Story of a Murderer.* 1985 (in German). Translated by John E. Woods. New York: Knopf, 1986.

Swarns, Rachel. "South Africa's Black Writers Explore a Free Society's Tensions." *New York Times,* June 24, 2002.

Tanner, Laura. "Sweet Pain and Charred Bodies: Figuring Violence in *The White Hotel.*" *Boundary* 2, 18 (1991): 130–49.

Taussig, Michael. *The Nervous System.* New York: Routledge, 1992.

———. *Shamanism, Colonialism, and the Wild Man: A Study in Terror and Healing.* Chicago: University of Chicago Press, 1987.

Terramorsi, Bernard. "Le Discours mystique du fantastique dans les contes de Julio Cortázar." In *Lo lúdico y lo fantástico en la obra de Cortázar,* 1:163–76. Madrid: Fundamentos, 1986.

Thiem, Jon. "The Textualization of the Reader in Magical Realist Fiction." In *Magical Realism: Theory, History, Community,* edited by Lois Parkinson Zamora and Wendy B. Faris, 235–47. Durham: Duke University Press, 1995.

Thomas, D. M. *The White Hotel.* New York: Viking, 1981.

Thomas, Nicholas. *Colonialism's Culture: Anthropology, Travel, and Government.* Princeton: Princeton University Press, 1994.

Thornton, Lawrence. *Imagining Argentina.* 1987. Reprint, New York: Bantam, 1988.

Todd, Richard. "Narrative Trickery and Performative Historiography: Fictional Representation of National Identity in Graham Swift, Peter Carey, and Mordecai Richler." In *Magical Realism: Theory, History, Community,* edited by Lois Parkinson Zamora and Wendy B. Faris, 305–28. Durham: Duke University Press, 1995.

Todorov, Tzvetan. *The Fantastic: A Structural Approach to a Literary Genre.* Translated by Richard Howard. Ithaca: Cornell University Press, 1975.

Torgovnik, Marianna. *Primitive Passions: Men, Women, and the Quest for Ecstasy.* Chicago: University of Chicago Press, 1996.

Trousson, Raymond. "Du fantastique et du merveilleux au réalisme magique?" In *Le Réalisme magique: Roman, peinture et cinéma,* edited by Jean Weisgerber, 33–42. Brussels: Le Centre des Avant-gardes littéraires de l'Université de Bruxelles, 1987.

Turner, Victor. *Dramas, Fields, and Metaphors: Symbolic Action in Human Society.* Ithaca: Cornell University Press, 1974.

———. *The Ritual Process: Structure and Anti-Structure.* Chicago: Aldine, 1969.

Ude, Wayne. "North American Magical Realism." *Colorado State Review* 8, 11 (1981): 21–30.

Updike, John. *Brazil.* New York: Knopf, 1994.

———. "Chronicles and Processions" (review of Ismail Kadare's *Chronicle in Stone* and José Saramago's *Baltasar and Blimunda*). *New Yorker,* March 14, 1988, 111–16.

Urbina, Nicasio. *"La casa de los espíritus* de Isabel Allende y *Cien años de soledad* de Gabriel García Márquez." *Escritura: Revista de Teoría y Crítica Literarias* 15, 29 (1990): 215–28.

Uslar-Pietri, Arturo. "Realismo Mágico." In *Godos, insurgentes y visionarios.* Barcelona: Seix Barral, 1986.

Valdez Moses, Michael. "Magical Realism at World's End." *Literary Imagination: The Review of the Association of Literary Scholars and Critics* 3 (2001): 105–33.

Van Delden, Maarten. *Carlos Fuentes, Mexico, and Modernity.* Nashville: Vanderbilt University Press, 1998.

Vizenor, Gerald. "Trickster Discourse: Comic Holotropes and Language Games." In *Narrative Chance: Postmodern Discourse on Native American Indian Literatures,* edited by Vizenor, 187–211. Norman: University of Oklahoma Press, 1993.

Volek, Emil. "Realismo mágico entre la modernidad y la postmodernidad: Hacia una remodelización cultural y discursiva de la nueva narrativa hispanoamericana." *INTI* 31 (1991): 3–20.

Walker, Nancy. *Feminist Alternatives: Irony and Fantasy in the Contemporary Novel by Women.* Jackson: University Press of Missouri, 1990.

Walsh, Roger. *The Spirit of Shamanism.* Los Angeles: Jeremy P. Tarcher, 1990.

Walter, Roland. *Magical Realism in Contemporary Chicano Fiction.* Frankfurt am Main: Vervuert Verlag, 1993.

Watt, Ian. *The Rise of the Novel.* Berkeley and Los Angeles: University of California Press, 1969.

Weisgerber, Jean. "La Locution et le concept." In *Le Réalisme magique: Roman, peinture et cinéma,* edited by Weisgerber, 11–32. Brussels: Le Centre des Avant-gardes littéraires de l'Université de Bruxelles, 1987.

———, ed. *Le Réalisme magique: Roman, peinture et cinéma.* Brussels: Le Centre des Avant-gardes littéraires de l'Université de Bruxelles, 1987.

Weisz, Gabriel. "Shamanism and Its Discontents." In *Methods for the Study of Literature as Cultural Memory,* edited by Raymond Vervliet and Annemarie Estor, 279–87. Vol. 6 of *Literature as Cultural Memory.* Amsterdam and Atlanta: Rodopi, 2000.

———. "Subliminal Body: Shamanism, Ancient Theater, and Ethnodrama." In *Primitivism and Identity in Latin America: Essays on Art, Literature, and Culture,* edited by Erik Camayd-Freixas and Eduardo González, 209–19. Tucson: University of Arizona Press, 2000.

Williamson, Edwin. "Magical Realism and the Theme of Incest in *One Hundred Years of Solitude.*" In *Gabriel García Márquez: New Readings,* edited by Bernard McGuirk and Richard Cardwell, 45–63. Cambridge: Cambridge University Press, 1987.

Wilson, Rawdon. "The Metamorphoses of Space: Magic Realism." In *Magical Realism and Canadian Literature,* edited by Peter Hinchcliffe and Ed Jewinski, 61–74. Waterloo: University of Waterloo Press, 1986.

———. "The Metamorphoses of Fictional Space: Magic Realism." In *Magical Realism: Theory, History, Community,* edited by Lois Parkinson Zamora and Wendy B. Faris, 209–33. Durham: Duke University Press, 1995.

Woolf, Virginia. "Professions for Women." In *Collected Essays,* edited by Leonard Woolf, 2: 284–89. London: Chatto and Windus, 1972.

Wyatt, Jean. "Giving Body to the Word: The Maternal Symbolic in Toni Morrison's *Beloved.*" *PMLA* 108 (1993): 474–88.

Yarbro-Bejarano, Yvonne. "The Multiple Subject in the Writing of Ana Castillo." *The Americas Review: A Review of Hispanic Literature and Art of the USA* 21, 1 (Spring 1992): 65–72.

Young, Robert, and Keith Hollaman. *Magical Realist Fiction: An Anthology.* New York: Longman, 1984.

Zamora, Lois Parkinson. "Magical Romance/Magical Realism: Ghosts in U.S. and Latin American Fiction." In *Magical Realism: Theory, History, Community,* edited by Lois Parkinson Zamora and Wendy B. Faris, 497–550. Durham: Duke University Press, 1995.

————. "The Magical Tables of Isabel Allende and Remedios Varo." *Comparative Literature* 44, 2 (1992): 113–43.

————. "Magic Realism and Fantastic History: Carlos Fuentes's *Terra Nostra* and Giambattista Vico's *The New Science.*" *Review of Contemporary Fiction* 8, 2 (1988): 249–56.

————. *Writing the Apocalypse: Historical Vision in Contemporary U.S. and Latin American Fiction.* Cambridge: Cambridge University Press, 1989.

Zamora, Lois Parkinson, and Wendy B. Faris, eds. *Magical Realism: Theory, History, Community.* Durham: Duke University Press, 1995.

Zizek, Slavoj. *Looking Awry: An Introduction to Jacques Lacan Through Popular Culture.* Cambridge: MIT Press, 1991.

Index

abiku, 11, 45, 73
Abrams, M. H., 65
Absalom, Absalom!, 30
absurdity, 88
Achebe, Chinua, 37
African American magical realism, 268n.33
   religious traditions in, 71
African art, 258–59n.63
African literature
   cultural hybridity of, 262n.101
   magical realism in, 8, 164, 232n.89,
      233n.94, 233n.97
   resemblance to Latin American, 268n.33
   traditional religions in, 149
After Death, 243n.78
Aizenberg, Edna, 41, 63, 234n.94, 243n.84,
   261n.92, 263n.106
Alaimo, Stacy, 190, 193, 272n.68
Alazraki, Jaime, 134
"Aleph, The," 89–90
Alexander, Marguerite, 224n.13, 255n.28
Alexis, Jacques Stéphen, 136, 149
allegory, 20–21, 74, 252n.4, 258n.60, 272n.73
Allende, Isabel. *See also The House of the*
   Spirits.
   as magical realist, 2, 37, 57, 179, 268n.33
   boundaries blurred in, 183
   defines magical realism, 222n.8, 247n.10
   feminist ideology of, 172, 176–77,
      266n.12, 269n.41
   history in, 38, 187, 261n.83
   shamans in, 168

   strategy in underdeveloped world of,
      183–84
   supernatural in, 183–84
Allie McBeal, magical elements in, 246n.111
Alter, Robert, 230n.73
alterity in magical realism, 133–69
   dynamics of, 4, 134–35
   encoded in magical realism, 36, 48
Anderson, Robert, 11, 249n.45
Andrews, Lynn V., 208, 210–11, 275n.113. *See*
   also Medicine Woman.
"androgynous mind," 176
"angel in the house," 180
angels in magical realism, 16, 57–58, 180–81,
   238–39n.32
   as encoding the ineffable, 56
   in "A Very Old Man with Enormous
      Wings," 64
   in *The House of the Spirits*, 276n.118
   popularity of, 238–39n.32
   trivialization of, 242n.72
animism, 60
Anna Karenina, 16
anthropology, 146, 149, 172, 240n.40
antinomy, 8, 17, 20
antitotalitarian. *See* political critique.
anxiety. *See* reader's response.
Anzaldúa, Gloria, 84, 105, 171
apartheid, 262–63n.101
apocalypse, 185, 187
Apollonian, 147
Appiah, Kwame Anthony, 36

appropriation
  in "Constancia," 152
  in *The Famished Road,* 158
  of fantasy, 166
  in *A Woman Named Solitude,* 153
  by magical realism, 145, 212
  of magical powers/of Other, 155–56
  of magical realism, 166, 264n.116
  of mythologies, 165
  of primitive cultures, 166, 168, 195,
    275n.113
  of shamanism, 198, 257n.47, 259n.71
  of suffering, 180
  of voice, 150, 154, 257n.46
  of women's bodies, 181
  resisted by magical realism, 264n.116
Ardener, Edwin, 182
Argentina, 198
Arguedas, José María, 166
art. *See* painting.
As I Lay Dying, 44, 106
Ashcroft, Bill, 111, 253n.10
Asturias, Miguel Angel, 33–35, 146, 161, 166,
    203–4, 267n.21
atavism, 62
Auerbach, Erich, 15
Aura
  as decolonization, 38, 152–53
  binary opposites in, 249n.40
  boundaries, blurred in, 213; of identity
    32, 173–76; of pronouns, 124; of time/
    space, 24, 101, 160, 194
  ending of, 173, 266n.14, 266n.18
  female spirit in, 181, 198, 211, 269n.40
  influences on, 16, 199, 243n.79
  narrative distance in, 123–24
  quoted, 24, 101, 174, 175, 199
  realism in, 15, 19, 21
  replenishment in, 267n.19
  spirit realm in, 71, 107
Aurélia, 195
Austen, Jane, 197
authority
  and hybridity, 156
  challenges to, 4, 103, 168, 179
  in magical realism, 126
  in narrative, 136–37, 178
  of realism, 154, 172, 177, 256n.38
autodiegetic narrative, 109

automatic writing, 241n.53
Autumn of the Patriarch, 248n.37
avant garde, 33
"Axolotl"
  as allegory, 258n.60
  as postcolonial, 258n.60
  Aztec myth in, 249n.44
  boundaries, blurred in, 26, 109, 132; of
    pronouns, 109, 249n.42
  narrative technique in, 27, 109, 123,
    249n.43
  quoted, 26, 109–10
Aztec motifs, 71, 132, 174, 200, 243n.79,
    249n.44

Babi Yar (massacre), 10, 16, 84, 124, 131, 140,
    192, 251n.66
Bach, Rebecca Ann, 250n.52
Bachelard, Gaston, 100, 182
Bak, Hans, 275n.106
Baker, Houston, 238n.30
Bakhtin, M. M., 144, 173, 227n.49, 241n.58
Balzac, Honoré de, 93
Balzer, Marjorie Mandelstam, 245n.104
Bambara ritual, 258–59n.63
baroque sensibility, 241n.57
Barth, John, 29, 168, 251n.65
Barthes, Roland, 14, 70, 236n.10
Bassi, Shaul, 229n.67
Bear, 177
Beckett, Samuel, 64, 88, 107
belief, 71, 76, 97. *See also* skepticism, spirit.
Bell-Villada, Gene, 248n.37
Beloved
  African traditions in, 149
  as decolonization, 136
  as fantasy, 162
  body in, 190–91, 272n.70, 274n.90
  boundaries, blurred in, 17, 24, 217,
    272n.71, 277n.132; of identity, 194–95
  cinematic technique in, 62
  compared to *Distant Relations,* 199–204
  ending of, 126
  femaleness in, 181, 188, 273–74n.89
  fetishes in, 60
  healing in, 81, 84–86, 138–39, 140, 187
  history in, 62, 138–39, 165, 185, 200
  house/domesticity in, 181–83
  location in, 160, 176

magical elements in, 9, 11, 20, 27, 69,
    121–22, 139, 193, 202
narrative techniques in, 107, 122, 124, 213,
    238n.29, 263n.106
political critique in, 70, 147, 274n.92
quoted, 9, 17, 24, 85–86, 181–82, 190–91
religious beliefs in, 71
revenants in, 194
Ben Jelloun, Tahar, 66–67, 187, 242n.66
Benhabib, Seyla, 271n.65
Benjamin, Walter, 147
Bennett, Arnold, 40
Bennett, Caroline, 183, 269n.44
Benstock, Shari, 171
Bergson, Henri, 272n.72
Bhabha, Homi, 134, 222n.5, 252n.3
Bible, influence of, 111, 201
Bigfoot Dreams, 105, 147, 188
Bingo Palace, 213
bird. *See* flight.
Black Elk, 259n.71
Blake, William, 75
Blanchot, Maurice, 67, 68
Blanco Aguinaga, Carlos, 260n.80
bodies, 16, 188–95
    and knowledge, 190, 213
    and language, 272n.70, 274n.90
    and place, 184, 208–12
    and spirit, 170–71, 213, 276n.120
    and writing, 195–204
    as bridge, 181, 187
    as inscription site, 271n.61
    as muse, 195
    commodification of, 212, 214–15
    disfigurement, 181
Boehmer, Elleke, 157
Böll, Heinrich, 240n.49
Bontempelli, Massimo, 33
Book of Laughter and Forgetting, The
    appropriation in, 169
    as allegory, 20, 62
    belief in, 72
    dreaming in, 104
    epistemological/ontological orientations
        in, 31
    flight motif in, 56, 58, 201
    history in, 15–16, 115
    loss of control as theme in, 93
    magical elements in, 27

metaphors literalized in, 114
metatextuality of, 115
political critique in, 11, 20, 70, 114, 140–
    41, 147, 150
polyvocality of, 145
quoted, 58–59, 141
Booker, M. Keith, 168, 227n.55
"boom, el," 2, 37, 39, 232n.87
border feminism, 171
borders. *See* boundaries.
Borges, Jorge Luis, 2, 35, 150
    about Franz Kafka, 40
    about Leslie Weatherhead, 243n.78
    as apolitical, 168
    as early magical realist, 246n.6
    blurring of reader/character, 236n.10
    influence on Salman Rushdie, 229n.70
    on the ineffable, 88–89
    use of Kabbalah, 71
Bound to Violence, 36
boundaries, in magical realism, 21–23, 88,
    115–22, 160, 206, 217, 223n.5, 243n.84.
    See also individual authors *and* iden-
    tity.
    and female magic, 208–12
    and female writing, 171
    between life and death, 152, 244n.87,
        248n.32, 248–49n.38
    between past and present, 22–23, 272n.71
    between polarities, 7, 21–23, 223n.5
    between self and others, 23, 25–27, 170–
        71, 277n.131
    between spirit/real worlds, 23–25, 62, 145,
        208–9, 277n.132
    overcome by angels, 276n.118
Braidotti, Rosi, 271n.65
Brazil
    as magical realism, 147, 251n.65
    boundaries, blurred in, 26, 118
    myth in, 127–28
    nonautonomous characters in, 137–38
    popularity of, 264n.116
    quoted, 26, 118–19
Brecht, Bertholt, 256n.37
Breinig, Helmbrecht, 251n.65
Brennan, Timothy
    on cosmopolitanism, 135, 222n.5
    on magical realism, 157, 256n.45
    on Salman Rushdie, 223n.4, 261n.92

Breton, André, 22, 46, 94–95, 112
  on seers, 72–73, 180
  on surrealism, 94–95
  on women and writing, 273n.81
bricolage, 32, 114
bridges
  between different discourses, 104, 114–15
  between different people, 108–10
  between different realities, 104–8
  between life and death, 105–6, 137
  between reality and discourse, 110–15, 154, 249n.45
Brink, André, 262–63n.101
Brontë, Emily, 197
Brooke-Rose, Christine, 95–96, 223n.13
Brothers Grimm, 134
Büchner, Georg, 134
Buci-Glucksmann, Christine, 170
Burkert, Walter, 70
Burnham, Sophy, 242n.72
Butler, Judith, 271n.65
Butterfield, Bradley, 242n.76
Buzzati, Dino, 150
Byatt, A. S., 215–16

Camayd-Freixas, Erik, 11, 21, 33, 35, 163
Campaign, The, 36, 198
cannibalism, xi, 144, 149
Cape of Storms: The First Life of Admastor, 262–63n.101
Caribbean culture and literature, 35, 50, 136, 235n.2
carnivalesque, 34, 227n.49, 226n.38
carpe diem, 174, 213, 221
Carpenter, Lynette, 271n.59
Carpentier, Alejo, 2, 28, 33–35, 161. *See also The Kingdom of This World.*
  as archival writer, 58
  compared to Heinrich Böll, 240n.49
  condescension in, 149
  defocalized narrative in, 50
  influences on, 147, 148, 208
  magical elements in, 166
  musicology of, 222n.5
  on surrealism, 147, 167, 231n.82
  on types of magical realism, 27, 28
  pessimism in, 36
  political critique in, 262n.96
  primitivism in, 35

resistance to magical realist label, 179
  spirit, realm of, 55, 66, 71, 146, 241n.57
Carter, Angela, 134
Castañeda, Carlos, 46, 257n.47
Castillo, Ana, 98, 172, 186, 267n.23. *See also So Far from God.*
  as magical realist, 2, 271n.60, 276n.113
  quoted, 8
Castle, The, 261n.89
Catholicism in magical realism, 71, 147, 209
  in *Ironweed*, 86
  in *One Hundred Years of Solitude*, 114
  in *The Tin Drum*, 72
Cezair-Thompson, Margaret, 37, 158, 165, 232n.90
"Chac Mool," 38, 71
Chait, Sandra, 262–63n.101
"Chambre Voisine, La," 115
Chanady, Amaryll, 8, 20, 28, 144, 228–29n.65, 247n.12
  on *The Kingdom of This World*, 52, 237n.23, 238n.28
  characters, boundaries between, 121, 131–32, 137–38
  magic associated with, 121–22
Chatterjee, Partha, 166
Cheever, John, 62–63
Cheney-Coker, Syl, 164
Chiampi, Irlemar, 11, 111, 164, 223n.3, 233n.101
  on Alejo Carpentier, 241n.57
  on marvelous realism, 133, 237n.19, 238n.25
  on metafiction, 236n.10
Chicana/o fiction, and magical realism, 164, 178, 242n.69, 264n.116, 266n.11
  So Far from God as, 276n.120
childlike narrators. *See* narrators.
children's songs, 201
Chilean poetry, 163
Chinese boxes. *See* narrative distance.
Chippewa, 208
Chocolat, 29, 147
Chodorow, Nancy, 270–71n.58
Christ, Carol, 276n.122, 277n.131
Christian tradition, 208, 274n.92. *See also* Catholicism in magical realism
Christopher Unborn, 38, 198–99, 273n.85
  quoted, 273n.85
Chronicle of a Death Foretold, 38–39

chronotope, 241n.58
chthonic imagery, 107, 181
civilization, escape from, 166
clairvoyance, 194
Clarke, Joni Adamson, 250n.53
Clifford, James, 3, 59, 60, 61
Cohn, Deborah, 183, 267n.23
collectivity. *See* communal voice.
Collette, Marianella, 266n.18, 267n.20
Colombia, 268n.33
colonialism, as appropriation, 150, 156, 158,
    171, 252n.3. *See also* decolonization
    and postcolonialism.
comedy, 221n.4, 255n.28
commercialization. *See* commodification.
commodification
    in "Chac Mool," 71
    of magical realism, 41, 162–66
    of primitivism, 154, 169, 257n.52, 258–
        59n.63
    of shamans, 166
    of women, 62, 140, 203, 212, 214–15
    vs. appreciation, 173
communal voices, 178, 181, 185, 270n.49
communism, 72, 93, 114, 141
community, 70, 172, 237n.20
computers, in *Ghost,* 86
concentration camp, 185–86
Conjugal Angel, The, 215–17
Connell, Liam, 231n.80
Conniff, Brian, 260n.81
Conrad, Joseph, 67, 145, 153
Constancia and Other Stories for Virgins, 150–
    52, 197, 198
cooking, 204–7, 274n.97. *See also* house.
Cooper, Brenda, 8, 20, 232n.89, 240n.50
    on Ben Okri, 248n.26, 251n.64
    on magical realism, 15, 164, 233n.97
Cornell, Drusilla, 171
corporality. *See* bodies.
Cortázar, Julio, 2, 35, 60, 71, 132
    alluded to in *One Hundred Years of
        Solitude,* 114
    boundaries, blurred in, 21, 26; of
        pronouns, 109
    doubles in, 243n.80
    female narrative voice in, 180
    magical elements in, 27–28, 77
    pessimism in, 36

political critique in, 262n.96
cosmopolitanism, 34–35, 134–35, 222n.5
counterdiscourse, 76, 154–55
Creole culture, 147
crossovers. *See* boundaries.
Crying of Lot 49, The, 224n.13
cultural identity, 3, 52, 66, 164
culture
    and reader response, 59–60
    decolonized by magical realism, 134, 137,
        154, 166, 168–69, 178
    patriarchal, 4
    trivialization of, 166, 167
    vanishing or emergent, 145, 240n.40
curative magic. *See* healing.

D'haen, Theo, 221n.2, 234n.104, 268n.30
Daisne, Johan, 150
Daly, Mary, 276n.122
Danow, David K., 226n.38
Dante, 64, 195
Dapprich-Barrett, Ute, 134
Darrieussecq, Marie, 2, 72. *See also Pig Tales.*
    and feminist ideology, 172, 271n.65
    as urban magical realist, 161
    boundaries blurred in, 21
    literalized metaphors in, 112
    realism/fantastic in, 23, 62
    social critique in, 140
Dash, J. Michael, 136, 138
Davies, Lloyd, 168, 247n.19, 261n.83, 276n.118
de Nerval, Gérard, 195, 201
dead, in magical realism, 80, 98, 137, 244n.87,
        248n.32
    boundaries with living blurred, 22, 105,
        248–49n.38
    in modernist novels, 106, 107
    voices of, 3, 14
Death in Venice, 33, 67, 104
Death of Artemio Cruz, The, 106, 115
decentered texts. *See* narrative.
decolonization, 139–69
    and commercial success, 162
    and myth, 147
    and spirit, 154
    as effect of magical realism, 36, 38–39, 40–
        41, 133–39, 149, 155, 158, 165, 167–68
    for women, 176
    in ethnic literature, 172

deconstruction, 173, 178
defamiliarization, 13, 50, 60, 224n.14,
    243n.84. *See also* reader response.
defocalization, in magical realism, 3,
    43–59, 68, 137, 154, 167, 201,
    241n.53
    and female voice, 177, 180, 187
    and history, 138
    and hypothetical focalization, 235n.4
    and otherness in, 74
    and spirit, 63–74, 227n.49
    and the ineffable, 64, 171
    as appropriation, 195
    as narrative effect, 80, 133, 104–22, 154,
        167
    in shamanistic accounts, 77–78
    in time and space, 97–98
DeKoven, Marianne, 274n.93
Delgadillo, Theresa, 275n.111
Delicka, Magdalena, 275n.109
della Grisa, Graciela Ricci, 223n.5
demarginalization. *See* marginalization.
democracy, 142
demystification, 163
depersonalization, 160
Derrida, Jacques, 67, 171
"Desdichada, La," 198
desire, 70, 190, 205, 212, 219
    in *Palace of the Peacock,* 100–101,
        122
destabilization. *See* narrative.
detachment. *See* narrative voice.
dialogical, 170, 227n.49
Díaz, Nancy Gray, 225n.36
Díaz, Porfirio, 187
Dickens, Charles, 30
diegesis, 109, 147, 236n.10
Dionysian, 147
discourse. *See* narrative *and* defocalization.
Discusión, 243n.78
disruption, disjunction. *See* boundaries *and*
    individual works.
Distant Relations, 2, 8
    as decolonization, 38
    boundaries/disruptions in, 22–24, 27,
        101–2, 129–30, 132, 142, 194
    compared to *Beloved,* 199–204
    fetishes in, 60

friendship in, 142–43
influences on, 122
hallucinations in, 100
hand motif in, 142–43, 203
history in, 16
location in, 160
magical elements in, 20, 69, 122, 193,
    202
metatextuality in, 115
narrative strategy of, 123, 128–30, 255n.36
political critique in, 142
polyvocality of, 145
quoted, 16, 102, 128–30, 142–43
distopic fiction, 62
Dixon, Paul B., 248–49n.38
domesticity. *See* house *and* location.
Don Quixote, 13
double-voiced discourse. *See* polyvolcality.
doubling. *See* repetition.
doubt. *See* reader response.
dreaming
    and shamanaism, 156
    in magical realism, 17–18, 100–104
    in women's novels, 265n.2
Dreaming in Cuban, 106, 213, 209
Dreamtime, 21
Dudley, Edward, 61
Duerr, H. P., 21
Duffy, Enda, 230n.72
Dupuis, Michel, 103–4, 227n.54, 251n.62
Durix, Jean-Pierre
    on magical realism, 40, 164, 227n.50,
        258n.59
    on Salman Rushdie, 158, 250n.50
    on Wilson Harris, 269n.38
Durrell, Lawrence, 67

Earle, Peter G., 270n.54
ecofeminism, 275n.104
eco-politics, 62
ekphrasis, 150
Eliade, Mircea, 76, 150, 167, 259n.71
Eliot, T. S., 88
Ellison, David, 67–68
"embodied subjectivity," 190
embodiment. *See* bodies.
emergent literatures, 37, 133–34
empiricism, 7, 28, 68, 133, 146

ending
  of *Aura*, 173, 266n.14, 266n.18
  of *Beloved*, 122
  of *Distant Relations*, 132
  of *Like Water for Chocolate*, 217–18
  of *One Hundred Years of Solitude*, 123, 187
  of *Palace of the Peacock*, 122, 180
  of *The House of the Spirits*, 184, 187,
    261n.83
  of *The Odyssey*, 185
  of *The Stone Raft*, 10
  of *The White Hotel*, 169, 184, 260n.81
Engel, Marion, 177
Enlightenment/post-Enlightenment, 38–40,
    48, 161, 242n.76, 243n.82
"Enormous Radio, The," 62–63
epic, 144
epic theater, 256n.37
epistemology. *See also* ontology.
  in magical realism, 27, 28, 30–32, 193,
    234n.101, 275n.106
  in *One Hundred Years of Solitude*,
    230n.73
  feminist, 190, 193, 213
  fictionalizing of, 272n.72
Erdrich, Louise, 2, 116, 176. *See also Tracks*.
  and spirit in, 276n.123
  and territoriality, 275n.104
  as magical realist, 275n.106, 276n.113
  location in, 208
  marginality in, 253n.11, 275n.106
  multigenerationality in, 213
eschatology, 252n.4
Esquivel, Laura, 2, 32, 276n.113. *See also Like Water for Chocolate*.
  and feminist ideology, 172, 205–6, 215
  and spirit, 215
  healing in, 186
  loss of control as theme in, 93
ethnology, 244n.88
Europe, as location in magical realism, 27–28
European
  appropriation, 144, 154, 263n.106
  fiction, 57, 228n.62. *See also* individual authors.
  history, 154
  influenced by Latin America, 157–58
  magical realism, 134, 149–50, 161

realism, challenges to, 137, 146, 156, 165–66, 253n.12
  political conservatism, 150
exaggeration, 157
existentialism, 8, 58
exploration narratives, 158
expressionist. *See* painting.

Fagunwa, D. O., 37
fairies. *See* boundaries.
faith. *See* spirit.
Famished Road, The, 2, 3, 10–11
  as decolonizing/postcolonial, 28, 37, 158
  boundaries, blurred in, 120–21, 226n.41,
    235–36n.8; of identity, 25–36, 137–38;
    of time/space, 99–100
  defocalized narrative in, 45, 94–95, 127
  hallucinations in, 100, 102, 150
  healing in, 102–3
  history/religion in, 71, 159, 165
  literalized metaphors in, 112–14
  metatextuality in, 115
  myth in, 158
  political critique in, 70, 113, 147
  quoted, 10–11, 25–26, 99–100, 102–3,
    112–14, 120–21, 159
  spirit in, 73, 202
  technology in, 63
fantasy/the fantastic
  and magical realism, 17, 20–21, 23,
    48, 76, 91–93, 147, 157–59, 161,
    228n.62
  and Nazism, 254n.26
  and realism, 149, 156, 241n.58
  as escape, 160, 185
  in women's novels, 265n.2
  marginalization of, 160
  meaning in, 225n.34
  reader response to, 260n.79
  psychic, 260n.81
Faris, David, 222n.6
fascism, 242n.76
Faulkner, William, 30, 44, 198
female, 270n.57, 275n.111. *See also* bodies *and* male.
  affinity with nature, 210, 275n.111
  attachment, 272n.71
  bodies, 188–95, 198

female, *(continued)*
  desire, 180
  healers, 186–88
  knowledge, 265n.1, 273n.74
  mysticism, 215–17
  narrative, 171–73, 176–78, 187, 195, 201,
    249n.40, 265n.2, 267n.25, 267n.27,
    274–75n.103
  seers (voyantes), 180
  sensibility, 170, 172, 178, 260n.79, 267n.21
  shamans, 186, 270–71n.58
  spirit, 213, 269n.45, 277n.127
feminism
  and critical theory, 4–5, 170, 171, 206,
    258n.58, 265n.1, 271n.61
  and magical realism, 4, 62, 134, 171, 178,
    183
  oppositional consciousness, 208
  postmodern/postcolonial, 171, 268n.36
  theologies, 277n.131
fetishes, 42, 60–61, 69, 147, 240n.45
Field of Dreams, 29, 62
Fijians, cannibal fork of, xi
film, magical realism in, 29, 62, 246n.111,
    264n.116
Finke, Laurie, 178–79
Flanagan, Kathleen, 228n.56
flight, 51–58, 246n.111
  by male shamans, 270–71n.58
  in *The Book of Laughter and Forgetting,*
    201
  in *The Conjugal Angel,* 215–16
  in *The Kingdom of This World,* 201,
    238n.28
  in *The Satanic Verses,* 201
  in *Song of Solomon,* 238n.30
Flores, Ralph, 136
focalization. *See also* defocalization.
  as "primitive," 147
  defined, 234–35n.1
  hypothetical, 235n.4
  in *A Woman Named Solitude,* 153
  in *Ironweed,* 86
  in "La Desdichada," 198
  in magical realism, 43–45, 47, 68,
    227n.49, 252n.2.
  in *Palace of the Peacock,* 122
  in *The Famished Road,* 236n.8
  in *The Kingdom of This World,* 50–53,

    237n.23, 238n.28
  in *The Tin Drum,* 64
  in *The White Hotel,* 187, 192
  in *The Woman Warrior,* 125, 178
  folklore, and magical realism, 35, 166,
    242n.69, 277n.127
Foreman, P. Gabrielle, 37, 260n.79, 261n.83,
    268n.33
Forest of a Thousand Daemons, The, 36–37
Forster, E. M., 145
Foster, John, 16
Foucault, Michel, 86, 135
Fox-Keller, Evelyn, 272n.72
Frazier, G. W., 35
Freeman, Barbara, 272n.71
French Caribbean, 115, 122
Frenck, Susan, 174, 243n.79, 266n.14
Freud, Sigmund, as character in *The White
    Hotel,* 114, 124, 192, 251n.66, 260n.81
Freudian thought, 69, 162, 187, 190, 240n.45
Frucht, Abby, 2, 185.
Fuentes, Carlos, 2, 8, 15, 32, 35, 38. *See also
    Aura, Christopher Unborn, Constancia
    and Other Stories for Virgins, Distant
    Relations, Where the Air Is Clear.*
  and female spirit, 199–200, 269n.40
  as character in own novel, 203
  as decolonizing writer, 37, 152–53
  as magical realist, 150–51, 161, 162
  as transnational, 150
  fantasy in, 160
  healing in, 185
  historical detail in, 16
  influence of, 115, 122
  influenced by, 197–99, 243n.79, 258–
    59n.63
  narrative strategies of, 32, 255n.36
  "oneiric optic" in, 101
  pessimism in, 36
  political critique in, 141, 273n.85
  repetition in, 128–31
  spirit in, 71
Fuguet, Alberto, 162–63
future perfect tense, 99, 123

Gablik, Suzi, 222n.10
Galsworthy, John, 40
Gandhi, Indira, 139, 141, 189, 207
Gandhi, Leila, 166

García, Cristina, 2, 106, 209
García Márquez, Gabriel. *See also* "Light Is
    Like Water," *Of Love and Other De-*
    mons, One Hundred Years of Solitude,
    "A Very Old Man with Enormous
    Wings."
  and apocalypse, 185, 187
  as decolonizing/postmodernist writer, 37,
    230n.79, 261n.92
  as magical realist, 2, 14, 35, 60, 150, 161,
    166, 179, 276n.113
  boundaries, blurred in, 224n.17, 253n.12;
    of identity, 32; of time/space, 99
  female magic in, 168, 207, 214–15, 268n.33
  flight motif in, 56
  history in, 15, 38, 261n.83
  hypertrophism in, 117–18
  ineffable in, 64
  influence of, 29, 157, 234n.103, 261n.92,
    264n.116, 273n.86
  influenced by, 35
  magical elements in, 27, 77, 80, 193
  metaphors literalized in, 110
  multiculturalism in, 221n.1
  narrative techniques of, 90–92, 117,
    248n.37, 253n.12, 260n.81
  pessimism in, 36
  political critique in, 37, 114, 141, 162,
    262n.96
  primitivism in, 35
  realism in, 12, 19–20
  time and space in, 99
García-Johnson, Ronie-Richelle, 183
Garro, Elena, 276n.114
Gelley, Alexander, 44, 254n.26
gender. *See also* bodies *and* female.
  and author's sex, 171, 176, 186
  blurred in magical realism, 4, 198, 202
  construction of, 153, 193
  stereotypes, 175–76, 271n.64
General in His Labyrinth, The, 36, 38
Genette, Gérard, 234n.1
genre, 41, 236–37n.13
German, influence on magical realism, 1, 134
Ghanaian music, commodification of,
    257n.53
Ghost (film), 86, 147, 246n.111
ghosts, in magical realism, 80, 212, 276n.114
  and female power, 266n.12, 271n.59

  in *Beloved,* 181–82, 190, 200
  in *Distant Relations,* 194, 200
  in *One Hundred Years of Solitude,* 182
  in *The Conjugal Angel,* 216
  in *The House of the Spirits,* 178
  in *The Woman Warrior,* 177
Gide, André, 66, 241n.66
Gilligan, Carol, 270–71n.58
Gimbutas, Maria, 276n.122
globalization. *See also* international.
  and need of healing, 83
  of American village, 198
  of literature, 2
  of magic realism, 5, 40, 161, 179,
    234n.103
  of realism, 172
goddess, 180–81, 184, 211–12
Goethe, Johann Wolfgang von, 115, 134
Gogol, Nikolai, 2, 12, 30
Goldberg, Whoopie, 86
Gómez, Sergio, 162–63
González Echevarría, Roberto, 27, 57–58, 146,
    233n.100
Gothic fiction, 160–61, 182
Govaert, Serge, 149–50
Goya, 161
Goyen, William, 276n.114
Graff, Gerald, 256n.38
Grass, Günter. *See also The Tin Drum.*
  and the ineffable, 64
  as decolonizing writer, 37
  as magical realist, 2, 29, 134, 161
  boundaries, blurred in, 225n.32
  history in, 16, 255n.33
  imagery of, 227n.53
  influence of, 229n.70
  influenced by, 254n.26, 261n.89
Gray, Richard T., 243n.82
Griffiths, Gareth, 111, 136
Grosz, Elisabeth, 189–90, 271n.61
grotesque, 224n.17, 241n.58
Guadeloupe (massacre), 154
guerrilla narrative, 229–30n.72
Guidotti, Valeria, 164
Guidry, Glenn A., 232n.93, 245n.105
Guyana, magical realism in, 136

Hahn, Oscar, 163
Haiti, 136

Halifax, Joan, 240n.40
hallucination, 100, 102–3, 150, 155. *See also*
    dreaming.
Hansel and Gretel, 181
Haraway, Donna, 272n.68
Harding, Sandra, 190
Harner, Michael, 80, 121, 240n.40
Harris, Trudier, 149, 238n.29, 273–74n.89
Harris, Wilson, 2, 213. *See also Palace of the
    Peacock, Tumatumari.*
    as magical realist/postmodernist, 136–37,
        230n.78
    commodification in, 168
    metaphor in, 100
    multiculturalism in, 221n.1
    narrative voice in, 46, 50–51
    on change, 145
    on realism, 137, 144
    political critique in, 269n.38
    spirit in, 65, 80, 100, 269n.38
Hart, Patricia, 223n.2, 266n.12
Hart, Stephen, 224n.17
Havel, Vlaclav, 135
Hawkins, Peter, 64
Hawthorne, Nathaniel, 161
healing
    and angels, 276n.118
    and land, 271n.59
    and magical realism, 105, 167–68, 196
    female, 186–88
    in *Palace of the Peacock*, 81–83, 101
    in *So Far from God*, 194
    in *The Famished Road*, 103
    in *The House of the Spirits*, 185
    in *The Tin Drum*, 245n.105
    in *The White Hotel*, 185
    of "primitive," 166
    shamanic, 75–87, 147, 149, 157
Heart of Darkness, 67, 153
hegemony, and magical realism, 144, 179
Heidegger, Martin, 58
"Heights of Macchu Picchu, The," 55
Hellens, Franz, 150
Herman, David, 235n.4
hesitation. *See* reader response.
heterodiegetic narrative, 109
"high realism," 160
Hindu traditions, 165–66, 206

Hispanic magical realism, 13, 264n.116. *See
    also* Chicana.
history. *See also* individual works *and* authors.
    as context for magical realism, 21, 81, 124,
        127–28, 138–45, 160, 165, 185, 221n.4,
        261n.83
    as patriarchal, 198
    ghosts localized in, 276n.114
    in Latin American fiction, 232n.87,
        239n.33, 262n.96
    inscribed on bodies, 190
    transformed by magical realism, 81, 136,
        185, 234n.106, 140–41, 225n.24,
        245n.103
Hoffman, E. T. A., 134
Hollaman, Keith, 7
Holler, Linda, 272n.72
Hollington, Michael, 224n.17, 243n.81,
    263n.104
Holy Place, 198
home. *See* house.
Homer, 199
Hong Kingston, Maxine, 2, 63, 125, 177,
    266n.12. *See also The Woman Warrior.*
Horrocks, David, 255n.33
Horseman, 262–63n.101
house/housekeeping, 180–88
    and women, 182–84, 196, 204–7
    as body, 184
    as cosmic space, 171, 181, 184
    in magical realism, 182–84, 205, 212
    in *One Hundred Years of Solitude,* 270n.46
    in *The House of the Spirits,* 270n.57
House of the Spirits, The, 2
    angels in, 57, 276n.118
    belief/skepticism of characters, 97
    boundaries, blurred between living and
        dead, 22; between realism and magic,
        117, 183, 270n.49; of space, 25
    female power in, 183, 266n.12, 270n.54
    ghosts in, 178
    healing in, 184
    history in, 187
    liminality in, 152
    location in, 160, 176
    magical items in, 193
    multigenerationality in, 213
    narrative perspective in, 57, 95, 247n.19

patriarchal discourse in, 267n.23
political/social critique in, 37, 147, 168,
    183, 261n.83
quoted, 57, 95, 97, 117, 183
smuggled into Chile, 196
"House Taken Over," 21
Hugo, Victor, 241n.53
Hundejahre, 254n.26
Hutcheon, Linda, 27, 124, 165, 228n.60,
    251n.60
Hutchinson, George B., 69
hybridity, cultural, 2, 4, 147, 167
    and authority, 156
    and defocalized narrative, 235n.2, n.3
    and primitivism, 167
    and shamanism, 75
    in angels, 238–39n.32
    in Caribbean literature, 235n.2
    in *One Hundred Years of Solitude,* 234n.103
    in *Palace of the Peacock,* 81
    in *Pig Tales,* 189
    in *The Famished Road,* 60, 99–100
    of Afrikaaner literature, 262n.101
    of female discourse, 170–71
    of Louise Erdrich, 250n.53, 275n.106
    of magical realism, 25, 28–29, 35, 39, 103–
    4, 134, 147, 149, 155, 161, 198, 226n.38,
    235n.2, 259n.71

identity
    and community, in Chicano fiction,
        266n.11
    and hallucination, 155
    and modernism, 31–32
    and postcolonial societies, 156
    and voice, 257n.46
    blurred in magical realism, 23, 25–27, 32,
        36, 128–30, 167, 168, 173, 190, 193,
        223n.2, 227n.50, 227n.55, 246n.6,
        259n.71, 272n.71
    Julia Kristeva on, 277n.131
    search for, 234n.103
    women's, 265n.2, 270–71n.58
Imagining Argentina, 66, 68, 187
    literalized metaphors in, 114
    political critique in, 70, 114, 147
    quoted, 68
IMAX theaters. *See* virtual realities

Immoralist, The, 66
immortality, 213
In the Labyrinth, 44
indeterminacy. *See* narrative.
India
    as setting for *Midnight's Children,* 29, 189
    literature/religion of, 37, 72, 115, 225–
        26n.36, 229n.67
indigenismo, 166
indigenous cultures, 21, 33, 147, 154, 240n.40
Indo-Pakistani war, 160
ineffable. *See also* spirit.
    and defocalized narrative, 73, 171
    and realism, 161, 178, 236–37n.13
    and self in text, 228n.61
    and the sacred, 63–64
    as challenge to materialism, 161
    as positive and negative, 64
    encoded in magical realism, 46, 56–57,
        67–69, 74, 88–132, 236–37n.13,
        243n.82
Inferno, 39
Ingalls, Rachel, 114, 161
initiation rites, 137
interchange between worlds. *See* boundaries.
international trend, magical realism as, 1, 2–3,
    5, 28, 33, 40–42, 150, 161, 163–64, 168,
    172, 179, 222n.8, 228n.62, 229n.70,
    230n.74, 253n.12, 262n.93
Interpreters, The, 232n.90
intertextuality, 41, 115, 201
Ionesco, Eugene, 141
Iranian Nights, 144–45
Ireland, 230n.72
Ireland, Kenneth, 229n.70
Irigaray, Luce, 4, 170, 173, 212, 276n.118
    on "la mystérique," 218–19
Ironweed, 2, 71, 106, 147
    defocalized narrative in, 45
    film version of, 29
    healing in, 84–86, 187
    magic in, 62,92
    quoted, 22, 45, 86, 92
    revenants/dead in, 22, 84, 106–7, 194
irony, in magical realism, 20, 55, 64, 76
    in *Terra Nostra,* 185
    in women's novels, 265n.2
    of history, 124

irreducible element, magic as. *See also* nonverifiable phenomena *and* individual
   titles.
   and fetishism, 61
   and hallucination, 102–3
   and nonverifiable phenomena, 44
   and the ineffable, 64
   as counter to empiricism, 68
   as guerrilla attacks, 178
   embedded in realism, 77–78, 126, 171
   in "Constancia," 150
   in Jorge Luis Borges, 246n.6
   in *Like Water for Chocolate*, 205
   in magical realism, 7–9, 14–15, 23, 33, 46,
      50, 70, 80, 133, 137, 139, 154, 156, 158,
      173, 223n.2, 225, n.31, 252n.2
   in *Pig Tales*, 62
Irvine, Dean J., 228–29n.65, 230n.73, 231n.79
Isaak, Jo Anna, 229n.66
Iturriaga, J. E., 231n.82

Jackson, Rosemary, 162
Jaeck, Lois Marie, 266n.16
James, Henry, 2
Jameson, Frederic
   on desacralization, 64–65
   on Latin American literature, 39
   on magical realism, 221n.4, 233n.99,
      245n.103
   on realism, 23–24, 143–44
   on romance, 158–59
   on time, 160
Japan, 222n.9, 234n.103
Jenkins, Ruth, 266n.12, 267n.27
Jewett, Sarah Orne, 238n.30
"Josefine," 67–68
journey, 100, 112. *See also* location.
   in *Palace of the Peacock*, 137
   in *Pedro Páramo*, 137
   in *The Famished Road*, 127, 251n.64
"Journey to the Seed," 160
Joyce, James, 40, 171, 198, 201
Jünger, Ernst, 150
Jungian critical perspective, 69

Kafalenos, Emma, 252n.2
Kafka, Franz, 2, 19, 62, 67–68
   and Marxism, 261n.89

as doubly marginalized, 161, 261n.88
   influence of, 40, 198
Kahlo, Frida, 181
Kane, Jean M., 228n.55, 264n.121
Kawin, Bruce, 46, 228n.61, 236–37n.13
Keele, Alan F., 254n.26
Kennedy, William, 2, 22, 71, 161. *See also*
   Ironweed.
Kingdom of this World, The, 58, 146, 149, 201
   as fantasy, 162
   defocalized narrative in, 50–55, 237n.23
   ending of, 54–55
   folk belief in, 28
   quoted, 50–52, 54–55
   status challenged, 149, 238n.28
Kinsella, William, 62
Kirby, Vicki, 193–94
knowledge. *See* bodies *and* epistemology.
Koelb, Clayton, 225n.34
Kolmar, Wendy, 265n.5, 271n.59
Kristeva, Julia, 4, 171, 250n.53, 277n.131
Kundera, Milan, 2, 20, 56, 72, 160. *See also*
   The Book of Laughter and Forgetting.
   history in, 15, 58
   political critique in, 141
   women in, 168

Lacan, Jacques, 70
LaCapra, Dominick, 143–44
Laing, B. Kojo, 164
Lambek, Michael, 80, 155
Lampo, Hubert, 150
land. *See* location.
language, magical properties of. *See* reality.
Larrea, Juan, 231n.82
Larson, Janet, 269n.45
Latin America
   Catholicism, in, 147
   intellectual milieu in, 150, 231n.82
   influence on European colonizers, 157–58
   shamanism in, 147–48
Latin American literature
   and world culture, 39
   anthropology in, 146
   history in fiction, 239n.33, 262n.96
   influence on African literature, 233n.97
   influenced by German literature, 134
   magical realism in, 1–3, 28, 33–37, 133–34,

161–63, 164, 222n.8, 225–26n.36,
228n.62, 228–29n.65, 241n.57, 268n.33
myth in, 146, 163–65
new forms of magical realism in, 232n.92
poets, as characters in *Distant Relations,*
203
postmodernism in, 230n.78
testimonial novel in, 257n.47
transculturation in, 253n.12
Lawrence, David, 274n.90
legend. *See* myth.
Lermontov, Mikhail, 115
"lethetic reading," 225n.34
"Letter to a Young Lady in Paris," 60, 180
Letter to Seers, 112
Lévi-Bruhl, Lucien, 35
Lévi-Strauss, Claude, 231n.80
levitation. *See* flight.
Lewis, I. M., 268n.31
Licorice, 176, 185–86
"Light Is Like Water," 12–13, 79–80, 111, 193
lightness. *See* weight.
Like Water for Chocolate, 93, 176, 186, 194, 219
as magical realism, 29, 147
ending, 217–18
identity blurred in, 32
popularity of, 163
role of food in, 205–6
liminality, and magical realism, 29, 37, 69,
152, 198, 243n.84
in *Palace of the Peacock,* 101
in *Tracks,* 250n.53
in women's writing, 265n.5
linguistic magic. *See* reality.
Lloyd, D., 166
location, 209–10, 249n.43, 271n.59. *See also*
house.
and female power, 176–77, 180–88,
208–12
blurred in magical realism, 223n.2,
248n.26
ghosts localized to, 276n.114
importance of, 27, 34, 45, 212
influence on magical realism, 27–30,
35–39, 208, 253n.12, 275n.104
London, Bette, 145, 257n.46
Lord of the Rings, 95–96
Lost Steps, The, 58

Lotman, Jurij M., 58, 133
Love and Other Demons, 214–15
Lovesey, Oliver, 252n.4
ludic feminism, 173
Lukács, Georg, 161
Lyotard, Jean-François, 142, 145

Mabille, Pierre, 35
MacAdam, Alfred, 249n.42
Macchu Picchu, 55
Madero, Francisco, 199
Maes-Jellinek, Hena, 81–82, 237n.20
magic, 27, 70, 183. *See also* irreducible element.
acceptance of, 7–8
and disruption of logic, 10–11
and spirit, 69–70. *See also* spirit.
appropriation of, 157
embedded in realism, 90–104
volition of items, 193–94
magical realism. *See also* decolonization, history, ineffable, narrative, primitivism, shamanism, spirit.
alterity in, 133–69
and cultural recovery, 1, 134, 264n.116
and fantasy, 48, 91–93, 147, 158–59, 161–62
and historical romances, 239n.39
and metropolitan paradigm, 34
and modernism/postmodernism, 30,
32–33, 67, 69, 163–65, 231n.80
and primitivism, 62–63, 239n.39, 240n.50
and taboo/sacred, 64–65, 69, 135–36
artificiality in, 147
as challenge to contemporary culture, 142,
160, 166, 193
as challenge to realism, 28–29, 124–25,
147, 164, 172, 173, 177–78, 193,
236n.10, 263n.106
as combination of miraculous/ordinary,
7, 14–16, 48, 65, 69–70, 74, 91–93,
138–45, 157, 229n.66
as "enabling mockery," 146
as postcolonial, 29, 48, 76, 157, 133–69,
179, 234n.104, 234n.106, 240n.50,
258n.59
boundaries, blurred in, 21–23, 128;
between living and dead, 248n.32;
between worlds, 43, 115–22, 145,
193–94

magical realism, *(continued)*
  characteristics of, 2, 11, 17, 124, 144–45,
    147, 162–63, 172, 223n.2
  compared to shamanism, 75–87, 156–57,
    167, 251–52n.67
  definitions of, 1, 7–42, 222n.8, 227n.50,
    228n.62, 233n.100, 247n.10
  ethical questions raised by, 147, 263n.106
  healing of sensory/spirit split by, 75–87
  influence of, 134 166, 276n.113
  metafictional qualities of, 236n.10
  mystery in, 40, 55
  political/social critique in, 14, 33, 36,
    139, 149–50, 160, 162, 168, 243n.84,
    261n.92
  popularity of, 239n.38
  possible escapism of, 263n.106
  term coined by Franz Roh, 33
  women's issues in, 4, 170–219
magicians, 126
Maillard, Keith, 236n.11
male. *See also* female, gender, *and* women.
  desire, 215
  energies, 270n.54, 273–74n.89
  gaze, 189, 173
  narrative voice, 201, 269n.40
Mali, 258–59n.63
Malle, Louis, 197
Mann, Thomas, 33, 67
Manual for Manuel, 36
Maori, 257n.52
marginality, and magical realism, 29, 146–47,
    150, 203
  and the fantastic, 160
  angels as manifestation of, 238–39n.32
  cultural, 156, 242n.69
Mariátegui, José, Marxism of, 35
marketability. *See* commodification.
Marting, Diane, 203, 267n.21
"marvelous real," 144, 233n.101.
  See also magical realism.
Marxism, 35, 228n.56, 261n.89
Mason, Ann L., 254n.26
materialism, and magical realism, 40
Matlou, Joel, 262n.101
matriarchal, 185
Mauss, Marcel, 231n.80
Mayan culture, 203

McClintock, Barbara, 272n.72
McElroy, Bernard, 225, n.32, 254n.26
McGee, Patrick, 206
McHale, Brian, 21, 23, 30–31, 230n.73
McNabb, Pamela, 249n.43
McOndo, 162–63
Mda, Zakes, 262n.101
Medicine Woman, 210–11
Menton, Seymour, 222n.1, 228n.62
merging realms. *See* boundaries.
Merino, Blanca, 249n.40, 267n.19
Merivale, Patricia, 229n.70
metafiction, and magical realism
  and blurred boundaries, 22, 100
  and women's narratives, 181, 265n.5
  in Jacques Stéphen Alexis, 136
  in "Axolotl," 249n.42
  in *Beloved,* 181, 202
  in "Constancia," 151–52
  in *Distant Relations,* 202
  in *Midnight's Children,* 12, 112
  in *Palace of the Peacock,* 49
  in *That Voice,* 107
  in *The Moor's Last Sigh,* 13
  in *The Tin Drum,* 47, 195–97
  Irlemar Chiampi on, 236n.10
metamorphosis, function of, 19, 137–38,
    249n.42
Metamorphosis, The, 62, 94–95, 102, 161–62,
    261n.89
metaphors, 157, 181, 237n.20
  literalization of, 110–15, 272n.70
  material, 3
metatextuality, 114–15
Mexico, 194, 202
Meyer, Doris, 172–73
middle class, and rise of novel, 137
Midnight's Children, 2–3, 50, 250n.50
  and India, 29, 37, 72, 147, 189
  appropriation in, 169
  as parody, 132, 232n.92
  as postcolonial, 28–29
  body in, 188–89
  boundaries, blurred between dead/living,
    22; between real and magic events,
    119–20; between selves, 25, 131–32;
    between spaces, 24; or pronouns, 110
  cinematic technique in, 62

commodification in, 126
cooking as magic in, 204, 206–7
dreaming in, 104
female energy in, 204, 206–7, 211
history in, 15–16, 74, 159, 228n.56,
 255n.28, 261n.85
liminal space in, 152
literalized metaphors in, 111–12
magical elements in, 8, 44, 61, 69–70, 105,
 121–22, 159, 193
mirror imagery in, 139
narrative strategies in, 19, 88–89, 100, 112,
 127, 233n.93
ontological orientation in, 31
pessimism in, 36
political/social critique in, 139, 147
polyvocality in, 139, 145
quoted, 11–12, 16, 18, 25, 61, 63, 97, 112,
 115, 119–20, 126, 139–40
realism in, 11–12
transformation of victims in, 84, 254n.26,
 264n.121
Vedic traditions in, 228n.55
Milagro Beanfield War, The, 264n.116
mimesis, 34, 178, 227n.50, 256n.37
as realist program, 173, 177
decolonization of, 156, 157, 256n.37
mimicry, 158, 252n.3
Minden, Michael, 227n.53
Mingelgrün, Albert, 103–4, 227n.54,
 251n.62
Mínguez, José Miguel, 240n.49
miracles, 135–36, 187
mirroring, 127–32. *See also* repetition.
mise-en-abyme, 98, 99
Missing Persons, 164
Mitchell, Carolyn A., 274n.92
Miyoshi, Masao, 234n.111
Mobley, Marilyn Sanders, 238n.30
modernism
 and identity, 31–32
 and primitivism, 59, 145, 156
 and spirit, 66–67, 236–37n.13
 influence on magical realism, 30, 33–34,
  67, 104, 164–65, 230n.79, 231n.80
 influence on postcolonialism, 230n.72
 magical realism as disruption of, 239n.39

modernist fiction, 41, 107, 229n.66, 257n.46
Monleón, José, 146, 158, 160–61
Montaner Ferrer, María Eulalia, 274–75n.103
Moor's Last Sigh, The, 12–13, 63, 163, 232n.92
moral authority, 52
Moretti, Franco, 41, 239n.38
Morgan, Marlo, 275n.113
Morgner, Irmtrud, 134
Morrison, Toni. *See also Beloved, Song of
 Solomon.*
 as magical realist, 2, 9, 176, 268n.33
 female energy in, 172, 199–200
 history in, 37–38, 165, 261n.83
 influence of, 199
 influenced by, 199, 251n.65, 258–59n.63,
  273n.86
 narrative distance in, 123–24
 political statements in, 85
 realism in, 17
 religious beliefs in, 71
 resistance to label of magical realist, 179
 shamanism in, 168
Moss, Laura, 232n.92
Mountolive, 67
Mrs. Caliban, 114, 250n.52
Mrs. Dalloway, 30–32, 35, 44
Mudimbe, V. Y., 164
Mukherjee, Arun, 256n.37
Mulata, 203, 267n.21
multiculturalism, 1, 29, 88, 172, 221n.1
multigenerationalism, 71, 177–78, 185, 200,
 213
multiple worlds, 39
multivocality. *See* polyvocality.
Murphy, Patrick, 258n.58
muse, 196–200
Musical Trees, The, 149
Mutant Message: Downunder, 275n.113
My Life in the Bush of Ghosts, 36
"My Life with the Wave," 181
"mystérique, la," 212–19
mystery in magical realism, 15, 40, 46, 55, 64,
 241n.53. *See also* spirit.
 female, 212, 272n.72
 in modernism, 67
mysticism
 medieval, 178–79, 276n.120

myth
  and political critique, 150
  and realism, 164, 231n.80
  appropriation of, 165
  as decolonization, 147, 156
  as inscription, 190
  in magical realism, 27, 32–35, 70, 80,
    127–28, 169
  South African, 36, 158
mythic time, 164–65
mythopoeia and history, 158

Naipaul, V. S., 38
Napier, Susan, 222n.9
narrative. *See also* defocalization *and* repeti-
    tion.
  appropriation, 150
  as counterdiscourse, 154–55, 212
  authority, 3–4, 98, 133, 135, 137, 142, 146
  boundaries blurred, 108, 235n.4, 268n.30
  decentered, 135, 137, 170
  destabilization, 45, 129–30, 135, 137, 166
  diegesis in, 109
  distance, 112–26, 167, 247n.19
  indeterminate, 97–98, 123–26, 135
  narcissism in, 136
  strategies, 3, 9–10, 88–132, 133, 247–
    48n.25, 276n.123
narrative space
  and political critique, 160
  and spirit, 8, 44–45, 63, 67–68, 211
narrative voice, 3, 68, 147, 157, 166, 275n.107,
    275n.108, 275n.109. *See also* female
    and polyvocality.
  and the uncanny, 67
  appropriation of, 147–48, 150
  communal, 177–78
  disruption of, 160, 241n.53, 252n.2
  in modernism, 67
  indeterminate pronouns in, 106–7
narrator. *See also* identity.
  believing/skeptical, 20, 44, 71–72,
    93–96
  blurred identity of, 131, 160, 235–36n.8
Natarajan, Nalini, 188
nationalism, 166, 232n.89
naturalism, 160
Nazism, 83, 141

negritude, 37, 136
neoplatonism, 213
Neruda, Pablo, 55, 201
New Mexico, 187
"new shamanism." *See* shamanism.
Ngũgĩ wa Thiong'o, 252n.4
Nicaragua, 261n.92
Nicol, Mike, 262–63n.101
Nietzsche, Frederick, 58, 147
"Night Face Up, The," 28, 30, 132
Niobe, 196–97
Noel, Daniel C., 240n.40
nonlinear temporality, 35
nonverifiable phenomena, 44–50. *See also* ir-
    reducible element.
Noriega, Chon A., 264n.116
North America, magical realism in, 161
Northern Exposure, 246n.111
"Nose, The," 12
nouveau roman, 108
Novak, Maximilian, 61
"novel of persuasion," 137

objectivity. *See* subjectivity.
Odyssey, The, 39, 185, 30
Oedipus, 242n.66
Of Love and Other Demons, 18–19
Ojibway, 182
Okri, Ben, 2, 60, 102. *See also The Famished
    Road.*
  as decolonializing/postcolonial, 37, 158
  boundaries, blurred in, 10, 164, 226n.41
  compared to Wole Soyinka, 232n.90
  influenced by, 233n.94
  narrative techniques of, 247–48n.25
  shamanism in, 73, 244n.87, 244n.93
Oliva, Renato, 244n.87, 244n.93
omniscient narration, 43
One Hundred Years of Solitude
  appropriation in, 169
  as fantasy, 162
  as magical realism, 2, 60, 96, 121, 161,
    194
  as postmodern, 230n.79, 231n.79
  boundaries, blurred between dead/living,
    22; of logic, 10–11; of magic/reality,
    116–17, 249n.45; of time/space, 23,
    97–99

epistemology/ontology in, 230n.73
female energy in, 186, 207, 211, 214,
    274–75n.103
fetishes in, 60
healing in, 84
history in, 74, 104, 159
house in, 182–83, 270n.46
influence of, 29
lack of control in, 93
magical elements in, 20, 69, 94–95, 126,
    159, 193, 260n.80
metaphors literalized in, 110, 114
metatextuality in, 114
nonverifiable phenomena in, 44
political/social critique in, 70, 114, 140,
    147, 231n.79
popularity of, 163, 234n.103
quoted, 7–9, 11, 15, 16, 18–19, 22, 23, 91,
    96, 114, 116–17, 123, 140, 183
realism in, 12, 15, 18–19, 91–92, 222n.1
technology in, 63
"oneiric optic," 100
ontology
    and magical realism, 27, 28, 30–32,
        230n.73, 235n.2
    and women, 212–13
oppositional consciousness, 178, 187,
    208
oral cultures, 111, 146
oral narrative, 36
Orlando, 32
Ortega, Julio, 230n.79
otherness, xi, 4, 171
    and primitivism, 257n.53
    and shamanism, 244n.88, 257n.47,
        259n.71
    and spirit, 243n.82
    and women, 171, 198, 269n.44, 276n.118
    Luce Irigaray on, 218–19
    in "Axolotl," 258n.60
Ouologuem, Yambo, postrealism in, 36
oxymoron, 39–40

Pachita (shaman), 80–81
painting
    and magical realism, 15, 39, 59–60, 181,
        222n.10, 228n.62
    cave, animal focalization in, 258n.58

expressionist, 39, 65–66, 242n.75
postsurrealist, 181
Palace of the Peacock, 2, 137, 162, 168, 180
    as fantasy, 162
    as liminal space, 152
    boundaries, blurred between living/dead,
        22, 84; between worlds, 73, 101, 106
    duality of vision, 100–101
    hallucinations in, 100, 150
    healing in, 81–84
    narrative techniques in, 46, 49–50, 122,
        213
    quoted, 49–52, 73, 81–83, 100, 101, 122,
        180
    romanticization of folk in, 168
Palm Wine Drinkard [sic], 36
Paradiso, 64
Paris, as setting, 200–202
parody, 158, 228n.56, 232n.92, 257n.46
Parry, Idris, 224n.13, 248n.37
past. *See* history.
pastiche, 257n.46
patriarchy/postpatriarchy in magical realism,
    4, 215, 217
    critiqued, 206, 266n.12, 267n.23
patrilineal, realism as, 172
Paz, Octavio, 2, 181, 196, 201, 269n.40
Pedro Páramo, 2, 122, 137
    boundaries, blurred between living/dead,
        22, 84, 105–6; between worlds, 105–6,
        217; of time, 30
    epistemological/ontological orientations
        in, 31
    healing in, 84
    influence on, 13
    narrative voice in, 105–7
    quoted, 31, 84, 105, 107
    revenants in, 194
Pérez, Laura, 242n.69
performance art, 222n.10
Perfume: The Story of a Murderer, 2, 93, 100
    angels in, 59
    as horror, 242n.76
    as political/social critique, 140–41, 150,
        242n.76, 243n.82
    bodies in, 192–93
    boundaries, blurred between worlds, 118,
        of identity, 27, 193; of logic, 10–11; of
        space, 23, 160

Perfume, (continued)
hypertrophism in, 117–18
fetishes in, 60
history in, 15, 16, 159
magical elements in, 8, 27, 44, 69, 122, 159
metaphors literalized in, 114
outrageousness of reality in, 13
quoted, 9, 13, 15, 59, 117–18
satire in, 70
scientific elements in, 74
shamanism in, 83–84
Perrin, Michel, 78–79
Petrarch, 115, 195
Phelan, James, 263n.106
Phillips, Adam, 240n.45
Pig Tales, 2, 62, 173, 177
female body in, 188
magical elements in, 21, 70, 112
political/social critique in, 140, 150,
271n.65
quoted, 188–89
Pigafetta, Antonio, 157
Pinget, Robert, 2. *See also That Voice.*
place. *See* location.
plot. *See* narrative.
Plumwood, Val, 171
pluralism, 144, 168
point of view. *See* narrative voice.
political/social critique, 36, 50, 56, 70, 183,
242n.76, 261n.92
and gender, 140, 150, 153, 271n.65
in magical realism, 14, 33, 70, 139–45,
149–50, 153, 158, 160, 162, 164,
226n.47, 229–30n.72, 262n.96
politics, cultural, 162–69
polyphony, 144, 170
polyvocality
as female, 170, 172–73
in *The Book of Laughter and Forgetting*, 145
in *Distant Relations*, 142–43, 145
in magical realism, 4, 25, 45, 133, 137,
145–46, 168, 173
in *Midnight's Children*, 139, 145
in *The White Hotel*, 145
Popul Vuh, 111
pornography, for women, 177
postcolonialism, 133–69
and alterity, 135

and feminism, 171
and identity, 156
and modernism, 230n.72
and the sacred, 275n.105
appropriated by magical realism, 169,
179, 212
characterized by hybridity, 253n.10
in "Axolotl," 258n.60
magical realism as, 1–2, 4, 28–29, 34, 48,
147, 161, 221n.3, 222n.5, 234n.104,
234n.106, 240n.50, 243n.84, 245n.103,
253n.10, 256n.45, 258n.59
resemblance to colonialism, 166
post-Enlightenment. *See* Enlightenment.
post-expressionism, 65
Postmodern Condition, The, 145
postmodernism, 171, 230n.78, 231n.79,
257n.46
and anthropology, 149
and appropriation, 163–64, 257n.46
and fantasy, 21, 23
and feminism, 170–71, 268n.36
and magical realism, 1–2, 4, 30, 115, 165,
221n.2, 221n.3, 234n.104
and primitivism, 59–63
reader as cocreator in, 130
post-Nietzschean, 56
postsurrealism, 144. *See also* surrealism.
Powell, Joan Miller, 235n.2
power reversal, in magical realism, 147
pre-Enlightenment, 59, 70, 80
Pretty Baby, 197
Price, Sally, 59
priestess. *See* shaman *and* female.
primitivism, 59–63
and anthropology, 149
and magical realism, 32, 35, 59, 70, 75,
145, 149, 167, 211, 231n.80, 239n.39,
240n.50, 275n.113
and otherness, 166, 257n.53
commodification of, 169, 257n.52
European/modernist, 35, 67, 145
Prince, Gerald, 43, 234n.1
pronouns, blurred in magical realism, 107–8,
123–24, 130–31, 137, 141, 171, 194,
248n.37, 249n.40, 249n.42
Prose, Francine, 2, 105, 161, 187. *See also Big-foot Dreams.*

proto-magical realism, in exploration narratives, 158
Proust, Marcel, 85, 266n.16
psychic inflation, 245n.93
psychoanalysis, as source of magic, 70
psychology, and realism, 33, 190, 226n.47, 256n.38
Pyncheon, Thomas, 224n.13

Quayson, Ato, 60, 226n.41, 235–36n.8, 247–48n.25
Quetzalcoatl motif, 249n.44

Rahv, Philip, 165
Rainwater, Catherine, 276n.123
Rama, Angel, 253n.12
Ramchand, Kenneth, 136–37
rape, 174, 184
reader response
  as cocreator of text, 130
  as doubt/hesitation, 17–21, 50, 96, 103, 121, 130, 181, 225n.34, 275n.106
  as optimism, 168
  by gender, 173–76, 180
  increased by magical element, 9
  to magical realism, 52, 59–60, 121, 130, 167, 223n.3, 225n.34, 225–26n.36, 251n.62, 260n.79
  to surrealism, 260n.79
realism, 90–104. *See also* magical realism.
  and fantasy/the fantastic, 7–8, 91–93, 149, 156, 170, 241n.58
  and female body, 212
  and myth, 164
  and postrealism, 235n.4
  and psychology of the self, 256n.38
  and reader response, 20, 59–60
  and shamanism, 251–52n.67
  and spirit, 21, 69, 158, 178, 212
  as "bourgeois," 143–44, 236n.10
  as context for magical realism, 46, 48, 50, 52, 57, 65, 74, 157–58, 216–17, 277n.127
  authority of, 137, 142–44, 172
  challenged by magic realism, 2, 4, 17, 20, 28–29, 62, 75, 129, 133, 167, 169, 212, 223n.2, 224n.13, 224n.17, 225n.32, 236n.10, 237n.19, 238n.25, 249n.45, 252n.2

challenged by oral cultures, 146
definitions of, 43–44, 144
history in, 15
in Indian fiction, 229n.67
in South African fiction, 36
realistic novel, 50, 52, 137
reality, as created by language, 110–12, 141, 144–45
rebellion, co-opted by romance, 158
Reedy, Daniel, 249n.44
reflecting surfaces. *See* repetition.
Rege, Josna, 139, 233n.93, 254n.18
Reichel-Dolmatoff, G., 251–52n.67
religion, 64, 68–69, 71, 107, 242n.69
remystification, 3, 65, 80
repetition, 128, 131–32, 243n.80
  as mirror motif, 139, 150–51, 216
  effects of in magical realism, 127–32, 232n.92, 251n.62
replenishing effects of magical realism, 37, 137, 155–56, 168
representation, 48, 44, 160. *See also* narrative, modernism, *and* realism.
revenants, 106, 194
reverie. *See* dream.
reversals. *See* repetition.
Revista de Occidente, 33
revolution, 35, 147, 256n.38
Rhinoceros, 141
Rigby, Kate, 171–72, 212
Rimbaud, Arthur, 75–76, 88, 246n.6
Rincón, Carlos, 221n.2, 234n.103
Rite of Spring, 36
Robbe-Grillet, Alain, 44
Robertson, Mary, 251n.66, 265n.1, 273n.74
Rodgers, Catherine, 21, 271n.64
Rodó, José Enrique, 35
Rodríguez Monegal, Emir 233n.100
Roh, Franz, 15, 65–66, 224n.22, 241n.58, 242n.75
  coined "magical realism," 33, 39
Rojas, Mario A., 270n.57
romance, 61, 158–59, 166, 167, 239n.39
Romeo and Juliet, 219
Rubin, Linda, 270–71n.58
Rulfo, Juan, 2, 35, 105, 161. *See also Pedro Páramo.*
  localized ghosts in, 276n.114
  possible influence on Salman Rushdie, 13

Rushdie, Salman, 2, 8. See also *Midnight's Children, The Moor's Last Sigh.*
  appropriation of Hindu traditions, 165–66
  as decolonizing writer, 37
  as magical realist, 8, 150, 161, 168
  boundaries of identity blurred in, 137–38, 168, 227n.55
  cinematic technique of, 62
  cooking in, 274n.97
  history in, 15, 38, 255n.33, 261n.84
  influence of, 13, 30, 33
  influenced by, 13, 38–39, 157, 229n.70, 261n.92
  magical elements in, 2, 56, 61, 77, 158–60, 163
  multiculturalism in, 221n.1
  narrative voice in, 65, 97, 223n.4, 229n.67
  political critique in, 141, 168
  realism in, 11–12, 88, 144, 256n.37
  religious culture in, 72

sacred, 22–23, 63–64 111, 135–36, 146, 154, 156, 240n.50. See also spirit.
Sacred Night, The, 66–67, 187
Saldívar, José David, 199
Sánchez, Napoleón, 231n.82
Sandoval, Chela, 171, 178, 187, 208
Saramago, José, 2, 9. See also *The Stone Raft.*
Satanic Verses, The, 56, 144, 137–38, 201
satire, 14, 139, 144. See also irony.
Sauer, Michelle, 267n.23, 276n.120
Sauerberg, Lars, 226n.47, 260n.81
Scarano, Tommaso, 117
Schapiro, Meyer, 41
Scheherazade, 206, 207
Schotter, Anne, 64
Schrimpf, Georg, 66
Schwartz, Marcy, 258n.60
Schwarz-Bart, André, 2, 14, 153. See also *A Woman Named Solitude.*
Schweitzer, Albert, 80, 83
Scott, Nina M., 270n.46
Scott, Walter, 239n.39
"second reality," 37
seers, 72–73, 180, 186–88, 254n.26
self-reflexive text, 46
Senghor, Léopold Sédar, 37

Sered, Susan Starr, 268n.31, 270–71n.58
Serrano, Joaquín Soler, 231n.82
Seventh Heaven, 147
sexuality, 203, 205–7, 213, 219
shaman/shamanism
  and colonialism, 147–49, 154–57, 166–68
  and identity, 251–52n.67
  and spirit, 75–80, 120, 154, 156–58, 182, 244n.87
  appropriation of, 147–48, 154, 156–57, 240n.40, 257n.47, 259n.71
  as psychological facilitator, 245n.104
  boundaries, blurred by, 75, 105, 121, 244n.93
  female, 180–81, 196, 211, 238n.29, 270–71n.58
  healing, 149, 152, 184, 246n.111
  in *Brazil,* 118
  in *The Musical Trees,* 149
  in *The Tin Drum,* 245n.105
  Latin American, 166
  lodge of, 182
  magical realism compared to, 75–88, 105, 121, 155–57, 167, 215–17, 244n.87–88, 251–52n.67, 259n.71
  male, 270–71n.58
  "new," enacted by western practitioners, 240n.40
  possibility for hubris in, 145
  vision of, 154
Shields, Brooke, 197
Shirogarov, S., 245n.104
Shoeless Joe, 147
Showalter, Elaine, 4, 173
Sieroszewski, Wenceslas, 76–78
Silver, Carole, 277n.127
situated knowledge, 272n.68
skepticism, of characters, 96, 103
Slavonic Casubian folklore, 243n.81
Slemon, Stephen
  on alterity, 134–35
  on magical realism, 41, 48, 120, 234n.106
  on postcolonialism, 253n.10, 264n.118
Smith, Paul, 166
Snyder, Gary, 258n.58
So Far from God, 2, 96, 184, 176–77, 194
  boundaries, blurred in, 22, 106
  female energy in, 186, 206, 209–10, 275n.111, 276n.120

healing in, 186–87
narrative techniques in, 94–95
quoted, 8, 73–74, 96, 177, 194, 187
revenants in, 106, 194
spirit realm in, 71, 73–74
time in, 98
social critique, in magical realism, 139–45. *See also* political/social critique.
sociocultural exchange, 154
sociology and magical realism, 149
Song of Solomon, 123, 199, 213, 238n.30
South Africa, 36, 164, 232n.92, 262–63n.101
South America. *See* Latin America.
Soyinka, Wole, 37, 221n.1, 232n.90
space, boundaries of, blurred in magic realism, 23–25, 97–99, 110, 185–86, 190, 227n.50, 230n.75, 246n.6. *See also* time.
  female, 182–83
  sacred, 154
spirit, realm of, 63–74. *See also* individual authors *and* titles.
  and female energy, 170, 178–79, 214–15, 269n.45, 273n.81
  and magical realism, 70–73, 135, 155, 162, 167–68, 182, 227n.49, 234n.106, 237n.20, 238–39n.32, 240n.50, 241n.57, 243n.82
  and realism, 212
  as decolonization/postcolonialism, 154–55
  boundaries blurred with real, 154, 157, 187, 212, 272n.72, 277n.132
  in Chicana discourse, 242n.69
  in Latin America, 241n.57
  in precolonial literature, 136, 241n.53
  in South Africa, 36
  need for, 75, 80
  popularity of, 40, 275–76n.113
  shaman's ability to enter, 244n.87. *See also* shaman/shamanism.
spiritualism, 241n.53
Spivak, Gyatri, 146
Starhawk, 212
Stewart, Susan, 240n.43
Stone Raft, The, 9–10
story and discourse, differentiated, 100
story-telling, in magical realism, 185, 191, 203, 208, 229n.67. *See also* narrative.
stream of consciousness, 35

Suárez-Murias, Marguerite, 260n.79
subalternity, 152–53, 172–73, 178, 198
  and female voice, 267n.25
  in *Midnight's Children*, 206
  in *Ulysses*, 229–30n.72
subjectivity/objectivity in magical realism, 68, 104–15, 193–95, 227n.54
sublime, 69
succubus, 201
Suleiman, Susan Rubin, 180, 268n.36
supernatural. *See* ineffable *and* spirit.
  as female authority, 266n.12, 268n.31
  in magical realism, 64–65, 185, 224n.17, 247n.12, 255n.28
Supervielle, Jules, 115
surprise, as effect of magical realism, 135
surrealism, 4, 30, 35, 147
  and female energy, 180–81, 212, 269n.41
  and fetishes, 60–61
  European, 34, 35, 147
  influence on magical realism, 33–34, 38, 57, 73, 167, 180, 231n.82, 231n.83
  literalization of metaphors, 112
  Parisian, 147
  reader response to, 260n.79
  uses of, 94–95, 198
Süskind, Patrick, 2, 8, 83–84. *See also Perfume: The Story of a Murderer.*
Swarns, Rachel, 36
Swedenborg, Immanuel, 217

Tan, Amy, 176
Tanner, Laura, 260n.81
Taussig, Michael
  on magical realism, 135, 152, 166–67
  on shamanism, 147–48, 154–55, 166–67, 198, 259n.71
technologies, 62–63, 169, 190
Tempest, The, 114
Tenochtitlán, 243n.79
Terra Nostra, 36, 185, 211, 255n.36
Terramorsi, Bernard, 243n.80
territorial magic, 208–12. *See also* location *and* boundaries.
territoriality, 275n.104, 275n.105
That Voice
  as magical realism, 2
  boundaries, blurred between realms, 22, 106–7; of identity, 27; of pronouns,

That Voice, (continued)
  107–8; of time/space, 98
  hallucinations in, 100
  narrative techniques in, 107–9, 123, 146
  quoted, 107–9, 131
  repetition in, 128, 131
Theseus, 242n.66
Theweliet, Klaus, 274n.93
Thiong'o, Ngũgĩ wa. *See* Ngũgĩ wa
  Thiong'o.
Thinner, 29, 147
Third World, 38–40, 41, 197, 223n.4
Thomas, D. M. 2, 10, 260n.81, 235n.3,
  273n.74, 275n.113. *See also White
  Hotel, The.*
Thomas, Nicholas, 257n.52
Thornton, Lawrence, 2, 66, 147, 275n.113. *See
  also Imagining Argentina.*
Thousand and One Nights, 115
Tiffin, Helen, 111, 253n.10
time. *See also* space.
  boundaries of, blurred in magical realism,
    22–23, 97–99, 127, 160, 185–86, 199–
    200, 223n.2, 227n.50, 275n.106
  ceremonial, 276n.123
  in Ben Okri, 247–48n.25
  in Jorge Luis Borges, 246n.6
  in women's novels, 265n.2
  sacred, 154
Tin Drum, The
  as magical realism, 2, 92–93, 193, 227n.53,
    254n.26
  boundaries, blurred, 118; of pronouns,
    248n.37
  characters in, belief/skepticism of, 96–97
  compared to *Midnight's Children,* 206
  female figure in, 195–97
  Germany/Nazism in, 29, 37, 139, 243n.81,
    245n.105
  grotesque in, 224n.17
  healing in, 11, 84, 134
  history in, 16, 48, 254n.26
  narrative techniques in, 44, 47–48, 66,
    94–95, 139, 237n.17, 263n.104
  political/social critique in, 47–48, 139,
    141, 150
  quoted, 16, 44–45, 47, 72, 92, 94–97,
    195–97
  realism in, 18, 19

  response of critics to, 144
  spirit in, 11, 64, 66, 71–72
Todorov, Tzvetan, 7, 17, 40, 110
Tolkien, J.R.R., 95–96
Torgovnik, Marianna, 240n.50
totalitarianism, 142, 256n.45
Tracks, 71, 116, 208–9, 250n.53
traditions, 156, 164, 212
transculturation, 154–62
  and female creativity, 269n.41
  and magical realism, 134–35, 147, 253n.12,
    259n.71
transformation, poetics of, 252n.4
trickster, as male energy, 274n.89
Tumatumari, 80, 213
Tutuola, Amos, 36, 232n.89
Turner, Victor, 29, 139, 172
two-way streets. *See* boundaries.

Ude, Wayne, 227n.50
Ulysses, 30, 32, 229n.70
Unbearable Lightness of Being, The, 141
uncanny, 7, 17, 67, 127. *See also* spirit.
Uncle Tom's Cabin, 136, 201, 274n.92
unconscious, 171, 230n.78
univocality. *See* polyvocality.
Updike, John. *See also Brazil.*
  as magical realist, 2, 26, 118–19, 251n.65,
    264n.116
  on magical realism, 29, 168
urbanization, of magical realist fiction, 161
Ureña, Pedro Enríquez, 231n.82
Urhobo myth, 71
Uslar-Pietri, Arturo, 33–34, 64
utopia, 187

Valdez Moses, Michael, 239n.39, 253n.12,
  258n.62, 262n.93
Vallejo, César, 201
Van Delden, Maarten, 262n.96
Varo, Remedios, 269n.41, 269n.42
Vasconcelos, José, 35
Vedic traditions, 228n.55
ventriloquism, 145–54. *See also* narrative.
Veracruz, Mexico, 202
"Very Old Man with Enormous Wings, A,"
    56–57, 60, 162
  magical elements in, 20, 60, 64
  metaphors literalized in, 114

political critique in, 14, 114
Victorian female spirituality, 269n.45
video games. *See* virtual realities.
virginity, 195–98
virtual realities, 74, 111
vision, 113, 150
Vladislavic, Ivan, 164
voice. *See* narrative voice.
Volek, Emil, 230n.74
voyeurism, literary, 147

Walker, Alice, 176
Walker, Nancy, 265n.2
Walker, Steven, 246n.6, 258–59n.63
Walter, Raymond, 266n.11
Walter, Roland, 164
Warsaw ghetto, 154
Wasteland, The, 88
water imagery, 201, 274n.93
Watt, Ian, on realism, 137
Weatherhead, Leslie, 243n.78
weight/lightness, 55–57
Weisgerber, Jean, 27
Weisz, Gabriel, 244n.88, 257n.47
Wells, H. G., 40
West Africa, 8, 232n.89
Where the Air Is Clear, 198
White, Hayden, 255n.33
White Hotel, The
    appropriation in, 169
    as allegory, 74
    as magical realism, 2, 27, 162
    boundaries, blurred between reality/
        magic, 226n.47; of characters, 132; of
        logic, 10; of time/space, 25, 30, 194
    cinematic technique in, 62
    dissonant perspectives in, 235n.3
    embodiment in, 191–92
    female energy in, 183–84, 187, 211
    Freudian concepts in, 192
    hallucinations in, 100, 150
    healing in, 81, 84–85, 184, 185
    history in, 15–16, 159, 235n.3, 251n.60,
        251n.66, 260n.81. *See also* Babi Yar.
    loss of control as theme in, 93
    magical elements in, 20, 122, 159, 193
    metaphors literalized in, 114
    narrative techniques in, 123–24, 131, 145

political critique in, 70, 150
quoted, 84–85
role of dead in, 22, 84–85
Whitman, Walt, 69, 75
wild man, 61–62
"wild zone," 182
Williams, Gareth, 253n.10
Wilson, Rawdon, 226n.38, 230n.75
witch, 175, 176, 180–81, 196, 198
Witches of Eastwick, The, 29, 147
Wittgenstein, Ludwig, 46
Wizard of Oz, The, 114
Wolf, 19, 147
Woman Named Solitude, A, 14, 153–54
Woman on Top, 29
Woman Warrior, The, 2, 63, 125, 177–78, 210,
    266n.12
women, 170–219, 271n.64. *See also* female *and*
    feminist.
    and domesticity, 204–7
    and magical realism, 170–219
    and writing, 172, 179–80
    as narrative enablers, 4
    as other, 170
    bodies of, 4, 181, 212
    commodification/worship of, 203
    medieval, 178–79
    postcolonial status of, 269n.38
Woolf, Virginia, 32, 35, 44, 173, 176
    "angel in the house" of, 180
    narrative perspective in, 145
    on modernism, 30
    on James Joyce, 40
world culture, 39
World War II, 141, 228n.62
Wyatt, Jean, 272n.71

Xolotl, motif of, 243n.79, 249n.44

Yarbro-Bejarano, Yvonne, 271n.60
Yeats, William Butler, 241n.53
Yoruba myths, 71, 115, 158
Young, David, 7

Zamora, Lois Parkinson, 178, 183, 225, n.31,
    269n.41, 276n.113
Zizek, Slavoj, 70